EXPLORATIONS
IN THE
TEACHING
OF ENGLISH

EXPLORATIONS IN THE TEACHING OF ENGLISH

Third Edition

STEPHEN TCHUDI
Michigan State University

DIANA MITCHELL
J. W. Sexton High School

HARPER & ROW PUBLISHERS, New York
Cambridge, Philadelphia, San Francisco,
London, Mexico City, São Paulo, Singapore, Sydney

Sponsoring Editor: Lucy Rosendahl
Project Editor: David Nickol
Text Design: Mina Greenstein
Cover Design: 20/20 Services
Production Manager: Jeanie Berke
Production Assistant: Paula Roppolo
Compositor: ComCom Division of Haddon Craftsmen, Inc.
Printer and Binder: R. R. Donnelley & Sons Company
Cover Printer: Phoenix Color Corp.

Explorations in the Teaching of English, Third Edition

Copyright © 1989 by Harper & Row, Publishers, Inc.

Library of Congress Cataloging in Publication Data

Tchudi, Stephen, 1942–
    Explorations in the teaching of English/Stephen Tchudi, Diana
Mitchell.—3rd ed.
      p. cm.
    Bibliography: p.
    Includes index.
    ISBN 0-06-043466-X
    1. English language—Study and teaching. I. Mitchell, Diana.
II. Title.
PE1065.T35 1989
428′.007—dc19

88 89 90 91 9 8 7 6 5 4 3 2 1

For Wallace W. Douglas

Contents

Preface

ATTACHED to the deceptively simple title "Teacher of English" are responsibilities that could tax the capabilities of a dozen specialists in diverse fields. It is not enough that the English teacher takes on two-thirds of the three Rs. Beyond the teaching of fundamentals of literacy, he or she must be a reading consultant and diagnostician, literary critic, writing instructor, writer, librarian, reader of books, media specialist, linguist, psychologist, and counselor.

Given the complexity of the task of "teaching" English, it is tempting for teachers to look for *the* method, a clear-cut, no-nonsense approach that will reduce complexity and bring serenity. It is also tempting for the writers of a book on the teaching of English to develop a formula for instruction, a compendium of rules and "surefire" lesson plans purporting to solve the teacher's dilemma.

This book will not offer such a formula, though it does present what we regard as a consistent, integrated approach to English. Our writing draws on contemporary research, our observation of other teachers and classes, as well as our combined forty years of experience teaching high school and college English. What we offer is not a set program for teaching but a description of a set of principles about the teaching and learning of language, accompanied by numerous examples drawn either from our own experiences in the schools or from the professional literature.

We see *Explorations in the Teaching of English* as a source book for the teacher/learner, a teacher of any age and any amount of experience who wishes to explore systematically his or her approach to English in the elementary, junior high/middle school, or secondary classroom. It is a starting point for individual experimentation which, we believe, will help teachers discover and refine their own sets of methods for teaching.

The heart of the book is a series of Explorations—some problems to think about, talk over, and do—that appear at the close of each chapter. These are not mere discussion questions or homework assignments; they are open-ended suggestions that both prospective and experienced teachers can explore as a way of seeking information and ideas about the teaching of English.

Despite its many rewards, English teaching is sometimes difficult, painful, lonely work. It can cause stomachaches, headaches, heartaches, and sleepless nights. *Explorations in the Teaching of English* is intended to support the teacher who is willing to take some risks in the interest of better teaching and who will engage in trials and experiments to find more effective ways of helping students become literate in the fullest and best sense of the word.

A NOTE ON THE THIRD EDITION

The most obvious change in the third edition of *Explorations* is the addition of a coauthor, Diana Mitchell. She has taught junior high and high school English for over twenty years in a variety of Michigan schools. She thus brings to the book a wealth of practical teaching experience, and instructors familiar with the first two editions will recognize the book's new emphasis on practical, classroom-tested teaching strategies.

Diana's experience is further reflected in two new chapters in this edition, Chapter 7, "Literature and the Young Adult," and Chapter 16, "Managing the English Classroom." Chapter 15, "The Dimensions of the English Curriculum," was placed much earlier in the second edition, though users with a truly long memory will recognize that it appeared toward the close of the first edition. These shifts suggest another important feature of the book: its flexibility for use in a variety of situations. Reviewers of this edition had a number of suggestions for reordering chapters. Two felt that Chapter 11, "Exploring Language," should be placed earlier to provide a more solid linguistic base for the book. Another felt that Chapter 17, "Evaluation, Grading, Assessment, and Research," should be placed close to Chapter 3, "Creating Instructional Units," to emphasize that assessment schemes must be a part of classroom planning from the very beginning, not an afterthought.

We considered all recommendations carefully before settling on the present order, but we emphasize that, for the most part, the chapters can be presented in a number of different sequences depending on the needs and interests of instructors and their students. The literature chapters, 6 to 8, probably should be treated as a cluster, as should 9 and 10, the chapters emphasizing the teaching of writing. Otherwise, the arrangement possibilities are virtually limitless. Indeed, in our own teaching we have even explored the extreme possibility of teaching Chapter 1, "A Documentary History of the Teaching of English," as the *last* item in a course rather than the first, as an opportunity to sum up some crucial topics in the teaching of English rather than as an introduction to the history of our profession.

We extend our appreciation to Sheila Gullickson, Moorhead State University; Eleanor Michael, University of Idaho; Lynn Nelson, Arizona State University; and Monica Weis, Nazareth College of Rochester, who reviewed the manuscript of this third edition, and to our editor at Harper & Row, Lucy Rosendahl. Naturally, we assume responsibility for any errors or oversights in the text.

STEPHEN TCHUDI
DIANA MITCHELL

EXPLORATIONS
IN THE
TEACHING
OF ENGLISH

A Documentary History of the Teaching of English

Good Boys at their Books.

HE who ne'er learns his A,B,C,
    Forever will a Blockhead be;
But he who to his Book's inclin'd,
Will soon a golden Treasure find.

FIGURE 1.1
From *The New England Primer.*

WITH the short poem shown in Figure 1.1—one of the earliest recorded efforts to motivate a child to study—the history of English teaching in America began, over three hundred years ago. The book in which it appeared was physically small, about two inches by three, but it carried the weighty title of *The New England Primer, or an easy and pleasant Guide to the Art of Reading, Adorn'd with Cuts. To which are added, The Assembly of Divines and Mr. Cotton's CATECHISM.* After its motivational opening, the *Primer* presented the alphabet and, in sequence, "Words of One Syllable," "Words of Two Syllables," up through "Words of Five Syllables"—a course of instruction that ranged from "fire" to "fornication." Once students had mastered spelling and vocabulary, they read "The Lord's Prayer," "The Dutiful Child's Promises," "Lessons for Youth," biblical excerpts, and the catechism, or "Spiritual Milk For American Babes, Drawn out of the Breasts of both Testaments, for their Souls Nourishment" (Figure 1.2). For many years instruction in Colonial schools centered on books like *The New England Primer.* Few children received more than

FIGURE 1.2

From *The New England Primer.*

rudimentary instruction in English, and the academies and colleges concentrated their language teaching on Latin and Greek.

In the early years, much American schooling took place in the home. The Colonial "dame" schools, for instance, were conducted by a community member who took on the task of teaching her own and her neighbors' children to read and write. Thus many books were designed for home instruction (Figure 1.3). In fact, interest in home teaching persisted well into the early nineteenth century, as evidenced by the following passage from the popular book *Goody Two-Shoes,* by H. W. Hewit. "Goody" was a stereotypically well-behaved child, whose metaphorical name was Margery Meanwell. She received her nickname after expressing great joy over a new pair of shoes given to her by a clergyman, Mr. Smith (Figure 1.4). Goody was also wise enough to see how Mr. Smith was acquiring his learning and astute enough that she could actually teach herself:

> Little Margery saw how good and how wise Mr. Smith was and concluded that this was owing to his great learning; therefore she wanted, of all things, to learn to read. For this purpose she used to meet the little boys and girls as they came from school, borrow their books, and sit down till they returned. By this means she soon got more learning than any of her playmates. . . .

Later, Goody participated in the dame school tradition by teaching other children to learn to spell and read, once again following the "alphabetic method," which began with syllables *(ba, be, bi, bo, bu)* and moved to full words. Because a book like *Goody Two-Shoes* was meant to be read aloud to children, parents were given a basic course in "methods of teaching reading" simply by following the stages used by the precocious Goody in her teaching.

Yet the impulse toward public education—as opposed to home or private education—is deeply rooted in American culture. The Massachusetts Bay Colony school laws of 1648 required that any community of more than fifty families provide for public schooling in reading, writing, and arithmetic. Further, from the beginning, American education has always grown toward democratization, extending educational opportunities to more and more people. Especially important for our purposes, literacy has generally been at the center of that democratic education: Knowing how to read and write is regarded as an unwritten bill of rights for all Americans.

The movement toward literacy was soon extended beyond the basics of reading and writing (or word recognition and spelling). In his "Proposals for an Academy," Benjamin Franklin included recommendations for increased attention to the teaching of English at a secondary school level, and his own academy in Philadelphia emphasized English instruction for young men about to enter commercial life. Although English is today perceived as one of the humanities, allied with the fine arts and classics, language,

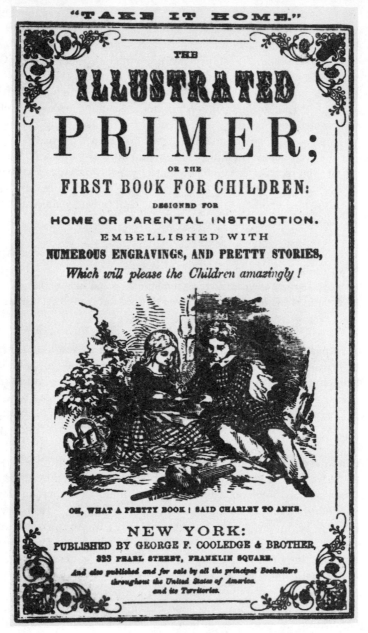

FIGURE 1.3   A PRIMER FOR HOME INSTRUCTION.

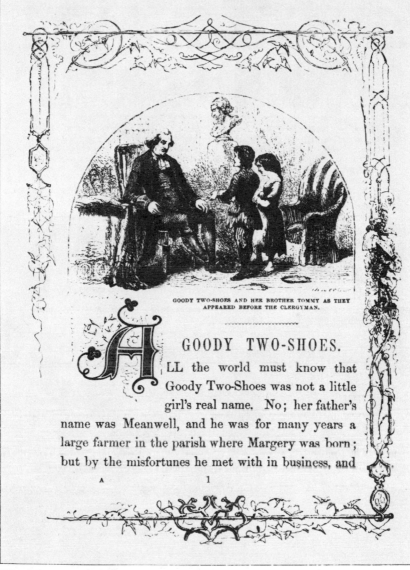

GOODY TWO-SHOES AND HER BROTHER TOMMY AS THEY
APPEARED BEFORE THE CLERGYMAN.

GOODY TWO-SHOES.

ALL the world must know that Goody Two-Shoes was not a little girl's real name. No; her father's name was Meanwell, and he was for many years a large farmer in the parish where Margery was born; but by the misfortunes he met with in business, and

A   1

FIGURE 1.4

From *Goody Two-Shoes,* by H. W. Hewitt.

composition, and literature initially made their way into the curriculum as subjects in opposition to more traditional education in Latin and Greek (Figure 1.5).

From the first, the secondary schools taught English "Grammatickally." In the late eighteenth century, a number of grammars competed in the

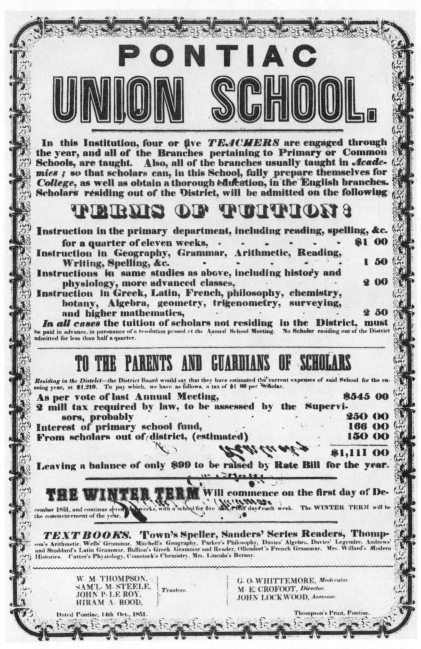

FIGURE 1.5   ANNOUNCEMENT OF THE TERMS OF TUITION AND TAXATION FOR AN EARLY PUBLIC SECONDARY SCHOOL, 1851.
Michigan History Collection

market, but at the beginning of the nineteenth, the grammars of Lindley Murray came to dominate. Murray's grammar centered on mastery of parts of speech, followed by syntactic analysis. His main pedagogical tool was "parsing," a form of sentence analysis that was said to discipline the mind while teaching students to speak and write "with propriety" (Figure 1.6).

Murray's work had a strong moral tone, one that linked the use of language to proper human conduct. Writing of "Guarding the Innocence: English Textbooks Into the Breach" (*The English Journal,* December 1974), Conrad Geller, an English teacher from Chappaqua, New York, cited this passage from a Murray grammar:

> [The author] wishes to promote, in some degree, the cause of virtue, as well as of learning; and with this view, he has been studious, through the whole of the work, not only to avoid every example and illustration, which might have an improper effect on the minds of youth; but also to introduce, on many occasions, such as have moral and religious tendency. His attention to objects of so much importance will, he trusts, meet with the approbation of every well-disposed reader. If they were faithfully regarded in all books of education, they would doubtlessly contribute very materially to the order and happiness of society, by guarding the innocence, and cherishing the virtue, of the rising generation.

It is said that Murray's books became so popular that his name became synonymous with language study, and students came to speak of studying their "Murray."

Lindley Murray may have been the first, but certainly was not the last, to be concerned with "guarding the innocence." Language instruction has

---

FIGURE 1.6   AN EXAMPLE OF PARSING

From Lindley Murray, *English Grammar Adapted to Different Classes of Learners,* first published in 1795. It should be noted that although Murray chose not to write out the rules in this example, he asked his students to recite or copy all rules, numbers, cases, &C, so that student response to a single exercise might run several pages. There are reports of students doing extensive parsing in school in the nineteenth century. Some high school students even parsed the entire first book of John Milton's *Paradise Lost.*

"Every heart knows its sorrows."

Every is an adjective pronoun of the distributive kind, agreeing with its substantive "heart" according to Note 3, under RULE VIII which says, &C. *Heart* is a common substantive *(Repeat the gender, person, number, and case.) Knows* is an irregular verb active, agreeing with its nominative case "Heart" according to RULE I which says, &C. . . .

been consistently linked to morality, with English teachers perceived as defenders of the language against the onslaughts of "barbarians," including their students.

After Murray, only one component was needed to round out the grammar curriculum as many living Americans know it. In 1877, convinced that grammatical parsing as a form of sentence analysis was unnecessarily time-consuming, Alonzo Reed and Brainerd Kellogg invented a shorthand version: the sentence diagram (Figure 1.7).

Composition followed grammar into the school program. Most nineteenth century texts emphasized analysis of structure—including discourse forms (narration, description, exposition, and argumentation), paragraphs (the "topic sentence" is a nineteenth century invention), and theme organi-

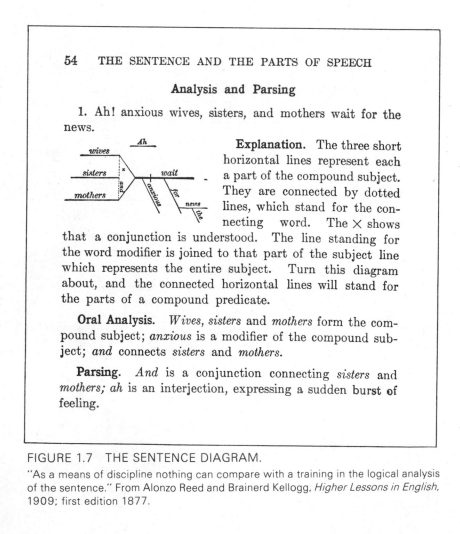

54   THE SENTENCE AND THE PARTS OF SPEECH

Analysis and Parsing

1. Ah! anxious wives, sisters, and mothers wait for the news.

Explanation. The three short horizontal lines represent each a part of the compound subject. They are connected by dotted lines, which stand for the connecting word. The × shows that a conjunction is understood. The line standing for the word modifier is joined to that part of the subject line which represents the entire subject. Turn this diagram about, and the connected horizontal lines will stand for the parts of a compound predicate.

Oral Analysis. *Wives, sisters* and *mothers* form the compound subject; *anxious* is a modifier of the compound subject; *and* connects *sisters* and *mothers*.

Parsing. *And* is a conjunction connecting *sisters* and *mothers; ah* is an interjection, expressing a sudden burst of feeling.

FIGURE 1.7   THE SENTENCE DIAGRAM.

"As a means of discipline nothing can compare with a training in the logical analysis of the sentence." From Alonzo Reed and Brainerd Kellogg, *Higher Lessons in English,* 1909; first edition 1877.

zation (including outlining skills). T. Whiting Bancroft's *A Method of English Composition* (1884) shows clearly this rule-centered approach to composition. (Figure 1.8).

Nineteenth century teachers were deeply concerned with training for correctness; they developed the in-depth marking of themes—with red pencil recommended for visibility—to a high art (Figure 1.9). At Harvard College, students enrolled in English "A," the forerunner of modern freshman English classes, wrote daily, weekly, and fortnightly themes, all of which were corrected as vigorously as the one shown and then sent back to the student for revision. The Harvard composition faculty made no secret of wishing secondary school teachers would pursue an equally rigorous course of instruction.

The teaching of literature was a relative latecomer to the English curriculum, added to the secondary schools only during the final quarter of the nineteenth century. Although *reading* had been central to American schooling since Colonial times, the study of literature had been largely limited to the Greek and Roman classics, read in the original. However, growing literary nationalism coupled with the increasingly pragmatic emphasis of public school education led to the introduction of selected works by American and British writers in the 1870s and 1880s.

Teachers were at first more concerned with literary history, biography, and criticism than with the actual content of literature. The last quarter of the nineteenth century saw the development of the literature "compendium," a handbook of information on authors and their works. Although the youngsters who studied Jennie Ellis Keysor's *Sketches of American Authors* might never have *read* anything by James Fenimore Cooper, they would know that Cooper's literary style was "pure, simple, strong, breathing of untrammelled outdoor existence; weakest in portrayal of character and strongest in description of scenes and narration of events." They would learn and recite that Cooper himself was "truthful, fearless, uncompromising, sensitive, impulsive, pure-minded, partisan, aristocratic, [and] ingenuous" (Figure 1.10).

The emphasis on knowledge about literature was promoted both directly and indirectly by the colleges, particularly through the medium of the entrance examination. Concerned about the preparation of entering students, many colleges created their own examinations requiring students to demonstrate their knowledge of grammar, literature, and writing skills. Classics of British and American literature were often set readings for the exams, and these books, in turn, found their way into the high school program. By 1880, *Silas Marner* was a staple in the high school curriculum, and a set of Shakespearean plays—*Julius Caesar, As You Like It, Macbeth, Hamlet, The Merchant of Venice*—had become established as a standard repertory for study by precollegiate high school students.

By the end of the nineteenth century, examinations had so proliferated

6

INTRODUCTION.

PART SECOND.

RULES FOR THE SELECTION OF A THEME.

BEFORE it can be determined what kind of composition should be employed, the theme must be selected. For this purpose the following rules should be observed:

RULE I. **Unity of Theme.** — A theme must have unity. As a sentence should contain but one thought, so an essay should have but one theme. A theme is a unit when it contains one predominant thought which can be developed throughout a discourse. Such a theme is definite, and susceptible of treatment. A vague theme will elude the mental grasp of the writer, and a theme without unity will be followed by a discussion without method.

RULE II. **Plan of Theme.** — Before there can be a clear discussion there must be a definite plan. Whately says: "Whether it be an exercise that is written for practice' sake, or a composition on some real occasion, an outline should be first drawn out — a *skeleton* as it is sometimes called — of the substance of what is to be said." For beginners, a general subject should be narrowed, until we reach a theme so definite as to have a uniform principle of division. This process makes the work of planning comparatively easy, as there is but

---

RULES FOR THE SELECTION OF A THEME. 7

one line of thought to pursue. For example, take the General Subject, *Rivers*. This is vague and not easily grasped or analyzed, as lines of thought may be drawn out in different directions. Should this be limited to *Uses of Rivers*, we should have a uniform principle of division — *Uses* — by means of which it may be methodically analyzed. This process of narrowing a general subject and analyzing a theme may be arranged in tabular form, as follows: —

GENERAL SUBJECT . . . . Rivers.
THEME. . . . . . Uses of Rivers.
A. NATURAL. { a. For boundaries,
              b. For irrigation,
              c. For navigation.
              d. For drainage.
B. ARTIFICIAL. { e. For manufactures,
                 f. For water supply.

Let us take another general subject, *Poetry*.[1] This is also vague and not easily analyzed, as lines of thought may be drawn out in different directions. Should this be limited to *Estimates of Poetry*, we should have a uniform principle of division — *Estimates* — by means of which it may be methodically developed. This process may be also arranged in a tabular form, as follows: —

GENERAL SUBJECT . . . . Poetry.
THEME . . . . Estimates of Poetry.
A. PERSONAL, founded on . . { a. Our affinities,
                              b. Our preferences,
                              c. Our circumstances.
B. HISTORICAL. { founded on the { d. Language,
                 development   e. Thought,
                 of natural   f. Poetry.

[1] Material taken from Matthew Arnold's *Essay on Poetry* prefaced to Ward's *English Poets.*

FIGURE 1.8 NINETEENTH CENTURY COMPOSITION TEXTBOOK.
From T. Whiting Bancroft, A *Method of English Composition*, 1884.

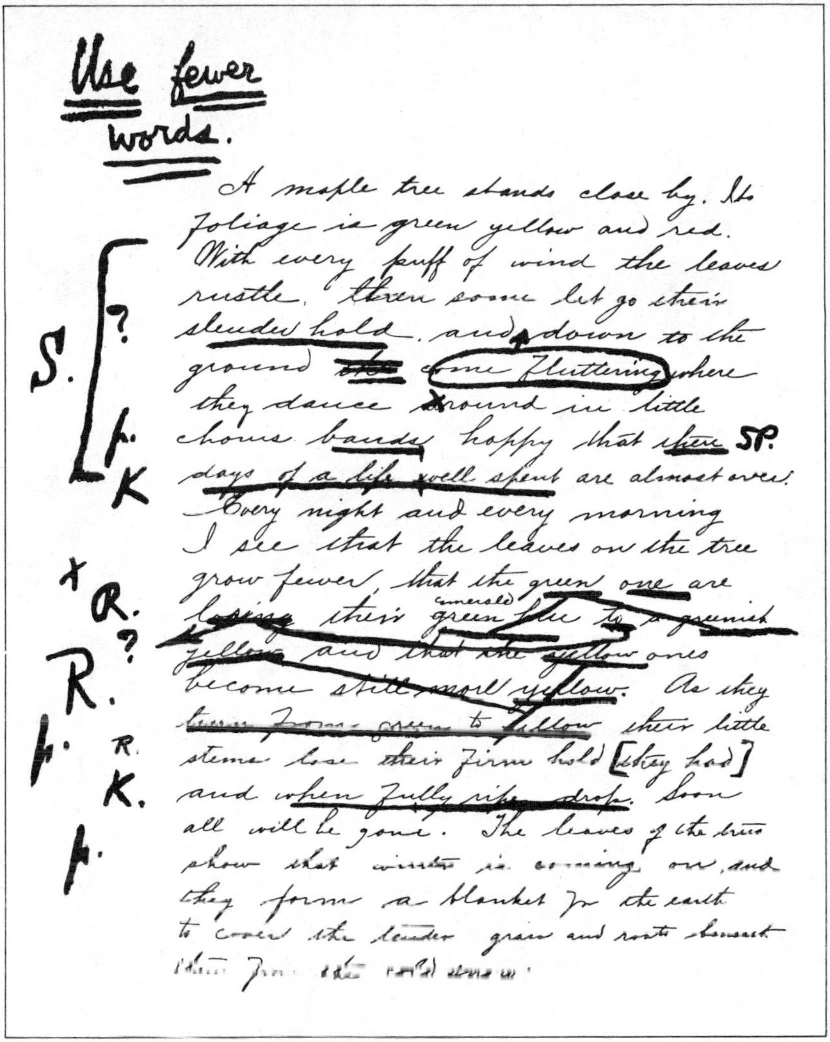
Use fewer words.

A maple tree stands close by. Its foliage is green yellow and red. With every puff of wind the leaves rustle, then some let go their slender hold and down to the ground come fluttering where they dance around in little chorus bands happy that their days of a life well spent are almost over. Every night and every morning I see that the leaves on the tree grow fewer, that the green ones are losing their green [emerald] hue to a greenish yellow and that the yellow ones become still more yellow. As they turn from green to yellow their little stems lose their firm hold [they had] and when fully ripe drop. Soon all will be gone. The leaves of the trees show that winter is coming on, and they form a blanket for the earth to cover the tender grass and roots beneath them from the cold snow.

FIGURE 1.9 HOW TO CORRECT A THEME.

From C. T. Copeland and H. M. Ridout, *Freshman English and Theme Correction at Harvard College,* 1901.

that many high school teachers demanded a unified examination and a single list of books. Regional groups such as the North Central and Middle States associations of school and college teachers were formed to help solve the problem, and these led to the founding of the College Entrance Examination Board in 1900. The resulting common book lists and exams had a standardizing effect, but they tended to reduce literary study to biographical, philological, or narrowly analytic drudgery. At least one critic—writing

40   AMERICAN WRITERS.

QUESTIONS ON COOPER.

How much younger was Cooper than Irving?

What new era in our national development began with his birth?

Where was he born? What fact in his father's life accounts for this?

Where is Lake Otsego? Describe the scenery about this lake.

Where is Cooperstown and why so named?

Give several reasons why this region was well adapted to be the residence of such a novelist as Cooper.

Speak of Cooper's opportunities at the Academy.

What sort of schools were the old Academies?

How was Cooper further fitted for College?

What college did he enter? What of his career there?

What business was selected as Cooper's life work? How was it learned in those days? How is it learned to-day?

Of what value was it to Cooper in his story writing? Illustrate your answer.

What can you say of the relations of Captain Lawrence and Cooper?

Why did Cooper give up his business? What can you say of its success?

What largely caused this result?

What difficulty did Cooper have to contend with that never troubled Scott?

What were some of the things which made "The Spy" a success?

Why did Cooper move to New York?

What was "The Bread and Cheese Club"?

Who were some of its prominent members?

Who was "Leather-Stocking"? What books are called by the name of this character and why?

What development did Cooper work out in this character in the course of the series?

AMERICAN WRITERS.   41

What can you say of the pay Cooper received for his books?

When did Cooper go to Europe and how long did he stay?

How did he defend us while abroad?

What features of the old country pleased him and how did he profit by them?

What country was his favorite? What city?

How did America impress him on his return? What reasons were there for this condition of things?

How did he show his disapproval of American manners?

What led to the famous quarrel with his neighbors?

How did the quarrel result? Was Cooper justified in the quarrel?

Why did interest in Cooper's novels decline during his last years?

Explain the difference between the *novel of adventure* and the *domestic novel*.

In what other kinds of writing did Cooper excel besides the novel?

What are some of the strongest points in Cooper's literary style?

What is his greatest work?

What character did he *create*?

Make a list of the good points in Cooper's character.

Name some of the bad points and show how the former outweighed the latter.

Where would you look for Cooper's grave?

SUBJECTS FOR LANGUAGE WORK.

1. The Scenery of Otsego Lake.
2. A Day with Leather-Stocking.
3. Cooper, Our Defender Abroad.
4. Cooper, Our Censor at Home.
5. Cooper and His Critics.
6. Cooper and His Neighbors.
7. Cooper and Irving Contrasted.

OUTLINE OF COOPER'S LIFE.

I. Birth in 1789, the beginning of the Constitutional period in United States History.
　1. At Burlington, New Jersey.
　2. Of Quaker parentage.

FIGURE 1.10 NINETEENTH CENTURY STUDY OF COOPER.
From Jennie Ellis Keysor, *Sketches of American Authors*, part of *The Young Folks Library of Choice Literature*, 1895.

FIGURE 1.11
From Oscar McPherson, "Reading Hobbies," *Library Journal,* September 15,
1931. Cited in *The English Journal,* October 1985, p. 21.

About twenty-five years ago, or just after the close of the nineteenth
century, adolescents in general stopped reading the classics of that
century for their own entertainment. I was and am convinced that the
demise of those classics, so far as the average boy or girl en route to
college was concerned, is traceable directly to the college entrance
examination boards. Those boards, then made up largely of members of
college faculties, composed their own restricted lists of thus formally
decreed classics. The old technique was soon to kill Greek and is now
partly responsible for the moribund condition of Latin, and had been and
was applied to the English classics. That technique has it as an axiom
that language, foreign or native, should be taught philologically. Well,
for boys and girls of today Scott and Thackeray and Dickens are no
more. True, they would have died even if we teachers hadn't chloro-
formed them in the classroom, because these books are written in an
idiom far different from that of today and because this is a tradition-
ignoring age. But we undoubtedly hastened their death.

from the vantage of the 1930s—held that the exams had effectively destroyed young people's interests in reading good literature (Figure 1.11).

Well before the twentieth century, then, a tradition had been established.
English consisted of three major components—language, composition, and
literature. *Language* meant grammar, including parts of speech, the nature
of the sentence, parsing, diagramming, and/or sentence correction exercises. *Composition* was principally the study of prose structures, followed
by the writing of practice themes, that followed by error correction. *Literature* centered on examining selected great works from a historical-critical-
philological point of view. This tradition has been challenged over the years,
and it is under considerable fire today. However, English teachers should
recognize that its roots run deep.

In 1917 a committee of the newly organized National Council of Teachers of English (NCTE) and of the National Education Association (NEA),
chaired by James F. Hosic, expressed concern at the academism of English
and its emphasis on preparation for college. This "Committee of Seventeen," which was powerfully influenced by the progressivism of John
Dewey, declared that English was preparation for life, not college, and
concluded that the best course of study for all students would serve nicely
to ready students for college. However, these recommendations suffered in
translation to classroom practice. Skewing Dewey's notions, the committee
argued that classic literature ought to be good preparation for life and

should appeal to all students by virtue of its greatness. Thus teachers continued with a literature program that was essentially college preparatory but were made to feel inadequate if they could not persuade students in the lower tracks that this reading would help them throughout life.

A second attempt at breaking with the tradition emerged in the middle 1930s, documented by a book titled *An Experience Curriculum in English* (NCTE, 1935). The report presented the work of a committee chaired by W. Wilbur Hatfield and emphasized both the social value of English and the role of the student's own experience in learning. Perhaps its two most significant developments were its emphasis on teaching literature by patterns, themes, and ideas (Figure 1.12) and its focus on teaching socially useful skills such as letter writing and conversation (Figure 1.13). Although perhaps overly concerned with language correctness and the values of the middle class, the *Experience Curriculum* presented a unique opportunity for English education to broaden its base and move into new domains of language.

Published just three years later, another NCTE committee report, *A Correlated Curriculum in English,* explored ways of fusing or correlating elementary, secondary, and college English with work in other fields. This document, which anticipated the current interest in "language across the curriculum," also offered English teachers an opportunity to break away from the tradition and to make language study something more than literary history, *belles lettres,* and syntactic correctness.

However, the potential of the *Experience Curriculum* and the *Correlated Curriculum* was never realized. Some educational historians feel that the outbreak of World War II and an ensuing interest in English as part of the war effort blunted the effects of the new programs. Others believe that the *Experience Curriculum* was too "permissive," too exclusively focused on social skills while ignoring academic knowledge, so that its own "softness" led to its dissolution. Some critics and teachers of the era also felt that the *Correlated Curriculum* would mean the death of English, which would become fragmented among other disciplines (a worry that surfaced again in the 1980s as part of the language-across-the-curriculum movement).

In any case, after World War II and a flurry of interest in English as promoting patriotism, the 1950s dawned with the traditional curriculum firmly in place. A few components of the *Experience Curriculum* remained in the schools, most notably the concern for teaching social graces such as answering the telephone (Figure 1.14). Interest in interdisciplinary teaching had been reduced to an occasional "core" humanities program that united English and social studies. The familiar chronological-historical approach to literature was back, and the thematic foci of the 1930s survived only in modified form in a few junior high school texts (Figure 1.15). The new look of the fifties was often graphic, not pedagogical (Figure 1.16). Texts were printed in multiple colors, with "amusing" drawings to illustrate traditional

LITERATURE, GRADES 7—12

5. PRIMARY OBJECTIVE: To observe man's industrial expansion.
   ENABLING OBJECTIVES: To compare industry as it was before our time with our own industrial age; to participate vicariously with men and women who worked and are working under conditions both good and bad; to analyze our present economic system, and to compare it with systems of other days.
   Typical Materials: Silas Marner (Eliot); David Copperfield (Dickens); The Last of the Mohicans (Cooper); The Slave Ship (Johnston); The Luck of Roaring Camp (Harte); Roughing It (Twain); Two Years Before the Mast (Dana); A Son of the Middle Border (Garland); The Oregon Trail (Parkman); The Crossing (Churchill); Seven Iron Men (de Kruif).

6. PRIMARY OBJECTIVE: To observe the effects of widening trade horizons on our daily lives.
   ENABLING OBJECTIVES: To see how new frontiers and new customs were the direct result of the desire of man to increase his trading area; to catch some idea of the need for invention, investigation, and discovery; to note the organization of big business and the resulting efficiency and economy which it implies.
   Typical Materials: I Hear America Singing (Whitman); Modern Pioneers (Cohen and Scarlett); Pete of the Steel Mills (Hall); Making of an American (Riis); Our Foreign Born Citizens (Beard); "The Thinker" (Braley); Andrew Carnegie's Own Story (Brochhausen); At School in the Promised Land (Antin); Greatness Passing By (Neihuhr); The Pit and The Octopus (Norris); The Harbor (Poole); I Went to Pit College (Gilfillan).

FIGURE 1.12   TEACHING LITERATURE BY PATTERNS, THEMES, AND IDEAS.

Note that in addition to expanding literary study into social domains, the Committee on the Experience Curriculum also drew on a wider *range* of literature, including contemporary works. At the same time, the tradition—here represented by *Silas Marner* and *David Copperfield*—continued as a strong component in the program. (From *An Experience Curriculum in English*, 1935.)

WRITING EXPERIENCES, GRADES 7—12

A. SOCIAL LETTERS

1. SOCIAL OBJECTIVE: To write appreciative and tactful notes of thanks.
ENABLING OBJECTIVES: To evidence cordial and sincere gratitude for the gift or favor or hospitality and appreciation for the consideration of the tastes and interests of the recipient. To write prompt acknowledgment as an evidence of appreciation. To use adjective prepositional phrases to add color unobtrusively (I.G.U. 11). To use appropriate paper with matching envelope, and ink, never pencil. To say "Dear John," or "My dear Mary," but never "Dear Friend." To end the letter "Sincerely yours," or "Cordially yours," avoiding "Respectfully yours."

2. SOCIAL OBJECTIVE: To write informal and courteous notes of invitation and acceptance or regret.
ENABLING OBJECTIVES: To write interesting, persuasive invitations. To make definite and concise statements concerning place, time of arrival, and extent of visit. To specify the type of entertainment and the size of party, which will suggest appropriate dress. To give directions and suggest convenient transportation. To arrange items in orderly sequence and to express them with direct simplicity. To omit confusing items and superfluous words. To accept or to decline graciously and sincerely so that appreciation for the invitation is evidenced. To capitalize important words in titles. To use infinitives as subjects for variety and vigor (I.G.U. 13). To capitalize proper adjectives.

FIGURE 1.13   TEACHING SOCIALLY USEFUL SKILLS.
From *An Experience Curriculum in English.*

rules and principles. Textbooks tried to stress the *fun* in English, as illustrated by such series titles as *Enjoying English* and *Enjoying Life Through Literature.*

Interestingly, the most influential textbook of the fifties emphasized neither fun nor graphics; it was a stern little volume called *Handbook of English,* written by a high school teacher, John Warriner (Figure 1.17). Just as Lindley Murray's books became synonymous with "grammar,"

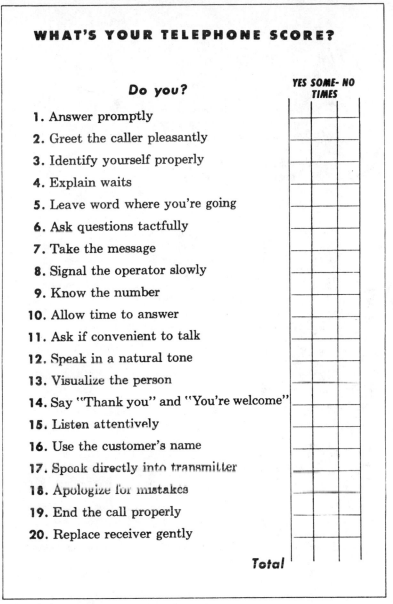

WHAT'S YOUR TELEPHONE SCORE?

Do you?	YES	SOME-TIMES	NO
1. Answer promptly			
2. Greet the caller pleasantly			
3. Identify yourself properly			
4. Explain waits			
5. Leave word where you're going			
6. Ask questions tactfully			
7. Take the message			
8. Signal the operator slowly			
9. Know the number			
10. Allow time to answer			
11. Ask if convenient to talk			
12. Speak in a natural tone			
13. Visualize the person			
14. Say "Thank you" and "You're welcome"			
15. Listen attentively			
16. Use the customer's name			
17. Speak directly into transmitter			
18. Apologize for mistakes			
19. End the call properly			
20. Replace receiver gently			
Total			

FIGURE 1.14   ANSWERING THE TELEPHONE.

From *Building Better English 9*, by Mellie John, Paulene M. Yates, and Edward N. De Lancey. Copyright © 1981 by Harper & Row, Publishers. Reprinted by permission.

The Concord Hymn

By the rude bridge that arched the flood,
  Their flag to April's breeze unfurled,
Here once the embattled farmers stood,
  And fired the shot heard round the world.

The foe long since in silence slept;
  Alike the conqueror silent sleeps;
And Time the ruined bridge has swept
  Down the dark stream which seaward creeps.

On this green bank, by this soft stream,
  We set today a votive stone;
That memory may their deed redeem,
  When, like our sires, our sons are gone,

Spirit, that made those heroes dare
  To die and leave their children free,
Bid Time and Nature gently spare
  The shaft we raise to them and thee.

Discussion

1. What makes this poem especially appropriate for the occasion for which it was written?
2. What is a "votive stone"?
3. To whom do the pronouns "them" and "thee" in the last line refer?
4. What does Emerson mean by "the shot heard round the world"?

Research

1. The Battle of Concord was an event of historical importance. Look up the facts and prepare a brief report.
2. Concord is important in literary and political history. Prepare a written report on both aspects of its history.

FIGURE 1.15 CHRONOLOGICAL-HISTORICAL APPROACH TO LITERATURE.
In contrast to the methodology recommended by the *Experience Curriculum*, the approach here makes no reference to the experience of the student. The poem is treated as a historical artifact for analysis and research. (From Gunnar Horn, *A Cavalcade of American Writing*, 1961. Copyright © 1961 by Allyn and Bacon, Inc. Reprinted by permission of the publisher.)

PRINCIPAL PARTS   PARTICIPLES AND INFINITIVES

Present Tense: *see* ⟶ Present Participle: *seeing*
                             Present Infinitive: to *see*
Past Participle: *seen* ⟶ Perfect Participle: having *seen*
                             Perfect Infinitive: to have *seen*

Practice 3 Using the Principal Parts

For each of the verbs below make two charts like those above. Use *I* as the subject of the verb when you write the tenses. Several pupils may each write the charts for one verb on the board.

1. go	5. come	9. bring	13. shrink
2. lie	6. hear	10. sever	14. acquire
3. sell	7. swim	11. write	15. discuss
4. walk	8. take	12. choose	16. flutter

Practice 4 A Verb's Progress in Outline

Write the forms of any six of the irregular verbs listed on page 173. Follow the model below.

    Example: PRINCIPAL PARTS

         Present tense: Today I *take*
         Past tense: Yesterday I *took*
         Past Participle: For a long time I have *taken*

Present tense: I *take*	Present perfect tense: I *have taken*
Past tense: I *took*	Past perfect tense: I *had taken*
Future tense: I *shall take*	Future perfect tense: I *shall have taken*

FIGURE 1.16   GRAPHICS AND GRAMMAR.

Handbook
of English

 JOHN E. WARRINER
Head of the English Department,
Garden City High School, Garden
City, Long Island, New York

The English Workshop Series

HARCOURT, BRACE AND COMPANY

NEW YORK   CHICAGO

FIGURE 1.17   TITLE PAGE FROM THE FIRST EDITION OF WAR-RINER'S *HANDBOOK OF ENGLISH,* 1951.

Reprinted by permission of Harcourt Brace Jovanovich, Inc.

"Warriner's" has come to mean "grammar" in our own time. Equally interesting are the similarities in content between Murray's and Warriner's books. Both men taught the basic structure of English, and each succeeded with his book because he told about this structure more clearly than anyone else in his time.

There have been other challenges to the tradition in the past several decades. One was figuratively "launched" in 1957, when the Soviet Union opened the space era by sending the first earth satellite into orbit. The American government and the public were greatly alarmed by Sputnik. No one had imagined the Russians possessed such technological skill, which, incidentally, could also be used to launch nuclear warheads at an enemy. Suddenly, American education found itself blamed for the "missile gap." If the schools had not been so "soft," so "progressive," it was argued, students would have learned more and American technological supremacy would have been preserved.

Initially, this concern, and even anger, was directed toward teachers of the sciences and mathematics. In 1958 Congress funded the National Defense Education Act, which provided funds for curriculum development and teacher in-service training in mathematics and science. The NDEA completely ignored English. However, the National Council of Teachers of English argued for the centrality of literacy studies in the schools and published a monograph with the propagandistic title *The National Defense and the Teaching of English* (1961). NCTE's effort was rewarded when, in 1962, Congress provided for a series of curriculum study centers in English as part of an expanded NDEA.

"Project English," as this network of research and demonstration centers was called, led to critical examination of all aspects of the English curriculum. Virtually all the centers agreed that the tradition had failed: Teaching grammar had not bred better readers or writers; red-penciling student themes had not brought about improvement in composition; treating literature as fodder for historical study had not created good readers or lifetime lovers of literature.

A variety of "new English" programs emerged. At one extreme, educators looked to the transformational grammar of Noam Chomsky to provide a structure for English. This, in turn, led to publication of a number of "linguistic" textbook programs for high schools, most short-lived because of their complexity and their remoteness from actual language use (Figure 1.18). Other teachers looked to what was called "student-centered" education, focusing the curriculum on young people's growth and development rather than on the structure of the disciplines. Textbooks growing from this school of thought featured high interest, accessible reading materials along with writing that emphasized expression of self rather than mastery of set forms (Figure 1.19).

The "new English" revolution was catalyzed by several related broader developments in education:

Syntax — **Number**

We will note one other optional element that may occur in the determiner of the noun phrase. This is **number**:

Det → (pre-article) + Art + (demonstration) + (number)

As the rule shows, **number** occurs after D_1 or D_2, if they occur, and in any case after **article**.

Number is of two sorts:

number → cardinal
      ordinal

cardinal → one, two, three, four, five . . .
ordinal → first, second, third, fourth, fifth . . .

With the inclusion of number, we can account in the grammar for noun phrases of the sort shown in the following:

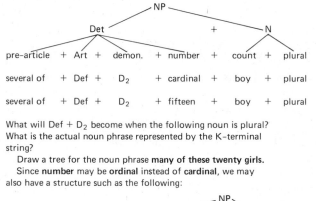

pre-article	+	Art	+	demon.	+	number	+	count	+	plural
several of	+	Def	+	D_2	+	cardinal	+	boy	+	plural
several of	+	Def	+	D_2	+	fifteen	+	boy	+	plural

What will Def + D_2 become when the following noun is plural? What is the actual noun phrase represented by the K–terminal string?

Draw a tree for the noun phrase **many of these twenty girls.**

Since **number** may be **ordinal** instead of **cardinal**, we may also have a structure such as the following:

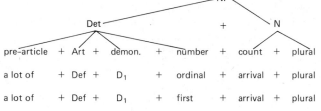

pre-article	+	Art	+	demon.	+	number	+	count	+	plural
a lot of	+	Def	+	D_1	+	ordinal	+	arrival	+	plural
a lot of	+	Def	+	D_1	+	first	+	arrival	+	plural

What noun phrase is represented by the K–terminal string?
Draw a similar diagram for **most of those second floors.**

FIGURE 1.18

From Paul Roberts, *The Roberts English Series* [Complete Course], probably the most widely used of the 1960s linguistic approaches to a new English. Copyright © 1967 by Harcourt Brace Jovanovich, Inc. Reprinted by permission.

You can also tell about yourself by describing some of your favorite things. In *The Book of Myself* make a list of your "favorites", including your favorite

song
singer
singing group
sport
school subject
item of clothing
athlete
musical instrument

food
color
car
animal

Are there any other "favorites" in your life? What does each of these tell about you? If you wish, share your list with someone else and talk over your favorites.

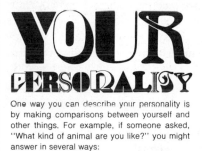

One way you can describe your personality is by making comparisons between yourself and other things. For example, if someone asked, "What kind of animal are you like?" you might answer in several ways:

"A *dog*, because I am friendly and agreeable."

"A *cat*, because I am very independent."

"A *fish*, because more than anything, I enjoy swimming."

What kind of animal *is* like you? Write down the answer and then explain why. Then answer some of these comparison questions and put your answers in *The Book of Myself:*

What kind of *automobile* is most like you? (an old-fashioned model-T Ford? a bright red Triumph Spitfire? a blue Chevrolet sedan?)

 What kind of *flower* or *plant* or *tree* is most like you? (Are you like an oak tree? a rose? a cactus? a poison ivy bush? In what ways?)

What piece of *furniture* is closest to your personality? Why do you think so?

If you were a pair of *shoes* what would you be like? (an old pair of sneakers? a dusty set of loafers? a freshly shined pair of dress shoes?)

Describe a *day* that is like your personality. (Are you a rainy day in March? a pleasant day in October? a blazing August day? a blizzardy day in December? Why?) What other comparisons can you make between yourself and other living things or objects? Write these in the *Book of Myself* too.

The Creative Word III   **10**

FIGURE 1.19

From *The Creative Word 3*, by Stephen Judy. Copyright © 1973 by Random House, Inc.

- In the mid-1960s a group of "romantic" critics of education—John Holt, Jonathan Kozol, Herbert Kohl, and George Leonard, to name several—wrote indictments of the schools for being oppressive. Learning, the critics argued, must be natural, positive, and pleasurable.
- Paperback books became common in the schools along with hardbound textbooks. Formerly relegated to "blue" literature sold at drugstores, paperbacks made a wide range of classic and contemporary literature available to English teachers at low cost.

- An Anglo-American Seminar on the Teaching of English held at Dartmouth College (1966) emphasized the role of language learning in personal growth, stressing, for example, the importance of self-expression in writing and in response to literature.
- Elective English came into vogue, replacing the traditional high school courses—English I, II, III, IV—with a range from "Shakespeare" to "Supernatural Literature."

As the 1970s dawned, then, a revolution from the tradition seemed, if not complete, at least solidly under way. The traditional tripod of literature, language, and composition, with common course content for all students, seemed to have been replaced by student-centered programs based on a wider range of reading materials than had ever been seen in the schools.

But the revolution was by no means complete. Nor, as it turned out, had the schools entirely discarded tradition.

For one thing, much revolutionary activity took place only in the pages of professional journals and in conference meeting rooms. Teachers "in the know" were often department heads who kept up with the latest in professional ideas. The classroom teachers, too busy to read the journals and not having their way paid to conventions, inherited only the trappings of student-centered learning. They placed the students' desks in circles, and they spoke of the need for creativity along with correctness. But, in large numbers, they kept on teaching their Warriner's.

Further, beneath the glitter, the "new English" had some obvious weaknesses. Students sometimes found that the choices offered in elective programs were limited to course selection; once enrolled, they discovered that the actual course content was fixed and frequently traditional—the clichéd old wine in new bottles. Electives also tended to cloud the curriculum: If only one section of a course was offered, no one other than the teacher ever knew what was being covered. Although electives improved faculty morale and created a sense of community, they also tended to dissolve the curriculum and result in chance coverage of basic topics.

Even as these new elective programs were being introduced, some unfamiliar terms began to crop up in the professional literature: "behavioral objectives," "accountability," "assessment," "mandated goals." While some English educators had been moving toward a curriculum based on language growth, others had been looking toward assessment and quantification as a means of creating a more efficient, effective school curriculum. Robert Mager's influential *Preparing Instructional Objectives* (Figure 1.20) was originally written as an instructional guide for programmed learning materials, reflecting another interest of the 1970s: teaching machines. It articulated a call for increased specificity of learning goals. The "behavioral" objective became linked with state and nationwide assessment of educational progress and the preparation of lists of minimum objectives.

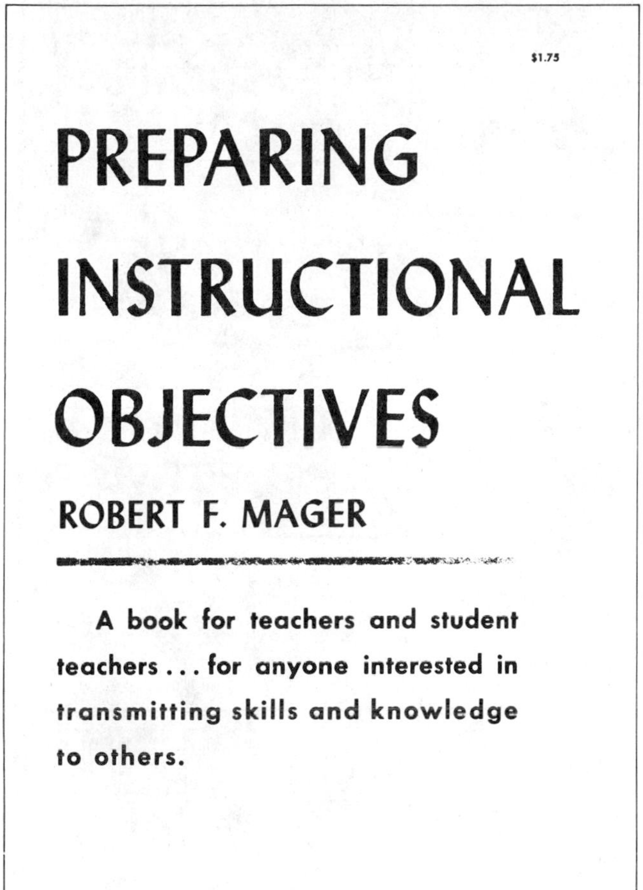

$1.75

PREPARING

INSTRUCTIONAL

OBJECTIVES

ROBERT F. MAGER

A book for teachers and student teachers ... for anyone interested in transmitting skills and knowledge to others.

FIGURE 1.20

From *Preparing Instructional Objectives,* first edition, by Robert F. Mager. Copyright © 1962 by Fearon-Pitman Publishers, Inc., Belmont, California. Reprinted by permission. This book represents the origin of the behavioral objective.

Many English teachers agreed that curricula should have clear statements of purpose. However, the language form of the "behavioral" objective meant that many of the aims of the new English simply wouldn't fit. On the other hand, the goals of traditional English, particularly grammar instruction, could easily be translated into the terminology of the accountability movement. Behavioral objectives thus tended to make the curriculum conservative (Figure 1.21).

The accountability models spread so rapidly that by the mid-1970s, state departments of education and local school districts all over the country

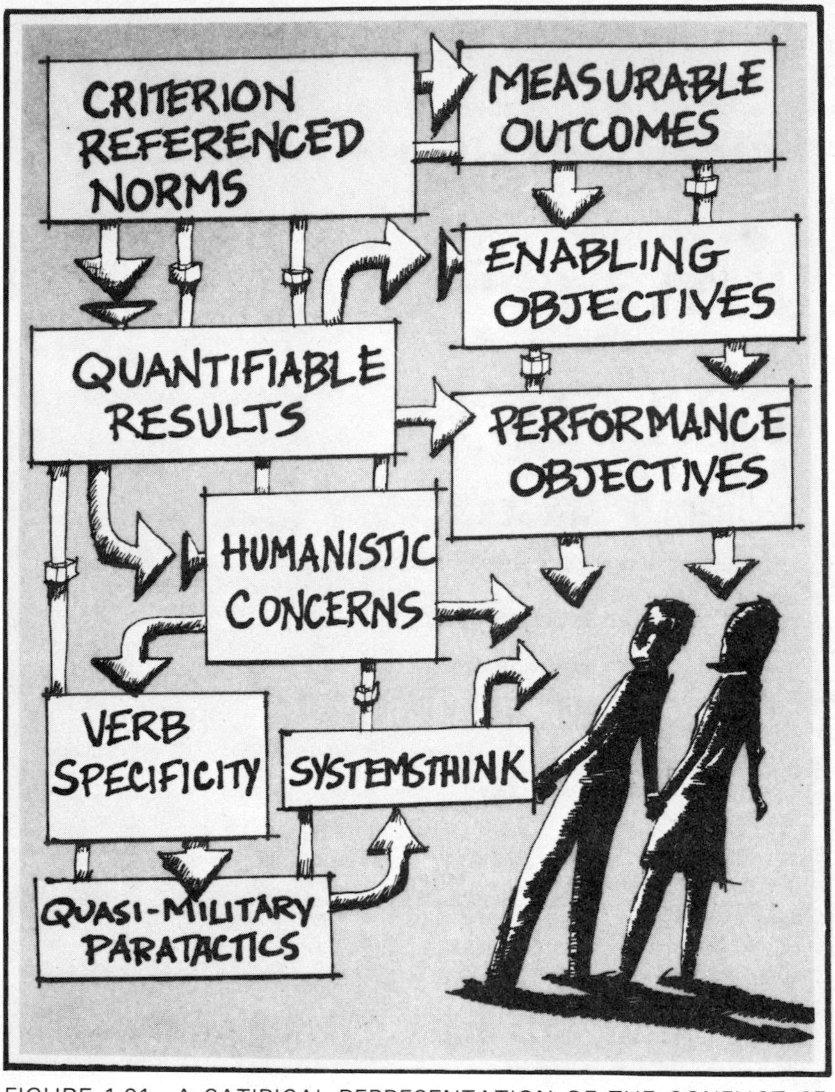

FIGURE 1.21 A SATIRICAL REPRESENTATION OF THE CONFLICT BE-
TWEEN THE ACCOUNTABILITY MOVEMENT AND THE STUDENT-CEN-
TERED APPROACH TO ENGLISH.

David Kirkpatrick's cover for *The English Journal,* April 1975. Copyright © 1975 by
the National Council of Teachers of English. Reprinted by permission.

were industriously engaged in writing objectives and developing assessment programs. Although the proponents of behavioral objectives, including Mager himself, argued that such programs need not be limited to rote skills or simple learnings, in most cases the new curricula concentrated principally on "minimum essentials."

The conservative movement gained enormous strength when, in 1974, the College Entrance Examination Board announced that scores on the Scholastic Aptitude Test verbal measure had been dropping for over a decade. The public and the media were aghast. *Newsweek* magazine devoted an entire issue to the "crisis" in literacy and asserted:

> If your children are attending college, the chances are that when they graduate they will be unable to write ordinary, expository English with any real degree of lucidity. If they are in high school and planning to attend college, the chances are less than even that they will be able to write English at the minimal college level when they get there. If they are not planning to attend college, their skills in writing English may not even qualify them for secretarial or clerical work. And if they are attending elementary school, they are almost certainly not being given the kind of required reading material, much less writing instruction, that might make it possible for them eventually to write comprehensible English. Willy-nilly, the educational system is spawning a generation of semiliterates. [December 8, 1975, p. 58. Copyright 1975, by Newsweek, Inc. All rights reserved. Reprinted by permission.]

The analysis offered by *Newsweek* proved inaccurate in a number of ways; most notably, it was biased by its outdated notions of language correctness and learning. Nevertheless, the impact on English teachers was marked: In large numbers, sometimes forced by the administration, often by their own volition, teachers went back to the basics. (Some, obviously, had never left.) Schools replaced electives with general English courses stressing grammar and punctuation. The bright readable anthologies of the late 1960s and early 1970s disappeared, and publishers brought out new editions of older books, in some cases with methodology that had been largely discredited by the research of the new English years. (In conjunction with the American Bicentennial in 1976, Harcourt Brace Jovanovich put new covers on John Warriner's *Handbook* and called it the "Heritage Edition"; the book enjoyed its best sales ever.)

Not all teachers responded by retreating into traditional approaches. Many argued that the new English was not responsible for the test score decline. They pointed to the success of paperback reading programs and the great interest in student writing as evidence that new methods had not failed. Yet the attacks persisted, and well into the 1980s media criticism of literacy education was common. The notion that literacy skills had decayed was widely maintained, along with the belief that the situation could be remedied with more frequent testing and assessment.

Nor was the back-to-basics movement limited to teachers in the United States. At a gathering of English teachers from Australia, New Zealand, Canada, Great Britain, and the United States in 1984, leaders in the profession discovered a worry about regression toward the tradition. James Moffett, the American most responsible for popularizing the term "student-centered," asked, "Why are most schools going backwards? Why are most schools retrenching into materials and methods long ago tried and found untrue?" Australia's Garth Boomer said that in his country the "new way" teacher was not only cutting against the grain of public views of "proper" education but also "quite likely going against the common practices of teachers in her own school." John Dixon of Great Britain, the chronicler of the influential Dartmouth Seminar, lamented the "baleful economic and political context in which we live," forcing teachers to adhere to conservative and outdated principles. A study group led by David England of Louisiana State University reported its impression of teachers "being right, but not yet having carried the day." (All cited in Stephen Tchudi, ed., *Language, Schooling, and Society*. Upper Montclair, N.J.: Boynton/Cook Publishers, 1985.)

To be sure, there were also many encouraging signs and promising practices in the English teaching profession in the late 1970s and into the 1980s. The negative effects of the media were partially blunted by a growing body of research and teaching expertise in writing. A National Writing Project centered at the University of California, Berkeley, established in response to the writing crisis, led to a network of over 150 training sites, which have taught hundreds of thousands of English teachers new approaches to writing. Unquestionably, the NWP has developed a "grass roots" that has reached virtually every part of the country.

Further, a national interest in "language across the curriculum" has generated cooperation between teachers in many disciplines and heightened awareness of the importance of language in schooling. From elementary school to college, English teachers and their colleagues in mathematics, science, history, social studies, vocational arts, and even physical education have joined together to discuss the writing problems they perceive in their students and to develop a shared responsibility for improving literacy instruction.

In some respects, then, the intense criticism of English teaching over a fifteen-year span has led English teachers, the public, and teachers in other disciplines to recognize something our Colonial forebears knew: that language is *the* central element of schooling. Such a commitment to language creates a solid base on which English can grow as a discipline and a teaching field as we approach century twenty-one. As Ernest L. Boyer wrote in his influential *High School: A Report on Secondary Education in America:*

> The first curriculum priority is language. Our use of complex symbols separates human beings from all other forms of life. Language provides the connecting

tissue that binds society together, allowing us to express feelings and ideas, and powerfully influence the attitudes of others. It is the most essential tool for learning. We recommend that high schools help all students develop the capacity to think critically and communicate effectively through the written and spoken word. [From *High School.* New York: Harper & Row, 1983, p. 85. Reprinted by permission.]

Still, English teachers today often find themselves split into "two personalities," as described by Charles Bonnici in *The English Journal* (September 1978): one personality that of a mechanic concerned with teaching the rote mastery of "basics," the other that of "artist," dealing with human concerns in a more subjective way through the teaching of literature and writing. Theory, research, and the taxpaying public differ on what is "right" to teach. The inherent subjectivity and vastness of the discipline called "English" create more divisions, and colleagues often disagree sharply over what is "fundamental."

That the two personalities need not make teachers schizophrenic is a central premise of this book. In the chapters that follow, we will show that correctness is not in conflict with self-expression, that the reading of literature can be as disciplined as any other activity. Whether in the future English teachers will be able to bring about a fusion of their subject, treating it as an integrated whole, or, failing that, will allow the English teaching profession to be split hopelessly into two personalities must be of continuing concern to us all.

EXPLORATIONS

• Throughout the history of English teaching, a number of central issues and questions have been debated. Why do we teach English? How can we teach students to write? What good is literature? Where does language study fit in? Answers have been offered, tested, modified, accepted, and rejected—sometimes following repetitious cycles.

What follows is a collection of statements about the teaching of English made over the past two centuries. It constitutes a brief overview of the kinds of questions this book will explore. Write down your reactions to each of these statements. Do you agree or disagree? In what ways? Save your notes (perhaps use them as a bookmark). When you have finished studying *Explorations in the Teaching of English,* reread the statements to see how your thoughts on the teaching of English have changed. (Note: Don't let the vintage of these statements shape your opinions. Not all good ideas are new, and not all of our contemporaries have profited from the mistakes of history.)

Purity of language expresses and aids clearness of thought: vulgarity, profanity, coarseness, carelessness in language, deepen the characteristics they express.

> J. M. Blodgett, *Journal of the Proceedings of the American Education Association,* 1870

"When I use a word," Humpty Dumpty said in a rather scornful tone, "it means just what I choose it to mean, neither more nor less."

"The question is," said Alice, "whether you *can* make words mean so many different things."

"The question is," said Humpty Dumpty, "which is to be Master—that's all."

> Lewis Carroll, *Through the Looking Glass,* 1872

The province of the preparatory schools is to train the scholar, boy or girl, and train him or her thoroughly in what can only be described as the elements and rudiments of written expression—they should teach facile, clear penmanship, correct spelling, simple grammatical construction, and neat, workmanlike mechanical execution. And this is no slight or simple task. . . . It demands steady, daily drill, and drudgery of a kind most wearisome. Its purpose and aim are not ambitious—its work is not inspiring.

> The Committee on Composition and Rhetoric of the Harvard College Board of Overseers, 1898

Language is acquired only by absorption from contact with an environment in which language is in perpetual use. Utterly futile is the attempt to give a child or youth language by making him learn something about language. No language is learned except as it performs the function of all speech—to convey thought—and this thought must be welcome, interesting and clear. There is no time in the high school course when language will be learned in any other way.

> Samuel Thurber, teacher, Girls' Latin School, Boston, 1898

[In literature] the pupil should be given experiences that have intrinsic worth for *him,* now. No matter how much the story may thrill us sophisticated adults who make and teach the courses, no matter how much the play may inspire us or the poem charm us, if it is beyond the intellectual and emotional range of our pupils, we are worse than wasting time to attempt to impose it on them.

> *An Experience Curriculum in English,* 1935

Ideally the teacher should not only read every paper and mark its formal errors, but should write detailed comment. The comment should not necessarily be complete for each paper read, but it should always be constructive and specific, showing the student exactly what he might have done to improve the theme and what has been done successfully in the theme as presented. In the course of a year, the comment should make as coherent a progress as the classroom teaching, directing each writer to examine and correct his worst faults, one by one, so that at the end of the year he can look back on measurable improvement.

> The Commission on English of the
> College Entrance Examination Board, 1965

For the sake of both proficiency and pleasure the student should be able to understand implied as well as surface meanings, to make critical judgments as a basis for choice in his own reading, to recognize the values presented in literature, and to relate them to his own attitudes and values. He should be familiar with the "reservoir" literature that forms a common background for our culture (classical mythology, European folk and fairy tales, Arthurian legends, the Bible, etc.), with a range of selections from English and American literature and with some from other literatures in good translation. So far as possible, he should have some "time sense"—not a detailed, lifeless knowledge of names and dates, but an imaginative sense of the past.

> Study Group on "Response to Literature,"
> Anglo-American Seminar on the
> Teaching of English, 1966

Standard English is not just a bourgeois dialect, after all, but the most common and widespread form of English, and no education for life in a democracy can be complete without some knowledge of it. Call the preference for it ignorant or snobbish, the fact remains that it is the language of educated people everywhere, and no person can hope to talk or write effectively for all his purposes unless he can use it with a fair degree of naturalness and correctness. Democratic idealism itself calls for the teaching of it to all children as an essential means to sharing the heritage of their society and the opportunities for realizing their potentialities, bettering themselves, both intellectually and socially. Refusing to teach it to poor children would automatically condemn most of them to remaining poor and underprivileged, seal the division into sheep and goats.

> Herbert Muller, *The Uses of English,* 1968

We affirm the students' right to their own patterns and varieties of language—the dialects of their nurture or whatever dialects in which they find their identity and style. Language scholars long ago denied that the myth of a standard American dialect has any validity. The claim that any one dialect is unacceptable amounts to an attempt of one social group to exert its dominance over another. Such a claim leads to false advice for speakers and writers, and immoral advice for humans. A nation proud of its diverse heritage and its cultural and racial variety will preserve its heritage of dialects. We affirm strongly that teachers must have the experiences and training that will enable them to respect diversity and uphold the right of students to their own language.

Conference on College Composition and Communication, 1974

The history of American education is the triumph of hope over experience.

Fred and Grace Hechinger,
Growing Up in America, 1975

Everyone has the right to be literate.

Study Group on Language, Politics, and Public Affairs;
Conference of the International Federation for the
Teaching of English, 1984

We leave you, dear reader, with a final thought to consider, a thought on the profession of teaching English that may cause you to look deep into your pedagogical soul:

The teacher who has not a passion and an aptitude for imparting instruction in English, who does not feel it is a great thing to live for, and a thing, if necessary, to die for, who does not realize at every moment that he is performing the special function for which he was foreordained from the foundation of the world—such a teacher cannot profit greatly by any course of training . . . he lacks the one thing needful.

G. R. Carpenter, F. T. Baker, and F. N. Scott,
The Teaching of English, 1909

ADDITIONAL READING

For those interested in reading further about the history of our profession, Arthur Applebee's *Tradition and Reform in the Teaching of English* (Urbana, Ill.: National Council of Teachers of English, 1974) is a standard reference. Also useful is J. N. Hook's *A Long Way Together* (Urbana, Ill.: NCTE, 1980), a history of the National Council of Teachers of English since its founding in 1912. For those who prefer a briefer history, David England and Stephen Judy's "Historical Primer on the Teaching of English," which appeared in the April 1978 issue of *The English Journal,* includes a range of articles on issues in English teaching from spelling in Colonial times to literacy in the age of Sputnik. Finally, to center one's readings, we recommend *Consensus and Dissent in Teaching English,* edited by Marjorie Farmer, the inaugural yearbook of the National Council of Teachers of English, published in 1986, which puts a number of long-standing issues and problems into clear focus.

Language, Experience, and the Teaching of English

> . . . I am waiting
> to get some intimations
> of immortality
> by recollecting my early childhood
> and I am waiting
> for the green mornings to come again
> youth's dumb green fields
>   come back again
> and I am waiting
> for some strains of unpremeditated art
> to shake my typewriter
> and I am waiting to write
> the great indelible poem
> and I am waiting
> for the last long careless rapture
> and I am perpetually waiting
> for the fleeing lovers
>   on the Grecian Urn
> to catch each other up at last
> and embrace
> and I am awaiting
> perpetually and forever
> a renaissance of wonder.

ONE summer evening some years ago, Steve's three-year-old son was standing on the balcony of the apartment, resting his chin on the railing and staring off into the sunset—one of those rare quiet times for a pre-schooler. His mother, concerned about paint and lead poisoning, called to him, "Are you chewing on that railing?" He thought about that for a moment, then turned and said, "No, I'm *wondering* on it."

Such uses of language by the young continue to amaze and delight us. We wish we still had the freshness of vision and language that would allow us to make that kind of imaginative and syntactic leap. Most adults recognize that the ability to "wonder" with language tends to diminish with age, and we know that the loss comes about, in part, as a natural result of refining language skills. As children learn more and think more, they employ language with more precision and at the same time lose some of their ability to make broad, poetic jumps. This increase in the precision of children's language is an important part of growing, and thus it is natural for some of children's "wondering" capacity to disappear.

When Steve's son was eight, his language growth had taken on new dimensions. While father and son were pedaling their bikes down a back street, they paused to watch a mangy, battle-scarred tomcat sniff the contents of a garbage can. The boy thought, then asked, "Is this an alley?"

In that instance he was using language not to create a metaphor, but to pin down a definition and to learn the "right" kind of label for the cat. As both semanticists and logicians have observed, the more mature and sophisticated our labeling systems, the less able we are to jump outside the restrictions imposed by our own language.

However, one must also examine the effects that *schooling,* specifically the teaching of English and the language arts, has on children, for despite good intentions and carefully planned language curricula, book reports and poetry discussions, weekly themes and careful evaluation, schools have rather consistently blunted children's use of language and created an unhealthy fear of errors among adults. It is ironic but telling that as of this writing, Steve's son, the wonderer and alley-cat-definer, is just finishing his first year of college, where he received a poor mark on his most recent freshman paper because of his failure to follow the footnoting conventions of Turabian's guidebook exactly to the comma and parentheses. (Kate L. Turabian, *Student's Guide for Writing College Papers.* Chicago: University of Chicago Press, 1976.)

THE CONCERN FOR ADULT STANDARDS

One clue to the problem of diminishing imaginative capacities with language can be found in the attitudes of adults to the language of children. Although adults sometimes delight in "childlike" utterances, there seems to be a great rush to propel young people through their linguistic childhood. Spelling errors are attacked in the early grades, even as children are first

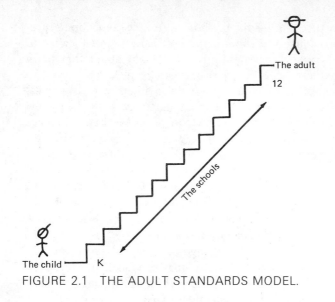

FIGURE 2.1   THE ADULT STANDARDS MODEL.

learning to write. Kids are pushed to write in complete sentences, even though their natural oral language is quite flexible in this regard. In general, throughout the history of English teaching (as described in Chapter 1) there has been an overwhelming concern for adult language standards—what adults say, do, read, and write—with the schools requiring young people to meet these standards as early in the game as possible.

The adult standards model is visualized in Figure 2.1, with the adult standing at the top of the stairway of learning, the child at the bottom. Since adults perceive adulthood as a generally desirable end product, adult knowledge is parceled out along the K–12 stairs. Children pause at each level to learn the required materials—this year, nouns and topic sentences; next year, gerunds and the three-paragraph theme. Sometimes children get stuck and must spend an extra year on a step; occasionally a bright child comes along who can take the steps two at a time. In terms of the school system, the diploma symbolizes the attainment of adulthood.

In English classes, this approach creates an obsession with "good English" and leads to grammar and usage lessons, vocabulary and spelling drills, and endless correction of errors in student writing. It leads to undue monitoring of reading "grade levels" and to a mistrust of youngsters' tastes in reading matter. It kills off imaginative writing after grade school and leads to four and a half points off for each error in footnote form.

A prospective English teacher in one of our classes wrote:

I feel sad that we can't capture the "wondering" part of the language in childhood and adolescence, and I keep seeing the image of us pushing kids so hard into adulthood that like caterpillars becoming butterflies, we lose part of the metamorphosis and end up with older caterpillars that have sprouted wings but can't fly.

Now, we don't want to be overly dramatic about the effects of the adult standards approach; nor do we want to be among those who get their kicks "teacher bashing"—complaining about the alleged inadequacies of the schools and the incompetence of teachers. Nevertheless, the evidence is clear that in a great many schools the adult standards approach is the dominant mode of instruction, despite the fact that it is pretty well discredited by research.

So what's wrong with the adult standards view? Why not identify the end product and direct instruction to it? Why fool around ignoring errors when we know that in the end, in adulthood, youngsters will be expected to produce grown-up work? Isn't all this just one more "progressive" scheme of education that fails to deal with the realities that kids face?

In fact, our attack on the adult standards model is not just "progressivism revisited." The adult standards approach seems logical and simple enough on the surface, but it makes several false assumptions about the nature of language, thought, and experience. It ignores a growing body of research in language and language learning that offers other models. For instance, it clearly implies that adult language behavior is both fixed and exemplary: because adults think and talk one way, future generations must continue to do the same. This assumption fails to take into account the flexible, changing nature of language and dialect (if it were valid, "icebox" would still be the common term for the plug-in refrigerator). Thus it tends to discourage language explorations and excursions, cutting down on the very sort of wondering with language that is so vital to children.

Another weakness centers on its metaphorically expressed assumptions about the relationship between thinking and language. Adult standards draw on the idea that "language is a mirror of thought." The reflection of thinking in language is seen as so exact that many teachers believe that "unclear" or "ungrammatical" speech—any deviation from the adult norm—represents unclear thinking or reasoning. This belief, in turn, has created an almost moralistic tone in language instruction: Teachers of English are not simply teaching language forms, they are teaching *right thinking* through the medium of language. If the mirror of thought—language—is not shiny and spotless, the mind of the child is dull and blighted. Thus English textbooks have made heavy use of metaphors centering on disease, decay, and warfare as teachers "diagnose and cure" language ills, "attack and defeat" illogical phrasing, and "clean up" language that is "polluted" by undesirable words. These metaphors at best oversimplify the thought/language relationship and ignore such phenomena as intuition, uncomprehended experience, subconscious thought, and the exploratory, expressive role of oral language.

Perhaps the most damning indictment, however, is that the adult standards approach denies the language competence of young people. In Figure 2.1 the child is shown at the *bottom* of the stairway, far removed from the ideal of adulthood. Yet we know that virtually all children perform quite competently in many language situations from the very time they learn to speak. Sometimes they say "he don't" or "me and him," but young people of school age—five to seventeen—exhibit a remarkable amount of language competence. They send most of their messages successfully, to adults as well as to one another. They talk, chat, and gossip; they question, challenge, and inquire. When you think about it, in a short span of time, young people have mastered an incredible number of language skills.

From David Ciotello, "The Art of Writing: An Interview with William Stafford." *College Composition and Communication,* 34 (May 1983), p. 176. Copyright © 1983 by the National Council of Teachers of English. Reprinted by permission.

William Stafford: I can't help feeling that discourse is learned and enhanced though social process insofar as that involves imitation. I mean, you know, you hear someone make a sound, and that seems to bring a result. And you make the sound again and it brings the same result and it turns out to be a hamburger you both ordered or whatever. I suppose that's the way in which one learns a vocabulary. And so I suppose the imitation is in it, but it is not imitation of writing. It's imitation of discourse flooding in on me all the time.

However, the adult standards approach sees *any* error, *any* deviation from the ideal, as something wrong, rather than as an experimental groping. Thus it imposes a doctrine of *anticipatory remediation,* calling for every student to be treated as a *remedial adult,* even though he or she is still in the process of reaching adulthood. If adults applied the same hypercritical standards to their *own* language, they might find themselves plunked on the bottom step of the stairway of learning.

THE RELATIONSHIP BETWEEN LANGUAGE AND EXPERIENCE

Language learning is more complex than the adult standards model admits. Figure 2.2 shows a model derived from contemporary research in education, linguistics, and psychology. (See Related Readings at the close of this chapter.) It consists of four central parts:

1. *Experience* (here represented by the "real" world, a globe)
2. *Perceiving*

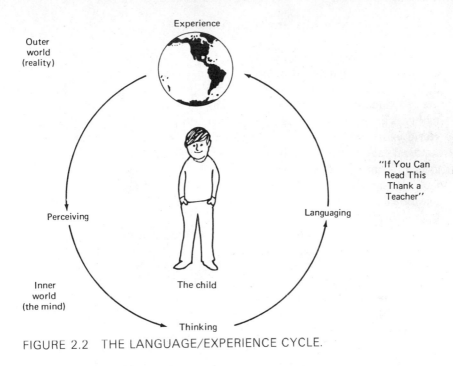

FIGURE 2.2   THE LANGUAGE/EXPERIENCE CYCLE.

3. *Thinking*
4. *Communicating*

A fifth component, shown at the center of the model, is the *child*. In Figure 2.2 the child is represented as an individual human being—a kid—to stress that although one can talk about the cycle in general terms, it is unique for every individual. (The reader can paste a photograph of himself or herself over the drawing of the kid, by the way, or a photo of a son, daughter, niece, nephew, or student.) The cycle gains its power—is "energized" so to speak—by the fact that human beings have the power and desire to convert experience into symbols and symbols into language.

From James Moffett, "The Word and the World," *Language Arts*, February 1979, p. 115.

The human child was made to symbolize. Language is one especially useful way to do so because it parcels out, labels, and links material according to social practicality.

Experiencing and Perceiving

We have spoken of the world out there as the "real" world, yet each of us perceives that world differently. The seventeenth century empirical psychologists got themselves into a logical dilemma, in fact, by following the individuality of perception to a reductio ad absurdum: that the *only* reality is a person's perceptions, so there is no way one can prove that the world exists independently. Children today play a variation of this philosophical game: "How do I know that 'blue' really is 'blue'?" asks a second grader, meaning "How do we know that the color I see and call blue is, in fact, the same as the color you see and call blue?" One answer to that question is, "We don't." Another answer was provided by the philosopher Bishop Berkeley three hundred years ago, when he refuted the empiricists by kicking a stone to show its reality: "I refute them *thus.*"

Granted, we know there's a world out there, even though each of us may perceive it differently. "Blue" is "blue" because everybody says so. A rock exists because if you or we or somebody else kicks one, we can agree that the rock is solid and the toe hurts.

In addition, language is bound up with the process of mutual realities. Walt Whitman wrote of the child who "went forth every day" to look upon objects and to become those objects. However, as Ernest Cassirer observed, this process of "becoming" involves both conceptualizing and naming, recognizing objects and attaching labels to them. Language becomes the link between what people perceive in the world and the concepts they store in their heads. Words do more than send messages, then; they help tabulate, classify, name, and conceptualize. Spoken language provides a particularly important link and is only the tip of the iceberg. It does not always reflect the depth of thinking, and it is not always the end product, sometimes being an important part of the process.

From Walt Whitman, "There Was a Child Went Forth."

There was a child went forth every day.
And the first object he look'd upon, that object he became,
And that object became part of him for the day or a certain part of the day,
Or for many years or stretching cycles of years.

From Ernest Cassirer, "An Essay on Man."

By learning to name things a child does not simply add a list of artificial signs to his previous knowledge of ready-made empirical objects. He learns rather to form the concepts of those objects, to come to terms with the objective world.

This role of language has long fascinated linguists and psychologists. In the early part of this century, they believed that language systems actually placed limits on perception. People who spoke "simple" languages were said to be limited to "simple" ideas. Linguistics has since shown that (contrary to the portrayal of savages in the movies) there are no "simple" languages, and psychologists have shown that all people are sophisticated thinkers, whether or not they happen to be living in a "high-tech" industrial culture. Further, we know that language systems expand to accommodate people's experience, culture, and need to communicate.

What we're saying, then, is that language and perception have a reciprocal arrangement, with language evolving, expanding, altering to take in people's needs as observers and communicators about the world.

There is a danger, however, that once language symbols have been established, they can become a substitute for reality. "The sky is blue," people say, and others nod in agreement. Yet often the sky in our part of the world is a bleak gray, and even if the weather were bright and sunny, any painter will tell you that blue pigment is not a very accurate representation of the sky.

To say that the sky is blue is a useful verbal shorthand that will do for most purposes. Yet language users must regularly test their verbal abstractions against the reality of what they are seeing, hearing, and feeling. A good user of language—the child at the center of Figure 2.2—will come to learn that although language can simplify the process of recording experience, it must be used with great caution as well.

Thinking

In contrast to Berkeley and his stone kicking, Descartes verified his existence by saying, "I think, therefore I am," finding reality within his rationality. He might as easily have said, "I language, therefore I am," for just as perceiving is a linguistic process, what we label as "thinking" involves language as well. The words we use generate some of the raw material for our thinking; we "talk to ourselves"; we think in language (or possibly several languages); we rehearse what we are going to say before we say it; we review what we have said after we have said it. Philosopher Susanne Langer once remarked that although not all thought is verbal, it's pretty difficult to reveal such thought without words. That is, even for "thought without words," language is ultimately required to get that thought out of one's head. "I gotta use words when I talk to you," said T. S. Eliot's Sweeney in "Sweeney Agonistes."

Just as with perception, language simplifies and endangers clear thinking. The general semanticists remind us that the more abstract a word becomes, the less direct its connections with reality. Compare the specificity of "animal" (abstract) to "dog" (more specific) to "poodle" (more specific still) to

From David Holbrook, *English for Meaning* (Atlantic Highlands, N.J.: Humanities Press, 1979).

The use of words in English is a discipline of meaning in what I shall call a phenomenological way—as a way of understanding what goes on in human consciousness.

"Fifi" (a particular pet). Abstraction allows us to manipulate large chunks of meaning in our heads, but it also results in a blurring of distinctions and differences. Consider the amount of abstracting involved in a term like "freedom" or "equality" or "professionalism" or "justice." Think about the problems involved in making statements about poodles or dogs in general on the basis of Fifi's tendency to bite people with red hair. It is quite easy for thinking to go astray because of inaccuracies induced by the abstracting process.

In the 1980s a "critical thinking" movement attracted great interest in the teaching profession, with workshops of various kinds proposed to help teachers handle these skills. Predictably, lesson plans and workbooks were developed to teach students patterns of critical thinking. As the reader might suspect, we found such approaches quite simplistic, teaching the superficial forms and conventions of adult thinking and expecting that better reasoning in children would result. One might as naively teach rules of grammar and expect changes in speech and writing patterns. We believe that because thinking is so firmly rooted in language, English teachers are already centrally concerned with "critical thinking," not in the abstract, not even in the concrete of stone kicking, but in the practical reality of helping students harness their natural powers of using language *thoughtfully*.

In *Children's Minds* (New York: W. W. Norton, 1978), Margaret Donaldson argues for helping intellectual powers develop by giving children some awareness of what they are thinking about: "The child . . . cannot control it while he remains unaware of it." She argues further that it is through oral and written language that this awareness is best developed.

Communicating

The final phase of the language/experience cycle is where the schools and English teachers have traditionally spent the most time: the sending and receiving of messages. It is important to recall, however, that beneath all utterances lies much previous language activity. Through perception and thinking, people structure a view of reality and a view of themselves. When it comes to creating language, they formulate that experience, sometimes for their own scrutiny, sometimes for others to consume and respond to. It is important to recall, too, that each "consumer" of language has a structure of words and experience in his or her mind, so there is a matching of language/experience at the point of communication, and the correspondence—the fit between what I think and say and what you hear and respond to—is not always perfect.

To see these functions more clearly, it is useful to draw on the work of several teachers and language researchers who allow us to see language on three scales or continua as shown in Figure 2.3.

James N. Britton, a language researcher formerly with the University of London, distinguishes between language that is *expressive* and that which is *transactional*. *Expressive language* is very close to the inner worlds of perceiving and thinking. It is created not so much for the benefit of the listener or reader as to help the language user clarify the sense of self and reality. For instance, writing in journals and diaries is done principally in expressive language, allowing one to pin down thoughts and ideas for analysis. Talking to oneself is also an example of expressive language.

At the other end of the scale is *transactional language,* which carries messages to others: transacting business. Britton laments that this form has received almost exclusive attention in the schools (as one might expect with the adult standards approach in operation). There is nothing "wrong" with transactional language, of course; we've written it and you're reading some right now. Nevertheless, Britton argues, students must develop skill in expressing things for themselves as well as transactional business with teachers and employers. Further, it is important to note that messages can be "transacted" in many forms of discourse—including so-called "imaginative" forms of film, television, video, song, story, and poem. And, of course, there is probably no such thing as "pure" transactional or expressive language; there will always be elements

---

FIGURE 2.3   THREE VIEWS OF LANGUAGE.

James Britton

EXPRESSIVE _____ POETIC

James Moffett

PRIVATE _____ PUBLIC

Louise Rosenblatt

EFFERENT _____ AESTHETIC

of both in any utterance. (Readers familiar with Britton's work know that he also makes a distinction concerning *poetic* language, but we find that function of language more conveniently described through the work of Louise Rosenblatt, to follow.)

James Moffett helps us see another use of language with a distinction between *personal* and *public language*. *Personal* language may be created for ourselves (similar to Britton's expressive writing), but Moffett's interest here is in audience rather than the role of language. *Personal* language may also be composed for a circle of close friends and acquaintances, people who know us and recognize our values and interests. *Public* language is directed toward a broader audience, often strangers. Moffett urges a natural evolution of teaching emphasis in the schools, beginning with personal language and, as youngsters develop their powers of abstraction and conceptualization, moving to more distant audiences. Thus the kindergartner will focus on oral "show 'n tell" for friends, while the adult will reach large audiences through the relatively impersonal form of writing. Similarly to Britton, Moffett worries that the schools do too much with public language, failing to provide sufficient development for the personal. We want to repeat, too, that the extremes do not exclude one another, and that even when one reaches adulthood there is a need for personal expression to be maintained along with public.

The ways of classifying language are, we suspect, infinite. One could theoretically create as many scales, dichotomies, and distinctions as there are utterances. However, we'll introduce just one more distinction that helps us round out the uses of language and complete Figure 2.3.

Louise Rosenblatt distinguishes between *efferent* and *aesthetic* language. *Efferent* speech and writing concentrates solely on the message, on getting the point across, somewhat like Britton's category of transactional language. *Aesthetic* language not only transmits information, but engenders and carries affective response—response to the quality of the language itself (as in poetry) and response to the experience transmitted (as in a reader crying at the end of a novel or film). As John Rouse has told us, creating language, whether in poetry or prose, in speech or writing, or in the aesthetic or efferent domains, is an essential part of being human, and it is Rosenblatt whose categories most neatly encompass this human dimension.

From John Rouse, *The Completed Gesture* (New York: Skyline Books, 1979), p. 8.

We need the poem, we have an insatiable hunger for story, as through understanding it we understand our own life experience.

Completing the Cycle

With the creation of language, the experience cycle is complete; the speaker/writer establishes contact with the "real world." When a person creates language, he or she asks a fundamental question of an audience: "Is my sense of the world an accurate one?" While that question sometimes leaves the person at the mercy of an audience, it is much more sensible than kicking rocks to prove that one is alive.

The language/experience cycle, at first glance a simple one, is in fact quite complex. Figure 2.4 shows it again, with the processes of language overlaid on the original diagram. Of particular interest is the dotted line which connects the world of the speaker/writer with that of the listener/reader. For as important as it is for people to remain in touch with "the real world," it is extraordinarily convenient to use language as a form of and substitute for experience. If you want to fix your car, you don't just open the hood and start pulling wires. Rather, you read a book or look up a good mechanic in the Yellow Pages and ask for help. It is not necessary for people to have

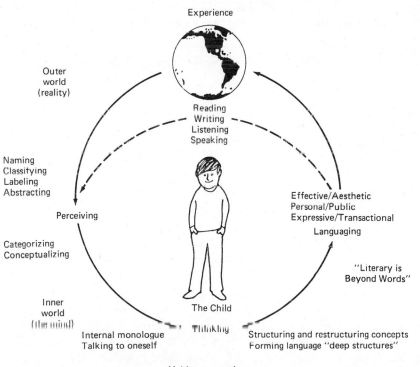

Experience

Outer
world
(reality)

Reading
Writing
Listening
Speaking

Naming
Classifying
Labeling
Abstracting

Effective/Aesthetic
Personal/Public
Expressive/Transactional

Languaging

Perceiving

"Literary is
Beyond Words"

Categorizing
Conceptualizing

Inner
world
(the mind)

The Child

Thinking

Internal monologue
Talking to oneself

Structuring and restructuring concepts
Forming language "deep structures"

Making connections

FIGURE 2.4   THE FUNCTIONS OF LANGUAGE.

every possible human experience and emotion directly, the materials of language provide a very solid substitute.

So you can see why the teaching of English is such a complex affair. When someone complains, "I wish children nowadays could write a decent English sentence," you can see the unconscious complexity of the demand. "English" is vastly more than mastering parts of speech or learning some of the conventions of the current adult standards. It involves an incredible number of processes and skills, all of them basic, not only to communication, but to living as a fully functioning, imaginative, moral, aesthetic, critically alive human being.

PRINCIPLES OF LANGUAGE LEARNING

Another important question remains: How do people actually *learn* to use this amazingly complex and multifaceted phenomenon called "language"?

There is a short answer to that question (which we'll present here, with apologies), a longer and more complex set of answers (which we'll also offer as an overview), and answers that lie well beyond the scope of this text (see the Related Readings at the close of the chapter as well as the Bibliography).

From James Britton, "Second Thoughts on Learning," *Language Arts,* January 1985, p. 74. Copyright © 1985 by the National Council of Teachers of English.

We learn to read by reading and we learn to write by writing . . . . In taking part in rule governed behavior, individuals may internalize implicit rules by modes that are indistinguishable from the modes in which those rules were socially generated in the first place—and by the modes which they continue, by social consensus, to be adjusted or amended.

The short answer to the question "How do people learn language?" is "By using it." Language seems to be one of the original learn-by-doing skills.

The middle-sized answer is based on three basic principles of language learning which have emerged from research in this century.

1. *As people grow, their language grows with them.* Growth in language is most obvious in babies learning the basic structures of English. No one needs to "motivate" the infant to want to communicate, to want to make contact with mommy and daddy. In fact, short of isolation, it is virtually impossible to prevent a normal child from acquiring language. From the beginning of life, the baby searches for ways to

communicate, to express needs, and this drive for communication continues throughout life.

As people gain experience, they naturally assimilate what has happened to them, and they share it with others. In doing so, they search for the language that will help them say what they want. Language is not a *limit* to what people think and do; rather, it is an outgrowth of their thought and experience. Nor is language a mere reflection of thought patterns; both mind and syntax are more complex than that. Although there is an element of truth to the cliché "You don't understand something until you write it," one can also accurately argue that "You may write about something clearly and articulately and not even begin to touch the depth of your thought."

2. *The learning of language is naturalistic.* Given time, almost all people will discover a way of saying what is important, just as a baby, trying to find a way to describe his or her needs, discovers all kinds of strategies for communicating with others—especially at 2 A.M. No one gives the baby "babbling lessons." In fact, by the time children begin to string two words into short sentences, they are creating original speech, combining words in ways they have not heard to express needs that are, for them, unique. Through a complex process of probing, testing, receiving feedback, listening, and absorbing language patterns, children learn the complex rules of English.

It appears that the same process takes place in other kinds of language learning, even complex matters of structure and style. Language learning is a process of wondering and exploring, of discovering the conventions of language in society so that people can use language fully for their own purposes. One of the greatest problems with the adult standards approach has been that it underestimates the enormous capacity people have for learning language (or anything else that interests them, for that matter).

I do not believe that language, in any of its manifestations, is regarded as something "different" by the child. Children do not learn language differently from the way they learn anything else. Nor are they motivated to learn about language for different reasons. Indeed, children do not want to learn "speaking," "listening," "reading," and "writing" as isolated skills or abstract systems; they want to understand the world in a far more general sense and to achieve their own ends in a far more general sense, and the learning of language in any of its external aspects is entirely coincidental. Language only becomes complicated and difficult to learn when it is separated from other, more general, nonlanguage events and activities in the world.

3. *People learn language when that language is being used purposefully.*
One hundred years ago, Samuel Thurber of Boston recognized that it is
"utterly futile" to teach language through direct study of rules and regulations (see Chapter 1). No one learns very much about language by studying
it in isolation or completing practice exercises. Naturalistic language occurs
when people are using language for self-selected purposes, doing what they
see as important with it. No amount of "motivation," threats, challenges,
or browbeating will change this. In other words, one cannot teach language
unless the language user sees it as important. (There are times when direct
instruction seems to "work." As we'll note in the next section, however, this
comes about only when students are ready to seek explicit information. It
is their decision, conscious or unconscious, that makes direct information
transmission effective or ineffective.)

SKILL LEARNING: A MODEL

The idea of language learning as "naturalistic" is unsettling to
many teachers. It seems to imply that language learning happens by magic,
without any intervention from the outside. Since many of us were reared
in school systems that used a more traditional approach, we wonder where
the teacher fits into all this.

To gain a sense of the relationship between learner and teacher in an
experience-based program, it is useful to look at one more model, this one
on the process of skill acquisition. Alec Hinchliffe has suggested (in Leslie
Stratta, ed., *Writing.* London: National Association of Teachers of English,
1968.) that "skill getting" and "skill using" are reciprocal and interdepen-
dent processes. Only as people employ existing skills, Hinchliffe suggests,
do they create a need to develop new ones. Further, as people search for
new skills, they strengthen and refine their existing ones (the "use it or lose
it" equation). Thus we, as teachers, need to create situations in which
students employ present skills productively but are nudged, through the
nature of the activity, into reading and writing that go beyond their present
limits.

Borrowing from Hinchliffe's model, we can visualize a cycle of skill
acquisition as shown in Figure 2.5. This cycle shows how language skills—
from basics to complex thinking—grow and develop. Speakers or writers,
whatever their age, have an intuitive knowledge of their reservoir of skills—
that is, what they can *do* with language. "I have these skills," they say to
themselves, "therefore I can do these kinds of things." However, no member of the community of language is static; each person is growing, so
speakers or writers come to feel, "I want to do new things to express and
share my growing experiences." Thus, they conclude, "I will need new skills
to accomplish this task." As they enter into the new task, they reinforce
their present skills while adding to them.

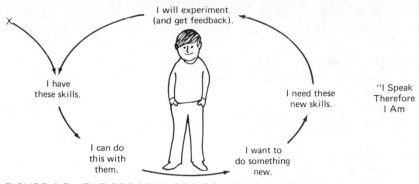

FIGURE 2.5   THE PROCESS OF ACQUIRING LANGUAGE SKILLS.

But how are the new skills actually *learned?* Obviously, many complex processes operate, but three main sources, in order of importance, can be identified:

1. *Imitation and generalization.* We absorb language from our surroundings. We imitate what we hear. In this way we begin and continue to master the systems and conventions of language. Sometimes imitation is direct—as when, alas, a child starts using the four-letter words daddy just expleted while failing to saw off a board just right. More often imitation is less direct: After being immersed in a language for any period of time, people begin to pick up its traits. You've probably experienced this if you have ever found yourself in a different dialect community; after a day or two you start to pick up some of the speech traits of the inhabitants.

There is a school of teaching writing that attempts to use the imitation impulse by presenting writing as model to be imitated by novice writers. This approach is based on a misunderstanding of the process of imitation and, in our experience, produces wooden writers. What happens in "real" (i.e., naturalistic) imitation is a process of learning underlying rules and systems, not just copying surface structure. Through imitation, the child (or adult) comes to discover or intuit a complex network of rules or, more accurately, principles. From an imitative "Mommy bye-bye" comes "Mommy come home," which reveals the child's powers of generalization at work. So, too, the child who unknowingly says "$%#!" in direct imitation will, if daddy's modeling continues, eventually come to discover the situations where such language fits and where it does not.

In this way, language grows. By the time children are four or five, they have mastered thousands of linguistic rules and tens of thousands of vocabulary words. Beyond that, they have a considerable knowledge of language customs and conventions, a broader (and in some ways more important) collection of rules and linguistic generalizations. All this is done without a single lesson in grammar, without a textbook or schoolteachers, without exercise sheets and drill.

For the system to work, however, the child does need to have examples (not models to be slavishly imitated) and opportunities to practice. It is thus axiomatic and automatic for parents to talk to their babies and young children, to read to them, to discuss their interests and their lives. In that way examples are provided and youngsters are integrated into the society of language users.

2. *Trial and error.* Closely bound to imitation and generalization is experimentation, testing out new language structures to see whether they work. The baby experiments with one- and two-word utterances, babbling and cooing and shifting sounds until language gets results. Young people and adults experiment as well. In using oral language, for example, people watch for cues in body language and quiz their listeners—"You know what I mean?"—to make certain their message is coming across. In writing, people draft and revise, trying to find the words they want, and seek feedback from peers and potential audience members—"How is this coming? Can you understand it?"

It seems to us that the schools have been much too eager to assist children with the "error" part of trial and error. In fact, trials of language often provide feedback on errors quite naturally, without the intervention of a teacher or a linguist. If people are testing out language in real situations, for real audiences, they also collect feedback—information on errors—that allows them to make corrections, not only in their surface utterances but also in the deep structure of their understanding of the language. Teachers would be a good deal more effective in language instruction if they concentrated on helping students arrange for some realistic trials with words rather than pointing out mistakes.

Thus we are led back to our short answer to the language learning question: *One learns to use language by using language.*

3. *Information sources.* Of course, there are times when language cannot be learned entirely by imitation or by trial and error. In reading, for example, it seems evident that students need to be told something about the print code in order to be able to crack it. And, although one can learn to spell through trial and error, it is sometimes much more efficient to master a few rules or study and even memorize some spellings. Still, one should not underestimate the extent to which the imitation process works in these arenas. A great many readers *are* self-taught, and recent research in spelling shows that if children are permitted freely to use "invented" spellings, before long they move toward conventional patterns.

But there are times when a teacher may want to present some rules or facts about usage and spelling to the students. Our main pedagogical principle along these lines is to provide overt help *when it is needed.* By that we mean that we don't spend much time presenting language facts to whole classes of students; rather we try to individualize our teaching so that we can provide particular instruction to particular students when they have particular needs.

We also encourage our students to ask for help. When students ask for assistance or identify a problem, they need prompt, useful assistance, not a lecture on adverbs.

It is important to recall, too, that not all students will master information about language (information that generally reflects the adult standard) at the same pace. The teacher needs to be very cautious about supplying information or giving overt instruction.

STUDENT-CENTEREDNESS AND THE LEARNING OF LANGUAGE

From Sybil Marshall, *An Experiment in Education*. Copyright © 1963 by Cambridge University Press. Reprinted by permission.

However good the children are, they will not produce adult work. Their work will be essentially child-like, and to assess this work anyone is up against a very real difficulty. For though he was a child once, though he may have made a serious study of child psychology and development, though he may have spent years at work among children, the fact is inescapable that [the teacher] is an adult now. His memories of childhood are remembered with an adult memory, his knowledge of children is an adult's knowledge, and his conception of what is child-like is adult, too. The absolutely impossible thing for most people is to see anything as a child sees it, unclouded by maturity, and not through the mirror of assimilated experience.

As Sybil Marshall has suggested, it is difficult for any adult to predict what a young language learner will see or not see as vital in learning at any given moment. We have suggested in our overview of the language learning process that language will be learned when students are pursuing their own interests, and it is obviously difficult for teachers to know what those interests will be and when they will emerge. This philosophy has been labeled "student centered" and has been subject to a good deal of misinterpretation. Some see it as implying that teachers cannot intervene in language learning at all or must wait about idly until something happens with language, then leap in to fix what's wrong. We hope it is clear that we do not see student-centered language education as at all passive, for student or teacher, and the remainder of this book is devoted to discussing ways in which teachers can generate, promote, and respond to student language use. We wish to argue, then, that if students begin to develop confidence in their ability to use language in new situations, and if the teacher gives them confidence in their skills and a feeling of security about exploring new territory, they will, in the end, at their own and natural pace, come toward the language behaviors identified by the "adult standards" model. We want to argue further that if teachers will approach language from this student-centered perspective, the adult standards will be acquired in a much more solid fashion.

THE COMMUNITY OF LANGUAGE

From Jerome Bruner, "The Process of Education Revisited," *Phi Delta Kappan,* 53 (1971), pp. 18–21.

A community is a powerful force for effective learning. Students, when encouraged, are tremendously helpful to each other. They are like a cell, a revolutionary cell. It is the cell in which the mutual learning and instruction can occur, a unit within a classroom with its own sense of compassion and responsibility for its members.

We visualize the young person as a growing, inquiring member of a community—all of humankind—linked together by its use of language. The range of participation varies from one person to another, from one age level to another. The baby in the cradle participates only to a minor extent, making contact with one or two people in limited ways, sharing with them and learning from them. As young people mature, as they meet new people and probe new ideas, their participation in the community of language naturally broadens until it becomes full and "adult." In coming of age, young people learn the language that supports their needs.

The English class, at its best, offers a particularly rich language community, a place where students can explore their ideas and experiences through language. The English teacher is anything but passive in this classroom, as subsequent chapters will show. However, we have also argued that the role of the English teacher must be reconceptualized, as research and practical experience provide evidence that the teacher should be much more of a coach and a mentor than a dispenser of adult standards. A central aim for the English teacher must be to help students participate in the community of language to the fullest extent by providing situations and experiences that allow them to use language naturally and pleasurably. This is no small task.

EXPLORATIONS AND RESOURCES

• Make a list of your principal encounters with language during a busy hour of your life, say, the first hour of the day or en route to school. What division do you note among various language forms—the amount of language you receive orally, in print, or through the media? Dazzle yourself by seeing how central and constant a role language plays during your waking hours.

• Have students keep a log of their own uses of language for a period of time, a day or part of a day. Elicit their opinions on the functions of language in their lives. (In doing so, you may well help them raise their awareness of language, the sort of metalinguistic awareness of which Margaret Donaldson writes.)

• Choose a nonverbal medium—photography, painting, clay or junk sculpture, drawing, montage—that you have never used before and compose or create something. Keep note of the skills that you master in the process of composing. Where do the ideas come from? Could a teacher have helped you before you started? In what ways? What questions would you ask someone skilled in that medium?

• Apply the three scales of language presented in this chapter:

EXPRESSIVE———————— TRANSACTIONAL	(Britton)
PERSONAL ———————— PUBLIC	(Moffett)
EFFERENT ———————— AESTHETIC	(Rosenblatt)

Look at some works in print, from the newspaper, from a literature text, from your own journals and correspondence. Where does the writing fall on each of these scales? Capture some oral speech (either in memory or on tape) and do the same sort of classification.

• Observe a class for a 20-minute period and make a list of the language skills exhibited and learned—question asking, discussion, teacher lecture, even student sass. If this seems to be a successful class, describe one or several of the language components that make this community work. If it is unsuccessful, think about some of the changes that seem to be required.

• Here is a letter of complaint to a daily newspaper. Like many such letters, this one makes its point but does so through extreme statements and by ranting. Analyze this letter and its language. If schooling should have some carryover into adult life, what did the schools owe this writer?

To the Editor:

In response to the recent letter about the noise of the Foundry: I realize that the factory is noisy but there are a lot of men and their families who depend on that noise for a living. My husband is one. One thing you don't know is the terrible heat and heavy lifting all the guys do there.

Also, we live about a mile from the airport and talk about noise and not being able to hear tornadoes. Those big jets sound just like a tornado. We are right in the take off and landing pathways and if one ever comes down God help us. So you may have noise but the Foundry isn't going to drop on your home.

I'm not saying stop the planes and put a lot of men out of work. So you see, we all have things we don't like, but we have to think of others, too.

RELATED READINGS

There are numerous books about language and learning that one "ought" to have read, the authors included. In the Bibliography of this book we list a number of basic reference books on theory and practice in teaching English, including titles that do not receive direct reference in the text but are part of its philosophical and practical foundations. We suggest that you skim the Bibliography early in reading the book and look for titles which concern aspects of the teaching of English that seem especially important or that you feel could strengthen your own background.

For basic reading, John Dixon's *Growth Through English* is central; it is the originating book of the current movement toward enfolding language instruction into a broader perspective of human experience. James Britton's *Language, the Learner, and the School* is also critical reading. Every teacher should, at one time or another, look at some of the classic background work that supports a naturalistic language-learning approach: John Dewey's *School and Society,* Jean Piaget's *Language and Thought of the Child,* L. S. Vygotsky's *Thought and Language,* and Susanne Langer's *Philosophy in a New Key.* The past two decades have also seen the evolution of some of the finer details of this philosophy. See the Bibliography for books by Britton, Moffett, Mayher et al., Knolblauch and Brannon, Berthoff, Murray, Graves, Rosenblatt, and Goodman.

Creating Instructional Units

3

THE term *units* is one that teachers use loosely. "I've just finished a unit on vocabulary," says Teacher A, who has spent a week having students master word lists while studying prefixes and suffixes. "I'm about to start my popular culture unit," says Teacher B, who will spend the next eight weeks having her students explore mass media. "I'm falling behind in my New England Poets unit," says Teacher C, who is halfway through a chapter in a literature anthology.

An *instructional unit* can range from a few days of concentrated study to an entire course. Some teachers may have several units going at once: a Fridays-only writing unit, taught along with a Monday-Wednesday literature unit, while a Thursdays-only free reading unit is in progress.

In this chapter we use the term "unit" to mean all of the above, consistent with popular usage. A *unit*, then, is simply an organized block of instruction. However, we place particular emphasis on units that extend over a period of time—several weeks to a month or more. In general, it is fairly easy to put together short units where the end is in sight right from the beginning. By contrast, teachers often have difficulty planning and sustaining experiences for their students working over a period of many weeks or several months. If a unit is not carefully structured, it can degenerate into a string of loosely related activities, and, to borrow from Shakespeare, "Tomorrow, and tomorrow, and tomorrow, creeps in this petty pace from day to day."

Of course, there are some very good reasons for keeping a unit flexible, not planning it so tightly that there is no opportunity to change course or direction. If teachers are responsive to the needs, interests, and abilities of the students, then some of the outcomes of an instructional unit will emerge as students react to the material. In the course of reading a novel such as William Sleator's *Singularity,* students may become fascinated by scientific concepts such as black holes, in which case the teacher may want to schedule library time so that students can find information they will share orally or in writing. Still, it is one thing to individualize by providing options for students *within* a well-designed unit framework and quite another to teach from day to day with no real sense of direction. This chapter presents a pattern for planning units—whether a ten-day "mini-unit" or a full-term course—that allows for careful, comprehensive design, yet still allows room for meeting individual needs. Much of unit building depends on the teacher and his or her individual style and values. You must discover patterns of organization and activity that are comfortable for you while still being productive for your students.

It is also important to state two axioms about unit building:

1. A good instructional unit will be based on careful assessment of students' needs and interests. This may seem self-evident to the reader, but we have witnessed (alas, sometimes in our own classes) students plodding through ingeniously designed units that simply do not make connections. In some cases the failure grows from inappropriate content (e.g., a unit on eighteenth-century British poetry for a class of developmental freshmen); in others it may simply be a result of expecting too much (e.g., the formal, footnoted research paper for seventh graders).

2. A good instructional unit will be consistent with the teacher's articulated philosophy of the discipline and of instruction. That is, a unit should reflect the teacher's absolute conviction that this work *is* something valuable for students to know, and it should further reflect his or her understanding of how young people go about learning in and through language. It is with this second axiom that prepackaged units, whether in textbook or school curriculum guide, may cause problems, and the teacher needs to make some careful decisions before teaching from or adapting such materials.

TOPICS FOR UNITS

An instructional unit can be created on just about any topic in the known, or for that matter *unknown,* universe. In English programs, units have traditionally been centered on the following:

Literary history—covering periods in British, American, and world literature.

Literary genre—focusing on a particular kind of literature: poetry, short story, the novel, or a subgenre such as science fiction.

Literary theme—with an emphasis on driving ideas that are common to a number of works.

Elements of language and composition—ranging from "grammar" to "personal writing" to "analyzing public doublespeak."

While very good units can be built using any of these organizing principles, each kind places some limitations on the concepts and materials that a teacher can naturally introduce, and it is useful to consider these limitations. For example, in a literary history unit, matters that go outside historical interest are often ignored or introduced accidentally, and literature is presented from a single point of view: its location in a chronological parade. Similarly, genre units run the risk of becoming "self-centered," dealing only with the elements of a single genre: the rhyme and meter of the poem, for example, or plot and character in the short story. Language and composition units may be taught in isolation from literature (or language in use) and sometimes treat language fragmentarily rather than as an organic whole.

Our preference for teaching is the *thematic* or *topical* unit, although this pattern, like the other three, can foster its own kind of blindness to some aspects of teaching. For example, "theme" may be taken to mean exclusively literary themes or recurring motifs: "courage," "identity," "the westward movement." If literary theme is the sole concern, the unit, like a genre unit, may become self-centered, with the theme providing the central quest and teachers and students looking for little beyond it. Thus, once the students find a reference to "innocence" or "experience" or "love and hate," they conclude they have correctly solved the puzzle of a particular piece of literature.

We like to treat the concept of theme or topic very broadly (there are dangers in that, too, we acknowledge), so that thematic units take on a wide range of issues. Perhaps most important, a broadly selected theme invites integration: of youngsters' personal experiences and interests, their oral language, their reading, their knowledge of disciplines beyond English, their writing, even their understanding of literary history and genre. A good thematic unit will offer a variety of writing, reading, research, and speaking activities without unduly limiting kinds of materials or methods of response.

As Figure 3.1 shows, units can center on topics as diverse as the "The Literature of Labor" and "Eskimo Literature." They can include authors ("Twain and Woody Allen"), literary topics ("Civil War Stories"), social issues ("American Ethnics"), and civics ("Literature and Politics").

FIGURE 3.1 TOPICS FOR THEMATIC UNITS.

This list is adapted from several publications: *Miniguides,* by the editors of Scholastic (New York: Citation Press, 1975); Sylvia Spann and Mary Beth Culp, eds., *Thematic Units in English and the Humanities* (Urbana, Ill.: National Council of Teachers of English, 1977); Susan Judy, ed., "The EJ Curriculum Catalog," *The English Journal,* September 1977, p. 53; and Stephen Judy, *The ABCs of Literacy* (New York: Oxford, 1980).

Loneliness and Alienation	Songs of America (or your region)
American Folklore	Inner Space of the Mind
Supernatural Literature	Whodunit?
Science Fact/Fiction	Surviving
Maturity and Mortality	A Study of Humor
Life Experience: Biography	The Art of Criticism
Violence in America	The Literature of Labor
The Voice of the People	Life on Other Planets
New Journalism	The Exodus Theme
Handicappers	American Technology
Divorce	Gods and Goddesses
Twain and Woody Allen	Eskimo Literature
American Ethnics	People in Crisis
Literature from Prison	Police Stories
Working	Fire and Ice
Our Town	Civil War Stories
Truth and Fiction	Quality and Classics
Future Shock	Ambiguities
Contraries	Frailties
Foibles	Literature and Politics
Innocence and Experience	

We are particularly convinced of their usefulness because of three advantageous characteristics of *thematic/topical units.*

1. *They accommodate a wide range of literary and other linguistic materials.* Not limited to any genre or in many cases to any era or national literature, a thematic unit can contain poetry, prose, drama, and nonfiction that range over a spectrum of literature from classic to contemporary, from all areas of the globe, from highly accessible reading to that which challenges the most able. Further, thematic units invite the use of language in various forms, including films, videotapes, television programs, talk, conversation, speech, and drama. In a unit on "Violence in America" students would certainly explore the theme of violence in literature, but they could just as easily make a study of contemporary television programming. They might look at violence in literature reflecting various cultures, or they might compare some of the eyeball-spearing classics to violent books from our own time to reflect on similarities and differences.

2. *They are naturally interdisciplinary.* A unit on "Technological Dreams and Nightmares" can easily include history (tracing industrial growth in American history), science (examining scientific and technological progress and problems), vocational arts (the effect of labor-saving devices on the quality of products), social studies (the impact of automation on employment), and even futuristics ("Where is our technology taking us?").

3. *They allow a natural integration of reading, writing, listening, and speaking.* The traditional unit often isolates the components of English: literature is studied alone; language is treated by itself; writing is separated from both. Thematic and topical units, by contrast, invite students to apply all the language arts to the topic at hand. One day they write or talk about it; they next day they read or listen.

It should be noted, too, that thematic/topical units can often be worked into courses or curricula that have been structured along other lines. For example, within a chronological American literature course, a teacher may subdivide to create topical clusters of readings: "American Identity," "City Life and Country Life," "The Quest for Technology." Recognizing this flexibility, some textbook publishers provide alternative tables of contents for their books, showing how an anthology can be used to teach by theme, genre, or chronology. If your textbook lacks such helpful apparatus, you can do the same thing simply by browsing through the book and looking for literature that flows together in a thematic pattern. Even composition courses can be structured by themes, often beginning with units on personal experience and moving toward social or academic issues and problems.

We do not wish to oversell the thematic/topical approach, for there are drawbacks and abuses. When Steve was visiting and teaching in Australia in 1986, teachers there told him they had a sense of déjà vu when he preached the virtues of teaching by themes. That approach had swept Australia in the 1960s and was now being rejected, generally in favor of teaching by genres. The problem, he was told, was that teachers picked their themes and taught them year after year, seldom adding new material. Or they became "theme hunters" and would read a piece of literature only if it matched their teaching interests. Further, the Australian teachers complained that they had problems managing the individualized reading that was going on in their classrooms. Lastly, there was worry about coverage: In Australia, even more than in the United States, set examinations for high school certificates stress mastery of selected great books.

We acknowledge that the sorts of abuses mentioned above are possible with thematic teaching. There are also solutions to each of those problems (an issue we invite you to consider in the Explorations that conclude this chapter). However, it is important to distinguish between *practical* or *applied* abuses and the *theoretical power* of an approach. No method—genre, chronology, language, or themes—should be rejected solely because some teachers abuse it; probably any style of teaching can be turned into a satire of itself through excess. The critical question is which approach (or combination of approaches) can offer students the greatest access to language; for us, the answer to that question is teaching by themes.

What follows, however, applies to any approach to unit development and should help teachers who value a variety of patterns of organization in creating well-organized units. We'll discuss this in four stages:

Setting objectives
Choosing materials
Structuring the unit
Orchestrating activities

There is a fifth stage, creating an evaluation plan, which we will leave for discussion in a later chapter.

SETTING OBJECTIVES

The setting of goals or objectives has been a subject of considerable debate ever since the publication of Robert Mager's *Writing Behavioral Objectives* in 1962 (see Chapter 1). Mager objected, rightly, that many teachers phrase their goals fuzzily, and valid criticism has been directed toward English teachers because of their failure to make objectives explicit.

"I want my students to *appreciate* literature," says the English teacher.

"What do you mean *appreciate?*" asks a skeptic. "How will I know that your students 'appreciate'?"

"You're a boor and a philistine," replies the English teacher. "Appreciation cannot be defined, only recognized; I will recognize it when it occurs in my students."

The skeptic, perhaps rightly, concludes that the English teacher doesn't have a firm grasp on the objective and how it can be achieved.

Although some English teachers may hide behind the vagueness of a word like "appreciate," part of the problem may be in terms of language; it's not that English teachers don't know what they're doing, it's simply that it is difficult to get it into words.

From James Hoetker, "Limitations and Advantages of Behavioral Objectives in the Arts and Humanities," in John Maxwell and Anthony Tovatt, eds., *On Writing Behavioral Objectives for English* (Urbana, Ill., 1970), pp. 49–50. Copyright © 1970 by the National Council of Teachers of English. Reprinted by permission.

There are three sorts of behaviors that educators are concerned with. I am going to call these "can-do" behaviors, "may-do" behaviors, and "will-do" behaviors. "Can-do" behaviors are those specific things that a student can do at the end of a particular unit that he could not do at the beginning of it; in terms of Bloom's *Taxonomy*, the "can-do" behaviors include knowledge, comprehension, and the application of knowledge in familiar situations. "May-do" behaviors are things a student may be able to do in a novel or unfamiliar situation because he has mastered certain "can-do" behaviors. These would include, among cognitive behaviors, the application of abstractions in novel situations, analysis, synthesis, and evaluation; plus, among affective behaviors, attending, responding, valuing, and in some cases, organizing. "Will-do" behaviors are the choices and preferences that describe the quality of an adult's life, and which are present only fractionally during the school years. . . ."

"Appreciation" is what James Hoetker calls a "may-do" behavior, involving synthesis of a variety of skills in a new situation. When students face a new literary work, the teacher hopes that they "may" be able to respond to it creatively and imaginatively and thus to "appreciate" it. One way to describe a complex "may-do" skill is to subdivide it into components, the "can-do" behaviors.

What can students who appreciate literature do? Here are some possibilities:

- They might be able to choose from among many works some that they find particularly satisfying.
- They will certainly be able to express their reactions to literature orally or in writing.
- They will probably do some reading on their own beyond that required in school.
- They may even become frequent library users or book buyers.

In that last example we are beginning to move toward Hoetker's third kind of behavior, the "will-do" behavior, the acid test of whether students apply what they have learned in later life or away from the schoolhouse.

Nevertheless, we hope the point is clear that even something as seemingly vague as "appreciation" can be broken down into observable processes and skills. There is a danger, of course, of fragmenting a global skill—appreciation—by trying to specify its component behaviors too tightly, and many of Mager's followers made that error when they tried to apply the behavioral objective in English. Although one can identify a number of discrete skills mastered by a good reader—who may, for example, respond to metaphors in a text—it is not necessarily appropriate for the teacher to turn around and teach that skill directly: "The student will be able to identify eight of ten metaphors in a passage from literature."

A way out of the dilemma of specificity may be to worry less about the exact form of the objectives than about their rationale and their theoretical underpinning. The lack of focus that concerns many critics of education results not from lack of a proper statement but from failure to develop a rationale for teaching. Perhaps the question should not be "What is appreciation?" A better one might be "Why are you teaching something called 'literary appreciation' in the first place?" That seems to us a valid and important question, especially in an age dominated by media and a powerful national will to succeed in the "practical" domains of business and industry.

Any objective needs to be clearly justifiable in terms of the following questions:

> Is this objective consistent with what we know about the nature of the learning process and the aims of schooling?
> Is there any evidence from research or critically examined experience that having students do this will actually help them use language more successfully?
> Is this goal consistent with the developmental levels of the learner?
> Is it based on real expectations (i.e., what we know students *do*) rather than on wishful expectations (what we think students "ought" to do)?

If these criteria are met, the objective can be described in a number of ways:

> As skills or processes that the students will master during the unit.
> As course activities: what the students will read, talk about, write on, or experience.
> As a set of "exit skills": activities the students will be able to perform after the course is over (moving into the domain of the "will-do" behaviors).

Objectives can be phrased as infinitives ("to learn," "to read," "to write") or imperatives ("you will _____"). They can also be written as aims for teachers, sketching out what is to be accomplished in a course. Some teachers we know write a "scenario" instead of a list of objectives, describing what they want to have happen in the "drama" of the forthcoming class. Others put their aims into the epistolary mode, writing a plain English letter to parents and students outlining what will be happening in the course and why that's a good thing.

In themselves, objectives are a dime a dozen. Most of us can generate long lists of trivial to significant goals on any topic in English. *Clearly stated* objectives that mesh with current research and understanding of teaching are not so easily produced, because one is constantly thrust back to the real question, "Is this objective a *worthy* one?"

CHOOSING MATERIALS

One of Steve's first experiences in the world of educational consulting was a visit to a small school district in southern Illinois which was engaged in developing a new English curriculum. Another consultant had preceded him and had issued to the teachers some complex forms on which they were to list objectives, materials, classroom activities, and evaluation processes as a way of creating a new program. Steve found the teachers quite frustrated by the empty squares on the "curriculum pad," as they called it, and he eventually figured out that the teachers were going at the whole process backward. On the sly, while the consultant was not looking, they were selecting the works they liked to teach from their anthology, then recopying the study questions from the book, finally inventing an objective for teaching (or flipping to the teachers' manual, where objectives were conveniently listed). The highly touted new curriculum was, in fact, a spelling out of the existing adopted textbook.

Too often the adopted textbook, rather than the teacher's own philosophy, sets the curriculum. Of course, the adoption of texts allows schools to guarantee a degree of consistency in courses that are taught by a number of different teachers; it ensures some continuity between grade levels; it simplifies the selection of materials for teachers; and it cuts down on paperwork in ordering books. Unfortunately, adopting textbooks creates a great many pedagogical problems.

For one thing, educational publishers see that the largest sums of money are to be made through getting series of books adopted by large systems. The effects of large-system adoptions—particularly the state adoptions in Texas and California—are notorious in educational circles. The massively adopted series are designed to satisfy large numbers of teachers and to be as inoffensive to as many people as possible. Thus they are often conservative in tone, reflecting not the best of current practice, but simply the practices of a majority.

Closer to home, adoption can be time-consuming for a school staff and, once completed, it locks a school or district into a fixed curriculum for the period of time it takes the books to wear out. Nevertheless, most teachers do work from an adopted text, and in many schools it is the only resource provided to the teacher. In the next chapter, we'll offer some suggestions for pre-September activities to supplement the adopted text. For the moment, we'll suggest two stages in working with the text:

1. *Choosing the best of a text.* In most school districts, teachers have broad flexibility to select portions of the adopted text for teaching. The truly "lockstep" curriculum where everybody covers "Mending Wall" on the third Thursday of October is an anachronism or a myth. Your first step, then, in working with the adopted text is to survey it, listing its resources that mesh with your goals.

2. *Supplementing the text.* Except for occasional problems with censorship, we've never seen a school district that objected to teachers using supplemental or enrichment materials. In selecting materials for your instructional unit, then, you will probably want to consider, in addition to the adopted texts:

Clusters of four or five titles for small-group reading.
Individual titles for solo reading.
Library books as well as books you can order.
Free and inexpensive print materials—newspapers, magazines, brochures.
Nonprint materials: films, filmstrips, slide tapes, videos, cassette recordings.
Community resources: speakers, consultants, guests.

Before putting something on a book list or a resource list, a teacher should consider:

How the material supports the course or unit objectives.
A rationale for its selection.
Whether the material is meant for whole class or individualized use.
Whether material required of all students may be objectionable to special interest groups.
Whether it has been approved or recommended by a professional organization or listed on an established bibliography for young readers.

We are believers in presenting students with a richness and variety of resources and materials, not to dazzle or confuse them but to make the most of our possibilities as teachers for engaging students with language. As we'll show in this and subsequent chapters, the strict one-book, one-assignment approach to English is a method from the past.

STRUCTURING THE UNIT

In creating plans for a unit, the teacher will probably want to choose from among the following kinds of management structures:

Whole Class.   Meeting the class as a whole is the time-honored mode of teaching. It allows the teacher to convey common content efficiently and to involve students in whole class discussions. If handled well, this approach can create a sense of community. The obvious disadvantages of whole class teaching are that it tends to force the teacher into a dominant role, it allows for relatively little student interaction, and it permits little time for students to work on their own. Steve seldom uses whole class sessions for presentation of material, but Diana likes to use whole class time to introduce core material and to pique the students' interest and begin to get them involved. Additionally, both of us use class meetings as show-and-tell sessions for presentation of students' work or to organize along the several patterns that follow.

Small Groups.   A student in one of Steve's classes once remarked, "This is the 'groupiest' class I've ever been in." Both of us like to use groups, and we find them an effective middle ground between whole class instruction and a totally individualized program. Groups usually involve a high degree of interaction among students, yet control is still maintained. The major disadvantages of small groups are that the teacher cannot always tell what is happening within them and that students don't always know how to work well in groups (a problem we will take up in Chapters 8 and 16).

Individual or Independent Study.   Involving individual students in their schooling in a meaningful way has long been a goal in education, one complicated by the economic necessity of clustering students in groups of thirty or more for efficiency. It's difficult to find ways to meet all students at their interest and need levels when English teachers have at least five classes and 150 students. However, if students have some choice about selections and also have a variety of appealing writing assignments, the teacher has made a good start toward individualizing. Time can be set aside in class for students to work individually on such tasks as composing, researching, and reading.

Individualization can, of course, be taken too far if students work in isolation and never come together to share and discuss what they have done. Some schools in the 1970s developed programs based so heavily on individualized study that both students and teachers became downright *lonely.* Although individual study may be important, education seems to require the sharing of ideas and information as well.

Peer Learning and Tutoring. Jean Jacques Rousseau's educational ideal was an adult working one-to-one with a child. Contemporary educators have discovered that face-to-face learning need not always involve an adult, that young people of almost any age have much to learn from one another. Babies who have older brothers and sisters learn to talk more rapidly than those who don't. Why? Because the older siblings interact with the baby and help the infant to learn to talk. In elementary school classes, peer learning can be used in everything from spelling to reading. In the secondary schools, peers can edit each other's papers, pair up to generate ideas related to literature, and work through more difficult assignments together. We are just beginning to understand how peer learning works; it is an area that deserves exploration and experimentation in English classes.

Contracts. Extremely popular as a form of organizing individualized classes, contracts require that the teacher and student agree on an amount of work to be done by the student to receive a certain grade. Quality controls are built into the contract so that students must do more than produce rote work on assignments or breeze through the reading and writing work mindlessly. In some schools, projects have point values assigned—e.g., 10 points for a book report, 15 points for an essay—with grades depending on point accumulation. Contracting sometimes has the effect of generating work simply for its own sake—the more students do, the higher their grade—but handled cautiously, it allows teachers to control individualized work and manage it effectively in rather large classrooms. Further, contracting offers clearly defined structures and expectations for students who may get lost in totally individualized classrooms.

Resource Areas. English teachers often have students working on several activities and projects at one time. The classroom can have resource areas where students can find writing topics; a wide selection of poetry; art supplies to complete projects; tape recorders so that student work can be saved or shared; reference materials including dictionaries, thesauruses, and books on editing; shelves of books for browsing; and a table where students who need to plan a project can discuss their ideas. As teachers collect more resources on particular units such as science fiction they can also create resource areas that include supplementary readings, suggestions for writing (say creative writing topics on science fiction), pictures and photographs (with a science/sci-fi theme), as well as lists of recordings or filmstrips available in the library. (Additional ideas for developing resource units are presented in the next chapter.)

ORCHESTRATING ACTIVITIES

How objectives, materials, and structures are woven together to create a class is as much a matter of art and intuition as it is of science and rationality. We call it "orchestrating" activities, creating a sequence that allows the course objectives to be met while providing a variable mix of activities for the students.

Wolfgang Amadeus Mozart claimed that there was a moment of inspiration when a symphony came to him all of one piece, where he could hear it from beginning to end. Few teachers will be fortunate enough to be able to visualize the orchestration of a unit all at one moment (much less find the model students who will play that masterfully composed symphony precisely as written). Nevertheless, we often have an "aha" moment when the grand plan comes into mind:

"Yes, if I begin with poem X, then introduce short story Y, then send the kids off to the library for free reading, that will get the flow started so I can play the recording of novel Z on Tuesdays and Thursdays and have their first writing due on Friday the umpteenth."

At other times orchestrating moves more slowly, and our desks and briefcases are filled with scraps of paper showing charts and diagrams and possibilities. In general, however, the patterns of orchestration for our teaching run along several sequences:

1. *From large group to small group.* Initial class sessions describe the course or unit, stake out the class ground rules, clarify objectives, and provide some common experiences such as reading several stories or writing on a central or introductory topic.

2. *From assigned work to individualized projects.* We want our students to work toward exploring topics on their own terms and generating their own assignments for response and writing, so we move toward that goal by offering them lots of choices in assignments and encouraging them to create their own activities.

3. *From small group or solo work back to large.* At the conclusion of group or individualized work, students have ideas, projects, and writing to share. This sharing helps the class to operate as a cohesive group rather than as a collection of individuals or subgroups.

There are many other sequences that we recognize as part of our teaching, and perhaps you will find some of these familiar from your own teaching or learning:

From writing that draws directly on personal experience toward writing about acquired experience (either from the world or from reading).
From private response to public display or demonstration.
From contemporary literature, easily accessible, to older, more difficult pieces.

From shorter works to longer (the latter often read individually, with
support from the teacher).

However, we can find examples of contrary movements in our teaching
as well. There are times, for example, when we may begin with a complex
work, one which requires our sponsorship or leadership, then move to
"simpler" works (are any literary works truly "simple"?) which the students can handle on their own.

As a teacher/artist, you will certainly want to develop your own patterns,
techniques, and strategies. It is important to note, however, that good art
is seldom improvisational, random, or chance. There is science to our
discipline, some widely accepted principles of good teaching, and they must
underlie our artistry. Further, good teaching happens when we *plan* rather
than improvise.

We would like to end this chapter by presenting a detailed, well-designed
unit plan (selected from the many we've collected over the years). Susan
Mead teaches English, social studies, and science at John Hannah Middle
School in East Lansing, Michigan. Her unit on "Dreams" (Figure 3.2)
seems to us especially well planned and workable without overwhelming the
teacher, and it is filled with activities that involve students. It also demonstrates the positive traits of thematic/topical units which we invoked earlier
in this chapter.

EXPLORATIONS AND RESOURCES

• Learn about common goals that have been prescribed for a school or
district. Do common skills lists exist? Is there a set of goals that every
teacher is expected to cover? How is mastery of these goals measured or
monitored? Evaluate the list in terms of your own knowledge and beliefs
about the teaching and learning of language. How can you mesh the mandated goals with your own as a teacher?

• Review the adopted textbooks for a school or district. Read the preface
to see what the authors have stated as the aims or goals of the text. Read
some of the study questions or exercises to see how those goals are actually
put into practice, in fact or by implication. Are there consistencies? How
well do the goals of the text mesh with your own aims and beliefs? Consider
strategies for drawing on the adopted textbook in your own teaching.

• Make a list for yourself of the potential uses and abuses of the various
kinds of units we have described: genre, language, historical/national, the-
matic/topical. Also list what you see as the strengths and weaknesses of
each from a theoretical perspective (i.e., how well the unit style meshes with

FIGURE 3.2

DREAMS: A CALL TO ADVENTURE.

People have always been fascinated with dreams and fantasies. Even thinking about dreams and fantasies appears to put us into a creative state of mind and increase our capacity for understanding, discovery and renewal. Dreaming forces us to reach inside ourselves and think about tomorrow. In a classroom, sharing and attempting to analyze dreams and fantasies has the potential for being exploitive; but handled properly, it can help unearth our common thoughts, desires and fears. This commonality can be extremely reassuring to the adolescent.

Objectives

To introduce students to past and present visionaries—their dreams and accomplishments; to promote concepts of self-awareness, self-discovery and identity; to confront universal conflicts of man (fear, anxiety, isolation); to write imaginatively, allowing natural imagery to unfold; to learn the skills that will enable students to do biographical research; to dramatize dreams; to identify real or imagined conflicts in reading about dreams.

Materials

Required textbooks, 8th grade:

Counterpoint in Literature, Robert C. Pooley (Glenview: Scott, Foresman, 1967)
Physical Science, William L. Ramsey and Lucretia A. Gabriel (Holt, Rinehart and Winston, 1986).
America: Its People and Its Values, Leonard Wood and Ralph H. Gabriel (Harcourt Brace Jovanovich, 1975).

Informational/background books on dreams:

Dream Power, Ann Faraday, 1972.
Creative Dreaming, Patricia Garfield, 1974.
Sleep, Gay Luce and Julius Segal, 1966.
Brainstorms and Thunderbolts, Carol Madigan and Ann Elwood, 1983.
Applied Imagination, Alex F. Osborn, 1963.
The Power of Fantasy in Human Creativity, Steven Parker, 1985.

Course Sequence

Begin by sharing definitions for the word *dream* (a goal, an inspiration, a wild fancy, or something that happens when sleeping). After reading Langston Hughes' "Dreams" students discuss the purpose of having a dream or goal. Discuss attainable and unattainable dreams and then discuss what a utopia could be like.

In pairs create six questions to use interviewing four people outside of class about their dreams. Categorize responses with four other students charting similarities and differences. After reading much material from required texts and resource books from the library, have students discuss such people as Martin Luther King, Emma Goldman, Marie Curie, Joan of Arc, Alfred Hitchcock, Jonas Salk, Nat Turner, Adolf Hitler, Lewis Carroll, Buckminster Fuller, Douglas MacArthur, Robert Louis Stevenson, Louis Pasteur, Galileo, Amelia Earhart in terms of being "visionaries" and "predictors" as well as dreamers. Discuss accomplishments as well as failures.

Students now turn to their own dreams and take a poll on such questions as "do you dream in color?" and "are you in your dreams?" They then investigate answers to similar questions using the library (some areas to investigate are Jung, Freud, REMs, stages of sleeping).

Assignments: Journal writing topics are linked to dreams; students create a utopia through a drawing, poem, or writing; students compose interview questions, interview four subjects, and chart answers; students each find one person in textbooks or other resources who was a dreamer and write a two page paper dealing with the accomplishments as well as the failures of the person/persons chosen; students through interview, videotape, radio show, role playing, puppet show, experiments, or creation of displays must tell how the dream of the person portrayed originated and explain what the person did to achieve his dream. Students end the unit by writing a biographical poem that expresses their own dreams and their own uniqueness.

your understanding of basic principles in English teaching). On the basis of your lists, consider which kinds of unit structures would work best for you.

• Create a list of units that you would like to teach some day. (This is a list that will grow over the years as you teach.) How can your particular areas of interest and expertise be focused for students (without, of course, imposing your own literary hobbyhorses on your students)?

• Learn about textbook adoption procedures in a school district or your state. How often are books adopted? For what kinds of courses? Who decides which books are chosen? Is there a written policy? Also investigate the ground rules for use of supplemental materials. How free are teachers to supplement the required texts with books of their own choosing?

• Develop plans for a unit along the lines suggested in this chapter.

RELATED READINGS

The professional literature is surprisingly sparse when it comes to course and unit planning. It is almost as if it is assumed that through experience, teachers will somehow know how to put together a well-organized, coherent plan. *The English Journal* publishes outlines of courses and units from time to time. In addition, the National Council of Teachers of English publishes *Thematic Units in English and Humanities,* which is updated from time to time.

Perspective on the specific content of English teachers' courses worldwide is offered by Stephen Tchudi's *English Teachers at Work: Ideas and Strategies from Five Countries* (Boynton/Cook, 1986), edited on behalf of the International Federation for the Teaching of English. In it, elementary and secondary teachers from England, Canada, New Zealand, Australia, and the United States describe their classroom practices in such areas as *literature and reading, the teaching of writing, oral language and drama,* and *language instruction.* Although specific unit plans are not explicitly included in this volume, the reader can easily infer unit designs and structures from the description of classroom practices and procedures.

Perhaps the best source of ideas for units, however, is fellow teachers. "Idea exchanges" are popular at professional meetings, and frequently conference organizers will invite teachers to bring one hundred or so copies of a unit plan, course design, or teaching idea to share. Join these exchanges to enhance your collection of good unit plans. If such exchanges don't exist in your area, you might even want to organize one for the school district where you teach.

The Classroom— Environment and Resources

4

I N they come that first day of school, thirty or thirty-five students presenting a diversity of opinions, attitudes, skills, and interests which the teacher cannot fully anticipate. Some teachers don't bother to worry about that diversity; they crank out a syllabus and, like it or not, the students must conform to it. The style of teaching we advocate in this book suggests that the good teacher will adapt aims, resources, and even teaching style to accommodate (not "cater to") the individual personalities of students. It is difficult, under such a "student-centered" style of teaching, to prepare for September.

Something teachers *can* do well in advance is take steps to ready the environment and resources for the variety of students they will face. Whether a course is being taught for the first time or the tenth, reviewing resources at the beginning of the year and taking a look at the physical setting of the class can be a stimulus to new ideas.

THE CLASSROOM

The setting in which learning takes place has been a neglected aspect of education. Whether one considers the institutional lime green of hallways or the uniformity of cinder block classrooms, the school environment is too seldom interesting or attractive to students, kids who spend their free time in the glitzy environments of fast-food joints and malls. Industrial psychologists long ago recognized that the pleasantness of an environment strongly influences productivity. There seems to be no reason why language arts classrooms cannot be similarly "engineered" to enhance students' involvement with their work. Although one doesn't want to compete with the plastic environment of the commercial world, the teacher can certainly create a room that will be modestly memorable to students and will simplify and catalyze their engagement with the oral and printed word.

John Artman, an English teacher from Keokuk, Iowa, claims to have made himself an "interior decorator," using student work and posters to transform his classroom. In addition to serving the cosmetic function of covering plain walls, his practice offers a substantial audience for student work and also provides models on which students can draw for future projects and ideas.

From John Artman, "The English Teacher as Interior Decorator." *The English Journal,* February 1972. Copyright © 1972 by the National Council of Teachers of English. Reprinted by permission of the publisher and the author.

. . . If you come to my classroom you will see that I have become an accomplished interior decorator. . . .

Hanging on the wall, hanging from the ceiling, and scattered all over the floor of the room are projects which the senior Individualized Reading classes have made. At the end of this one semester course, the students are asked to interpret in some art form (model, mobile, drawing, painting, or sculpture) the book they enjoyed the most. Leaning against the blackboard in the back of the room is a large oil painting of *In Cold Blood.* It shows a black shotgun leaning against an orange wall that has blood splattered on it. To the right of the shotgun, on the scales of justice stand Perry and Richard. Another picture on the blackboard is of *Alas, Babylon.* It is painted in bright yellows, oranges, reds, and blues and shows a mushroom explosion and distorted people gathered in a circle in front of it.

Hanging from the ceiling is a mobile representing *Exodus.* It is a round ball of barbed wire with a yellow wooden star of David hanging in the center of it. On one of the shelves of a huge bookcase is a wooden model of *The Bad Seed.* A wooden body with black wire legs and arms has a black seed in its stomach. From one of the arms hangs a pair of shoes. Another arm has a burnt match and an ax. Long strands of gray hair are twisted around the arm. Also in the bookcase is a huge stone literally covered with faces cut out of magazines and glued on. It represents *A Single Pebble.*

Besides these Individualized Reading projects, there are posters hanging on two bulletin boards that students asked to make. These posters are for Individualized Reading, and they show one or more scenes from a book. Again these are not required. The students become fired up over a book and want to paint or draw a poster. At present there are two student posters on the board. One is a huge one of *All Quiet on the*

> *Western Front* and the other is *On the Beach.* The first one shows death dressed as a German soldier standing in a trench. The second one shows an Australian officer standing outside a building. He is waiting for the end of his world.
>
> As you stand in my room, you exclaim, "How do you ever get around in this room?" I say, "I don't. I stumble through, but it's nice stumbling."

However, decoration alone is not sufficient to prepare the physical or intellectual environment of a classroom. *Mad* magazine once ran a satire entitled "The Senior Prom," in which students spent their money to rent a hotel ballroom and then decorated it to look just like the school gym, where they usually held their dances. Cosmetology won't transform students' learning styles and habits. In planning the learning environment, then, teachers need to consider aims and goals, the focus of the curriculum, and the expressed and latent interests and needs of the students. Then the environment—classroom, resources, use of space—can be planned to enhance the odds of achieving what the teacher wants to accomplish.

THE GATHERING PLACE

Here it is, Room 31, thirty-five feet by thirty-five feet, with insufficient closet space and too few bookcases. Over the summer the janitor has waxed the floor and scrubbed the graffiti off the desks. Those desks have been lined up to face front, flag, and lectern. What to do? As a first step, the teacher might push the desks against the wall—physically or in the imagination—and have a look at the space available. (If you're in a school that still has desks bolted to the floor, lodge a protest with the principal; then skip this section of the chapter and move on to projects where you have more options.) The actual floor plan of Room 31 can vary over a broad range to meet various needs as projects, students, and furniture come and go. In our teaching we like to avoid the traditional classroom grid, which implies a teacher-centered class. Desks can be pushed into patterns of circles, semicircles, horseshoes, grape bunches, or bananas to create functional designs for small- and large-group discussions, workshops, and resource centers. Just a few of many possible classroom floor plans are shown in Figure 4.1.

Preferable to individual desks, we think, are worktables, which lead to much more flexible and efficient use of space. (They're also cheaper to buy than individual desks, an argument you might offer to the principal.) Six to eight folding tables with individual chairs—preferably stackable chairs—give one an enormous range of possibilities for large- and small-group work. Some designs with larger tables are shown in Figure 4.2.

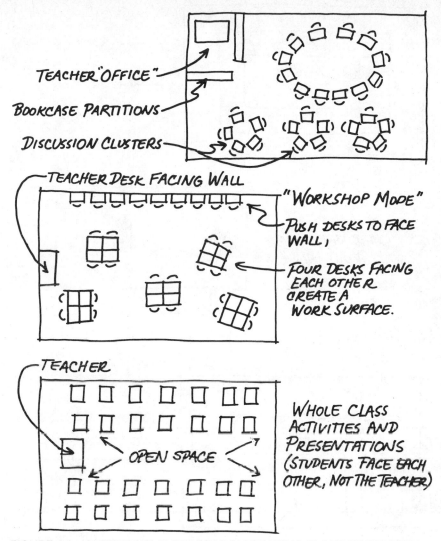

TEACHER "OFFICE"

BOOKCASE PARTITIONS

DISCUSSION CLUSTERS

TEACHER DESK FACING WALL

"WORKSHOP MODE"

PUSH DESKS TO FACE WALL,

FOUR DESKS FACING EACH OTHER CREATE A WORK SURFACE.

TEACHER

OPEN SPACE

WHOLE CLASS ACTIVITIES AND PRESENTATIONS (STUDENTS FACE EACH OTHER, NOT THE TEACHER)

FIGURE 4.1 ALTERNATIVE CLASSROOM SEATING PLANS USING MOVABLE DESKS.

USING THE WALLS

We're assuming here that you'll have your own classroom (and will not be one of those "peripatetic" teachers who is assigned to wander from one "free" room to another). We assume further that you are pretty much free to decorate the room as you see fit. However, even if you have restricted space or are assigned to several different classrooms during the school day, you should think imaginatively about what can be done with the available

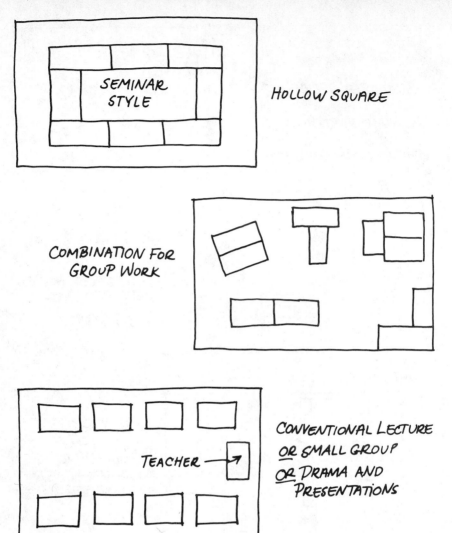

FIGURE 4.2 ALTERNATIVE CLASSROOM SEATING DESIGNS USING FOLDING TABLES.

wall space. We've heard that in British schools, student teachers are penalized if their supervising teacher observes the same bulletin board display two days consecutively—stiff upper lip, chaps. By contrast, in many American schools bulletin board displays, once on the wall, remain there until the construction paper has paled. To keep the bulletin boards fresh, use them for a kaleidoscope of student work (rather than displaying your own cleverness at designing displays). Let student productions create an ever-changing show of themes and compositions (drafts and final copies), artwork, photography, book reports, reviews, announcements of interest, "chain" letters or novels, notes of reaction and response. You can also use the bulletin board as a way to keep students informed about forthcoming events—around the school, around town, on television—or to display book jackets or photocopies of the covers of recently acquired paperbacks. (More suggestions for bulletin board displays are given in Chapter 10.)

In any case, prepare the walls for September with the thought of setting an example of what the class will be about. You might hang posters that touch on themes or books that will be discussed during the year, record-keeping maps or charts that will encourage students to keep track of their own progress, professional art, record album covers, fliers and posters from the plays you saw last summer in London or Kalamazoo, culminating projects from last year's class.

RESOURCE AND ACTIVITY CENTERS

In addition to arranging the furniture to enhance communication, the teacher can make the English classroom a place where students have ready access to the tools and materials of literacy. Books and supplies can be collected and stockpiled over the summer and made available in the fall. One way of organizing materials is through the development of resource centers—actually just corners of the room or tables set aside for certain purposes.

Among the centers or areas you might develop are:

Paperback Displays. Paperback distributors have long recognized that displaying books with the covers face up attracts a readership. To the greatest extent possible, the classroom library should be presented in open-faced shelves or bookracks. (Talk to your paperback distributor about obtaining some of the "spinner" racks that maximize book display space in a small area.)

Bins and Files. Create a filing system where students can find looseleaf materials easily. You can efficiently maintain a set of boxes or baskets or even plastic bags, appropriately labeled, to hold your collectings. Perhaps the easiest system is to file material by type: pamphlets, newspaper clippings, photographs. A more useful arrangement for teaching is to file by themes or topics: animals, ecology, current events, Romantic literature, Shakespeare. Once students learn the system, they can clip and file materials they find in their everyday reading.

Current Magazines. Too few teachers have a subscription budget for classroom magazines, but there are many other ways to obtain magazines for classroom use. Paperback book distributors often shred outdated periodical literature and would be pleased to give it away. Notify your friends with hobbies that you want the back issues of their magazines, whether they focus on cycling, cars, photography, or computers. Bring in your own leftover magazines as well. Ask a relative to contribute that collection of *National Geographic* for your students.

Newspapers.   Schools all over the country participate in "Newspapers in Education" programs, which make sets of papers available for the classroom at low cost. In addition, you can contribute your own daily paper to the classroom and invite students to bring in newspapers their families have finished using at home.

Book Carts.   Even if the supplementary reading materials you can display permanently in your classroom are limited, you can still extend your resources through book carts if the librarian or media center director is willing to bring in forty or fifty titles from time to time.

Writing Center.   This resource center is a near must for virtually any classroom. Your writing center might contain:

Ideas for Writing.   "What can I write about?" is one of the most common questions asked of the English teacher. The writing center might provide students with:

Activity or index cards with writing ideas and suggestions. The National Council of Teachers of English has published lists of thousands of composition topics, and you and your students can come up with an equally good list.

Samples of writing, either by other students or by professional authors, with suggestions for related projects.

Photographs or posters to serve as inspiration.

Topics of the day/week/month as set by the teacher or proposed by the students.

Editing help.   When students have completed the draft of a paper, they might go to the writing center to talk with others about their writing, to work on revision, or to examine selected reference books for help with mechanics, style, usage, and form.

Graphics Materials.   Much school writing is done on cheap paper by students using smudgy pencils or spotty ballpoints. We have all seen and spilled coffee on the stacks of papers that result. In *Gifts of Writing,* Stephen and Susan Judy propose that young people make their writing "look as good as it reads" by turning final drafts into books, magazines, posters, displays, greeting cards, etc. The writing center can make the materials for this sort of graphic enhancement available. Supplies can include construction paper in a variety of colors; scraps of poster board; felt tip pens in a rainbow of colors; string and yarn for book-binding; magazines for cutting up; paste, glue, and scotch tape.

Drama Center.   Many dramatic activities can be woven into the English program: creative dramatics, improvisation, reader's theater, dramatic interpretation, oral presentations of students' work. The tools of the drama trade need not be terribly complex, and many dramatic activities require no equipment at all. Often the "stage" will simply be an area of the floor cleared away for the purpose—this becomes the drama "center." Reader's theater and oral readings are aided by tall stools so that readers can sit and be seen. Music stands help hold papers and manuscripts. For elementary and junior high students, a costume box will be an excellent resource; just a supply of hats, shirts, skirts, jewelry, etc. will do.

THE TEXTBOOK AS RESOURCE

Experienced teachers will recognize that the resource centers we've described can be built up over time; after a few years of developing centers, the problem becomes less finding materials than chucking the old stuff. (We will, incidentally, offer more suggestions on how to use resource centers throughout the remainder of the book.) However, inexperienced and experienced teachers alike recognize that the major teaching resource for any classroom is likely to be the required textbooks, often selected by a committee to which the teacher may or may not have had an opportunity to provide advice. Late in the summer, prior to the arrival of that unpredictable mix of students, careful review of the textbook as resource is in order.

Some texts provide helpful teachers' manuals; sometimes teachers either find the manual missing or discover that its philosophy and organization do not mesh with their own. Since the textbook alone or with a guide should not be allowed to dictate the structure of *your* course, you will need to figure out how to make the material useful. Hopping from one section of the text to another is confusing to students, who need reasons to read a text and need to see pattern and organization. If you keep these ideas in mind, using a standard or adopted textbook need not be deadly.

In the magical world where everyone wants to dwell (that world where everybody wins the lottery), there would be time before school begins for the teacher to read the book cover to cover, picking out the most teachable materials and leaving out the rest. Unfortunately, most teachers have far less time available. A good way to prepare, therefore, is simply to skim the contents and look at the organization of the text. If it's a literature book, does it use a genre approach or does it operate by chronology, themes, or some combination? Where is the poetry placed? Is it integrated throughout the book or is it in clusters? Which old literary favorites are there? Which classics that are readable by your students? Which new pieces that you'll want to read yourself? If it's a composition text you can sense its philosophy from the table of contents: Is this a book dedicated to writing-as-process, structural rhetoric, grammar/correctness? How well does the book's table of contents coincide with your own philosophy? Glance at some of the exercises and rate them on an imaginativeness scale of 1 to 10 or A through F.

From these skimmings you can begin to work out the details of a course, even to plan for the first week or more. Do you want to begin with literature or composition (or neither—perhaps oral discussion or drama)? Which stories in the literature text might be reasonably surefire for the first days of teaching? Which topics in the composition book will most directly make contact with the students and help them see that English really can be of some help to them in school?

At some point, you'll probably want to draw a map or chart of your teaching journey, tentatively identifying textbook chapters you want to use, in what sequence, and for what purposes. That, in turn, helps you begin to think about other resource needs for your class. Conclude the text survey by writing down what *isn't* there. How will you have to supplement the book to enrich your class? Will you need to find a wide range of novels related to a theme? Will you have to develop your own writing topics to substitute for dry-as-dust topics in the textbook? Make a shopping list and then start looking for more resources.

FINDING OUT WHAT'S AVAILABLE

Talking to other teachers who have taught the course may prove useful. One of them can probably discuss additional resources that teachers use with particular courses. Other teachers can tell you which novels are traditionally taught in that grade and the kinds of films and videos that are available; colleagues may even discuss suggestions for units or writing assignments or share lesson or unit plans they have developed.

The Book Room

Almost every school contains a book room for the use of the English department. It may be an old dusty closet or a well-stocked departmental office. In spite of the dust and battered covers, the books there may be quite helpful. There will certainly be dictionaries, class and small-group sets of novels, and single copies of a number of books. After a book room scan, check out copies of books that seem to have possibilities for use in your particular course.

Older literature anthologies are a rich and underused source of stories and poetry that can supplement the current glossy textbook. Inspect the contents of one of the old-timers to see if any authors or titles seem appealing. There will be poetry collections in the book room, too, as well as drama anthologies that can be used to supplement the adopted textbooks.

Somewhere on the shelves of the book room may rest books of quotations, pamphlets on word origins, or texts on dialects or other aspects of language. There may be back issues of student magazines such as *Scope, Read,* and *Literary Cavalcade,* and there may be a stack of magazines like *Time* or *Reader's Digest* that you can acquire for your classroom for the low cost of physical labor (probably yours).

A key to using the book room successfully is to see its potential for helping to *individualize* your program. If you go there with the idea that you must find thirty or thirty-five copies of anything, you'll likely be disappointed.

The School Library

Another valuable and often underused resource in the school is the school library. We regularly hear teachers complain about the poor quality of their school library, but it often turns out that they simply haven't explored the full range of available resources. Librarians commonly provide services ranging from giving a classroom orientation to the library through doing book talks for entire classes of students to preparing reserve shelves on specific topics. The library will also house audiovisual resources, along with AV catalogs for the school or district. The librarian can often give practical advice on the availability of movies and how long it takes to obtain them. Ordering films may, in fact, help you organize for the year, for in many districts the demand for films is high and the waiting lists are long. School districts frequently have access to media centers for regional agencies, and even teachers who have worked in the same district for years are not always in the know about the availability and location of all the AV resources in the area.

Records, filmstrips, and, increasingly, videos are more often stored in the school library itself. Before school, scan the lists of in-house records and filmstrips and note any that seem especially interesting or appropriate for your courses. Preview all these materials at your relative leisure before the hordes arrive in September, thus sparing yourself the embarrassment of showing something of poor quality or inappropriate content. (Diana once showed a condensed film version of a famous book by Herman Melville only to find that the role of Captain Ahab was played by the nearsighted Mr. Magoo!)

The library is centrally about *books*. We find it helpful to spend time browsing the shelves before school opens looking for interesting titles (jotting down call numbers as we go to save a second trip to the card catalog during the school year). Check nonfiction titles to locate books and topics that students might find interesting. Then inspect the biographies to see if there are heroes and heroines your students might enjoy studying. Explore the reference section to remind yourself of the kinds of materials there—it's more than just dictionaries and encyclopedias. Review the vertical files and look into the clipping and pamphlet collections on such topics as gardening, disasters, alcoholism, riots, refugees, prisoners, sod housing, whaling, spies, and slums.

The librarian can also show you which magazines your school subscribes to, and you can skim them quickly to catch the drift of magazines you might not ordinarily read, like *Hot Rodder* or *Teen Idols*.

Look through the poetry section in the library, paying attention to the amount, variety, and quality of poetry on the shelves. Often you will have to supplement the library holdings, but the librarian may also be willing to pick up poetry anthologies to supplement your class topics and themes.

Lastly, look through the fiction to familiarize yourself with titles you can recommend to your students and use to augment your course themes, topics, periods, or genres. We believe that you *can* judge a book by its cover—at least a sound enough judgment to determine whether you want to list the book for possible individualized reading. Further, if you reveal yourself to be a serious user of the library, the librarian will often call on you to help build up the holdings in particular areas.

The Public Library

Another helpful planning strategy is to review the holdings of the public library. A section particularly rich in resources and possibilities will be the children's literature. The name can be misleading, and one might assume that this collection has only books for elementary school children. However, Diana in particular has found that books for younger readers are often highly successful with older students. Biographies from the children's section, for example, are often more appealing to secondary school readers because they deal with the lives of contemporary heroes and heroines who are not yet or may never be the subject of "adult" biographies.

The nonfiction section in the children's area is usually filled with titles on topics that will appeal to students. You'll find usable books on witches, werewolves, ghosts, wild foods, hot-air ballooning, jazz, minicycles, bug hunting, magic, dinosaurs, pirates, buried cities, and knives, as well as books on adoption, death, and living with a single parent. Familiarity with the range of topics in this section will serve you well later in the year when you formulate plans for assignments and units.

Also in the children's section will be collections of legends, fairy tales, myths, and folklore. Here you'll discover tales of tricksters, giants, witches, dragons, kings and queens, ogres, and demons. There will be wonderfully entertaining stories about distant lands: China, India, Scotland, Africa, Poland, France, and England. And there will be tales of enchantment, wonder, superstition, and nonsense. Check with the librarian, too, for various reference and guidebooks to resources in these areas, books such as Margaret Reed MacDonald's *The Storyteller's Sourcebook* and Norma Olin Ireland's *Index to Fairy Tales.*

The children's poetry section will contain many collections that appeal to secondary students. Students don't find this sort of poetry childish, especially if they've been prepared for it. Here, too, a number of indexes and resource books exist to help one find poetry on such topics as loneliness, pioneers, executions, revenge, family life, trains, storms, wolves, twins, odors, stars, names, or space travel.

Don't pass by the picture book section of the public library, which can provide sources of many writing ideas and can even be used with less able readers. Examine a subject index such as Caroline Lima's *A to Zoo—Subject Access to Children's Picture Books* or Sharon Spredemann Dreye's *The Bookfinder—A Guide to Children's Literature about the Needs and Problems of Youth Aged 2–15,* which have subject categories in such areas as attention getting, freckles, child abuse, cooperation, dropping out, friendship, hostility, and shyness.

Elsewhere in the public library you may find paintings to rent for a dollar or two per month, a way of brightening up your institution's walls. You may find an inventory of posters that can lead to writing assignments. Videos can be rented here, too, and you may be able to supplement the school's AV holdings by borrowing records, filmstrips, and cassette recordings.

THE FINE ART OF SCAVENGING

It's a shame that the public schools are not well funded and that classroom resources are often at the bottom of the list for expenditures. In many schools, paperback libraries paid for by school funds are out of the question, and the meager annual book budget is consumed by replacement copies of adopted textbook series. The teacher—experienced or inexperienced—can either accept that state of affairs or aggressively work around it. We've both become scavengers over the years, and we've found that there are innumerable resources around town that can be helpful in the classroom. We're also willing to open our wallets and spend the occasional

Air

Fire

Earth

Water

FIGURE 4.3 ENHANCING THE CLASSROOM ENVIRONMENT.

These visualizations of the classical four elements, air, earth, water, and fire, were done by the students of Sister Mary Clare Yates at Our Lady of Mercy High School, Farmington, Michigan. (In Stephen Judy, ed., *Lecture Alternatives in Teaching English.* Copyright © 1971 by the Michigan Council of Teachers of English.)

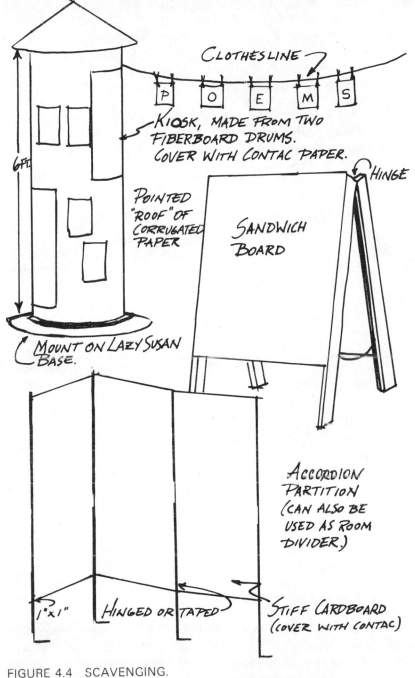

CLOTHESLINE

P O E M S

KIOSK, MADE FROM TWO FIBERBOARD DRUMS. COVER WITH CONTAC PAPER.

6 FT.

POINTED "ROOF" OF CORRUGATED PAPER

HINGE

SANDWICH BOARD

MOUNT ON LAZY SUSAN BASE.

ACCORDION PARTITION (CAN ALSO BE USED AS ROOM DIVIDER.)

1"×1"   HINGED OR TAPED   STIFF CARDBOARD (COVER WITH CONTAC)

FIGURE 4.4   SCAVENGING.
Some classroom display centers created from low-cost materials.

buck for something that looks like a bargain, but if you're opposed to this, either on principle or by virtue of an empty billfold, you can still find plenty of material free. We've seen creative use made of scavenged rope, tin cans, an army surplus parachute, scrap wood, Christmas lights, wallpaper remnants, Styrofoam, pasteboard drums, cloth remnants, chicken wire, and orange crates. You can also find an extraordinary amount of reading material free in almost any community, material ranging from promotional brochures to full-length books. You need not be limited by a barren Room 31; a bit of imagination and persistence can transform it into the reading/writing environment you want for your students. Figures 4.3 and 4.4 illustrate some possibilities.

EXPLORATIONS AND RESOURCES

• Design a floor plan for your classroom. Following the example of interior decorators, you might even cut out paper scraps to represent desks, bookcases, tables, etc. and move them about on a classroom grid to find designs that you think would best use your available space.

• Resource centers (or simply resource boxes) can be developed on almost any topic and need not be limited to reading, writing, and drama. Below are listed some possible topics for centers. Choose one and develop a list of materials you'd like to include. Or, better, start collecting the resources.

Language Play	Biography
Language History	Media Study
Discussion	Short Stories
Media Production	Script Writing
One-Act Plays	Nature of Language
Careers	Biography
Science	Computers
Classic Literature	Modern Classics

• Hunt through the bookshelves of other English teachers' classrooms (with their permission, of course) looking for still more usable materials. Encourage fellow teachers to exchange freely single copies of materials that would enhance one another's teaching.

• Make the trip to your public library and inquire about the services librarians will provide. Do they have a storyteller who would meet with your class? Will they allow you to check out large quantities of books for use with your class? Do they have a librarian knowledgeable about young adult literature who would be willing to give book talks in your class?

• Haunt garage sales, library sales, and secondhand bookstores for inexpensive books to build your classroom library. Often secondhand bookstores are willing to take "trashy" books in exchange for those suitable for schools.

• See Stephen and Susan Judy's *Gifts of Writing* (New York: Charles Scribner's, 1980) and *Young Writer's Handbook* (New York: Charles Scribner's, 1984) for additional ideas on ways to create writing centers, including suggestions for the kinds of materials to include in a graphics or book production center.

Getting Started

5

The summer is over. You've prepared and planned, thought about the school year, and possibly even cleaned out the book closets in preparation for the fall.

What do you do once the students arrive?

We like to borrow from the great thinker and futurist Buckminster Fuller and think of the English class as a potential *synergistic* structure. Fuller's geodesic domes illustrate the principles of synergy: a number of separate parts act in concert to create a structure that is stronger than any of the individual parts. As Fuller pointed out, the human body is also a synergistic unit, with separate organs—each one incapable of surviving alone (except in science fiction)—all working on different tasks for a common purpose.

Teaching language arts class can be perceived as the task of creating a synergistic structure using *people*. On the opening day of class, the teacher is faced with students of widely diverging interests and expectations. Each of these students has special strengths and individual weaknesses; the teacher's task is to figure out how to design a class to maximize strengths and help every student succeed, thus creating a strong unit, a community of learners who are willing to work together. If the class comes together and works well, it will become self-supporting—like a geodesic dome. Unfortunately, unlike dome builders, teachers don't know quite what the final structure will look like, and there are no clear-cut engineering principles or mathematical formulas to guide them. As much as they would like to produce a smooth, geometric unit, the English class will probably be more like the human body: subject to malfunctions and disease, with parts that need glasses, or braces, or occasional shots to keep operating. But, like the body, a class is capable of doing some marvelous, unanticipated things.

OPENINGS

Where to begin? Given all the pieces and parts, how does the teacher start the class-building process? We think teachers often underrate the competence of young people, failing to see the abilities and skills they bring with them. In an age in which there is lack of public confidence in the schools, teachers can easily fall into the trap of expecting their students to come in unlearned and unskilled. Although, as we have acknowledged, few kids will come to class as skilled as one would like, most young people (like adults) have developed powerful skills already. Perhaps one of the first things a teacher should do is discover the human resources of the class and take a brief glimpse at the attitudes and ideas the students bring with them.

An introductory letter from the teacher to the students (Figure 5.1) can serve many purposes and lets the teacher begin to get a sense of the students in the class. Students like the chance to show a bit of their uniqueness to the teacher, and they usually respond enthusiastically to this type of letter. The questions in the letter can be varied for different kinds of classes and levels of students.

These letters are responded to (not graded) and given back to the students within a day or two. The immediate response, including comments on what the students have said or even questions for them to answer in a further interchange, builds rapport between the student and the teacher. Students often feel they have received personal attention from and thus have a personal connection to the teacher as a result. Thus, letters can help establish the tone and atmosphere of the class, since students feel from the start that what they think *does* matter. This letter can also help to defuse any antagonism or hostility from some students. Diana encourages the students to state right away what bothers them about the required English class and about teachers. Not all hostile students will answer—some preferring to wait to see if the teacher can be trusted—but the fact that the option of responding negatively exists will have been duly noted.

Before having students write their introductory letter, we usually explain each question and emphasize that any question can be skipped. This is the place for the teacher to explain that when they describe their personality, students may just be stating that they're talkative and friendly or quiet and thoughtful. We also emphasize that this letter is a guide to help us know how best to treat each student so that they can do well in the class. We invite students to tell us if they respond to prodding or do best when left alone. Or if they like to be called on or cringe at the thought of it. Or if they appreciate a literal pat on the back or recoil from any kind of physical

FIGURE 5.1   LETTER OF INTRODUCTION.

Write a letter to me telling me about yourself. What are you like as a student? How do you usually behave in class? How would you describe your personality?

How do you like to be treated? How is it easiest to get along with you? What behavior in a teacher really bothers you?

Explain how you feel about reading aloud in class or doing a presentation in front of others. Tell me about yourself as a reader. Describe any experiences you have had reporting on books.

Describe your writing/composing abilities. Do you consider yourself a good writer? What kinds of things do you like/hate to write about? What are your strongest and weakest skills in English? What areas would you like to improve in?

Think back to the last few years in English classes. Describe assignments or activities that you loved and those that you hated.

What would you like to accomplish in this class? What do you like/hate to be evaluated on in an English classroom? What do you like to be graded on?

What are your interests/talents/skills/hobbies? What are you proudest of that you have accomplished in school or outside of school?

What can I do that will be most interesting or helpful to you? Is there any other advice you'd like to give me or any questions you'd like to ask me? Is there anything else you feel I should know about you?

Don't forget to sign your name.

touch. These letters give the teacher more information about each student than can be digested at one time, so it's a good idea after students have read the responses for the teacher to collect the letters and reread them. (We also find that the letter has the practical consequence of helping us learn students' names early in the game.)

Another good way to break the ice in a class is through interest inventories and questionnaires. We've often been astonished at the amount of information less-than-fully "educated" students bring to the class with them. The inventory created by Robin Jackson (Figure 5.2) is a good way not only to see what students are concerned with but also to initiate library or research work for the year. If students know that this information will be used or be part of another assignment, they're often eager to take the time to fill out the inventory thoroughly.

We don't particularly care for assigning a "theme" the first day of class, since in the past students have often had such essays used "against them" as diagnostic instruments. "You write," the students say to themselves, "so the teacher can find out how rotten you write."

FIGURE 5.2
From Robin Jackson, "The Reading Inventory: A New Twist," *Notes Plus,* November 1983, p. 15. Copyright © 1983 by the National Council of Teachers of English. Reprinted by permission.

THE READING INVENTORY: A NEW TWIST

For years I've relied on a reading inventory in getting to know my students and their interests. Occasionally I've referred them to their completed inventories when they've complained, "I don't know what to read." Only recently, however, have I glimpsed the possibilities an inventory offers.

Let me begin with twenty typical inventory questions.

1. What are three questions to which you'd like the answer?
2. Have you ever wondered how something works? Name a mechanism or object you'd like to know more about.
3. What is your favorite after-school activity?
4. List three favorite weekend activities.
5. What two places would you most like to visit?
6. When you are alone, how do you occupy your time?
7. If you could have three wishes (you can't wish for more wishes), what would they be?
8. What do you dislike about school?
9. If you could talk to any three people in the world, living or dead, who would they be?
10. If you could live at any time in history—past, present, or future—what time would you choose? Be specific.
11. When you are thirty years old, what do you think you will be doing for a living?
12. If you had $1000, how would you spend it?
13. Name the skill you possess of which you are most proud.
14. What skill would you most like to improve?
15. List three things you hope to accomplish before you die.
16. If you could ask anybody in the whole world any question, who would you ask and what would the question be?
17. Where (aside from school) is the last place on earth you'd like to be right now and why?
18. Name something you are now or once were terrified by.
19. Since you have to study history, which period would you choose to study?
20. If you were to recommend a book to a friend, what book would you recommend and why?

. . . These inventories . . . help me learn about my students, and they gain some information about me because I post my responses to the inventory. . . . I also develop a book list around student interests that we use for required reading assignments throughout the year. In addition, I have access to a valuable source for composition and discussion topics.

Nevertheless, letters, inventories, and the discussion that surrounds them do provide some insights into students' language skills and how these skills can be used in the class. Some students are good talkers; others are good writers. Somewhere in the class are a potential spelling champion and a student who is a walking dictionary. The class probably has one or two crossword puzzle addicts, along with a few students who read and write poetry on the sly. One student likes to type; another does hand lettering. Someone has read the Bible cover to cover, and somebody else has read every single Star Trek book and comic.

The experience and language of the students should interact constantly. In the synergistic classroom, everything a student knows or does through language becomes a critical contribution to the class. Sharing knowledge and experience is an important event for the language community.

The tasks of those first few weeks of school are, first, finding the skills and interests each student brings and, second, shaping a climate where the students will share freely with each other. These are no easy tasks, and the first few weeks of any class are likely to be rocky and rather unpredictable—a period of trial, error, and groping.

GETTING TO KNOW YOU

Although some students may have pals in your class, in large schools many of the students will be strangers. The teacher may also be a stranger to the students. Students generally respond positively to teacher attempts to get to know them. However, as important as that teacher–student relationship is, student–student awareness of each other is even more important. Before the class will function as a unit, the students and teacher will need to get to know one another—not only by name but also as personalities.

If teachers explain why it is so vital that students know each other before beginning any getting-to-know-you activities, students will tend to see the activities as more than beginning-of-the-year time fillers. The teacher can explain that they will be working together in groups frequently and that to develop as a community, a group who will work together helping each other, it is necessary and an act of common courtesy to know each others' names.

The payoff for students is that they are more comfortable with each other. Working hard at the beginning of the year to learn each others' names can save them the embarrassment of having to ask someone his or her name after they have been in the class two or three months. It can also save them from feeling unimportant or not valued when no one knows their name.

There are many different ways in which students can begin to get to know each other. The most common one is "going around the circle," with

members of the class—including the teacher—talking a bit about themselves and their interests. Diana often asks students to use alliterative words
to describe themselves. She begins by telling them that she is Mrs. Mitchell
and can be both Marvelous and Mouthy. Though this sort of "round the
circle" device is useful, it is usually not enough to bring about solid acquaintances. To become partners and functioning peers, people have to
work and talk together, exchanging ideas and information. On the next few
pages are activities that supply opportunities for the students to work
together on cooperative ventures while eliciting expressions of interest,
abilities, and problems.

WORKING TOGETHER

SILHOUETTES.   Have students pair off with other students in the class
whom they haven't met. Using contrasting colors of construction paper,
each partner makes a cutout profile of the other, using a source of light (an
overhead projector works well) to cast a shadow on the paper. (See Figure
5.3.)

After the silhouettes have been completed, have each person interview
the partner about interests, beliefs, ideas, and background and then write
a thumbnail sketch of the person directly on the silhouette. It often works
well to have students generate these questions in groups so that the burden
of creating them doesn't fall on each pair of students.

Hang the completed silhouettes with written commentary around the
room for a week or two. This display provides an interesting and colorful
"rogues gallery" but in addition proves to be a help in learning names.

Although the above activity seems complicated in terms of the students
taking turns using the overhead and seems almost elementary in its use of
construction paper, scissors, and glue, we've used it very successfully in
grades seven through graduate school. Without overselling, the teacher
should show that this assignment includes a number of language arts skills
that are part of the overall curriculum, thus encouraging students to take
the assignment seriously even while enjoying it.

PERSONAL SURVEYS.   Another good way to get students to work together and learn more about one another is to have them work in groups
sharing the results of a class survey they have made. Possible items to
include in the survey are numbers of brothers and sisters; hours spent
watching TV per week; hours helping out at home; hours talking on the
phone; work; favorites—foods, books, colors, animals, music, movies, TV
programs, comic strips, sports; and hobbies. For older students, surveys can
move into local, state, and world affairs; careers; thoughts on marriage and
family; and plans for further education. Encourage students to keep the

FIGURE 5.3   SILHOUETTES.

questions light and not too personal so that everyone will be willing to share the responses with others. After students have completed the survey, have them work in groups to compile the results. Each group can report to the class on its findings, and results can be posted on the board. From these survey results, have students write up news articles describing the profile of the class or have them create a radio bulletin or essay describing teenagers today. By integrating group work with getting-to-know-you activities and with writing activities, students will begin to get a sense of what the teacher means by saying that thinking, reading, writing, and talking are all part of the language arts class and are all related to each other.

ASSESSING THE ANTHOLOGY.   One especially good way to get students acquainted with each other and to show them that you value critical thinking and their opinions is to conduct an anthology survey (Figure 5.4). Have the students work in pairs to find materials in the text and to evaluate and respond to some of those materials. Aside from giving students another opportunity to work together, this task should also help them see that the teacher views the text as containing a range of materials and that not every student is expected to love every last selection. Doing this sort of activity also gives the students a needed sense of purpose and direction for the class, and, with luck, they may even plunge in and begin reading some of the selections that seem particularly inviting.

SHORT-STORY GROUPS.   As a beginning assignment, have students review several short stories and select one or two for reading. Ask them to take notes justifying their choices and to share their reasons with the class. Among the features that may catch their eye are length, introductory comments, title, pictures, interesting first paragraph, topic, and content. They can then report their selections to the whole class and the teacher can note the kinds of selections that seem to appeal to most kids. Thus the students are providing invaluable information to the teacher about their interests.

SHARING WRITING

When students share what they have written, others in the class begin to see them as distinct people. Students also get to know the interests of others in the class and to learn more about the collective composition skills of the class. If handled sensitively, sharing writing can be a bonding experience that helps create a real community of learners and helpers. Most people feel vulnerable about their own writing. If they can be induced to share writing in a nonthreatening situation and can see that their feelings are not isolated, they will become more willing writers.

Following are writing ideas that we have found to work well at the beginning of the year—neither too personal nor too staid. They invite students to breathe life into their writing because they are writing about something they know about or feel strongly about.

FIGURE 5.4 ASSESSING THE ANTHOLOGY.

1. What is the title of the textbook?
2. Who are the authors? From information you find at the front of the book explain whether you think they were qualified to write the book or not.
3. What is the copyright date? What might this mean about what will be included or excluded from the text?
4. Look in the Table of Contents and together write down unit headings. Comment after several of these headings whether they seem interesting or not. Try to explain why.
5. List any authors or selections you have heard of before. Did either of you like the author's work or the selections you have heard of?
6. Skim the Table of Contents for titles of selections that sound interesting to you. Each of you should write down two or three.
7. Turn to the text itself. Pick a story and look at what you are asked to do with the story after you have read it. List the names of the sections after each selection (For Discussion, Language, and Vocabulary). Discuss with your partner how you feel about the way the authors ask you to respond to selections. Record your reactions. Have you ever had to respond in ways suggested by this book? What was your reaction to it?
8. Browse through the text looking for sections or selections that look interesting to you and for those that don't seem too interesting. Each of you write down two or three appealing sections and two or three unappealing ones. Try to explain your reactions.
9. Look at the pictures in the text. Discuss whether you think they add interest to the text or not. Record your reaction. Then each partner should look for a picture that he or she likes or hates. Describe the picture briefly and in a few words explain your reaction.
10. Spend a few minutes looking through the poetry sections. Find a poem each of you likes or hates, explain your reactions to each other, and record titles of poems, reaction, and two or three words to explain your reaction.
11. Find the glossary and write down two or three words that you each know the meaning of already.
12. Find the index and write down the kinds of information you can find there.
13. Are there any other sections or parts of the book? Write down the names of those sections and explain what can be found there.

• *Letter writing.* Susan Tchudi has had success meeting new groups of students by providing a different kind of letter-writing activity (*The Writing Interests of Children and Adolescents,* doctoral dissertation, Michigan State University, 1976). Students are given a variety of audiences for whom they can write, ranging from personal and private (write a letter to yourself) to public (write a letter to the mayor or the governor) to the imaginary (write to a Martian who is thinking about visiting our planet). Students can write anything from personal narratives to discussions of world issues. By studying topic choices, audience, and the quality of writing, the teacher can make significant statements about the abilities and interests of the students. Further, through sharing letters in small groups or talking about choices of topics, students will also become more aware of these differing interests and attitudes.

• *The Fib.* Often students feel hesitant to write much at the beginning of the year and even more hesitant to share what they've written. An idea offered by Jeff Golub (Figure 5.5) seems to solve both problems. Students become fascinated with the idea of lying about anything they choose. They come up with such topics as "Whales Spotted on Great Lakes," "The Loch Ness Monster Speaks," "President Promises No More Foreign Intervention," and "Russian Leader Wins Awards for His Humorous Writing." Diana has seen the positive results this assignment brings when students see how clever or creative their classmates are. The nature of this assignment seems to spring open the doors of creativity, and after sharing their "fibs" the students often have a deeper appreciation of the talents and individuality of others in the class.

• *Controversial articles.* To get a good sampling of another kind of student writing, the teacher can bring in a controversial newspaper article that speaks to students' interests. Students can then write a reaction, a letter to

---

FIGURE 5.5   LIES, LIES, LIES.

From *Ideas Plus,* Book 1. "Obtaining an Honest Writing Sample," by Jeff Golub. Copyright © 1984 by the National Council of Teachers of English. Reprinted by permission.

At the beginning of each school year, I want a writing sample from each student. . . . I used to have trouble getting a sample of more than a few sentences until I began using this topic: "You may write a poem, a letter, a story, a newspaper report; use any form you feel is appropriate. But whatever you do, fib! The entire composition is to be one outrageous fabrication—the wilder, the better." Using this topic, I routinely receive papers that are one to three pages in length. There is no problem persuading students to share their writing with classmates, either.

the editor, or a countereditorial. This project can be discussed first in groups to give the students a chance to explore how they feel while seeing how others' opinions differ from their own. The teacher can use the products to assess how well students handle essay writing, while the students see that the real stuff of life is being brought into the classroom.

All of these writing-and-sharing activities can be used anytime during the year, but they work especially well early on because they are assignments with which students can readily succeed. Equally important, these first successes can shape a student's attitude toward writing for the rest of the year.

RECOGNIZING AND ENCOURAGING INDIVIDUALITY

Since one of our goals is to create a community of learners, we find it useful to offer activities that focus on the uniqueness of every student while providing still more information to students and the teacher on the varied interests and skills of people in the class.

• *Signatures.* Handwriting says a lot about us, and our signatures are usually as distinctive as thumbprints. This activity requires students to think about similarities and differences in handwriting while focusing on their own uniqueness. We begin by explaining the thinking/writing connection in this activity, then ask that students write their signature across the top of a piece of notebook paper. Next they are to describe their own handwriting in terms of slant, shape, embellishments, loops, tightness, floridity, etc. After students see many of the ways handwriting can be described, they pass their papers to another person, who writes just one comment about a signature, e.g., "squished together," "open circles over the i's," or "all bent to the right." The papers are then passed to other students, and each one makes a fresh comment, sometimes responding to other observations that have been written on the page. Eventually, the students get their signatures back, and they can write a reaction to the comments, summarize them, or even compose a poem that describes their signature.

In a related activity, we sometimes invite students to explore different kinds of signatures for themselves, changing handwriting to explore their personalities (Figure 5.6).

• *Student-generated trivia.* This activity draws on the knowledge of each individual in the class. Students each generate five to ten trivia questions—any bit of obscure information will do, but they must know the answer. The last few minutes of class can be used to read these; students soon have a better appreciation of how much knowledge each student possesses.

FIGURE 5.6 SIGNATURES.

• *Skills exchange day.* All students have some things they do very well—hobbies, sports, outside interests. Skills exchange day consists of arranging for students to share their knowledge with one another. This can be done on a single, special class day in a "country fair" atmosphere, or it can be spread out over a term with, say, Fridays reserved for presentations by one or two students. To add to the interest, invite students to do their presentations using media, or have students write and read advance advertisements about their skills or presentations. Skills exchange can be taken "on the road" to other classes, thus helping build solidarity within your class.

To further enhance the language aspect of this activity, have students write about skills exchange day in a classroom bulletin or newsletter or interview one of the presenters, focusing on how the person became interested in the topic.

• *Library interest search.* It seems as if an introduction to the library is done every year in every English class, yet each September kids give you blank stares when you ask how one would go about finding information in the library. A partial cause of this bibliothecal amnesia may be that students don't often have experience looking up topics that genuinely interest *them*. The purpose of this assignment is to show students the library in a "hands-on" way. Instead of having them go directly to the card catalog, have them browse the shelves. Have them list two or three titles that interest them in the 100s, 200s, 300s, etc. Encourage them to go to the magazine rack and write down two titles they'd be interested in reading. Send them to the biographies to locate titles that sound interesting, and have them do the same at the record collection. In the fiction section, they can write down titles of three or four books they might be interested in reading (or, better, check out a title or two). In the reference area they can discover reference books besides encyclopedias by flipping through the pages. Finally, send them to the subject section of the card catalog to discover at least five topics that sound interesting.

The following day, students can share topics and book titles that appealed to them. They will have a clearer idea of how the resources of the library can be used and will have identified some interest areas for themselves and the teacher. Once again, the teacher is sending a message that people's interests differ and that a diversity of opinions is acceptable in this class.

We hope we've shown that "getting started" activities can be woven into the fabric of the course so that students immediately get a sense of direction from the teacher. Students need to know that the teacher understands that a "deep structure" exists for the class, even though they will have a choice of assignments and selection of materials. Students should see that there is a purpose to what they are being asked to do and that what they are doing fits in with their own interests as well as those of the teacher.

A LITERACY ATTITUDE SCALE

In addition to the various informal methods we have reviewed, the teacher may want to make a formal assessment of students' attitudes toward the main content of the course—reading, writing, and speaking. Elton McNeil developed an attitude scale for use in the *Hooked on Books* reading program that can be used for this purpose (Figure 5.7). In addition to helping the teacher learn how students assess the importance of reading and writing as compared to cars, television, sports, and food, this scale can be used as an informal pretest for the English class. Administered again at the end of the course, the scale will presumably show that students think better of reading, writing, and speaking than they did when

Example			Money			
			is			
very good	good	sort of good	not good or bad	sort of bad	bad	very bad
very weak	weak	sort of weak	not weak or strong	sort of strong	strong	very strong
very interesting	interesting	sort of interesting	not interest- ing or dull	sort of dull	dull	very dull
very small	small	sort of small	not small or big	sort of big	big	very big
very important	unimportant	sort of important	not important or unimportant	sort of unimportant	unimportant	very unimportant

Test Items (using above dimensions)

1. Cars are	2. Television is	3. Classes are	4. Newspapers are
5. I am	6. Sports are	7. Writing is	8. Food is
9. This place is	10. Reading is	11. Tests are	12. Teachers are
13. Home is	14. Magazines are	15. Work is	16. Books are

FIGURE 5.7   A LITERACY ATTITUDE SCALE.

From Daniel Fader and Elton McNeil, *Hooked on Books*. Copyright © 1966, 1968 by Daniel Fader and Elton McNeil. Reprinted by permission of the publisher, Berkley Publishing Company.

they entered the class. Since research has shown correlations between skill performance and the attitude of students, demonstrating such changes in students' views of English can provide a helpful bit of evidence of a teacher's competence.

Teachers will probably want to adapt this device to their own classes, adding some items and eliminating others. One notable omission from McNeil's list is reference to the listening/speaking/dramatizing domain of English. One might add items such as:

Talking with friends is _____.
Class discussions are _____.
Seeing plays is _____.
Debating is _____.

One could also add specialized questions about particular kinds of reading and writing:

Poems are _____.
Writing stories is _____.
Writing letters is _____.
Reading about people's lives is _____.

ASSESSING ABILITY LEVELS

Much has been written about the use of diagnostic tests and assessments to determine individual pupil needs. While we strongly support the idea of learning about students' needs on an individual basis, a great many commercial tests are not especially helpful and are even detrimental to establishing rapport with a class or obtaining quality information.

Reading tests, for example, generally offer students a series of passages for silent reading followed by a number of comprehension questions. Depending on whether they remember the facts of the passage, students are given a reading grade-level score or shown to be weak or suspect in various reading skills. One can also find on the market many so-called tests of writing skills that do not even ask students to write, preferring to base the assessment on spelling, vocabulary, or sentence correction.

Such tests are suspect on two counts.

First, the results—too often given as some sort of raw score or percentile—tend to bias teachers about the skills and abilities of their students. Johnny is labeled a "second grade reader" in the teacher's mind and remains that way throughout the year. Jane is perceived as "having language skills two years above norm," and her linguistic growth is ignored as a result. The scores are too easy to substitute for actual evaluation and observation of young people and their language.

Second, the tests themselves are inaccurate. No collection of passages followed by a series of questions can even begin to measure adequately what children can read. What do they read? Can they read street signs? The daily paper? TV commercials? The textbook? These are the crucial questions that are seldom answered by a diagnostic test score. Similarly, the tests of writing—even if they do involve a writing sample—are done under conditions of testing that blur whether or not people are functioning well with language. The question is not how well Jane does responding to a standardized "prompt" in a thirty-minute test frame, but how well she writes and uses language daily: for notes, for letters, for her personal diary, for a variety of classroom purposes.

In the course of a semester or term, a conscientious English teacher will compile information on his or her students that is far more detailed and specific than that accumulated through commercial tests. Even so, the teacher needs to do some preliminary assessment as well. To that end, we suggest that teachers look closely at what they learn from the broad range of activities and ideas we presented above. For example, if the opening letter is used the teacher can note writing strengths and weaknesses from this one assignment. By taking note of how students reacted to the library work or the textbook hunt, teachers should get many ideas about materials to use and strategies students seem to enjoy. Teachers should not undervalue their own skills of assessment, which are exercised every day in the classroom.

EXPLORING THE RANGE OF LANGUAGE

Another technique we employ in our own teaching is to deliberately expose the students to a wide range of language and language activities during the early weeks of the term, not only to assess what they know about and can do with language but also to provide them with a sampler of what we see as important in "English." Thus we will alter the diet in reading, bringing in, over several weeks, contemporary poetry; good, engaging short stories; a drama to be read aloud, by either the students or the teacher; and a boxful of paperback books and magazines for browsing. We'll do some formal writing of essays and editorials, but we'll also offer varieties of free writing, group writing, and journal keeping to give students a sense of how they can use the written word. We will show the students some magazine advertisements and have them analyze the language, then do the same for a newspaper article or editorial, looking for biases and slants. We'll start the directed, individualized reading program and teach the students to use in-class time for a writing workshop, and those two strategies, in turn, create time for individual conferences with students. Much of this work can be done in conjunction with a regular class unit, say a thematic or topic unit in literature, so we are "covering material" as well as testing the class to see what kinds of activities work most satisfactorily and to assess areas that require more work. In a sense, then, the opening weeks offer students a language arts smorgasbord. We hasten to add that this is *not* a collection of leftovers or of whatever happens to be on hand, but a systematic survey of the resources and possibilities of English.

These first few weeks are followed by evaluation through questionnaires and/or class discussion:

Which of the activities proved most interesting to you? Why?
Which *didn't* you care for? Why? Was this due to lack of interest or lack of skills?
From which activities do you think you learned most? (Be cautious about answers to this question, since many students have come to think of "real" learning as painful.) Which were least helpful?

From the answers, the teacher can proceed with related questions:

Which kinds of activities would you like to continue? Why?
What other kinds of things should we be doing in an English class?
Are there special issues or topics you would like to take up?

This is a good time, too, for the teacher to review the initial class syllabus or course requirements. Now the students will have enough background and sense of how you operate to ask better questions about the course than they might have on the opening day of the semester.

TAKING YOUR TIME

The kind of schedule and activities we have proposed in this chapter is obviously time-consuming: helping students get to know one another, assessing their interests, offering a variety of language activities, discussing results. This use of time may be frustrating to many teachers and, for that matter, to many students.

Yet this seems to us time well spent. Our experience suggests that classes where "getting started" is done carefully and thoroughly tend to be more productive than those where the preliminaries are gotten over with quickly. People are not interchangeable like the parts of a car; the "breaking in" period of a class is necessarily less mechanical and more time-consuming. And, to repeat, most of these activities can be deliberately integrated with course subject matter, so getting started is not an alternative to the "real" content of the course; it is a basic part of the program, though a first stage. It is the foundation of a synergistic structure, not a diversion from the main business of the class.

A NOTE ON TEACHER EXPECTATIONS

From a freshman orientation booklet of a large urban school.

Who Owns This School?

Surprisingly, you do! This building and its equipment, including the buses, was paid for by tax dollars contributed by your parents. Thus you and your family own a share in the school, and it is your responsibility to protect that investment for your family. This means that you must take care of all school property—books, desks, and classrooms—as if it were your own, and if you see other persons damaging or defacing the school, you must turn them in to the proper authority. Remember, MOST TROUBLE STARTS AS FUN.

Surprisingly, the students to whom this message was delivered resisted the temptation to take the school apart—brick by brick—and divide it into equal shares. Perhaps the warning was developed in an honest attempt to cut down on vandalism, but it is not an honest message, and it is typical of the negative attitudes many adults have toward young people. It is coy and patronizing. Instead of coming directly to the point, it plays a game, trying to trick students into feeling they have a stake in the school. The final sentence presents a stereotypical image of the young person, the kid whose "fooling around" invariably leads to catastrophe. The expectations of the adult who wrote this are low, and they are plainly communicated to the students.

Young people understand such messages, both the overt and hidden meanings. In significant research into teacher attitudes, Robert Rosenthal and Lenore Jacobson discovered that students are quite sensitive to what the teacher perceives to be their capabilities. They discovered a Pygmalion effect, the allusion being to George Bernard Shaw's play in which a cockney flower girl is transformed into a standard-English-speaking society lady by her professor. When teachers believe students are bright, students tend to perform well. When teachers are negative about student capabilities, performance drops to match. Rosenthal and Jacobson argued that students become "self-fulfilling prophesies," coming to behave in class just about the way their teachers believe they will.

From Robert Rosenthal and Lenore Jacobson, "Teacher Expectations for the Disadvantaged," *Scientific American,* April 1968. Copyright © 1968 by Scientific American, Inc. Reprinted by permission of the publisher.

We have explored the effect of teacher expectations with experiments in which teachers were led to believe at the beginning of a school year that certain of their pupils could be expected to show considerable academic improvement during the year. The teachers thought the predictions were based on tests that had been administered to the student body toward the end of the preceding school year. In actuality the children designated as potential "spurters' had been chosen at random and not on the basis of testing. Nonetheless, intelligence tests given after the experiment had been in progress for several months indicated that on the whole the randomly chosen children had improved more than the rest.

Skinny Malinky's foster mother observes much the same thing in Stanley Kiesel's *The War Between the Pitiful Teachers and the Splendid Kids.* When called into school yet another time to discuss Skinny's poor performance, she looks directly at the teacher and says, "Skinny got a good head, but you don't know about heads like his. Just because he different you don't expect much. He's not your background so you don't try hard."

This is not to suggest that all teaching failures are a result of negative expectations or that, conversely, by stating high expectations one can magically achieve results. One can visualize teachers abusing the Rosenthal–Jacobson research by raising inappropriate standards higher than ever: "I *know* you can read Anglo–Saxon, Charles; I *expect* it of you." However, it is clear that if the teacher is operating with a concern for adult standards (see Chapter 2), seeing children as essentially *in*complete, *in*articulate, and *in*capable, he or she will often be strongly influenced by that expectation. Nowhere is this more evident than in classes of general, average, or remedial students, who often have negative self-concepts to begin with.

A college student of our acquaintance, in reflecting on the "games" played in high school, said, "The whole point was to find out quickly what the teacher expected (i.e., if they ask a question and you don't know the answer, will they tell it to you or will they grill you until you talk) and then you would do that and nothing else." Her observation is reinforced by the observations of an elementary school child, Pippilotta Delicatessa Window-shade Mackrelmint Efraim's Daughter Longstocking—Pippi for short—in Astrid Lindgren's *Pippi Longstocking*. Pippi, however, refuses to play the game, refuses to meet the teacher's expectations, and thus gets herself into deeper trouble.

"Now," said the teacher [the first day of school], "suppose we test you a little and see what you know. You are a big girl and no doubt know a great deal already. Let us begin with arithmetic. Pippi, can you tell me what seven and five are?"

Pippi, astonished and dismayed, looked at her and said, "Well, if you don't know that yourself, you needn't think I'm going to tell you."

All the children stared in horror at Pippi, and the teacher explained that one couldn't answer that way in school.

"I beg your pardon," said Pippi contritely. "I didn't know that. I won't do it again."

"No, let us hope not," said the teacher. "And now I will tell you that seven and five are twelve."

"See that!" said Pippi. "You knew it yourself. Why are you asking, then?"

The teacher decided to act as if nothing unusual were happening and went on with her examination.

"Well, now, Pippi, how much do you think eight and four are?"

"Oh, about sixty-seven," hazarded Pippi.

"Of course not," said the teacher. "Eight and four are twelve."

"Well now really, my dear little woman," said Pippi, "that is carrying things too far. You just said that seven and five are twelve. There should be some rhyme and reason to things even in school. Furthermore, if you are so childishly interested in that foolishness, why don't you sit down in a corner by yourself and do arithmetic and leave us alone so we can play tag?"

There is no way we can directly persuade teachers that young people are fundamentally positive, capable creatures, and no amount of study of psychology or children's writing can substantially change a negative attitude toward the young. Further, we want to caution teachers about falling into the trap of praising all virtues—real or imagined—and ignoring all faults.

Our emphasis in this "getting started" chapter is on direct and realistic observation of youngsters, what they can and cannot do. Youngsters continually surprise us with their talents, interests, and successes.

Taking this positive (but not Pollyannish) view of youngsters allows us to shift away from the conventional metaphor of the teacher as diagnostician and remedialist. Instead, the teacher may be a coach or catalyst, a resource person, advisor, or guide. Perhaps the best metaphor we have heard is that of the teacher as midwife—one who assists in the process of bringing something forth but who does not directly give birth herself. As a midwife, the English teacher is constantly at work helping students give birth to language. The birth metaphor is neither erroneous nor accidental. And, like most times of birth, the beginning of a class should be a time of great, not small, expectations.

EXPLORATIONS AND RESOURCES

• It is Tuesday night, the evening of school opening, and an English teacher sits at her desk, writing with a quill pen on foolscap. She is working on her opening comments to her first period class.

"Hello, boys and girls," she writes, "My name is Miss Hendall, and I'm your English teacher. We'll be seeing a lot of each other this year."

That won't do. She scratches it out and begins again:

"Hiya, kids. I'm Becky Hendall, and we're going to have a lot of fun in here this year."

Nope.

In desperation: "Good morning class. My name is written on the chalkboard. Now who can tell me why it is important for you to do well in English?"

Enough. What *does* a teacher say on the very first day of class? Work out some tentative opening lines. Share ideas with others. Observe how successful teachers begin their classes and see if you can work out adaptations for yourself.

• School lore is filled with generalizations about managing a class in the opening days. "Let 'em know who's boss right from the start." "Don't ever turn your back on a new class." "Don't smile until the second week of class." "Give rotten grades on the first quiz to scare them into performance." Such statements are obviously based on a negative view of students' capabilities (and on some real-world bad experiences as well). In consultation with other teachers, work out some ideas for classroom management of the opening days of class. What rules and ground rules need to be set? How can you "be yourself" and be the teacher in control as well? (See also Chapter 16, on classroom management, for some ideas.)

• The various inventories, questionnaires, and activities in this chapter seek answers to questions we feel are important for the teacher to ask about students. No doubt your list of questions differs. Develop some questions you think need to be answered during the getting started stage; then create some activities tied to your own course plans that will partially reveal answers.

• In a tutorial or small-group setting, talk to students about their feelings about reading and writing. Survey their interests and their sense of their own abilities. Then look up the record of their performance in English as measured by grades and by standardized test scores. To what extent do your own observations conflict with or confirm the formal record? How might your expectations have differed if you had looked at the records first?

• Also in a small-group setting, interview students about their out-of-school pastimes, from TV watching to art to music. What language-related skills are required for each? For example, TV watching requires that one respond to a plot, no matter how banal; playing a musical instrument requires that one have a sense of the "togetherness" of a piece, rather like the coherence of a poem. How might these skills be drawn into an English class? Is there evidence that skills are transferred, or do out-of-school and in-school skills remain separated?

• *Four case studies.* Here are four hypothetical situations in which teachers must make decisions about beginning a class. What kinds of getting started activities do you recommend for each?

1. *Julian Harris* takes over a reportedly "wild" tenth grade class that drove the previous teacher to the edge of madness. Julian discovers that the previous teacher used lots of work sheets and fill-in-the-blanks dittos in an attempt to maintain order. How should he begin?
2. *Mary Anthony* gets to teach the advanced placement senior English class. These students are go-getters; they come to class with sharpened pencils, and if Mary comments about the weather, they write it down in their notebooks and ask whether it will be on the final. What kinds of getting started activities should she try? To what end?
3. *Benjamin Lews* gets the "C"-stream eighth grade class, a group of low-ability students who have been placed together for remedial help. They don't seem interested in reading and writing; they won't do homework; they are very

skilled at avoiding work in class. Propose some ideas for Benjamin to try with these students to get them started on a fresh tack.

4. *Lorrie Knight* teaches a fourth grade class in an affluent suburb. Almost every student has advantages such as ballet lessons, symphony concerts, and world travel (few of which Lorrie herself has experienced). Two or three of the students come from "across the tracks," a low-income neighborhood; fellow teachers claim they can always recognize such students by their poor performance. What is Lorrie to do to get started with this class?

RELATED READINGS

Suggestion 1: Don't buy or read any book with a title like *How to Survive Your First Year in the Classroom* or *Making It as a Teacher: Putting Students in Their Place.*

Suggestion 2: Don't expect any book, including this one, to offer solutions that can be directly transferred to your own classroom.

Values in Teaching, by Louis Raths, Merrill Harmin, and Sidney Simon (Columbus, Ohio: Merrill Publishing, 1966), is a slightly dated but very useful book that grew from the "values clarification" movement of the 1960s. It provides many teaching strategies that help students explore their own values and interests. *Hooked on Books,* by Daniel Fader and Elton McNeil (New York: Berkeley Medallion, 1976), also contains a number of questionnaires and evaluation forms that can help one create an organized survey of student interests and abilities. Two publications of the National Council of Teachers of English, *Notes Plus* (for high school teachers) and *Livewire* (for elementary school teachers), provide collections of practical teaching ideas, many of them self-contained or one-shot (rather than being part of a sustained unit), which can be adapted for introductory sessions. Also helpful is Walter Lamberg's "Helping Reluctant Readers Help Themselves" (*The English Journal,* November 1977, pp. 40–44), which contains a number of interest inventories that are very much in the spirit of this chapter.

Engagement with Literature

6

IN this chapter we use the term "literature" to include what is sometimes treated as a separate subject in the schools: "reading." In fact, we also frequently use "reading" to include what is traditionally included within the school "literature" program. We want to break down the traditional distinction between the two. Reading skills and literary skills are not separate and clearly distinguishable, any more than it is possible to neatly separate literature from nonliterature or even poetry from prose. We do, of course, discuss various kinds of reading/literature skills and examine a range of potential materials for use in literature/reading programs, materials that range from the daily newspaper to accepted classics. There is room for both in the schools, as there is a concern for factual comprehension along with literary criticism and analysis. However, from the outset we want to make it clear that we have a *single* purpose in mind for this chapter: helping teachers help more students engage successfully with print, call that process what you will.

SOME QUESTIONS FOR THE TEACHER OF LITERATURE

Did people read to you when you were a child? What stories did they read? Can you recall the details of the place where this happened? Who taught you to read? What can you recall from those days? What were the first books you read by yourself?

Did you ever go on reading jags when you were younger, reading book
after book by the same author or books linked together in a series?
Who was your best elementary, junior high, or senior high school teacher
of literature? What made that teacher good? Did you have any
negative experiences with books and reading? What can you recall
about that?

That you either teach or are interested in teaching English suggests that
your engagement with reading has generally been positive. The vast majority of English teachers come into the profession because of their love of
literature, and their interest in sharing literary experiences with young
people has consistently led to literature as the core of the language arts
curriculum, sometimes to the detriment of writing and oral language development.

From Larry Cohn, "The Medium That Matters," *Saturday Review,* December 22,
1969. Copyright © 1969 by Saturday Review, Inc.

According to the headline of an article that appeared late last May in
The New York Times, buried with the film advertisements on page 36,
"Young Writers Say They Don't Read." The five interviewed authors, all
of whom were respectably under thirty, announced that they rarely if
ever opened a book. "It's just easier to go to a movie and let it all wash
over you," one of them said. . . . Reading was regarded as an academic
pastime, and most books were relegated to the level and enthusiasm of
a chore. The article came to an abrupt close with one of those statements that must have chilled the warmest hidebound heart. One of the
young writers, Sally Grimes, who had previously spent some time composing obituary notices for the *Philadelphia Bulletin,* committed her own
cool piece of manslaughter by concluding, "I find I'm reading less and
less. I really don't know why."

Unfortunately, though the literary experiences of teachers may be rich,
those of many public school graduates are not. The schools have aimed at
producing people who love literature, who can read it and respond to it
skillfully, who know the great ideas and values of civilization. Yet too many
of the students who leave our schools are book haters and functional illiter-
ates. As even the most idealistic humanist will admit, the reading of literature seems to have had almost no impact on our nation's values and mores.
  Some teachers blame the "reading problem" on the influence of mass
media on the way youngsters spend their time. Although few people take

Marshall McLuhan's assertion that "print is dead" literally, in many areas of society the media have taken over many tasks formerly given to the printed word, and futurists tell us that we are just at the starting point of the electronic communications medium.

Yet, as G. Robert Carlsen reassures us, "We are literature-creating and literature-consuming animals." Even in an age of media there is evidence that people like to read and that reading satisfies some fundamental needs not met by other forms of communication and artistic expression.

Every once in a while groups of self-appointed intellectuals get themselves up tight about the status of literature and the status of reading in a culture. They feel that something must be done to defend a fragile flower against the trampling of barbaric boots. Really this seems nonsense to me. Literature is not so delicate that it needs any special protection. . . .

Man, we are told, is a tool-making animal. I suggest that equally we are story-making animals. . . . And something deep within us impels us to cherish the product of the writer. I have watched it happen over and over. Given a modicum of reading skill, some free time, and accessibility to literary materials, people read . . . not every person, but most. People read in cramped bunks under the arctic ice. They read 40,000 feet above the earth. They read as they have their hair cut or dried, and while they wait for the dentist. People read in bed, in the bath tub and occasionally, sitting upright in a chair.

We are literature-creating and literature-consuming animals.

What has often gone wrong in literature instruction is that programs have consistently ignored the individual experiences and interests that young people bring to their reading. A college model of literature instruction has been pushed down into senior high school and even into junior high, with a powerful emphasis on literary surveys, reading by genres or types, and mastery of the terminology of criticism: *plot, character, meter, rhyme, rising action, falling action,* . . . . Too often, classes focus primarily on analysis and explication, on wringing all possible meaning from a text or making "acceptable" judgments about literary works. Thus the texts chosen for analysis are those which (often deservedly) have a place in the canon of classic literature, but which speak to students in faint voices and unfamiliar languages.

From Diane Divoky, ed., *How Old Will You Be in 1984?* New York: Discus Avon, 1969.

Ivanhoe, Silas Marner, Christmas Carol, The Merchant of Venice, Julius Caesar, Lady of the Lake: The names of these books are familiar to us. Why? Have these books ever been on the best seller list? Have we ever seen them being bought up feverishly at the newsstands? Are these books the ones that our friends recommend? No! We know these books only because they are the sole stock of the English Book Room. . . . Someone long ago told that long dead original department head that those were the only truly good authors. This false idea has been perpetrated from year to year and remains with us today.

—High School Student

Under this "college model," we can visualize the literature curriculum as a giant vat or cauldron containing all the great works, all the accumulated literary scholarship and criticism, all the knowledge of form, style, figures of speech, and prosody. The cauldron gurgles from time to time as new critical discoveries break loose and rise to the surface. Like children in a Dickens orphanage, the students line up and pass by, each to receive a draught in a battered tin cup. The younger children pass by first, and the teacher draws off the lighter liquids for them; only the older, more mature students are allowed to drink of the dark, viscous fluids from the bottom.

This may seem like an unnecessarily bleak description of what happens in literature classes and may be unfair to college teachers of literature. After all, most of us—the present writers included—enjoyed a great many college classes that involved a dispensing of literary knowledge. (It's also important to note that most of us came to value that sort of direct instruction after we had reached the advanced age of eighteen or so; we learned an adult appreciation of adult texts as we neared adulthood.) Our purpose here is not to denigrate what works well (or, dare we say, not so well?) in many university classes, nor are we out to dislodge the classics from their place in education. Yet it is clear to us that the emphasis of a vat-and-tin-cup approach is inappropriate for most youngsters in elementary and secondary schools.

LITERATURE AND THE READER

One alternative that has emerged in the past twenty years (with historical origins much older than that) is to look toward the *engagement* of the reader with a text rather than concentrating on explication of the text by a teacher or professor. If we look at the experience of literature from the point of view of a reader, we realize that reading is a dynamic activity—no less creative than writing.

Louise Rosenblatt, whose pioneering book *Literature as Exploration* was first published in 1938, has suggested that in this respect literature is a "performing art." Not only do books "perform" for a reader, each reader "performs" on a text to create meaning as well. As readers become more experienced in responding to texts, their performances become more and more complex.

From Louise Rosenblatt, *Literature as Exploration*. New York: Noble & Noble, 1968. Reprinted by permission of the author.

No one else can read a literary work for us. The benefits of literature can emerge only from creative activity on the part of the reader himself. He responds to the little black marks on the page, or to the sounds of words in his ear, and he makes something of them. . . . Out of his past experience, he must select appropriate responses to the individual words, he must sense their interplay among one another, he must respond to clues of tone and attitude and movement. He must focus his attention on what he is structuring through those means. . . . The amazing thing is that critics and theorists have paid so little attention to this synthesizing process itself, contenting themselves with the simpler task of classifying the verbal symbols and their various patterns in the text.

The role of literary education, then, becomes far more than filling students' heads with nuggets of literary wisdom or the chowder of cultural history. It becomes a matter of helping individual readers improve their ability to engage with a wide range of books successfully.

Figure 6.1 shows four areas of reading/literature that we want to take up in this chapter:

1. Reading skills.
2. The process of engagement.
3. Analysis and criticism.
4. Knowledge of literary and cultural history.

The figure places a young person—an individual reader—at the center. The message we will repeat consistently is that teachers must keep that reader in mind. We must guard against the tendency for instructional concerns

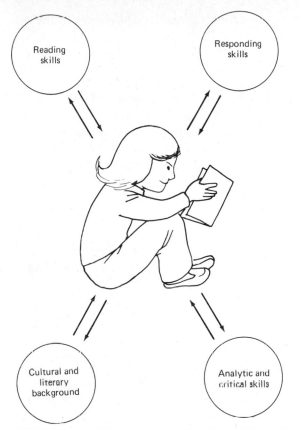

FIGURE 6.1 THE ELEMENTS OF READING AND
LITERARY STUDY.

about course or syllabus to take precedence over actual reading or for the
teacher's well-meant assistance to become an end in itself, destroying the
intrinsic pleasure in books.

READING SKILLS

We want to repeat our concern that reading and literature have
become separated in the professional mind. Reading even has its own
organization, the International Reading Association, while literature is
generally given over to teachers who belong to the National Council of
Teachers of English. It is a positive sign in our profession, however, that
in recent years IRA has become increasingly concerned with a whole language, reading/writing/literature model of learning, while NCTE has in-

creasingly extended its concerns to the act of reading as well as the processes of teaching and learning literature.

Both groups are increasingly skeptical of what we might call a "skills approach" to the teaching of reading, which consists of breaking reading into a series of discrete, identifiable skills—from phonics to paragraph patterning—teaching those skills, testing for their mastery through comprehension questions, and assuming that the same skills will be transferred by students engaged in reading. Unfortunately, even as professionals in IRA and NCTE have recognized that reading is such a complex act that one can't even begin to analyze all the possible skills, much less teach them, there has been growing pressure by parents and some academic conservatives to resurrect a basic skills or particle approach to reading.

From Peter Sanders, "Reading and the English Teacher," *The English Journal,* September 1974, p. 59. Copyright © 1974 by the National Council of Teachers of English. Reprinted by permission of the publisher and the author.

The number of students who *can not* read is small. The number of students who *will not* read, who have been taught again and again to think of themselves as inadequate, slow, and disabled—and who therefore behave as if they are—is considerable. We are not always successful in distinguishing between the two.

This "disabled" reader . . . is quite likely to be an authority on the subjects of failure and frustration. Where print is involved, he has long since learned that his chances for success are minimal. He has been conditioned to expect, though not necessarily to accept, embarrassment and even ridicule. His self-image, his ego, have been severely bruised. Small wonder, then, that he may also have learned that it is oftentimes easier to permit and, indeed, even to encourage his teachers to say, "Well, he can't read . . . ," than it is to risk once again his sense of who and what he is.

At the risk of seeming simplistic, we want to argue, along with Peter Sanders, that many reading problems are not matters of skill deficiency at all; they result from lack of interest in the material, lack of motivation, lack of confidence, lack of practice. Our "reading program," then, consists of focusing on engagement by the students and providing support, even tutorial help, as it is needed—as problems arise. Our program is thus antiworkbook, antitest, antidrill and probook, proreader.

One simple way we can develop reading in the English classroom is to follow the old and sound advice to "match the book with the child." Chapter 8 will provide more detail on individualized reading programs. At this point it is sufficient to suggest that a major cause of reading "malfunctions" is material that is inappropriate for the student: too tough, too distant, too removed from experience. As John Steinbeck remarked, books must "have some points of contact with the reader." Sometimes the point of contact will be the students' own interests and problems as these are reflected in the book, but it may also be the free play the book gives to imagination or fantasy. As teachers gain experience with books and students, their sense of appropriateness grows. It is a lifelong teaching quest for many of us to read constantly in a search for materials that will make connections with our students.

From John Steinbeck, *The Winter of Our Discontent.* New York: Viking Press, 1961.

A man who tells secrets or stories must think of who is hearing or reading, for a story has as many versions as it has readers. Everyone takes what he wants or can from it and thus changes it to his measure. Some pick out parts and reject the rest, some strain the story through their mesh of prejudice, some paint it with their own delight. A story must have some points of contact with the reader to make him feel at home in it.

This does not mean abandoning the classics or letting students read any old thing or encouraging them to be indifferent to literary merit. Teachers should make certain that students establish contact with their reading but should systematically introduce the students to new ideas and materials that will stretch both their minds and their reading skills.

People read for many different reasons: to learn, to be entertained, to escape the world, to seek solutions to problems. They seldom read simply for the sake of learning to read *better.* Yet a great many reading programs are based on the assumption that reading is done *for practice.* Students read passages and answer questions as a way of proving that they have understood; they read literary classics and write essay exams to show that they have mastered the central ideas. However, if we recall that the reader must be kept at the center of the process, we can see that unless reading serves a purpose, it is not likely to improve either reading skills or attitudes toward books.

If the match between student and book is a good one, the student will naturally sense a purpose for finishing the book. Although students should do some "reporting" after they read, the old-time book report traditionally calls for a rather wooden plot summary. Alternatives to that sort of reaction are offered by NCTE in "Thirty-Four Alternatives to Book Reports" (Figure 6.2). By providing such a variety of outlets for the students' responses, the teacher brings reality to the reading process, making it a part of the students' conscious concerns, not just a schoolroom exercise.

From Robert Probst, Response and Analysis—Teaching Literature in Junior and Senior High School. Portsmouth, N.H.: Boynton/Cook, 1988, p.4. Reprinted by permission of the publisher.

When literature is *read*, rather than worked upon, it draws us into events and invites us to reflect upon our perceptions of them. It is not at that point a subject to be studied as an artifact illustrating an age or a product representing an artist; it is rather an experience to be entered into. "Entering into" literature, however, may be different from most of our other experiences. The literary work invites us in not only as participants, but also as spectators, giving us the opportunity to watch ourselves. It freezes events and holds them still for examination. Few other moments in our lives allow us that time for thought; events move too quickly and we are too deeply and thoroughly involved. Literature, however, allows us both to experience and to reflect upon experience, and thus invites the self-indulgence of those who seek to understand themselves and the world around them.

A vast number of so-called reading skills are not unique to reading at all. Most young people are able to find the main idea in a television program or summarize the plot of a film they have seen, so it is redundant to teach such skills as if they were unique to reading. Further, from grade one on, most students are capable of basic decoding—translating printed words into sounds, either orally or silently—and need little help with phonics. Although it may seem to cut against our common sense (a "common sense" often conditioned by conventional schooling), the evidence *against* continuing to teach decoding skills is powerful. Instead, we suggest that the teacher create an environment that supports the development of reading abilities and skills. The teacher can:

Present a rich variety of reading materials: classic and contemporary novels, poetry and play collections, short story anthologies, books written for young adults, newspapers, magazines, monographs, brochures, pamphlets.

Provide time for students to read. Young people don't have a lot of time to give to reading. By providing in-class time, the teacher not only

FIGURE 6.2 THIRTY-FOUR ALTERNATIVES TO BOOK REPORTS

From *Ideas for Teaching English in the Junior High and Middle School,* edited by Candy Carter and Zora Rashkis. Urbana, Ill.: National Council of Teachers of English, 1980. Reprinted by permission of the publisher.

1. Design an advertising campaign to promote the sale of the book you read. Include each of the following in your campaign: a poster, a radio or TV commercial, a magazine or newspaper ad, a bumper sticker, and a button.
2. Write a scene that could have happened in the book you read but didn't. After you have written the scene, explain how it would have changed the outcome of the book.
3. Create a board game based on events and characters in the book you read. By playing your game, members of the class should learn what happened in the book. Your game must include the following: a game board, a rule sheet and clear directions, events and characters from the story on cards or on a game board.
4. Make models of three objects which were important in the book read. On a card attached to each model, tell why the object was important in the book.
5. If the book you read involves a number of locations within a country or geographical area, plot the events of the story on a map. Make sure the map is large enough for us to read the main events clearly. Attach a legend to your map. Write a paragraph that explains the importance of each event indicated on your map.
6. Complete a series of five drawings that show five of the major events in the plot of the book you read. Write captions for each drawing so that the illustrations can be understood by someone who did not read the book.
7. Design a movie poster for the book you read. Cast the major characters in the book with real actors and actresses. Include a scene or dialogue from the book in the layout of the poster. Remember, you are trying to convince someone to see the movie based on the book, so your writing should be persuasive.
8. Make a test for the book you read. Include ten true-false, ten multiple choice, and ten short answer essay questions. After writing the test, provide answers to your questions.
9. Select one character from the book you read who has the qualities of a heroine or hero. List these qualities and tell why you think they are heroic.
10. Imagine that you are about to make a feature-length film of the novel you read. You have been instructed to select major characters in your novel from your English classmates and tell why you selected each person for a given part. Consider both appearances and personality.
11. Plan a party for the characters in the book you read. In order to

do this, complete each of the following tasks: a) Design an invitation to the party which would appeal to all of the characters. b) Imagine that you are five of the characters in the book and tell what each would wear to the party. c) Tell what food you will serve and why. d) Tell what games or entertainment you will provide and why your choices are appropriate. e) Tell how three of the characters will act at the party.

12. List five of the main characters from the book you read. Give three examples of what each character learned or did not learn in the book.

13. Obtain a job application from an employer in your area, and fill out the application as one of the characters in the book you read might do. Before you obtain the application, be sure that the job is one for which a character in your book is qualified. If a resume is required, write it. (A resume is a statement that summarizes the applicant's education and job experience. Career goals, special interests, and unusual achievements are sometimes included.)

14. You are a prosecuting attorney putting one of the characters from the book you read on trial for a crime or misdeed. Prepare your case on paper, giving all your arguments and supporting them with facts from the book.

15. Adapt the prosecuting attorney activity outlined above to a dual-role project: In one role, present the prosecuting case, and in the other present the case for the defense. If a classmate has read the same book, you might make this a two-person project.

16. Make a shoebox diorama of a scene from the book you read. Write a paragraph explaining the scene and attach it to the diorama.

17. Pretend that you are one of the characters in the book you read. Tape a monologue (one person talking) of that character telling of his or her experiences. Be sure to write out a script before taping.

18. Make a television box show of ten scenes in the order that they occur in the book you read. Cut a square from the bottom of a box to serve as a TV screen and make two slits in opposite sides of the box. Slide a butcher paper roll on which you have drawn the scenes through the two side slits. Make a tape to go with your television show. Be sure to write out a script before taping.

19. Make a filmstrip or slide-tape show picturing what happened in the book you read. You can make a filmstrip by using Thermofax transparency material, but be sure it is narrow enough to fit through the projector. You will have to work carefully on a script before making your tape.

20. Tape an interview with one of the characters in the book you read. Pretend that this character is being interviewed by a magazine or newspaper reporter. You may do this project with a partner, but be sure to write a script before taping.

21. Make a book jacket for the book you read. Include the title,

author, and publishing company of the book on the cover. Be sure the illustration relates to an important aspect of the book. On the inside flap or on the back of your book jacket, write a paragraph telling about the book. Explain why this book makes interesting reading when writing this "blurb."

22. Write a letter to a friend about the book you read. Explain why you liked or did not like the book.

23. Make a "wanted" poster for a character in the book you read. Include the following: a) a drawing of the character (you may use a magazine cutout), b) a physical description of the character, c) the character's misdeeds, d) other information about the character that you think is important, e) the reward offered for the capture of the character.

24. In *The Catcher in the Rye,* Holden Caulfield describes a good book as one that "when you're done reading it, you wish the author that wrote it was a terrific friend of yours and you could call him up on the phone whenever you felt like it." Imagine that the author of the book you read is a terrific friend of yours. Write out an imaginary telephone conversation between the two of you in which you discuss the book you read and other things as well.

25. Imagine that you have been given the task of conducting a tour of the town in which the book you read is set. Make a tape describing the homes of the characters and the places where important events in the book took place. You may use a musical background for your tape.

26. Make a list of at least ten proverbs or familiar sayings. Now decide which characters in the book you read should have followed the suggestions in the familiar sayings and why. Here are some proverbs to get you started: He who hesitates is lost. All's fair in love and war. The early bird catches the worm. A stitch in time saves nine.

27. Write the copy for a newspaper front page that is devoted entirely to the book you read. The front page should look as much like a real newspaper page as possible. The articles on the front page should be based on events and characters in the book.

28. Make a collage that represents major characters and events in the book you read. Use pictures and words cut from magazines in your collage.

29. Make a time line of the major events in the book you read. Be sure the divisions on the time line reflect the time periods in the plot. Use drawings or magazine cutouts to illustrate events along the time line.

30. Change the setting of the book you read. Tell how this change of setting would alter events and affect characters.

31. Make a paper doll likeness of one of the characters in the book you read. Design at least three costumes for this character. Next, write a paragraph commenting on each outfit; tell what the cloth-

ing reflects about the character, the historical period, and events in the book.

32. Pick a national issue. Compose a speech to be given on that topic by one of the major characters in the book you read. Be sure the contents of the speech reflect the character's personality and beliefs.

33. Retell the plot of the book you read as it might appear in a third-grade reading book. Be sure that the vocabulary you use is appropriate for that age group. Variation: Retell this story to a young child. Tape your story-telling.

34. Complete each of these eight ideas with material growing out of the book you read: This book made me wish that, realize that, decide that, wonder about, see that, believe that, feel that, and hope that.

supports reading but also creates an opportunity to offer specific help to students who need it.

Include recorded literature in a classroom library for those who find reading difficult or for those who simply enjoy listening to a good story.

Use oral presentations and classroom drama to bring literature to life. Students should not be forced to read or dramatize if they find it extremely difficult, but in most classes, many students enjoy dramatic work. (See also Chapters 10 and 13.)

Provide reading warm-ups. Before students plunge into a new book or story, provide them with appropriate background and discuss the key issues and problems. Give students a preliminary sense of what is likely to happen so they don't become lost.

Use television and film tie-ins. Draw on novels for television and films made from books. Look for video versions of classic and contemporary books to show the class.

Let students quit reading books they are not able to comprehend or enjoy. With hundreds of thousands of books in print, the teacher can usually find acceptable alternatives.

Read aloud to students regularly, letting them follow along in a text or just listen.

Provide help with difficult textbook assignments. There are times when students will need to read material they do not find especially appealing as part of their course work. Rather than having them struggle in silence, the teacher can offer help for both English and other assignments. Create tutorials, partnerships, or discussion groups.

Provide class time for students to get into groups to talk to other students about what they are reading.

THE PROCESS OF ENGAGEMENT

A useful metaphor for literary study suggested itself as Steve watched a son playing with two lumps of modeling clay, one yellow and the other red. As the boy worked with the two lumps, a third color emerged— orange. In literature, the same kind of transformation occurs: a new color results from the mixing of red—the book—and yellow—the students' previous experiences. Orange then represents engagement.

Yet it is difficult to get this sort of chemistry going in the schoolroom. Most of us have experienced classes where discussions fell flat, where, despite the teacher's best intentions, the text remained dead on the page. Sometimes that may be due to the selection of texts, but it is also frequently due to students' lack of experience with probing discussion.

English teachers are not the only ones who face this difficulty. Hilda Taba, who was at one time a student of John Dewey, found a similar kind of reluctance in history and social studies classes, where students became oriented toward factual, cognitive responses and lost the ability to react in personal terms to historical experiences. Consequently, she devised a series of teaching strategies which can be used by teachers to lead students away from strict cognitive responses. Her work anticipated the later development of a "taxonomy" of cognitive and affective processes by Benjamin Bloom of the University of Chicago. Although Bloom's formulation is more detailed than Taba's, we prefer the simplicity of her design.

We have adapted some of her strategies to four levels of questions that the teacher can use in leading discussions of literature. Although the questions are listed by numbered levels, this is *not* a sequence that should be followed strictly or rigidly. Nor is one level necessarily "higher" or "better" than another. How these questions are actually used will depend on the individual teacher, the class, the literary work, and the intangible variables that surround any teaching situation.

Level I: Understanding. The teacher asks questions to make certain the students have understood the basic meaning of the poem, play, or story.

The types of questions asked at this level can be: What happened? What happened after that? What do you think the poet is saying in the first two lines? Describe the parts you didn't understand.

Level I questions tend to have single, right–wrong answers. The teacher asks only enough questions to make certain that understanding has taken place. Although most teachers want to avoid questions that have single answers, some group dynamics experts have noted that asking a few short questions of this type at the beginning of a discussion often helps to break the ice, providing opportunities for several students to speak and thus initiating a dialogue.

This first level deals with understanding, with the teacher conducting a brief survey to ensure that students understand the essence of the plot of a story or play or the basic content of a poem. The teacher wants to make certain all members of the class can follow the subsequent discussion. No member of the class should be left behind because of vocabulary problems or obscure meanings. The purpose is not to find out who did or didn't read the assignment; the aim is checking understanding, not conducting a police action. With some literature, a question or two will assure the teacher that students have gotten the meaning. With other pieces—say, an e. e. cummings puzzler or a complicated short story—a class may need to spend a fair amount of time figuring out meanings. However, if discussion at Level I takes up an unusual amount of time, the teacher might want to question the choice of literature. After all, it's probably true that one can drag junior high students to the point where they understand the language and meaning of a sophisticated adult play or novel, but is it a good idea to try? To force reading of difficult works violates the principle of matching the student to the book that we emphasized previously.

Level II: Interpreting. The teacher asks these questions to help students explore the relationships within the literature and to get them deeper into the piece.

Questions at this level might include the following kinds: How do you think this character felt? What did the heroine mean when she said this? Why do you think the hero reacted that way? What evidence did you have to suggest that the ending was going to happen that way? Why do you think the poet said all this? What do you think might happen next if we continued the story?

A variety of opinions will come out in this discussion. In most cases a class will be able to come to a consensus view, since the text itself provides evidence to support various interpretations. Nevertheless, the questions are generally open-ended, creating opportunities for sustained discussion.

This second level deals with seeing relationships between the parts of a poem or story. It calls for understanding characters beyond the surface, seeing levels of meaning, and probing into the parts of a work of literature to see how it is put together. Most students will enjoy this kind of discussion *if* the teacher doesn't overdo it by running an exhaustive analysis. Further, it has been the case traditionally that analysis is the *end* of the process—the draught of liquid from the vat of literature. However, if students see a connection between their own experiences and those described in a play, for example, they will be a good deal more interested in analyzing the play in depth.

The following are samples of Level II classroom applications. Ask students to:

Write the events of the story from another character's point of view.

Discuss what the main characters in the story would look for in a best friend.

List the issues raised in the story and rank them from least important to most important as they see them and then as a character would see them.

Choose a poem that they think one of the characters would like.

Select a character to be granted three wishes by a genie. What does the character wish for? Why? Will the character be better or worse off by getting these wishes?

Write an autobiography for one of the characters. What was his or her life like before and after the story?

Script a particularly compelling scene and perform it for the rest of the class.

Level III: Relating.   The teacher encourages the students to bring their own values and experiences to the literature.

The types of questions asked at this level might include: How did you like the hero? Explain why you would/would not want this character for a friend. What would you have done? Describe any similar situations you have found yourself in. What did you do? Why did you do it that way? Explain why you would/would not do it that way again. Why do people act that way?

Answers to these questions are obviously wide open. There are no right answers to them (although each student will have some answers that are personally right). Some of the questions direct the students toward the text; other send them into their own experiences. Occasionally the teacher can touch base with the story, bringing the student's experiences and those of the literature together: "That's an interesting reply, John, but don't you remember what happened to the heroine when she tried something like that?

At this third level—relating—the students bring meaning *to* literature. The teacher encourages students to put themselves and their values into the story or poem, drawing on their own experiences, concerns, interests, and ideas. Typically, in college, Level III questions are discussed only in dormitory rooms or over coffee at the grill, because much literary criticism is not prepared to deal with open-ended questions to which only the reader has the answers.

The following are samples of Level III teaching applications. Ask students to:

Talk about the character they disliked the most.

Pick out a specific emotion experienced by a character in the story and

write about their experience with the same emotion in a poem, diary
entry, letter, or short story.

Discuss whether they would ever do something that a character did, such
as save someone else's life or reject parental advice.

Talk about whether they have ever known someone like the character in
the story and what their reactions were to that person.

Write a letter to a specific character explaining how they felt about that
character's treatment of someone else in the story.

Share their ideas about how they agree/disagree with a character's view
on an issue.

Level IV: Exploring Beyond the Text.   Using literature as a jumping-off
point, the teacher searches for related ideas and ways of extending the
discussion into new areas.

Questions at this level might include: What other questions does this
bring to mind? What additional issues do you want to take up? What should
we do about it? Who is interested in writing a play (or poem or story or
essay) that expresses our view? What areas/issues would a small group like
to investigate more thoroughly? Here are two poems that also take up the
idea—what is your reaction?

The answers are unpredictable and unlimited in direction.

At Level IV, the literary experience extends *beyond* the text as the
students explore additional ideas that grow from their response. Formalist
critics might throw up their hands at this kind of questioning, arguing that
such discussions have nothing to do with literature. However, if the teacher
has been able to get students to stretch and explore, moving into new areas
of experience, the literature will have served its purpose well—the students
will have grown as a result.

The explorations that grow from literature need not be limited to talk.
We like to encourage students to experiment with many different ways of
describing their reactions to reading. Students can:

Look for other books on the same topic.

Imagine they are psychiatrists. Which character would they want to talk
to? What questions would they like to ask him or her? How do they
think he or she would respond?

Research an idea or issue that aroused their curiosity.

Choose an issue from the novel and create an ad campaign on it (e.g.,
drunkenness, cruelty to animals, cruelty to people).

Rewrite the story as a fairy tale.

Write a satire on the values or antivalues portrayed in the story.

Make a videotape on the same issue or theme.

In addition, many of the book report alternatives suggested earlier can be used as Level IV activities.

If the teacher supports a range of responses to literature, the students often become interested in one another's work. At this point, the traditional distinction between literature and composition vanishes. A class will flow freely from reading to creating responses to reading its own creations. The students' own work becomes part of the literature under examination.

Approaching a Poem

Although poetry is certainly a part of literature, we feel it deserves a special section for several reasons. First, from our work with prospective teachers we have learned that this is the area of literature where they feel particularly insecure about teaching. Second, poetry seems more difficult to get inside since it does not have the direct avenues of characters and plot that are present in fiction—here we can give suggestions that can be applied directly to poetry. Third, even experienced teachers who seem to have no problems dealing with other genres often ask, "What do I do with a poem besides read it?" We hope to give many activities that will help deal with this problem.

Thus, since poetry does offer some separate kinds of challenges and concerns, we deal with it apart from the rest of literature. We emphasize, however, that as with other genres, the reader's engagement with the poem is still at the heart of the matter. A useful set of premises describing that engagement was developed by a group of Australian teachers under the direction of Geoff Fox and Brian Merrick of Exeter University, England (Figure 6.3).

To illustrate this whole approach to poetry (and to all literature, for that matter), we describe an approach that we have used with Stephen Spender's "My Parents Kept Me from Children Who Were Rough."

My parents kept me from children who were rough
Who threw words like stones and who wore torn clothes.
Their thighs showed through rags. They ran in the street.
And climbed cliffs and stripped by the country streams.

I feared more than tigers their muscles like iron
Their jerking hands and their knees tight on my arms.
I feared the salt-coarse pointing of those boys
Who copied my lisp behind me on the road.

They were lithe, they sprang out behind hedges
Like dogs to bark at my world. They threw mud
While I looked the other way, pretending to smile.
I longed to forgive them, but they never smiled.

In our experience, most students react strongly and directly to this poem, because they can make contact by bringing a number of personal experiences to it. Because of its brevity and content, the poem is a good one to read aloud to a class. It is straightforward, and thus there is probably little need for detailed discussion at the understanding level (I). As a prereading activity, the teacher might want to check on one or two unusual words—"lithe" and "salt-coarse," for instance—to guarantee understanding. One or two questions would probably be enough to convince the teacher that the students understand the poem:

What image do you have of the boys Spender is talking about?
What did they do to him?
What did he say and think about them?

FIGURE 6.3   PREMISES FOR POETRY TEACHING
Geoff Fox and Brian Merrick. *The Times Educational Supplement,* February 20, 1981. Reprinted by permission of the authors.

1. Poetry is to be experienced before it is to be analyzed.
2. The enjoyment of a poem is often deepened by analysis, though such close study can be carried out obliquely, not only through line by line study.
3. Any classroom activity in teaching a poem should bring reader and text closer together; not come between them.
4. We need to discourage any message, implicit or explicit, that poems are really puzzles in need of solutions to be gradually pried from teachers by their pupils.
5. A poem rarely "belongs" to its reader on one or two readings, particularly when such readings are immediately followed by an all-class discussion of an evaluative kind; in fact, "Do you like it?" questions about the whole poem or its diction, rhythm, rhyme etc. are best deferred as long as possible.
6. Whether a poem is finally valued or rejected, we need to provide means for reflection upon it, the opportunity for readers and listeners to work in and out of the text.

Interpretive questions (Level II) may be a bit more challenging to the students, because some of Spender's attitudes and feelings are not explicit in the poem. In the discussion, the teacher might use some of the following questions:

How do you think Spender felt toward these boys?
Why did he say he "longed to forgive them"?
How do you think he felt toward his parents?
In what ways does he seem to imply/not imply that his parents did something wrong in keeping him from children who were rough?

That last question would lead quite naturally to some Level III discussions:

Do you think Spender's parents should have kept him from rough children? Why or why not?
How would you have handled this if you were one of his parents?
How would you have reacted if you had been Spender?
Would you have "longed to forgive" the boys?

If the students respond well to these questions, you might ask some additional, more personal questions at Level III:

Can you recall having been pushed around by rough children when you were younger? How did you feel? How did you react?
Have you ever done this sort of thing to someone else? How did you feel then?
Have you ever had to call on your parents to interfere on your behalf?
Have you ever had the feeling that your parents protect you too much?

Finally, the discussion might move into additional areas (Level IV). The teacher might want to bring in other poems and stories related to the theme of protection, roughness, and coming of age. For instance, Richard Wright's *Black Boy* contains a number of scenes in which Richard fights back against both young people and adults. In fact, literature is filled with stories of confrontation of this kind at many levels.

One outcome of this lesson might be role playing, with improvisations on a range of related issues and problems:

A student who is being pushed around by some older students talks it over with her friends.
A student feels he is receiving unfair treatment from a teacher and goes in to discuss it. What stand should he take?
A new student comes to school, and the other students decide to test her to see how she is going to fit in.

Other topics for exploration might include:

Interviewing other students and parents to develop ideas on whether youngsters nowadays are overprotected.

Writing a short story or play that illustrates the problem.

Conducting a panel discussion or debate on the process of raising children.

Reading more about the theme in fiction, nonfiction, poetry, or drama.

Digging into Literature. Besides the whole class discussion, there are times when we really want students to dig in and work with a poem (or any work of literature) and find meanings. We want them to respond to it. But just what does it mean to react or respond? Robert W. Blake and Anna Lunn gave students unfamiliar poems and asked the students to describe their reactions. The results of that study are shown in Figure 6.4. To *perceive, interpret,* and *enjoy* were the general processes the reader followed.

FIGURE 6.4   STAGES IN THE RESPONDING PROCESS
From Robert W. Blake and Anna Lunn, "Responding to Poetry: High School Students Read Poetry," *The English Journal,* February 1986, pp. 68–73. Paraphrased. Reprinted by permission.

The student responding to poetry:

- reads, rereads, and rereads. Words and phrases are reread over and over to support an initial interpretation.
- associates. First words and phrases are associated with personal experience and she associated items in the poem with her personal knowledge.
- interprets. At the heart of the response was interpretation. She interpreted frequently by hypothesizing, she questioned the interpretation, admitting her lack of understanding, she stated interpretations of lines, words, stanzas, literal and figurative meanings of words, of themes and of the meaning of the overall poem.
- restated, paraphrased lines in her own words.
- frequently quoted verbatim from the poem.
- responded emotionally.
- looked back.
- connected elements of the poem, both perceiving structures and creating her own.
- revised her initial interpretation and evaluation.
- evaluated the worth of the poem, showing pleasure with her judgment.

One of the authors' conclusions was that the process of reading a poem is not a simple, easy, linear, instantaneous task.

We are not suggesting that each piece of literature a student reads will be given such close scrutiny. This process can be used only with literature students are willing to get involved in. We bring this material to your attention so that you can understand the complexity of responding to a work of literary art. It is not at all as simple as the anything-you-want-to-say-is-fine approach.

More Avenues into Literature. Consider some of the following strategies:

After students have read several poems, divide the class into groups and have each group select a poem to read dramatically. Their arrangement and how they divide the poem up to be read will reflect their interpretation of the poem.

Get students involved in the meaning of literature by having them work in groups to create a new title. Each group should agree on its new title and present justifications for its choice. It is more interesting if several groups are retitling the same work.

Omit several words from a poem and ask groups of students to propose words that would best fit in. Compare the groups' results.

Read more difficult poems aloud several times. Then ask students to write down a response to the poem. After giving them a few minutes to complete this, have them move into small groups of three or four and discuss their initial responses. Have one member from each group report to the class on some of the group's responses and questions. Other class members can offer possible answers to questions and discussion can continue from this point.

After reading several works of literature on a theme, ask students to bring in a drawing, photo, or picture from a magazine that represents their response. The picture is mounted on one side of a sheet of paper; on the back the student writes an explanation of how he or she sees the picture connecting with or speaking to the theme. The teacher collects the pictures and then, while holding each picture up for the class to see, asks students to describe what work they think the picture represents.

Make up the story behind a story, play, or poem. What has happened before, "off stage," and what will happen later?

Have students rework a piece of literature into another genre such as a newspaper story, an essay, or a story. What has been gained and what lost?

Give students a poem cut into stanzas or a story cut into paragraphs. They are to figure out the best arrangement of these segments. They can compare their arrangement with the way the author wrote the work and see how meanings shift when the arrangement shifts.

Have students read a short story and a poem and, in groups, describe a relationship or a connection between the two.

While students are reading a novel, ask them to bring in a poem that speaks to the theme, setting, mood, tone, or plot of the novel.

Have students read a number of poems and find those which go together. Let them explain the connection or dramatize it through an oral reading and/or panel discussion.

Ask young readers to find a poem that could be placed at the beginning of a novel or short story as an epigraph.

Encourage students to find literature they would be willing to read to the class.

Have students create anthologies of favorite short literary works. They can start with the classroom anthology and then use books from the library. (Limited photocopying of literature for nonprofit classroom use of this sort is generally permitted by copyright law.) When the anthology is finished, have students share their two or three favorite works in small groups. Anthologies can be kept in the room and used as reading material at the end of the hour or as part of the classroom reading library.

ANALYSIS AND CRITICISM

Criticism—talk about likes and dislikes—is a natural part of making contact with literature, something that will emerge at *all* levels of discussion with students of all ages. Given a chance, students will talk about good stories and bad ones, poems they like and poems they don't like, and those assessments will become more sophisticated over time. In his book on the response-centered literature curriculum, *How Porcupines Make Love*, Alan Purves notes that the objectives of a good literature program involve helping students understand why they respond the way they do and why other people's responses differ from their own.

His objectives, shown in Figure 6.5, provide a bridge between purely personal, idiosyncratic reactions and the responses of large numbers of people that essentially stand as the critical judgment of a work. While acknowledging the validity of the individual's reaction—a reaction that will differ with a person's tastes and past experiences—Purves also insists that readers must take time to see how and why their responses differ from those of other people.

The sorts of activities and questions we have offered in this chapter naturally lead to that kind of criticism, but discussion of the quality of the literature emerges as a planned by-product of student engagement. Analysis

FIGURE 6.5   FOUR OBJECTIVES OF A RESPONSE-CENTERED
PROGRAM

From Alan Purves, *How Porcupines Make Love.* New York: Macmillan, 1982.
Reprinted by permission of author and publisher.

a. An individual will feel secure in his response to a poem [or other
   literary work] and will not be dependent on someone else's response. An individual will trust himself.
b. An individual will know why he responds the way he does to a
   poem—what in him causes that response and what in the poem
   causes that response. He will get to know himself.
c. An individual will respect the responses of others as being valid for
   them as his is for him. He will recognize his differences from other
   people.
d. An individual will recognize that there are common elements in
   people's responses. He will recognize his similarity with other people.

and criticism are thus not in opposition to a reader-centered program. They
occur as students read, react, and articulate their responses. We often use
the following sequence in moving from response to criticism:

1. *Discuss engagement and reaction.* What did the literary work mean to
   the students? What meanings did they find in it? What meanings did
   they bring to it?
2. *Explore the role of language in creating response.* What words,
   phrases, and structures helped create a particular response in the
   reader? One might, at this point, introduce some literary terminology·
   plot, character, style, tone, word choice, etc. However, what works
   best for us is "finger-pointing analysis": having students point directly
   to portions of the text that led them to respond as they did.
3. *Discuss how successfully the author has generated and controlled response.* Authors write with aim, purpose, and intent. If readers are
   confused or come up with wildly divergent opinions, the writer has not
   been particularly successful in realizing his or her goal. We often
   remind students that published authors go through the writing process, too: planning, drafting, and revising. Recognizing that readers
   differ and that tastes change and mature, we invite students to describe
   candidly how well they think the author did the job. And that's called
   "criticism."

What we eschew (*eschew* is one of those words that look like the opposite
of their meaning, so as authors we'll choose an alternative phrasing)—what

we avoid like the plague are the usual sorts of critical/analytical questions which are lined up at the close of selections in virtually any school anthology. Such questions, we find, largely ignore the reader's response and plunge directly into matters of literary criticism and analysis. They fail, we think, because they don't ever encourage students to connect their own responses with the writer's attempt to shape and control response.

Write your own study questions. But don't call them study questions.

CULTURAL AND LITERARY BACKGROUND

In recent years there has been considerable discussion of a concept called "cultural literacy," frequently linked to University of Virginia English professor E. D. Hirsch, Jr., and his book of the same title (Boston: Houghton, Mifflin, 1987). Hirsch and his followers feel that youngsters have gotten out of touch with essential cultural background knowledge, and they propose systematic teaching of great books, great names, and great ideas in the schools.

As the reader no doubt anticipates, we do not find the arguments of the cultural literacy advocates particularly persuasive. Certainly, youngsters don't always recognize classical allusions or references to the standard canon of literature. (Did they ever, we wonder?) More important, we think, is that the notion of indoctrinating students into the canon of ideas and literature is very much a vat-and-tin-cup approach.

What's to be done, then, about this traditional material? We suggested earlier that literary criticism and analysis can grow naturally from response to reading, and we would like to argue that cultural and literary background—knowledge of dates, periods, styles, and linguistic and literary conventions—can emerge in the same way. Literary background does become useful and relevant as students read more and more sophisticated works. Conversely, less experienced readers fail to appreciate literary history and culture when those materials are presented for information and "enculturation" rather than for assistance in reading. In our experience, young people seem genuinely fascinated with life in, say, Shakespeare's or Twain's time and enjoy studying the historical/cultural background *if* that information genuinely contributes to their understanding of a work.

There is a fine line between cultural history that enlightens and that which becomes extraneous to the students' responses. One key is the length of time required to present the necessary background. If teachers must spend almost as much time providing background reading as they do discussing the work itself, it would seem that background has gotten out of hand. In addition, teachers should recall that in-depth historical and cultural analysis is basically an adult or college-level activity. Relatively few school-age students will reach a stage where background study becomes an end in itself.

In Chapter 1 we presented a statement from the Anglo-American seminar on the teaching of English that students "should be familiar" with the "reservoir" literature "that forms a common background for our culture." We can agree with that statement only if *should* is taken to mean *opportunity* rather than *compulsion.* In the course of a literature program that focuses on meaning, students will be given an opportunity to gain a great deal of cultural background. Over time, many students will read and delight in a wide range of works by the masters, and they will enjoy gaining insights into periods of history and cultures other than their own. Some students will read Dickens and Austen; some will discover James Fenimore Cooper. Other students will read science fiction and discuss contemporary and historical culture as it is reflected in intergalactic sagas. Some will read travel and geography books; others will read history and social science texts. Probably just about every student will read (or better, watch) a Shakespearean play. Probably everyone will read or hear some myths, legends, and folklore. Not every student will read every book in common, and not all students will know every last tidbit of cultural history. (Did they ever, we wonder?) What we *can* say is that students will have absorbed considerable amounts of literary and cultural history and will have done so in service of the central aim of the literature/reading program: to engage with print.

EXPLORATIONS

• Think about the ways in which you respond to literature. How do you react when you are reading a good book? How does a book affect you? What happens after you have finished reading?

• Write in your own journal analyzing how your literary training helps you when you are engaged in personal or private reading.

• Start an argument in the teachers' lounge: "Print is dead. Literature is dying. We ought to abandon literature classes and teach TV!" What counterarguments do people offer? Who agrees with that statement? What counterarguments (if any) can *you* offer? Ask students to write about or debate the same question. (Prepare yourself for a possible surprise. We've discovered that students tend to argue in favor of preservation of a literary culture.)

• Give a poem to a small group of students and let them discuss it with no teacher present. Tape-record the discussion. Study its ebb and flow. How do students respond to literature on their own? Compare your results with those of Blake and Lunn in Figure 6.4.

• Choose a poem or short story that you think students will like and teach it to several groups, varying your approach each time. Try some of the response ideas suggested in this chapter. Explore the amount of historical/ cultural material required for reader comprehension. Write your conclusions in a journal or share them with a colleague.

• Examine the study questions in an anthology commonly used in the schools. Critique them. Write your own sets of study questions for several selections. (Don't call them "study questions.") Develop your skill at moving beyond any perceived weaknesses in the adopted anthology.

RELATED READINGS

Louise Rosenblatt's *Literature as Exploration* (New York: Noble and Noble, 1968) is a powerful book on teaching literature and deserves reading and rereading. Her more recent book, *The Reader, the Text, and the Poem* (Carbondale, Ill.: Southern Illinois University Press, 1978), provides a fuller theoretical view of her "transactional" approach to reading. The best practical book on teaching this approach is Alan Purves's *How Porcupines Make Love* (New York: Macmillan, 1972). A particularly good contemporary book on the topic is *Response and Analysis—Teaching Literature in Junior and Senior High School* by Robert Probst (Portsmouth N.H.: Boynton/ Cook, 1988).

Readers wishing more information on the teaching of poetry might begin by looking at Robert W. Boynton and Maynard Mack's *Introduction to the Poem* (Upper Montclair, N.J.: Boynton/Cook, 1985), which suggests ways of approaching poetry that will remove the bewilderment many people feel about it. *Reading and Writing Poetry: Successful Approaches for the Student and Teacher,* edited by Charles R. Duke and Sally Jacobson (New York: Oryx Press, 1983), can also be helpful since it emphasizes student interaction with the text. The Spring 1987 issue of *The ALAN Review,* published by an affiliate group of the National Council of Teachers of English, not only is packed with suggested resources for teaching literature but also has articles on aspects of involving students in poetry.

Literature and the Young Adult

7

From Aidan Chambers, *Introducing Books to Children*. Portsmouth, N.H.: Heinemann Educational Books, 1983, p. 103.

Wide, voracious, *indiscriminate* reading is the base soil from which discrimination and taste eventually grow.

T HE title of this chapter is deliberately ambiguous. A major focus is on so-called young adult literature ("Y.A. lit" in trade jargon), but we also emphasize that our central concern is the relationship between literature *and* the young adult, that much of what we say in the chapter applies to teaching any book to the young reader, whether that book is one of the classics or a hot new Y.A. title. Thus, in addition to finding suggestions for teaching Y.A. titles, the reader will be invited to explore ways of engaging readers in familiar classics, folktales and stories, and even books written for children.

YOUNG ADULT LITERATURE: AN EVOLVING GENRE

Not too many years ago teachers were wary of using books labeled as "young adult," believing that the content was light and frivolous. Many articles in *The English Journal* in the 1950s and 1960s, for example, were devoted to defenses of an emerging genre—the book about the teenager written especially for teenagers. Academics still attack Y.A. books from time to time, arguing that they water down the cultural heritage and are used as a substitute for teaching "great books." However, the merit of using young adult books in the classroom is no longer questioned by most specialists in reading and literature. The literary richness and variety of reading that teachers desire for their students can be enhanced by contact with the young adult novel, and often Y.A. books serve as a natural bridge into adult reading. There is as much of a range in the quality of young adult literature as there is in any other genre. Top-notch writers such as Sue Ellen Bridgers, Robert Cormier, Susan Cooper, Madeleine L'Engle, and Cynthia Voigt write with skill and grace, use vivid imagery, intertwine complex plot lines, and give depth to their characters while telling engrossing stories. Skilled writers are not the exception in young adult literature, and more and more excellent writers seem to be joining their ranks.

Using young adult novels in the classroom provides the teacher with a source of reading materials that can involve students while strengthening their reading/writing/thinking/speaking skills. Many of these novels deal with issues that students can respond to immediately, characters they can easily envision or identify with, and language that doesn't create a barrier between the reader and the text. Because so many books in this genre are accessible and available, many students read them readily.

Junior high/middle school teachers have been using young adult fiction in their classes for years because it engages students and works for them in providing a positive educational experience. High school teachers in the "general" classes—the students not destined for college—seem more willing to use Y.A. literature, but as teachers of higher level literature courses become aware of the quality and the depth of much Y.A. literature, they too seem to be more open to trying the genre, especially by pairing a Y.A. novel with one they are used to using (e.g., *Cages of Glass, Flowers of Time* by Charlotte Culin [Laurel-Leaf, 1983] with *The Bell Jar* by Sylvia Plath [Bantam, 1972]). Unfortunately, some teachers have used Y.A. lit as a starting point for lectures on symbol, theme, form, and plot, finding that it makes such aspects of literature more visible to students. We think that's a misuse of Y.A. literature, just as we have suggested that we think engagement with literature must come prior to literary analysis.

KNOWING YOUNG ADULT LITERATURE

Once teachers see ways in which young adult literature can be worked into their programs and see how positively students respond to it, they will be ready to try more and more of it. The next step for teachers is to become familiar with a broader range of Y.A. fiction. We present some suggested reading lists in this chapter, but Y.A. literature is a rapidly changing field. We offer some book lists and periodical sources at the chapter close, all updated frequently, that the teacher can use to discover new and established books recommended for young readers. It's also useful to find the librarian in your school or city who is interested in this area and get him or her to make suggestions.

Most colleges and universities now have courses in young adult literature, but perhaps the best way is simply to locate a few titles in the bookstore or library and begin reading. Seek recommendations from your own students. Diana became an avid fan of the Y.A. genre when enthusiastic students pressed her to read such books as *The Lion, the Witch, and the Wardrobe* by C. S. Lewis (Macmillan, 1950) as well as the works of Madeleine L'Engle, Susan Cooper, and Paula Danziger. When she saw how much it meant to students to have a teacher who could talk to them about books they were reading, she was sold on the importance of knowing the field well.

But since one can't become an expert overnight, another good way to get to know many different novels is to have students read them. Figure 7.1 shows a technique known as the Book Pass. With the help of the librarian, bring in enough titles for the whole class. On the Book Pass form, students record the title and author of the book on their desk. At a signal from the teacher the students start to read from the first page of the book. After three or four minutes the teacher has them stop, record their first reaction to the book, pass the book to the next person, and record the title and author of the next book. Diana has used this activity both in junior high and in high school to acquaint students with a large number of books and give them a chance to pick out a book they are interested in reading.

It's surprising how many students *don't* want to put down books after even a three-minute sampling. At an appropriate point, the teacher has students select books and assigns them to discussion groups; each day they come to class and discuss the books. The Book Pass is not only a good way to engage students in reading, it educates the teacher as well.

RESPONDING TO LITERATURE

Here are some suggestions for ways to engage young adults with literature, novels in particular; they are an extension of the ideas we proposed in the previous chapter in concentrating on poetry.

Make lists of rules. Have students select a character who has very definite ideas on a topic such as *friendship, raising children,* or *getting along in school.* Then have the students make up a set of "rules" about that topic as that character might state them. Do students share these values? Powerful whole class discussions can result.

Divide the text. In groups, students divide the novel into three to five parts, explaining the rationale for their decisions. Where does the "beginning" come to a close? Where are the pauses? If this book were on television, where would the commercials fall? In this way,

FIGURE 7.1

From *Ideas for Teaching English in the Junior High and Middle School,* edited by Candy Carter and Zora Rashkis. 1980, p. 79. Reprinted by permission.

BOOK PASS

Purpose: 1. To acquaint students with a variety of books available in your classroom or library.
2. To encourage students to begin individualized reading programs.

Preparation: Assemble a variety of books—in reading level and in subject matter. Try to select books that have interesting beginnings; your librarian may be able to help. You will need as many books as there are students in the class. Number each book with a removable sticker or insert a numbered file card between pages.

Presentation: Book pass can involve a class for half an hour or for an entire class period, depending on the age and attention span of students. Begin by asking each student to mark off four columns on a sheet of notebook paper and to label them as follows: book number, book title, author's last name, number of lines read. Explain that each student will be given a book at random. When "start" is called, students record the book number, title, and author and begin to read, starting at the first page of the book. When "time" is called, students stop reading immediately, count the number of lines read, and record that number in the fourth column. Allow one to two minutes per reading. Each student then passes the book on to a neighbor, receiving in turn another book.

At the end of book pass, nearly every student will have found at least one book that looks interesting. Additionally, students will have worked on reading speed.

students come to think about plot and structure without having the terminology imposed on them prematurely.

Question the text. Students brainstorm lists of questions they want to ask about the novel. This can be done before they begin reading, based only on the title, cover, and jacket blurbs, or it can be done throughout the novel.

Construct a time line of events. Pupils work up a linear representation of events in the book. They can also construct symbols or icons to represent each event.

Prepare diagrams. Students map the actions, events, or character relationships in the novel. One group might choose an event and show each character's relation to it, while another group might decide to show other characters' relationships. These diagrams can usefully be displayed on the bulletin board, with complexity emerging as the book progresses.

Change actions. Students choose a character in the book and look specifically at how he or she handled a specific situation. Then they discuss or write about how they would have liked to see the matter handled.

Propose characters' poetry choices. From a collection of poetry, students pick out poems they believe specific characters would like. The poems are then read to the class for discussion.

Discuss similar situations. Students discuss a situation in the book that moved them or angered them and share situations or feelings they have experienced which were similar.

Dramatize issues. Students list all the issues and problems they see being raised in the novel. Then they select several issues they see as critical and design role-playing situations about them, either using the characters from the novel or creating new characters and settings. (More about classroom drama in Chapter 13.)

Give advice to a character. Students choose a character and write all the advice they have to give to this character.

Study dialect. Discussion groups go through different chapters of the novel, gathering phrases and words that are used differently than they would use them. Students list the words and phrases and explain what they mean or tell how they would express the same idea.

Create new book titles. Many book titles are not appealing to some students or don't give an accurate idea of what the book is about. Have students in groups create new titles and explain their choices.

Compare the "good old days" with the present. Many books are set in earlier time periods and show what life was like back then. Students can discuss and then list what seems to be similar or different about these "good old days." As appropriate, the teacher can introduce material of literary or historical background, but don't use this as an excuse to become a history teacher.

Examine beliefs. Students choose a specific belief a character holds throughout the novel and discuss whether group members agree with this belief. Again, lively whole group discussions can result as students report.

Rewrite scenes. Students choose a scene that they feel didn't end up satisfactorily and rewrite it. Or they create a scene they would like to have included in the book. Is this a valid form of "literary criticism"? Is it appropriate for secondary school students? We think the answer is yes, provided students and teacher go back to the text as written from time to time to discuss how it created their responses.

Design advertising posters. If the novel lends itself to this, have students design posters advertising and promoting a specific event such as the Championship Coon Hunt in *Where the Red Fern Grows* by Wilson Rawls (Doubleday, 1961).

Write a eulogy. If an animal or character dies, students write a eulogy for him or her.

Present awards. Create a list of awards for both negative and positive actions and decide which character in the novel will receive each award.

IN PRACTICE: KEEPING THE NOVEL IN FOCUS

It is important that "catchy" ideas not be applied to novels at random. It is possible to engage students in a wide range of "fun" activities without helping them become much better as readers. To this end, it is important that the teacher consider aims and purposes in teaching the novel and focus activities appropriately. To illustrate how this can be done, we will apply several of the foregoing suggestions to a young adult novel that has become a popular classic with adolescent readers and with teachers: *A Day No Pigs Would Die* by Robert Newton Peck (Dell, 1972). It is a powerful novel of growing up on a Shaker farm and of a young man's search for identity and understanding. The following activities are designed to guide the students through their reading of the text and to help them sharpen their responses to it. Along the way, students regularly refer back to the text as well as to their own experiences.

After reading three chapters, students write out questions for Rob, the central character. They can ask about such things as his speech, his actions, his attitudes, or how he feels about his life. One student can play the role of Rob and answer the questions as he would probably have answered them.

When several chapters have been read, allow time for questioning the text. In groups, students brainstorm questions about all the events, attitudes, or people they are having trouble understanding.

Rewrite scenes. Many students are frustrated that Robert isn't able to get back at a boy who makes fun of his clothes. They might write a scene where Robert finally gets back at Edward Thatcher. Follow-up discussion can center on whether the revenge scenes, satisfying though they may be to the students, are true to the novel as written.

Propose characters' poetry choices. From collections of poems in the classroom, have groups find poems they think Rob would like and poems that might be selected by other adult and young adult characters.

Identify issues. The title of the book grows from Rob's experience watching the slaughter of his pet pig, Pinky. Invite students to write on such questions as, If your pet was seriously injured and your parents had it put to sleep because they couldn't afford to pay high surgical bills to save it, how would you deal with the situation? What would you feel? What would you say to your parents, who already feel bad?

Write a eulogy for Pinky that Robert might have written.

Compare the "good old days." Urban, suburban, and rural students can profit from thinking and writing about the farm life and values portrayed in this book. Groups can develop lists of behaviors, actions, attitudes, and objects that are the same today as they were back then, while other groups develop lists of differences. Students can talk about the merits and problems of living in the time in which the novel is set and can write their own evaluation of which period is better to live in and why.

Examine beliefs. Various views of wealth and "being rich" emerge in *A Day No Pigs Would Die*. Have students locate key statements in the text and then discuss their views of wealth.

Study dialects. Several groups take two or three chapters of the novel and hunt for expressions and words that Rob and his people use. Then students write down how this would be expressed today. Groups can compile their results into the Shaker Dictionary of Dialect.

FITTING IN YOUNG ADULT LITERATURE

Once teachers have decided to use the resource of the young adult novel, they will be surprised to see how easily it can fit into any type of English class. In "An English Teacher's Fantasy" (*The English Journal,* October 1980, pp. 35–36), Robert Le Blanc suggests pairing such novels as Sue Ellen Bridger's *Home Before Dark* (Knopf, 1976) with John Steinbeck's *Grapes of Wrath* (Covici-Friede, 1937), or Mildred Taylor's *Roll of Thunder, Hear My Cry* (Dial, 1976) with Harper Lee's *To Kill a Mockingbird* (Lippincott, 1960).

Teachers can also pick common themes or concerns. The American Dream is a theme frequently explored in teaching. Young adult materials can be found on diverse aspects of the theme, such as the early colonists' struggles for religious, social, political, and personal freedom. Students can be asked to read novels that deal with the inner conflicts of Americans and value clashes past and present. Other books focus on hopes and aspirations, survival, and emotional and physical needs. Students can also turn to books on discrimination and prejudice to see what conditions exist in America that keep some people from fulfilling their dream. Students can read biographies to see what the hopes and dreams of specific people have been. They can even turn to Y.A. science fiction to see what kinds of societies are touted as desirable and then compare them to our own society and address the question of whether our society makes it possible to achieve the American Dream. Of course, novels need not be looked at only in terms of one narrow theme. Students can branch out to discuss and write about a rich range of subjects.

Teachers may discover through discussion that students have become very concerned about such areas as abuse in families, reacting to the handicapped, handling the death of a loved one, or coping with divorce. Many students would welcome the opportunity to read further about these topics and would respond positively to suggestions of books that deal with the issue. Thus the lists in Figure 7.2 can be used in any number of ways: as a guide for students to books in areas of interest, as a source to help the teacher develop reading lists thematically, or simply as a place to begin exploring what's worthwhile in this genre.

Note: In a few cases these books contain language some teachers might not find appropriate for classroom use. It's a good idea to preview books before recommending them for individualized reading.

TEACHING THE CLASSICS

Steve recently taught a class to graduate students on the topic of teaching the classics. His central argument was that classics merit a place in the classroom because they deal with enduring issues and problems. The classics are classics because they have "sold" over time. In our class on "Literature and the Adolescent" at Michigan State we stress that classics—the so-called great books—are another type of literature young adults can get involved in and respond to, especially if classics are not treated differently than other kinds of literature. Naturally, one has to be concerned about accessibility: We don't advocate teaching great books that are remote from students' *young adult* concerns or that contain so much archaic language that they are difficult for the teenager to read. However, if activities planned for a classic are ones students can get into, they will generally have a good experience with the book. It seems that students lose interest in classics when they are told to read such books on their own and write academic essays on literary traits. The whole burden is then on the students to find their way through the novel and come up with an example of pseudocollegiate thinking when they're often not even sure what the novel was about. Teachers need to remind themselves that there are other ways besides the essay to get students thinking, analyzing, and writing. To suggest how to increase engagement between literature and the adolescent,

FIGURE 7.2   THEMES AND TITLES IN YOUNG ADULT FICTION

Abusive Situations

Abby, My Love, by Hadley Irwin (Atheneum, 1985).
The Boy in the Off-White Hat, by Lynn Hall (Scribner's, 1984).
Cages of Glass, Flowers of Time, by Charlotte Culin (Laurel-Leaf, 1983).
Cracker Jackson, by Betsy Byars (Viking Kestral, 1985).
Fly Free, by C. S. Adler (Coward, 1984).
The Girl, by Robbie Branscum (Harper, 1986).
The Girl Who Lived on the Ferris Wheel, by Louise Moeri (Avon, 1979).
Good Night, Mr. Tom, by Michelle Magorian (Harper, 1981).
Holding Me Here, by Pam Conrad (Harper 1986).
To All My Fans, with Love, from Sylvie, by Ellen Conford (Archway, 1983).

Death/Suicide

About David, by Susan Beth Pfeffer (Dell, 1982).
The Bumblebee Flies Anyway, by Robert Cormier (Pantheon, 1983).
Close Enough to Touch, by Richard Peck (Delacorte, 1983).
The Dark of the Tunnel, by Phyllis Naylor (Atheneum, 1985).
Hunter in the Dark, by Monica Hughes (Flare, 1984).
Mama's Going to Buy You a Mockingbird, by Jean Little (Viking, 1985).
Missing Pieces, by Sandy Asher (Delacorte, 1984).
Remembering the Good Times, by Richard Peck (Delacorte, 1985).
Sheila's Dying, by Alden R. Carter (Putnam 1987).
The Stone Silenus, by Jane Yolen (Philomel, 1984).
Tiger Eyes, by Judy Blume (Laurel Leaf, 1983).
Tracker, by Gary Paulsen (Bradbury, 1986).
Tuck Everlasting, by Natalie Babbitt (Bantam/Skylark, 1976).
Tunnel Vision, by Fran Arrick (Dell, 1980).
Waiting for Johnny Miracle, by Alice Bach (Bantam, 1982).
When the Phone Rang, by Harry Mazer (Scholastic, 1986).
The World Turned Inside Out, by Gail Radley (Crown, 1982).

Discovering Who We Are/What We Stand For

Answer Me, Answer Me, by Irene Bennett Brown (Atheneum, 1985).
Back Home, by Michelle Magorian (Harper, 1984).
The Bigger Book of Lydia, by Margaret Willey (Harper, 1983).
Coasting, by Barbara Cohen (Lothrop, 1985).
House Like a Lotus, by Madeleine L'Engle (Farrar, Straus & Giroux, 1984).

In Summer Light, by Zibby Oneal (Bantam, 1986).
Jacob Have I Loved, by Katherine Paterson (Flare, 1980).
The Lotus Cup, by Jane Louise Curry (Atheneum, 1986).
Night Cry, by Phyllis Naylor (Atheneum, 1984).
The Outsiders, by S. E. Hinton (Dell, 1967).
The Runner, by Cynthia Voigt (Atheneum, 1985).
Singularity, by William Sleator (Sutton, 1985).
Sons from Afar, by Cynthia Voigt (Atheneum, 1987).
A String of Chances, by Phyllis Naylor (Atheneum, 1982).
Tex, by S. E. Hinton (Delacorte, 1979).
Them That Glitter and Them That Don't, by Bette Greene (Knopf, 1983).
Walk Through Cold Fire, by Cin Forshay-Lunsford (Dell, 1986).
Wart, Son of Toad, by Alden R. Carter (Pacer Books, 1985).
Watergirl, by Joyce Carol Thomas (Avon/Flare, 1986).

Divorce/Remarriage/Abandonment

Dark but Full of Diamonds, by Katie Letcher Lyle (Bantam, 1983).
The Divorce Express, by Paula Danziger (Delacorte, 1982).
Downtown, by Norma Fox Mazer (Avon/Flare, 1984).
The Formal Feeling, by Zibby Oneal (Viking, 1982).
The Golden Pasture, by Joyce Carol Thomas (Scholastic, 1986).
The Liberation of Tansy Warner, by Stephanie Tolan (Scribner's, 1980).
Lindsey, Lindsey, Fly Away Home, by Stella Pevsner (Archway, 1983).
A Little Love, by Virginia Hamilton (Philomel, 1984).
Midnight Hour Encores, by Bruce Brooks (Harper, 1986).
The Moonlight Man, by Paula Fox (Bradbury, 1986).
Solitary Blue, by Cynthia Voigt (Atheneum, 1983).
Taking Terri Mueller, by Norma Fox Mazer (Morrow, 1983).
To See My Mother Dance, by Sheila Solomon Klass (Fawcett-Juniper, 1983).

Family Problems

Come Sing, Jimmy Jo, by Katherine Paterson (Avon, 1986).
Goodbye Pink Pig, by C. S. Adler (Putnam, 1985).
Hold Fast, by Kevin Major (Delacorte, 1978).
I Never Asked You to Understand Me, by Barthe DeClements (Viking Kestral, 1986).
I Stay Near You, by M. E. Kerr (Harper, 1985).
I Will Call It Georgie's Blues, by Suzanne Newton (Dell, 1983).
The Keeper, by Phyllis Naylor (Atheneum, 1986).
Notes for Another Life, by Sue Ellen Bridgers (Bantam, 1981).
Over the Moon, by Ellisa Haden Guest (Morrow, 1986).
Rainbow Jordan, by Alice Childress (Flare, 1982).

The Shell Lady's Daughter, by C. S. Adler (Coward-McCann, 1983).
Sweet Whispers, Brother Rush, by Virginia Hamilton (Flare, 1983).
A Taste of Daylight, by Crystal Thrasher (Atheneum, 1984).

Fantasy

The Beggar Queen, by Lloyd Alexander (Dutton, 1984).
The Blue Sword, by Robin McKinley (Greenwillow, 1982).
Crystal Singer, by Anne McCaffrey (Ballantine, 1982).
The Darkangel, by Meredith Pierce (Little, Brown & Co. 1982).
God Stalk, by P. C. Hodgell (Atheneum, 1982).
Heart's Blood, by Jane Yolen (Delacorte, 1984).
The Hero and the Crown, by Robin McKinley (Greenwillow, 1985).
Many Waters, by Madeleine L'Engle (Farrar, Straus & Giroux, 1986).
Seaward, by Susan Cooper (Atheneum, 1983).
'Ware Hawk, by Andre Norton (Atheneum, 1983).

Historical Fiction

Prehistoric
Maroo of the Winter Caves, by Ann Turnbull (Clarion, 1984).
Spirit on the Wall, by Ann O'Neal Garcia (Holiday, 1982).

Medieval
The Lady of Rhuddesmere, by Victoria Strauss (Warne, 1982).
The Way Home, by Ann Turner (Crown, 1982).

Early America
Brothers of the Heart, by Joan Blos (Scribner's, 1985).
Fawn, by Robert Newton Peck (Little, Brown, 1975).
A Gathering of Days: A New England Girl's Journal 1830–22, by Joan
    Blos (Scribner's, 1979).
The Gift of Sarah Barker, by Jane Yolan (Viking, 1981).
The Prospering, by Elizabeth George Speare (Houghton Mifflin, 1967).
Sarah Bishop, by Scott O'Dell (Houghton, 1980).
The Sign of the Beaver, by Elizabeth George Speare (Houghton Mifflin,
    1983).
War Comes to Willy Freeman, by James Collier (Delacorte, 1983).
The Witch of Blackbird Pond, by Elizabeth George Speare (Houghton
    Mifflin, 1958).
Witches' Children: A Story of Salem, by Patricia Clapp (Lothrop, 1982).

Early Twentieth-Century America
The Dark Didn't Catch Me, by Crystal Thrasher (Atheneum, 1975).
The Keeping Days, by Norma Johnston (Tempo, 1981).
Morning Glory Afternoon, by Irene Bennett Brown (Atheneum, 1982).

Illness and Handicaps

The Alfred Summer, by Jan Slepian (Scholastic, 1982).
And Don't Bring Jeremy, by Marilyn Levenson (Holt, 1985).
Before the Lark, by Irene Bennett Brown (Atheneum, 1982).
Friends Till the End, by Todd Strasser (Dell, 1981).
A Handful of Stars, by Barbara Girion (Dell, 1981).
Izzy Willy Nilly, by Cynthia Voigt (Atheneum, 1986).
Just One Friend, by Lynn Hall (Dell, 1981).
Passing Through, by Corrine Gerson (Dial, 1978).
Second Star to the Right, by Deborah Hautzig (Flare, 1982).
Tell Me That You Love Me, Junie Moon, by Marjorie Kellogg (2nd ed.
    Farrar, Straus & Giroux 1984).
Winning, by Robin Brancato (Knopf, 1977).

Inner Conflicts/Value Clashes

The Bennington Stitch, by Sheila Klass (Scribner's, 1986).
The Birds of Summer, by Zilpha Snyder (Atheneum, 1983).
The Burg-O-Rama Man, by Stephen Tchudi (Delacorte, 1983).
Far from Shore, by Kevin Major (Laurel-Leaf, 1983).
A Fine White Dust, by Cynthia Rylant (Bradbury, 1986).
God's Radar, by Fran Arrick (Dell, 1983).
Hit and Run, by Joan Phipson (Atheneum, 1985).
Justice Lion, by Robert Newton Peck (Little, Brown 1981).
No Safe Harbors, by Stephanie Tolan (Scribners, 1981).
One-Eyed Cat, by Paula Fox (Dell, 1984).
On My Honor, by Marion Dane Bauer (Clarion, 1986).
Running Loose, by Chris Crutcher (Dell, 1983).
Strike! by Barbara Concoran (Atheneum, 1983).

Mystery/Suspense

Blossom Culp and the Sleep of Death, by Richard Peck (Delacorte,
    1986).
The Death Ticket, by Jay Bennett (Scholastic, 1985).
Dragons in the Water, by Madeleine L'Engle (Laurel-Leaf, 1982).
The Executioner, by Jay Bennett (Flare, 1982).
Liar, Liar, by Lawrence Yep (Morrow, 1983).
The Other Side of Dark, by Joan Lowery Nixon (Delacorte, 1986).
Playing Murder, by Sandra Scoppettone (Harper, 1983).
Slowly, Slowy I Raise the Gun, by Jay Bennett (Flare, 1983).
The Stalker, by Joan Lowery Nixon (Delacorte, 1984).
To Be a Killer, by Jay Bennett (Scholastic, 1985).
The Twisted Window, by Lois Duncan (Delacorte, 1987).
The Watcher in the Mist, by Norma Johnston (Bantam, 1986).

Older People

Alive and Starting Over, by Sheila Klass (Scribner's, 1983).
Leroy and the Old Man, by W. E. Butterworth (Four Winds, 1980).
Nobody's Baby Now, by Carol Lea Benjamin (MacMillan, 1984).
The Pigeon's Legacy, by Paul Zindel (Harper, 1980).
Steps in Time, by Ruth Brodeur (Atheneum, 1986).
Sweet Bells Jangled Out of Time, by Robin Brancato (Knopf, 1982).
This Old Man, by Lois Ruby (Houghton Mifflin, 1984).
The War with Grandpa, by Robert Smith (Dell, 1984).
What About Grandma? by Hadley Irwin (Atheneum, 1982).
Won't Know Until I Get There, by Walter Myers (Viking, 1982).

Prejudice/Discrimination

As the Waltz Was Ending, by Emma M. Butterworth (Scholastic, 1985).
Because We Are, by Mildred Walter (Lothrop, 1983).
Beyond the High White Wall, by Nancy Pitt (Scribner's, 1986).
Chernowitz! by Fran Arrick (Signet Vista 1983).
In the Shadow of the Wind, by Luke Wallin (Bradbury, 1984).
Roll of Thunder, Hear My Cry, by Mildred Taylor (Bantam, 1976).
To Kill a Mockingbird, by Harper Lee (Lippincott, 1960).
Upon the Head of the Goat, by Aranka Siegal (Signet Vista, 1983).
The Wave, by Morton Rhue (Laurel-Leaf, 1981).
Words by Heart, by Ouida Sebestyen (Bantam, 1981).

Psychic/Occult Experiences

The Changeover, by Margaret Mahy (Atheneum, 1984).
Fingers, by William Sleator (Bantam, 1983).
The Haunting, by Margaret Mahy (Atheneum, 1983).
Locked in Time, by Lois Duncan (Dell, 1985).
The Silver Link, the Silken Tie, by Mildred Ames (Scribner's, 1984).
Stranger with My Face, by Lois Duncan (Little, Brown, 1981).
The Third Eye, by Lois Duncan (Little, Brown, 1984).
Who Knew There'd Be Ghosts? by Bill Brittain (Harper, 1985).

Relationships

The Changeover, by Margaret Mahy (Atheneum, 1984).
Corky and the Brothers Cool, by P. J. Peterson (Delacorte, 1985).
Facing Up, by Robin Brancato (Scholastic, 1984).
Finding David Delores, by Margaret Willey (Harper, 1986).
Harry and Hortense at Hormone High, by Paul Zindel (Bantam, 1984).
If Winter Comes, by Lynn Hall (Scribner's, 1986).

In the Middle of a Rainbow, by Barbara Girion (Scribner's, 1983).
Ludell and Willie, by Brenda Wilkinson (Harper, 1977).
The Moves Make the Man, by Bruce Brooks (Harper, 1984).
A Place to Come Back To, by Nancy Bond (Atheneum, 1984).
Pride of the Peacock, by Stephanie Tolan (Scribner's, 1986).
A Ring of Endless Light, by Madeleine L'Engle (Dell, 1980).
Stotan! by Chris Crutcher (Greenwillow, 1986).
Very Far Away from Anywhere Else, by Ursula LeGuin (Bantam, 1976).

Science Fiction

Anna to the Infinite Power, by Mildred Ames (Scholastic, 1981).
Devil on My Back, by Monica Hughes (Atheneum, 1985).
The Dispossessed, by Ursula LeGuin (Harper, 1974).
Earth Change, by Clare Cooper (Lerner, 1985).
Earthsong, by Sharon Webb (Argo, 1983).
Interstellar Pig, by William Sleator (Bantam, 1984).
The Mists of Time, by Margaret J. Anderson (Knopf, 1984).
Moon Flash, by Patricia McKillip (Atheneum, 1984).
Planet out of the Past by James Lincoln Collier (Macmillan, 1983).

Travels to Another Time

The Crime of Martin Coverly, by Leonard Wibberly (Scholastic, 1980).
The Dreadful Future of Blossom Culp, by Richard Peck (Dell, 1983).
Dream Lake, by Marietta Moskin (Atheneum, 1981).
The Ghosts of Austwick Manor, by Reby Edmond MacDonald (Atheneum, 1982).
Jeremy Visick, by David Wiseman (Houghton, Mifflin, 1981).
New Found Land, by John Christopher (Dutton, 1983).
Out of Time, Into Love, by Jean Marzolla (Scholastic, 1981).
Playing Beatie Bow, by Ruth Park (Atheneum, 1982).
A String in the Harp, by Nancy Bond (Atheneum, 1976).
Thimbles, by David Wiseman (Houghton, 1982).
The Tomorrow Connection, by T. Ernesto Bethancourt (Holiday, 1984).

Young People Surviving on Their Own

Center Line, by Joyce Sweeney (Delacorte, 1983).
Dear Lola or How to Build Your Own Family, by Judie Angell (Dell, 1980).
Dogsong, by Gary Paulsen (Bradbury, 1985).
Going for the Big One, by P. J. Peterson (Delacorte, 1987).
The Homecoming, by Cynthia Voigt (Atheneum, 1981).
Island of the Blue Dolphins, by Scott O'Dell (Houghton, 1960).

The Island Keeper, by Harry Mazer (Dell, 1981).
Island of the Loons, by Dayton Hyde (Atheneum, 1984).
Jo Silver, by Robert Newton Peck (Pineapple Press, 1985)
Julie of the Wolves, by Jean George (Harper, 1972).
Slake's Limbo, by Felice Holman (Dell, 1984).
Snow Bound, by Harry Mazer (Delacorte, 1973).
The Wild Children, by Felice Holman (Scribner's, 1983)

we'll show some activities for Charles Dickens's *Great Expectations,* which is frequently taught in ninth grade classes.

A book like *Great Expectations* is difficult enough that we like to read portions of it aloud or in some cases to read the entire book aloud in chapters across a term. In that way Dickens's stylistic and linguistic twists don't get in the way of his great story. Some teachers see oral reading as time wasting. We do not. In our experience, every minute spent in oral reading leads to increased understanding by students, something we can't say for silent reading. Whether or not the teacher chooses to read *Great Expectations* aloud, some of the following engagement activities will prove useful.

Have students report an incident from the book as if they were writing for a newspaper. They should remember to give the most important facts—who, when, where, what, why—in the opening sentences of their writing. They can add other details in descending order of importance.

On the board, make a list of the novel's most important characters in one column. In the next column have students suggest an intangible gift for each character (such as love, courage, or patience) that would dramatically change an aspect of that character's behavior. In the last column have them suggest a tangible gift that would help the character achieve the behavior or quality listed in column two, such as karate lessons, psychoanalysis, or a subscription to *Mad* magazine.*

Have students write a letter to a character in the novel, say a letter to Pip about his frightening experience in the cemetery. Have them write letters to themselves (or to younger brothers and sisters) about terrifying experiences of their own.

In groups, have students rewrite selected scenes as they might have been told from a different character's point of view. For example, a dinner scene might be written from the perspective of Pip's friend Joe or his wife, rather than through the eyes of Pip himself. Such a discus-

*Thanks for that idea to Joyce J. Swindell in *Notes Plus,* January 1984, p. 2.

sion of literature is especially useful when the narrator, like Pip, is blind to some of his own characteristics.

In groups, have students write new scenes for the characters and act them out before the class. They can present events that took place before or after the story or can place a character in an entirely different situation.

Let students write a list of rules of etiquette as Miss Havisham might have written them or a list of rules that children should obey as Pip's sister would have written them.

After reading the opening cemetery scene, ask students what Pip might dream about that night. Discuss the emotions he must have been feeling and possible dreams related to them. Then have each student write a dream for Pip.

Let students discuss an authority figure who treated them as brusquely and unfeelingly as Pip's sister treated him. What would they like to say to that person?

Discuss why Pip lied about what Miss Havisham's house was like. Discuss situations students remember where they felt they had to lie. What happened as a result of lying?

Explore history by having students write lists of characteristics (feelings, behavior of people, attitudes, living conditions, etc.) that are different today than they were at the time the book was written. Students can also describe the things that are the same. After sharing their lists with the class and discussing them, students can write on "Why I Prefer Living in the Twentieth Century" or "Why I Would Have Liked to Live in the Days of Dickens."

We hope it is clear from these activities that it is possible to engage students productively in the study of "serious literature." Steve vividly recalls from his first year of teaching, struggling with *Great Expectations,* assigning a chapter a night for silent reading, and flogging students through the discussion questions in the anthology on the following day. Teachers' options and alternatives are brighter now than they were in those shadowy times.

When a classic is used in upper level literature courses, the teacher can assume that students are capable of reading and will read the novel at home. (That does not diminish the need for oral reading in class, we believe.) Students will often write reactions in their response log after reading each night's assignment. Another often-assigned novel by Dickens is *A Tale of Two Cities.* Here again, students are often lost in complexities of language and plot. Assuming a class of relatively independent readers, we offer the following timetable to show how the sorts of activities we have been discussing can be "orchestrated" in a classroom sequence.

Day 1. Introduce the novel by asking students in groups to respond to the following prereading questions: If your parents strongly disapproved of your choice of a boyfriend/girlfriend, would you reconsider your decision to see him/her? Do you believe the violence of killing is ever justified? Explain. If someone in your family was brutally murdered, how would you want the killer to be punished? Under what circumstances would you give up your life for another? Do you consider unquestioning devotion to a parent or spouse a positive or negative quality? Do you believe that with the history of oppression in South Africa, there can be a peaceful and equitable distribution of political power? Have groups report to the whole class on their responses. Then explain that each of these issues will arise in the novel.

Day 2. Read some of the text aloud. Have students read parts of their response logs from homework reading. Share questions and reactions with the whole class.

Day 3. Have students in groups of four begin to synthesize information for one of the following projects for the parts of the book read so far:

a. Diagram the main plot and its subplots, with work presented as a poster or on the chalkboard. (The teacher may need to coach this group carefully as the plot is complex.)

b. Collect passages that illustrate attitudes and values of the aristocracy and of the peasants. Draw conclusions to share with the class.

c. Examine beginnings and endings of the chapters in the novel. What insights do these provide?

d. Create a "value chart" for the principal characters in the book, with quotations illustrating each value.

Day 4. Begin by having students in small groups share portions of their response log for 15 minutes. Then have each small group report to the class on questions or observations. If time permits, have students in groups make up a list of grievances the peasants had and a list of how the aristocrats would view those grievances. (These lists will be used later for a newswriting assignment.)

Day 5. Read aloud or organize a readers' theater presentation, with small groups bringing portions of the novel to life through oral reading.

Day 6. Divide the class into Patriots and Aristocrats (see Figure 7.3). Each student then writes two pieces—a news story, a feature, an editorial, or a letter to the editor—focusing on the events read about so far. If students are genuinely engaged with the novel, their feeling of moral outrage will be strong. (If the engagement isn't there, this might be a good time to pause for discussion of the barriers to comprehension.)

Day 7. Have students in groups of three, work on putting a newspaper together. They select stories, decide on a title, work on a layout, and develop other kinds of fillers such as weather reports, horoscopes, and ads. (Be

FIGURE 7.3

From Rita Little, "The Patriots vs. the Aristocrats in *A Tale of Two Cities*," in *Ideas Plus*, Book Four, pp. 33–34. (Urbana, Ill.: National Council of Teachers of English, 1986.) Reprinted by permission.

Students become intellectually and emotionally involved with the spirit of Dickens' *A Tale of Two Cities* when they "join" either the Patriots (the peasants) or the Aristocrats (the upper class). The moment they take on their new identities, students see events of the French Revolution, along with the story and the characters, from a particular point of view. As members of opposing sides, both the Patriots and the Aristocrats produce three editions of a newspaper (the Patriots' publication is an underground newspaper), one edition for each of the novel's sections.

Before beginning their news writing assignments, those members of the class who belong to the Patriots must understand what their purpose is: to stir the people to revolt. The Aristocrats, on the other hand, will try to reassure their audience, the upper classes, by telling them that because they are obviously superior, they are in no danger from the peasants' threats.

Before the students begin to write, guidelines will be given to them reminding them of the basic characteristics of a news story, a feature or human interest story, and an opinion article, such as an editorial or a letter to the editor. Each student group is then responsible for writing, revising, typing, and proofreading its newspaper articles.

careful here that they don't let gimmickry substitute for substance; at the same time, there is opportunity here for satirical representation of some elements of the novel.)

Day 8. Read some pages of the book aloud to the students, and have them share reactions from their reading logs. Then form groups and assign each group a specific character to analyze. Students list everything they know about the character, including appearance, mannerisms, speech patterns, best and worst characteristics, things that bother them about the character, behaviors that seem inconsistent or incomprehensible. During the last half of the hour, students report to the class and class members ask questions about the characters' actions, motivations, and so forth.

Day 9. For homework, have students locate a poem that exemplifies a particular theme, fits a specific character or setting, or captures the mood or events of the novel. (Keep your own anthologies available as a resource.) On the back of the poem, the students write the connections they see between poem and novel. Collect these documents and read each poem to the class, giving students time to write down a few sentences about how they think the poem connects to the book. After two or three poems have been read, stop and ask students to share their comments with the class. Some very interesting discussions can ensue.

Day 10. Finish sharing the poems. Give time for any additional work needed on the newspapers. Read some pages aloud toward the close of the day.

Day 11. Have students in groups pick brief scenes they'd like to rewrite, quickly rewrite them, and present them to the class. Students like this activity because it allows them to have input into the novel and change parts that annoy or bother them.

Day 12. Brainstorm with the class on critical issues, themes, and topics in the book. What is this novel *about?* Students can also suggest what makes *Tale of Two Cities* interesting as a piece of literature—its unique traits. Have the students comb their response logs for ideas which may have slipped between the cracks. This list of topics will serve as the starting point for the final writing associated with the novel. Students tentatively identify a topic they'd like to explore.

Day 13. Response logs for the whole novel are due. Spend the first part of the hour sharing responses either in groups or with the whole class. As a refresher, read some quotations from the book and play identification games with the class.

Day 14. Newspapers are completed. If the papers are duplicated or photocopied, have students assemble and distribute copies. If the newspaper is one of a kind, it is examined by students in small groups. Awards for best feature article, best headline, most creative paper, and the like may also be given by the class.

Day 15. For homework, have students draft an essay based on one of the topics listed on the board. Or they may choose one of the following activities:

You are Dr. Manette. Write a journal entry dated the first night of your imprisonment.
Translate a short passage from the novel into modern prose.
Write "How I Came to Lead a Double Life," by Miss Pross's brother.
Write on this is "The best of times, the worst of times."
Interview a character. In a group, construct a list of questions to ask that character. Then each person writes up the interview, having the character answer all the questions.
Write autobiographies for the characters in the novel. What were their lives like before and after the story? What kind of kid was Sydney Carton? What happened to his parents? How did his parents' deaths affect him? What made him loathe himself? Why did he feel stuck in the destructive cycle he was in? What was he attracted to in Lucie? Why did he fall in love with her? What made him determine to die for Charles? What did he learn about himself in the

end? Try to answer as many of these questions as you can in his life story.

As a class project, write and act out a new final chapter for the novel. Perhaps Charles Darnay is executed—would that change Sydney's relationship with Lucie? How would the doctor react to the death of his son-in-law? With Madame Defarge out of the way, will members of the doctor's family still be executed?

USING TALES IN THE CLASSROOM

Folktales, fairy tales, and myths are other good choices of literature for the English classroom, and they offer yet another dimension of the relationship between literature and the adolescent. Most of the stories are short and can be read quickly. The meaning is accessible to students, so they can deal very successfully with other aspects of the stories. Since values, conflicts, and issues can usually be recognized, students can more easily discuss them, think about them, and go more deeply into the literature. These kinds of tales also provide many opportunities for research and report writing. Drama activities can spring up, as well as a myriad of writing ideas. Literary elements such as use of figurative language, plot, stereotypical characterization, theme, setting, and point of view often arise naturally as discussion topics after students have done their reading.

From Bruno Bettelheim, *The Uses of Enchantment.* New York: Vintage Books, 1977, p. 12.

Fairy tales are unique, not only as a form of literature, but as works of art which are fully comprehensible to the child, as no other form of art is. As with all great art, the fairy tale's deepest meaning will be different for each person, and different for the same person at various moments in his life. The child will extract different meaning from the same fairy tale, depending on his intellect and needs of the moment. When given the chance, he will return to the same tale when he is ready to enlarge on old meanings, or replace them with new ones.

Discussion of the characteristics of fairy tales, folktales, and myths is often a concern of the students too. This genre provides many opportunities for the students to look at people and cultures as presented through literature and discuss the similarities and differences of such things as humans' hopes, expectations, fears, and joys. As a fringe benefit, the reading of myths and tales often provides students with a kind of cultural background that is useful in reading more traditional literature.

From Bruno Bettelheim, *The Uses of Enchantment.* New York: Vintage Books, 1977, p. 5.

For a story truly to hold the child's attention, it must entertain him and arouse his curiosity. But to enrich his life, it must stimulate his imagination; help him to develop his intellect and to clarify his emotions; be attuned to his anxieties and aspirations; give full recognition to his difficulties, while at the same time suggesting solutions to the problems which perturb him.

Many teachers are hesitant to use this literature because there is so much material in this genre that it is hard to know where to begin. Collections and anthologies are plentiful, and it is useful to enlist the aid of the librarian in finding some good resources. As in the Book Pass described earlier, we recommend that the teacher bring in collections of tales from the public or school library, keep them in the classroom, and have some class sessions in which students read and comment upon particular selections.

Classroom Activities Using Tales

We like to read selected tales aloud to the class from time to time, but there is obviously a great deal of room for individualized reading in a "tales" unit. Have each student read several stories in a collection and then choose three or four for response. Questions and subjects which students can address in writing, in group discussion, or in whole class discussion are:

What did you learn from reading about the characters' experiences?
What did you learn about the culture that was associated with the tales you read?
What were the various types of villians or heroes you found in the stories?
Compare different virtues between cultures. What's important to each? What are the similarities? Differences?
Do similar themes or motifs (such as questing) appear in any of the stories?
What different things do animals represent in different cultures? For instance, are wolves always seen as sly and crafty?

Compare the use of natural elements such as water and mountains in different stories.

If you were going to read two stories to your four-year-old relative, which two would you pick? Which one would you not want to read to him or her? Explain your choices. Did the use of violence or moral lessons influence your choices?

Television is said to be a bad influence on children, teaching them by bad examples to do bad things and form bad attitudes. Discuss violence, ugliness, and evil in the stories you have read. Would these stories be bad influences? Explain.

Why do you believe people tell these kinds of tales? To teach? To entertain? To explain phenomena? Cite stories as evidence to support your point of view.

Pick out three tales. List common elements such as beginnings and endings, characters, conflicts, and morals.

Discuss the role (or lack of role) of women that you find in these tales. How are women viewed?

How does the geographic location of the story affect its portrayal of nature and animals?

What values seem important in the stories you have read? Can any of these values be traced to the culture? Why do you think these things are valued?

Are there stereotypes in your tales? Are stepmothers always wicked? Old people weak or incompetent? What fears or values might these stereotypes be speaking to?

Who is seen as being the best person or animal in these tales? What made these people or animals best? What does this tell you about what is valued in this culture?

A folktales unit can also lead to some exciting culminating project work:

Select a tale with a theme or moral that your group liked. Then write and perform a skit that would give the same thematic message to your audience.

As a group, make a videotape of a news show. The anchor should be modeled after one of the characters in the tales you have read, as should the other members of the news team. They should report on the events in the other tales through news stories, weather reports, sports shorts, and features.

Research symbolic elements in the tales, such as what a hawk or a dove represents to different cultures. Present your findings to the class.

Make a fairy tale into a comic strip or booklet. Concentrate on the essentials in the story.

Draw illustrations for a tale. Explain why you drew them the way you did and why you chose what you did to illustrate.

Write a song or poem based on one of the tales.
Research different kinds of giants, ghosts, and witches. What traits do
they have? Are these traits consistent within specific countries? For
instance, are giants always evil and mean?

Reading Tales Aloud

Again, remember to do a good deal of oral reading of tales. In fact,
tales such as these can be read over and over because so many meanings
emerge. Even if you cannot fit a great deal of time for using tales into the
class structure, one way to expose students to this rich resource is to read
the tales aloud as time permits.

USING CHILDREN'S BOOKS IN THE SECONDARY CLASSROOM

Children's books often seem an unlikely resource to secondary
teachers, who worry that students would be insulted by their use. However,
Diana has used them for years in her urban high school classes, and thus
we present them as yet another way to extend the books/young adult
relationship. Diana finds that if students know *why* children's books are in
the classroom, even the oldest students find them a delight. She recalls, for
example, using *Horton Hatches an Egg* by Dr. Seuss and having teenage
sophisticates sitting on the edges of their seats in anticipation. Students were
remembering the fun of reading and the joy of being read to, and their
response to the children's books was extraordinarily positive.

From Michael Benton and Geoff Fox, *Teaching Literature—Nine to Fourteen*
(London: Oxford University Press, 1985), p. 74.

What do picture books offer children in their reading development?
Clearly those that achieve a successful integration of text and pictures
in telling their stories are capable of giving their readers an aesthetic
experience comparable to that gained through reading other forms of
literature. Moreover, in the best of these books the narrative skills characteristic of the mature novel are to be found in simplified but effective
forms. The use of juxtaposition, daydream, irony, the story within a
story, climax and anti-climax . . . are present in many of the books. Such
books provide not only a good, attractive introduction to more demanding literature; they are simultaneously an imaginative complement to
stories that are told primarily through print alone.

Aside from helping to recapture that zest for reading and language, there are several other sound reasons for giving secondary students the chance to read and respond to children's books. As Benton and Fox point out, children's books are an excellent way to introduce or enlarge upon literary elements in the context of response. Students can much more easily grasp the idea of *theme* after they read or listen to a book such as Maurice Sendak's *Where the Wild Things Are.* They can find the central topics in *Horton:* Why *does* Horton stay on that egg? How *do* we feel about Maisie and people like her who fly off and leave their responsibilities to others?

They can clearly see and explore character from the actions portrayed in a picture book such as Nicola Bayley and William Mayne's *The Patchwork Cat* (Knopf, 1981). Through a study of children's literature, older students see more clearly why people like to read and how literature speaks to people's fears and other emotions. It is a simple transition, then, to see some of the same traits in young adult and adult literature. Diana finds it much easier for many secondary students to be objective about why children would respond to literature than to discuss elements in their own literature that are just too close for comfort.

Finally, students can learn from children's literature that it takes *knowledge* to write about the essentials of a topic even in a "simple" way. Children's books can also be used to model *kinds* of writing or as a stimulus to writing (see Chapter 9).

Activities for Children's Literature

There are many ways to enliven the English classroom with children's books:

After reading adult stories on a topic such as death, fear, or loneliness, find children's books on the same theme. Discuss similarities and differences and assess how each genre handles the topic.

Have students use the basic plot line of a children's story and flesh it out, perhaps by adding dialogue. What kind of impact does this change have on the story?

Pictures draw in the reader and create interest in children's books. Examine how good short story writers do this in the stories they write for young adults and adults.

Study beginnings of several short stories and novels. Then study the beginnings of several children's books. How are these beginnings similar and different? What conclusions can students draw?

Since the text in picture books is so short, everything that is stated conveys a great deal of information. Have students take a novel or short story they have read and write it as a children's story, discussing what happens as they make changes.

Have students turn a children's story into a radio play. They can flesh out conversations between characters, remaining true to the characterization in the story. Was this difficult to do? Did they get enough information about their characters? How did they figure out what their characters believed and felt?

Have students read a dozen picture books and rank them from best to worst. Then list the criteria they used in judging the books, such as interest, pacing, being involved with the characters, and good use of language.

Help the students list the themes brought out in several picture books. How do they recognize themes?

Discuss book selection for children. Which characters in the books students have read could have a good or bad influence on children? Do you think some books should be kept from children? (And, by analogy, do the students feel they should be "protected" from some books themselves? This topic can lead to exciting explorations of the high school censorship cases.)

TEACHING SHORT STORIES

Short pieces of fiction also work well with young adults, particularly since they can be read in a single sitting and their often powerful impact can be experienced immediately. (Poe may have been right in arguing for fiction that can be read [as McLuhan hinted] "allatonce.") Short stories also allow a teacher to have students sample unfamiliar genres, such as fantasy or historical fiction.

We like to do a Short Story Blitz, where the teacher gathers short story collections from the library and the book room for the students to explore through browsing. The blitz exposes students to many kinds of stories at once, and almost all students will find stories they like. Keep an eye out particularly for story collections for teens such as *Imaginary Lands,* edited by Robin McKinley (Greenwillow, 1986); *Sixteen: Short Stories by Outstanding Writers for Young Adults,* edited by Don Gallo (Dell, 1984); *Short Takes,* edited by Elizabeth Segal (Lothrop, 1986); *Visions: Nineteen Short Stories by Outstanding Writers for Young Adults,* edited by Don Gallo (Delacorte, 1987); *Eight Plus One,* by Robert Cormier (Bantam, 1982); and *Spaceships and Spells,* edited by Jane Yolen, Martin H. Greenberg, and Charles G. Waugh (Harper & Row, 1987). Teachers should make it clear that the purpose of browsing through these books is to choose stories that can be used as part of the classroom experience. Part of the students' job is to get others in the class interested in these stories, so they are to look for stories that not only interest them but also would interest others.

After students have had time to go through the collections, each student picks out two or three favorites, shares them with two or three other group members, and then participates in some of the following activities:

Group members choose one of the stories and write a script based on the story. Students should remember to pick out a story that they considered dramatic or important. Dialogue in these playlets should be faithful to the characterization of each person used.

Group members brainstorm kinds of awards that could be given to characters in the stories. Then they choose the most dramatic or impressive awards and tell the class which characters got the awards and why.

Students choose a part of one story that the group would like to change. They write up the change and try to build interest in their story through a presentation to the class.

Students decide on two stories that could accommodate a change in characters. Discuss how story A would be different if a character from story B were put into it. How might this additional character change the story?

Students write pamphlets about any of the issues raised in the short stories: "How Not to Fall in Love," "Being Alone and Liking It," "Ten Things Parents Absolutely Should Not Do in Public," "Signs of Deteriorating Mental Health."

Students propose a new ending for one of the stories.

A group of students create a rap or a poem advertising one of the short stories they liked.

After they have reviewed a number of stories, the students figure out groupings. What themes are presented in these stories? Are the stories connected thematically or in other ways? Students explain their rationale for grouping the stories as they did.

In "story talks," students tell a story they've particularly enjoyed. When these talks are done, students in the class can vote on which three stories they would most like to read.

Students are asked: "Should some of these stories replace some of the ones in your anthology?" "If you were to put them in the anthology, what study or discussion questions would you raise?"

SUMMING UP

The relationships among books and young readers are extraordinarily complex. As the reader will recognize, the techniques we have suggested are models which can be applied to many other genres, including nonfiction and drama. The critical point is that there are a great many sound alternatives to the teacher's standing in front of a class flogging students through a "discussion" of literary elements. Without diminishing the need to "teach" literature, we can engage students in reading in vigorous yet enlightening ways.

EXPLORATIONS

• Try the Book Pass in the classroom or the library. Talk with other teachers about what went well and what didn't, and come up with strategies to improve the Book Pass.

• Interview several English teachers or prospective teachers about their favorite young adult novels. Then interview students on the same topic. After lists are made up, exchange the lists among your interviewees so that students can see what the teachers like and teachers can see what the students like.

• Talk to the school librarian about how young adult novels are selected for the school library and how he or she determines how much money can be allocated for them.

• Try one of the activities from this chapter that you've never done before with a novel. How would you evaluate its success and worth? How did you change or adapt this activity for your class?

• After you have read a novel, skim through the activities in this chapter and pick the five you'd most like to do and the five you'd least like to do with your book. Write up a set of notes for a lesson. This can be a valuable resource to you when you ask students to become involved in books.

• Take a young adult novel you know well and create ten activities you could ask students to do with the novel. Try to make up five kinds of activities that are *not* suggested in this chapter.

• Look through an anthology used in secondary English classes. Create the plans for a thematic unit that uses material from the text as well as from young adult literature. Then create a series of assignments, activities, or discussion questions you could use with the unit.

• From the school or public library, make up a list of biographies you think students would find interesting. Design a short unit that incorporates biography.

• Design short activities or units that include tales to get students acquainted with the idea of using folktales and fairy tales in the classroom.

• Go to the public library and browse through the picture book section. Pick out three to five books you like and design activities you could use with these books in the secondary classroom.

RELATED READINGS

Literature for Today's Young Adults, by Aileen Pace Nilsen and Kenneth L. Donelson (Glencoe, Ill.: Scott, Foresman, 1985), offers a comprehensive look at the whole field of young adult literature. It includes the history of the genre, sections on the different types of fiction and nonfiction in the genre, and extensive book lists; issues such as censorship of young adult literature are also covered. Arthea J. S. Reed's *Reaching Adolescents: The Young Adult Book and the School* (New York: Holt, Rinehart & Winston, 1985) focuses on getting readers together with the literature. Thematic units are emphasized, teaching methods are explained, and ways to share literary experiences are explored. *Teaching Literature—Nine to Fourteen,* by Michael Benton and Geoff Fox (London: Oxford University Press, 1985), is an excellent book on using literature in the classroom. The theoretical framework is solid and is illustrated with numerous teaching ideas.

For teachers who would appreciate annotated book lists on Y.A. fiction and nonfiction, the National Council of Teachers of English has three very thorough books: *Books for You—A Booklist for Senior High Students,* edited by Donald R. Gallo (NCTE, 1985); *Your Reading—A Booklist for Middle School Students,* edited by Jane Christensen (NCTE, 1983); and *Adventuring with Books—A Booklist for Pre-K–Grade 6,* edited by Dianne L. Monson (NCTE, 1985). These books are revised by NCTE committees on a regular basis.

If the idea of using fairy tales in the classroom enchants you, a full reading of Bruno Bettelheim's *The Uses of Enchantment—the Meaning and Importance of Fairy Tales* (New York: Vintage, 1975) will provide a rationale for their use. In addition, Betty Bosma's *Fairy Tales, Fables, Legends, and Myths: Using Folk Literature in Your Classroom* (New York: Teachers College Press, 1987) focuses on using folktales in upper elementary and junior high classrooms.

To keep up on the latest in Y.A. books subscribe to *ALAN Review,* published three times a year by the Assembly on Literature for Adolescents of NCTE. In addition to over thirty book reviews each issue, a full range of articles on Y.A. literature appears regularly. *The English Journal* includes a good review column on Y.A. books, and *Language Arts* reviews children's literature as well.

Organizing to Teach Literature

8

From Beecher Harris, "Helping to Read: A Proposal," *Phi Delta Kappan,* May 1969. Copyright © 1969 by Phi Delta Kappa. Reprinted by permission of the publisher.

I propose that we abandon the concept of reading as a subject and, as a consequence, the complex that has grown up around it. I propose, in short, that we stop "teaching reading." I propose that we adopt instead the concept of reading as an act, an act that children perform of their own volition, and that we develop a new set of practices to implement the concept, that is, to help children perform the act. . . .

First, a look at the kindergarten. Many children enter kindergarten already familiar with books. Their parents have read to them and the children have looked at books by themselves. In the kindergarten their teacher reads to them and they are free to look at books in the room collection. They experience many highly satisfying activities in their daily living and they find the activities reflected in the books. Before long the teacher arranges for them to take books home. Looking at books eventually becomes so engaging that the teacher and the class occasionally set aside a time to do just that.

Concurrently a number of other reading-related developments are taking place. One is that the children are acquiring myriads of concepts from their experiences. Another is that they are hearing language associated with the concepts and are using oral language extensively themselves. Still another is that they are experiencing reading in its origin: writing. They see the teacher writing on many occasions of practical importance and they become aware that reading what the teacher writes is the same as reading what is printed in books.

Of course in none of this kindergarten program is the teacher requiring the children to look at books. In none of it is he requiring them to speak or write. In none of it is he assigning, pressuring, checking, correcting, marking, testing. In none of it is he judging, labeling, grouping, or—certainly not—rejecting. In none of it is he using basal readers, workbooks, phonics charts, linguistic materials, individualized reading, language-experience reading, or any other method, means, approach, or system of "teaching reading." He is, in short, not "teaching reading" at all.

Yet several significant facts with respect to reading are soon making themselves apparent.

1. Without exception the children are continuing to use books. . . . The facts are that they do like the stories and information that come from books, that they will use books, and that they will continue to use them without harassment from us.

2. Using books means that the children are reading. . . . Ability ranges all the way from none at all to complete mastery. There is no practical value in trying to determine either extreme. The important fact is that after some zero point children are reading in some degree. They may be reading no words but they are getting meaning from the book and this is reading. And they do soon come to recognize titles and single words without instruction of any kind.

3. It is clear that when children choose books they choose them for certain purposes—their own purposes. We can interfere and force them to read for our purposes—to read what we think they should read, but the children's needs will be best served when the children are permitted from the beginning to read for their own purposes and therefore to select their own reading.

4. Children grow in their ability to read. They learn to read by reading. Each child learns as fast as he is comfortably capable of learning, given opportunity and help. He constantly pushes himself to keep abreast of his expanding interests and experiences.

BEECHER Harris offers an intriguing idea. Stop "teaching" reading. Harris looks at the free-and-easy way kindergartners use books for their own purposes and argues that reading is a naturalistic process. He suggests that teachers should adopt the same approach. If we abandon reading programs, he claims, a number of exciting things will happen:

More children will read better.
More children will read more.
More children will read more intelligently and with better taste.
Reading clinics and remedial reading will disappear.
Behavior problems now caused or aggravated by the pressurized reading
     program will no longer occur.
The money now spent on materials, gadgets, devices, and extra personnel
     will be entirely saved or partially channeled into libraries.

If only a third of Harris's claims prove valid, his idea seems well worth adopting.

If Beecher Harris is right, one can properly ask: "Why raise the topic of reading programs at all? In fact, if reading growth takes place without teaching, what is the point of even talking about the 'teacher' of reading and literature?"

We suggest two answers, one that is pragmatic and another that delves somewhat deeper into the nature of literature than Harris does in his broadside.

First, for practical purposes, simply leaving students alone to read doesn't work. Even though learning to read is a more naturalistic process than most teachers have imagined, without some structure in the schools and/or in the home, reading is not likely to be done in significant amounts. While Harris's point that reading programs have become overstructured is well taken, his program (or nonprogram) may well go to the opposite extreme.

Second, and possibly more important, Harris fails to acknowledge that reading and responding to what one reads are often community activities. The sharing of responses to reading is at least as important as the actual comprehension of print. A completely unguided program, then, fails to create opportunities for individuals to *do something* with what they read.

LITERATURE IN THE CLASSROOM

In *Response to Literature* (edited by James Squire [NCTE, 1968]), D. W. Harding described three "modes of approach" to literature; literature will be employed in three different patterns:

1. *Presentation of literary material accompanied by discussion.* This mode is one with which most of us are familiar from high school and college literature courses. It is guided by the teacher, but it need not be academic, dull, or divorced from the students' experiences, as we have suggested in Chapters 6 and 7.

2. *Literature as group experience.* In this mode, the class members share a common literary experience—"storytelling, folksongs and ballads, film viewing, listening to what others have written, creative dramatics, choral reading, oral interpretation, dramatic interpretation, role playing [or] listening to recorded literature" (p. 17). This is a shared experience, Harding suggests, with a concern less for intellectual analysis than for a kind of community response.

3. *The individual child with the individual book.* This, for Harding, is free reading—self-selected—with the teacher serving as a resource person. The teacher tends to remain on the sidelines, leaving students to read and

respond as they see fit. This is also the mode that Harris recommends in "Helping to Read."

It is fair to say that in the past, the presentation of literary material accompanied by discussion was allowed to dominate the literature curriculum, almost to the exclusion of group and individual reading experiences. As we discuss organizing to teach literature, we want to suggest the need for a balance among *whole class, group,* and *individual* approaches.

THE WHOLE CLASS APPROACH

Generally this involves assigning a single literary work—poem, short story, novel—to the class so that every student reads the same material. If the teacher assumes the role of lecturer or critic, the whole class approach can be deadly dull. There is a danger of what we call the "plod approach," the chapter-by-chapter, day-by-day, week-after-week stretching out of a book. However, the common class experience with a work of literature can also provide students with models of response that can be carried over to their small group work. Further, having read books in common builds the language community of the classroom and can provide a touchstone for experiences for the rest of the year. Students can also add to each other's knowledge and perceptions by sharing in discussions, projects, and writings over a period of time. Whole class books also can help balance what students would read on their own. Ethnic literature can be introduced through whole class novels; students might not choose a book on the Holocaust on their own but could get involved in a book like *Frederick* by Hans Peter Richter (Holt, Rinehart & Winston, 1970), or the *Diary of Anne Frank* (Doubleday, 1967). Students might be hesitant to pick up a book that deals with racism but could respond to *Roll of Thunder, Hear My Cry* by Mildred Taylor (Bantam, 1976) when they read it with a class. Teachers can also get students to try different genres such as fantasy (*The Dark Is Rising* by Susan Cooper [Atheneum, 1973]), introduce them to fairy tales for young adults (*Beauty* by Robin McKinley [Harper & Row, 1978]), or get them to look at what it's like to be picked on at school (*Mrs. Fish, Ape, and Me the Dump Queen* by Norma Fox Mazer [Flare, 1980]).

More challenging books that deal with philosophical (*A Ring of Endless Light* by Madeleine L'Engle [Dell, 1980]) or moral issues (*A Separate Peace* by John Knowles [Macmillan, 1960]) are also books that students may need a nudge to read. Whole class teaching provides an opportunity for the teacher to give that nudge and also creates ways for students to get involved with the novel on many levels.

Choosing a Book for the Whole Class

The use of literature as a common class experience calls for careful selection of books. One of the first questions teachers should ask is, "Is this a book that will engage virtually all my students?" It's important to recall that even though a title may appear on a great books list, unless it snares the vast majority of students in your class, you will likely fall into the plod approach and wind up having to "beat a dead horse" as well. Next you might ask: "What sort of response can I anticipate?" Are there issues and characters and actions that will lead to discussion? Can writing options be generated from the book? Are there research possibilities? Will the book give students a desire to read more and know more? Are there poems and short stories that could be used along with it? Are there films and TV programs touching on similar themes?

Teachers do not always consider the kinds of questions sketched out above when they select books for their students. Choices often seem almost idiosyncratic but may often reflect the books that teachers studied in college. Steve and his wife, Susan, conducted a poll of "English Teachers' Literary Favorites" for *The English Journal* (February 1979) and discovered some curiosities in the way teachers pick books. They discovered, for example, that a surprising number of teachers prefer to read contemporary literature on their own (e.g., poet William Stafford and playwright Neil Simon) but choose to teach older and more difficult writers (e.g., Melville and Ibsen). Now, personal reading is not necessarily a guide for curriculum planning, but one has to wonder at the inconsistency. Susan and Steve also found that in selecting books, teachers tended to stay with the tried and true "classics" that are frequently found in anthologies and were only gradually moving toward literature by and about minorities and women.

How does one avoid the many problems inherent in selecting and teaching common literary works to an entire class? Steve asked a group of experienced teachers in a workshop at Michigan State University to write down their suggestions. Here is a selection of their responses.

Teach short works rather than long ones, preferably choosing poems, plays, and stories that can be taught in one or two periods.

Don't teach classics just for their own sake. Teach books that will carry their own weight with young people.

Supplement reading with films, filmstrips, and recordings whenever possible.

Link classical and contemporary literary works together (e.g., *Romeo and Juliet* and *West Side Story*) so that students can see connections between great books and their own lives.

Accept the students' responses, even when they differ from your own. At the same time, students should have to explain why they respond as they do.

Pick and choose from the required anthology. Teach the works *you* want to teach. Never teach an anthology from cover to cover.

From Terry C. Ley, "Getting Kids into Books: The Importance of Individualized Reading," *Media and Methods,* March 1979, p.21. Copyright © 1979 by North American Publishing Company. Reprinted by permission of the editor.

In-common reading experiences, if wisely planned and carefully directed, are valuable for teaching literature/reading skills, of course. They become tools for teachers who wish to assist groups of young people to become independent readers. However, students whose reading experiences are selected almost exclusively by the teacher—often from a book which at least half the class cannot read independently and which may offer content of marginal interest to a minority of class members—may begin to associate even the reading of imaginative literature with failure, pain, duty—anything but pleasure. It is ironic and sad that so many teachers who feel it their duty to tour the anthology and its outlying paperbacks with their students (and who may do so with considerable flair) often work very hard to prepare students for other trips, trips those students will choose not to take.

Introducing the Core Text

If a whole class is to be involved in a book, getting them interested in reading it is crucial. Teachers need to show students what they can expect, build their sense of anticipation, or give them a preview or a tasty tidbit of what is to come. The following suggestions are aimed at getting the student to *want* to read the book:

Read the title and ask the students to speculate about its significance. What does it promise? How does it pique?

Begin with questions on issues that are part of the book. Before reading *Hamlet,* ask students a question such as, "If someone in your family was brutally murdered, how would you want the killer punished?"

Create a situation that parallels one in the book and ask students to react to it—for instance, a new kid at school for *A Separate Peace.* Then have them look for the way that a character reacted to the same situation.

Bring in poems that set the theme or center on the emotions of some of the central characters.

Read the first few pages of the novel or even the first chapter. Have students predict the kinds of situations that will develop or speculate about what will happen to the characters, based on those first few pages.

Draw students into the novel by asking them to share experiences that parallel characters' experiences. For instance, ask them about negative or positive experiences with pets before they read such a book as *Sounder* by William Armstrong (Harper & Row, 1969) or *Where the Red Fern Grows* by Wilson Rawls (Doubleday, 1961).

Make up startling or interesting statements about a key character. Before reading Steinbeck's *Of Mice and Men* (Covici-Friede, 1937), for example, tell students that in this story they will meet a gentle giant who loves animals and people but ends up killing them.

Give students a partial list of values that seem important to the character (acceptance, achievement, loyalty, honesty, etc.). Have the students rank these values from most important to least important and then look for the character who seems closest to or farthest from their own values.

Read a provocative paragraph or scene to raise student interest.

Once Under Way

Use response logs. We find this sort of journal writing effective in helping students prepare for class discussion. Logs are also a good way to help students understand what is going on in the novel by giving them a place to ask questions. Often these questions will be answerable by others in the class. Too, the questions students raise may not always be the ones you, the adult, would see as critical: "Why did Pip let his sister push him around?" "Why did Cassie's grandmother make her apologize to Miz Lillian?" Nevertheless, such questions can often lead to the sorts of critical discussions you want to initiate.

Teaching a single work to a whole class often invites productive small group work as well. For instance, if one or more groups in the class opt to write a newspaper based on people and events in the novel, they can subdivide tasks and choose to write editorials, feature articles, or news, draw cartoons, create the top ten hits of the time period, construct ads, and so on. The rest of the class will be interested in the end product because it knows the literary work under discussion.

Here are some activities for small groups working on a common text:

Create an eyewitness news team consisting of an anchor person, sports-caster, weather broadcaster, writers, and, if possible, a camera crew using home or school video. Use events in the book as a focus for one of the broadcasts. If several groups do this activity, they can focus on different events in the text.

Make a map of the area, including characters' houses and other locations mentioned in the story.

Create dialogue for a scene that is alluded to but not actually presented.

Do research on a topic related to the book and present the findings to the class. For instance, after reading *Roll of Thunder, Hear My Cry* by Mildred Taylor (Bantam, 1976), students can find information on sharecropping, the Depression, Reconstruction, carpetbaggers, and lynchings. When presentations are given, the class has a stake in knowing about the topics.

Take a main character and track his or her interests, likes, and dislikes through the novel or other work. Each group can take a different main character. They can come up with a list of books that their character might like, sharing book titles and justifying choices to the rest of the class.

While students are working in groups, the teacher can circulate from group to group, acting as a guide, which we also find a good way to monitor how well students are responding to the common novel as individuals.

SMALL GROUP READING AND DISCUSSION

Examining full-length books with an entire class can become difficult. Steve has reached the point where he seldom, if ever, compels a whole class to read a long work in common, preferring to limit the common class experience to short works. However, the teacher can often find several students in any class who would like to examine a single book and work together on it. Small group work also has the advantage of being self-supporting, with the group members, rather than the teacher, supplying the principal motivation and direction.

In moving toward small group reading the teacher uses a multitext approach, having students read a number of works simultaneously rather than study a single text. Multitext teaching can be as complex as a totally individualized reading program, with every student reading a different book, or it can be relatively simple, with students reading two or three different books in small groups. Multitext and single text approaches are compared in the accompanying box, where Roberta Riley and Eugene Schaeffer note the advantages of multitext teaching.

A COMPARISON OF APPROACHES

Multitext Approach

1. The problem of different levels of ability within a classroom can be addressed through content as well as activities.
2. Materials are diverse.

3. Participation in selection can be broad based and individuals or groups responded to simultaneously.
4. Group members become familiar with a wide range of varied books.
5. Teacher preparation and involvement can be personal and individual.
6. Reading for pleasure and out of interest can be encouraged.
7. Reading interests of the group may be expanded through variety of materials available and through use of peer recommendations.
8. Documentation of student learning can be highly specialized and individual. Record keeping may be a teacher's initial, dominant concern. On the other hand, some teachers are glad students are reading anything and precisely what they are learning or the depth of learning is not their main concern.
9. Occasionally, censorship may become an issue.

Single Text Approach

1. Since the content is the same, activities rather than texts vary.

2. Material is easy to keep track of.
3. Participation in selection may be narrow, idiosyncratic, and often determined by people outside the group concerned.
4. Intensity and in-depth study may be enhanced.

5. Teacher preparation can be focused on content rather than people.
6. Reading for structure and analysis is likely to be the focus.
7. Reading interests are directed toward a few prominent and well-known books.

8. The task of evaluation is simplified because it is focused on a single work; often paper and pencil tests are used.

9. Books are usually approved.

Multitext Approach	Single Text Approach
10. Enrichment is possible with this approach as well as time for the teacher (and possibly other students) to work one on one with students who cannot read.	10. Learning is rarely differentiated.

A convenient way to begin multitext teaching is to introduce several common readings to the whole class—four poems on a theme, three stories by a particular author—and then extend the range by having the students break into small groups to read several different full-length novels on the theme or to examine longer works by the same author. Students remain in their groups for a period of time for reading and discussion, then meet with the class as a whole to share their responses.

Until the teacher knows many novels well and can initially give guidance and structure to these small groups, the task may seem difficult. However, if teachers give the same kind of task to each group until they know several novels well, the problem of preparing separate discussion questions for each group each day is solved. Students can:

- Begin each small group with a sharing of questions and comments from their response log.
- Be responsible on different days for developing discussion questions.
- Fill out sheets (see Figure 8.1) ranking the values of the main characters.
- Make lists of the issues and themes presented in the book.
- Discuss where they would most like to intervene in the story.
- Discuss what seems realistic or unrealistic in the novel.
- Talk about what's most difficult to understand in the novel and how the author could have made this easier to grasp.
- Discuss conflicts in the book and what characters learn through resolving the conflicts.

Each day of class need not be spent in small groups. The teacher can vary the format by having students write about some aspects of the book during class. Also, whole class discussions on such topics as "the character who is hardest to understand" can help provide the variety needed in a class.

As the above suggestions imply, the teacher does not simply turn the students loose to proceed any which way. By preparing group activities and sometimes study guides—perhaps following the levels of response suggested

FIGURE 8.1

From *Writing about Literature* by Elizabeth A. Kahn, Carolyn Calhoun Walter, and Larry R. Johannessen, p.30. NCTE/ERIC, 1984. Reprinted by permission.

LITERARY CHARACTERS' VALUES PROFILE

Character: Rank the values in order from most important to the character to least important to the character. If the character's values change, then rank the values both before and after the change.

_____ 1. Acceptance (approval from others)

_____ 2. Achievement

_____ 3. Aesthetics

_____ 4. Altruism

_____ 5. Autonomy

_____ 6. Companionship (friend-ship)

_____ 7. Creativity

_____ 8. Health

_____ 9. Honesty

_____ 10. Justice

_____ 11. Knowledge

_____ 12. Love

_____ 13. Loyalty

_____ 14. Morality

_____ 15. Physical appearance

_____ 16. Pleasure

_____ 17. Power

_____ 18. Recognition

_____ 19. Religious faith

_____ 20. Self-respect

_____ 21. Skill

_____ 22. Wealth

in Chapter 6—the teacher will help students find a sense of direction in their reading. As students become more experienced in this sort of small group work, the teacher can reduce the amount of direction.

INDIVIDUALIZED READING

Individualized or "free" reading programs are relatively new in education, having become popular at about the time when the paperback revolution of the late 1950s and early 1960s made quality literature available inexpensively. Up to that time, common class reading of literary materials was the dominant mode of instruction.

Like multitext teaching, individualized reading calls for new roles for English teachers. Instead of being a lecturer, the teacher is often a book or reading resource, working closely with students to learn about and to suggest titles. Individualized reading programs also involve a fair amount of bookkeeping, and the teacher must develop some sort of management procedures to record student progress. Techniques range from cumulative reading folders that the students maintain themselves to large posters or charts on which the teacher or students can note the titles that have been read.

Launching an individualized reading program is not simply a matter of supplying books in profusion and letting the students "have at it." Most teachers find they need to supply additional structure to make the program work. Sometimes individualized reading can be linked to thematic or other kinds of instructional units. After the class has examined some common literary works, each student launches a personal reading program. In this way, the books read by individual students are related to the common interests of the class, creating a natural audience for sharing.

Many teachers have adapted the basic instructional idea behind *Reading Ladders for Human Relations,* a book first developed by the American Council on Education many years ago and currently in its sixth edition (Eileen Tway, editor, National Council of Teachers of English, 1981). The "ladders" consist of book titles, arranged by difficulty level, on a single topic or theme. Students can thus follow a series of titles that continually expands their interests. Most school and public librarians know of the concept of reading ladders and are willing to help the English and language arts teacher develop similar sequences using titles available locally.

In some schools, individualized reading programs become formal courses, frequently with a title like "Reading for Pleasure." Such courses have been controversial and have come under attack from both parents and other teachers. "Why should kids get credit just for reading for fun?" is the question most often raised. As far as we are concerned, the more fun connected with reading, the better. Given the wealth of reading materials available at all levels, K–12, there is no reason why the reading act need be unpleasant. Too often, individualized reading is slotted into the reading *course* only, while other English classes continue to plod with a one book, whole class approach. In some schools the "Reading for Pleasure" class is associated with students of low motivation or low reading ability. When this happens, the free reading course is seen as a last resort, a course to be recommended when the student cannot be compelled or cajoled into reading teacher-selected material. In short, individualized reading programs should be well integrated into the entire English or language arts curriculum.

Although individualized reading may sound like an unmanageable monster to the teacher, there are several ways it can be made to work in the classroom. One plan that can be followed is Jill VanAntwerp's "Twenty Students—Twenty Books" (Figure 8.2). Jill has successfully handled having each student read a different book by structuring the activities that each student responds to. Still, she has built in choices for students as well as outlets for their creativity.

Another way to work individualized reading into the regular class is to give students occasional reading days in class to supplement reading of

FIGURE 8.2 TWENTY STUDENTS—TWENTY BOOKS: A Sample Unit for Working with Self-Selected Novels. Created by Jill VanAntwerp, Lowell Senior High School, Lowell, Michigan.

This unit for the study of a novel can take two to three weeks depending on the length of the introduction to a novel, the amount of time given to select books, the amount of time given for in-class work on papers and projects, as well as time spent on the presentations themselves. Students are asked to read one-eighth of their chosen novel for each class day and to bring the novels with them to class.

Day One: An evaluation of the author's style. This is done by sampling pages throughout the book, checking on sentence structure, length of words, use of description, action, or dialogue, structure, and other observable surface features.

Day Two: Diad Quiz. The students trade books. Each student examines various pages in the first quarter of the book and writes down questions that come to mind about what he or she reads. The students spend part of the hour writing questions, then spend the rest of the time quizzing one another, a question at a time. Then each grades the other on the quiz.

Day Three: "The Friendly Strangers." I ask the students to picture themselves on a long train trip in a compartment with three other people. They are to be a character in their books and are to remain in character the entire hour as they talk to their fellow travelers about themselves. They break into groups of four or five for this exercise. Often I follow up with a request for each to cast a vote for the best performance in their compartment, writing their reasons for choosing the "stranger" they select.

Day Four: An examination of the setting and background of the novel. I spend part of the hour having the students respond by taking notes on their novels as I raise questions about the setting and background: place, time, references, etc. Then I ask for an essay from these notes.

Day Five: Do It Yourself Quiz. The students ask and answer questions which they feel bring out significant aspects of their novels.

Day Six: Group Book Talks. Each talk is followed by questions from the others. I stress: 1. Tell an event that aroused suspense. 2. How do you think your novel will end? 3. Do real people act like this? 4. How easy or hard is this book to read? Why? 5. Could a teen relate to this book enough to use it for inspiration or solace? 6. Tell the saddest, scariest, happiest, funniest, most tragic, or most ironic scene in the book.

Day Seven: Interview with the author. Each student role plays his/her author in a talk show format.

Final Day(s): Summing Up: Project. This takes several days. Students choose one of the following ways to respond to the book.

Paper—students select a thesis topic which they can support in a short reactive paper.

Creative—collage, oral interpretation, slide show, or dramatic scene.

Narrative—students write prequels, sequels, additional scenes, or put the character in another place or time.

Poetry writing or selection of a group of poems—students write or select poems which reflect in the student's mind his or her experience with the novel.

the rest of the text at home, have them read the bulk of the book at home, and then once or twice a month have them do group activities on their books. Whole class gatherings for book sharing are an important aspect of individualized reading programs. During each marking period students can make presentations to the whole class to build interest in their books. If students know that reading is an integral part of the class and that it "counts" for something by being evaluated or graded, they are much more likely to be enthusiastic about it. Simply assigning book reports without any other activities related to their reading or any other mention of reading in class does not produce the avid readers we would like students to be.

In addition, a free reading program opens unique opportunities for the teacher to individualize in other areas. For example, while students spend time reading, the teacher is free to consult with individuals about their work. A conference with a student on his or her writing problems can take place during this time. Further, as student reading is individualized, it becomes easier for the teacher to differentiate writing assignments, since students will often raise questions or make their interests known through their reading and the teacher can shape assignments around that new information. This differentiation in turn creates potential audiences for student writing, a topic we will take up again in Chapter 10.

THE TEACHER AS READING RESOURCE

As one moves toward multitext, individualized programs, the teacher needs to help each student find appropriate reading material. The reading process is supported powerfully if a teacher is present at the right times to suggest titles, without pressuring the students to accept recommendations.

In sheer quantity, the resources that *should* be made available to students are staggering. Paperback catalogs and book lists provide literally thousands of book titles that are appropriate at various levels of school. Moreover, at last count some twenty-five *thousand* magazines were being published regularly in this country, many of which are useful to a teacher of English. Add to that the newspapers, brochures, pamphlets, fliers, and booklets that are readily available and should be brought into a class at the appropriate times. A teacher must also know nonprint media in order to serve as a resource person on films, television, recordings, and radio.

This variety means that the English teacher must be "bibliographically agile." If a student develops a sudden interest in cacti or Strindberg or stage direction or poetry, the teacher should be able to help locate material that will satisfy those interests. Teachers of literature must know far more than the books covered in four years of college English. They must know and have access to many reading resources that may interest any growing members of the community of language. (In the previous chapter we mentioned several book review and selection guides to books appropriate for young readers.)

However, for many teachers, the problem is not so much locating titles as getting the actual books into the classroom. Book budgets are slim and are often consumed by the purchase of adopted anthologies. Libraries are poorly "booked," and in some cases the stereotypical librarian who doesn't like to have books circulate is still running things behind the desk. How do you bring more literature into the classroom? A group of students in Steve's teaching of literature class came up with this list of suggestions:

Contact your local paperback distributor for free or sample copies and for unsold back issues of newspapers, magazines, and even books.

Visit garage sales. Often you can find quality paperbacks at rock-bottom prices.

Sponsor book swaps, where students can exchange titles.

Rip apart anthologies and group the tear sheets by genre, theme, or author to create a loose-leaf file or "bin" of literature.

Seek contributions of reading material from the community and from the students. Many paperbacks rest unread on home bookshelves, and they can easily be obtained for school.

Raise money to buy books through a bake sale, car wash, or talent show. (The big money-maker, by the way is a car *wax,* which brings in much larger dollar amounts than a nickel-and-dime cupcake bake.)

Set up an in-school paperback bookstore with the assistance of your local paperback distributor, with proceeds used to buy more books, even as you promote books for purchase within the school.

Encourage students to join some of the paperback book clubs that are advertised through such magazines as *Scholastic.* These clubs supply books at bargain prices.

Write to the government with questions. These inquiries will often bring back a rich supply of pamphlets.

Rotate classroom libraries with other teachers.

There are other clever ways to get a supply of books inexpensively. For example, at MacDonald Middle School in East Lansing, Michigan, the principal hit on the idea of a nickel book drive/book sale. The students were paid five cents by the school for each paperback book they brought in; at the sale, they could buy as many books as they wanted for a nickel apiece. The students brought in thousands of good, readable books. (Parents were informed of the drive and told they must approve of the books their children brought in, thus anticipating censorship problems.) Students who couldn't afford to buy books were given a handful of nickels privately by a teacher, so that every child in the school was able to buy new reading material. The unsold books were then divided among the English teachers for use in classroom libraries.

Overall, our advice to the teacher who is just moving into the area of individualized reading is to start small and then expand. Initially, a class-room library may contain only twenty-five to fifty titles. That number can be gradually increased as the teacher locates new book sources and becomes more skilled at keeping track of individual student readers.

THE TEACHER AS READING PROPAGANDIST

Implicit, too, in multitext and individualized programs is the role of the English teacher as book promoter, one who unabashedly "sells" literature and reading to young people, telling them about books, placing books in their hands, reviewing books, sharing responses. One clue to the importance of this role is suggested by the success of TV novels. Such books, ranging from the *Star Wars* to the *Dynasty* spin-offs, sell well as a result of the publicity they receive. Apparently, most readers want to know something about a book before they plunge into it.

To propagandize about literature one can:

Put up attractive book posters advertising interesting reading.

Include many short books in your class library.

Habitually include free or individualized reading as part of any English course.

Have "hot" books available to the extent that school and community standards will allow it. Scan the best-seller list and get those books into the classroom.

Include series books: *Hardy Boys, Nancy Drew, James Bond,* the Dr. Seuss books, the *Wizard of Oz* books.

Provide book talks periodically, telling students what's available in an area or field. If you don't like to do book talks yourself, call on your librarian.

Sponsor field trips to bookstores or libraries.

Make audiovisual helps readily available: filmstrips, records, even filmed versions of books.

Start a book club that meets during lunch hours or after school where book lovers can talk about the books they are reading and recommend books to each other.

Another excellent list of suggestions, provided by Donna Brutten and her students, is shown in Figure 8.3.

ORGANIZING THE LITERATURE PROGRAM

Over the years, four principal ways of focusing literary study have predominated in the colleges and the schools:

1. *The historical/chronological approach,* featuring survey and period courses and a concern for literary history. (Often these surveys are done by individual nations, e.g., British literature.)
2. *The author approach,* with a concern for the collected works of a single writer and the relationships between the writer's biography and evolution as a writer.
3. *The genre approach,* which directs literary study through the examination of the principal forms of writing: poetry, essay, drama, fiction.
4. *The masterpieces or great books approach,* which unifies its study through the choice of widely accepted classics.

In any college or secondary school curriculum, one often finds a number of courses based on one of these four organizing features.

Without rejecting the value of dealing with literature in terms of history, biography, genre, or classic titles, we suggest that each takes the content of literary scholarship rather than human experience as its starting point. If one is teaching a genre unit such as poetry or drama, the common denominator of instruction is still the elements of a literary form, leading the teacher inevitably to such questions as, "What is the definition of poem?" "Why is *Dr. Zhivago* a 'better' film than *Gone With the Wind?*" "What is drama?" In a survey or period course, discussion emphasizes historical matters, concentrating on knowledge of times and writings. Each of the other approaches similarly initiates discussion in terms of critical content, and the students' personal involvement necessarily gets second billing.

To some extent, a fifth approach, *humanities,* has broken the tradition of criticism-centered courses by focusing on issues and ideas. Yet in practice, humanities courses are often simply grand survey courses in the historical/chronological mode, or they reduce truly interdisciplinary questions to a comparison of artistic genres.

FIGURE 8.3

From Donna Brutten, "How to Develop and Maintain Student Interest in Reading," in the English Journal Workshop, Betsy B. Kaufman, ed., *The English Journal,* November 1974, p.74. Copyright © 1974 by the National Council of Teachers of English. Reprinted by permission of the publisher and the author.

HOW TO DEVELOP AND MAINTAIN STUDENT INTEREST IN READING

How can we, as English teachers, motivate our students to read? In order to find possible solutions to this dilemma, we asked one thousand pupils at Nathaniel Hawthorne Middle School, Bayside, New York, the following two questions: *What has a teacher of yours done to interest you in reading? What could a teacher of yours do to interest you in reading?* The most frequent cited responses are listed below.

1. Let us choose our own book.
2. Tell us interesting stories.
3. Show filmstrips or films about stories.
4. Let us act out exciting scenes from stories and plays.
5. Suggest names of interesting stories.
6. Let us read along with taped stories.
7. Play records that tell stories.
8. Have free reading periods.
9. Assign creative projects, such as posters, collages, dioramas, and montages instead of book reports.
10. Have contests to see who reads the most books.
11. Assign different types of books.
12. Tell only the beginning of interesting stories.
13. Let us read comic books, magazines, and newspapers.
14. Have group discussions and panel discussions.
15. Let us tell the class about exciting books that we have read.
16. Decorate the room with interesting posters, book displays, and students' projects relating to books.
17. Take us to the school library.
18. Play reading games.
19. Award prizes.
20. Have a classroom library.
21. Bring book clubs, such as TAB or AEP, to the attention of students.
22. Prepare teacher and/or student annotated book lists.
23. Don't assign everyone the same book.
24. Let us read at our own pace.
25. Assign relevant literature.

Thematic courses and units provide a sixth alternative, which focuses first on issues and problems and second on literature. We confess to considerable partiality to teaching by themes. If a literature program begins with people and ideas rather than literary patterns, types, or histories, the teacher can effectively involve students' experiences in the reading process. By centering on ideas or topics rather than a form of literature, the teacher is free to bring in multiple resources in many forms and media and to provide direction for reading by allowing students to read for their own purposes. (A list of possible topics for thematic units and courses is given in Figure 8.4.)

A good many teachers, however, find themselves thrust into curricula that are patterned along traditional lines, with course titles like "American Literature," "The Short Story," or "Romantic Poetry." Obviously, curricula like these place limits on thematic teaching. But before teachers surrender by allowing the approach to dictate what they will do, they should explore how the traditional curriculum can be shaped along thematic lines and how they can involve students in the work.

For instance, if teachers find themselves in the position of teaching the early parts of American literature, they can mute the impact of a strictly historical/chronological approach by finding ways to involve students and by showing them connections between the literature and their own lives.

Thus, before tackling Benjamin Franklin's *Autobiography* and Jonathan Edwards' *Resolutions,* which focus on how these authors wish to improve

---

FIGURE 8.4 THEMES IN READING

Feelings	War and Peace
The Sea	Illusion and Reality
Animals	Ecology
Friendship	Futurism
The Supernatural	Coming of Age
The Seasons	Prison Reform
Holidays	Cities
First Relationships	Isolation
Anomalies	Dissent
Persuasion	Racism
Fantasies	Prophecy

their lives, the teacher can raise questions about how important self-improvement is in today's society. Students can:

- Brainstorm all the ways in which our society is involved in self-improvement (aerobics, weight loss, how to live without a man or woman).
- Read the selections with an eye to picking out the similarities and differences between what the authors think is important enough to change and what we think is important to change.
- Come to class having picked out five resolutions they strongly agree with and five they think are not important.
- Discuss what we can learn about the values and concerns of a people or a person by what they want to improve about themselves.
- Make up reading lists for Franklin and Edwards to help them achieve their goals (for example, Franklin might benefit from a book called *The New You—A Temperate Approach to Eating*).
- Think of the things they would like to change about themselves or their lives that could be accomplished by the end of the school year and then write a paper (possibly in the form of resolutions).

To cite another example from early American literature, students can look not only at issues but also at examples of a particular kind of writing and then begin activities based on that kind of writing. Thomas Paine's "The Crisis" and Patrick Henry's "Speech in the Virginia Convention" can be used as a springboard to persuasive writing or speechmaking and to a look at the ways we can be persuaded by the media today. Students can:

- Rewrite Patrick Henry's speech in modern English.
- Write a paper persuading the teacher of the need for more lenient or less work.
- Discuss why political speeches are in a literature book and why we no longer seem to treat speeches as literature.
- Discuss the media that our contemporary society uses most to convince people on political matters.
- Explore the issues that concerned Henry and Paine. Are there issues today that can make Americans equally impassioned?
- Debate whether the kinds of persuasive devices that were used by the early Americans work today.
- Bring in ads they consider effective. Then, using their knowledge of the early Americans, explain how they might have responded to the same ad. For instance, would the appeal to be like everyone else work for them? Students might rewrite the ad in such a way that the product would appeal to those early Americans.

Another way to deal with curricula organized along traditional lines is to do as a teacher we know did when presented with a class called "Poetry." "I'll be damned if I'll concentrate only on meter and rhyme schemes and versification," she told Steve. "The kids have had enough of that sort of thing and they hate it." Her solution was to purchase one copy each of the fattest paperback poetry collections at the bookstore—an out-of-pocket cost of under $20 for a dozen books—and then rip off the book bindings to create a loose-leaf collection of about two thousand poems. She parceled out this collection along the lines of thematic topics that she felt would be of interest to her students—Reminiscences, Coming of Age, and the Generation Gap, to name a few. Her poetry course was then structured topically.

A similar strategy, without ripping up books, can be applied to other courses. Thematic courses can be constructed from anthologies and collections that are exclusively American, exclusively British, exclusively drama, or exclusively in the classics. One could even build a topical course or unit around the works of a single author—say, Shakespeare or Mark Twain—by dividing the works into thematic units.

CREATING A LITERATURE RESOURCE UNIT

Whether one is teaching a topical, genre, chronological, thematic, or interdisciplinary course, it is useful to prepare in advance resource materials that promote a balance among the basic ways of presenting literature: whole class, small group, and individualized.

The Common Class Readings

You can use a good commercial anthology for this or create your own from books checked out of the library. Use short selections—poems, stories, essays, one-act plays—for the most part, perhaps punctuated with a novel. The function of these readings is to give the students a common background for the issue under discussion. These materials should have broad appeal and high readability. We like to use common readings as the focus of a class once or twice each week. The approach to discussion sketched out in Chapters 6 and 7 is most appropriate here.

The In-Class Library

This center is the heart of a program and the most interesting part of a course or unit to construct. It is based on the assumption that if teachers concentrate enough resource materials and enough project ideas in one place, they will be able to strike a spark with each student. The library should contain:

1. *Reading materials.* Select short to mid-length selections for the most part, and include all forms and genres: poems, articles, brochures, pamphlets, magazines, and so forth. Include some paperback anthologies. Clip appropriate articles from newspapers and magazines. Save your most interesting junk mail. As possible, dry-mount or glue the materials on construction paper, adding appropriate photographs. Make construction paper covers, envelopes, folders, and the like, or involve your students in making materials attractive and durable.

2. *Related materials.* Include photographs, prints, posters, comics, games, puzzles, records, filmstrips, film loops, tapes.

3. *Suggestions for projects.* Prepare a single list of suggested activities, or append writing, speaking, project, and related reading ideas to individual pieces. We have offered a number of suggestions in Chapters 6 and 7 about approaches to literature, and many of these can be applied to individual works. A few more for your files: students can:

Write newspapers that might appear in the various characters' towns.
Have a character from one story interview a character in another for a newspaper report or a magazine feature article, this done through writing or role-playing.
Assume that several of the families they have read about move into the same neighborhood. Who would live next door to whom? Who would live way down the street? Who would associate with whom? Why?
Choose several stories they have read and create an anthology or table of contents. What would they put on the cover of the book? What poems could be used in the beginning of the book to introduce the content? In what order would they place the stories? On the back cover, they can list some of the social issues the collection covers.
Fit selected stories into a time line representing a central issue. How have human rights, women's rights, views of freedom, or images of violence changed over time?
Design a proposal for a new public broadcasting series based on selected stories, plays, or poems.
Write imaginatively from the point of view of a character.
Imagine that characters went to school together and write their entries for the school yearbook. Students can include a nickname for each character and clubs, sports, and other activities. Certainly quotations about the character would be appropriate. Did the character win any of the nominations for person most likely to_____?

Individualized Reading Folders

As a supplement to the literature program, the teacher can develop individualized multidisciplinary reading folders, loose-leaf collections of materials. Steve asked his students simply to list some of their out-of-school interests. Their replies make a good sampling of possible folder titles:

Music	Politics
Crafts	Cacti
Philosophy	Calligraphy
Religions	Two-Cycle Engines
Theater	Pollution Control Devices
Parachute Jumping	Sewing
Knitting	Disc Jockeying
Printing	Terrariums
Jobs	Yoga
Making Snow	Plants
Communications	Journalism
Government	Cooking
Botany	Swimming
Sociology	Advertising
Girls' Sports	Almanacs

Folders can begin with a half-dozen clippings and expand to fill a box with several hundred related pieces of reading material. In response to their reading folders, students might:

Make a dictionary of new terms learned about the topic.
Write an encyclopedia entry based on information gleaned.
Rank the pieces from most to least informative or interesting.
Write an opinion piece based on a reading about which they felt strongly.
Construct a pamphlet giving others concise information.
Interview a person working in a field mentioned.
Construct a survey about others' attitudes or knowledge and then report on the results.

An afternoon spent cutting up the bulky Sunday *New York Times* will provide you with enough material to begin two dozen folders, as will an evening spent browsing through back issues of magazines you probably already have lying around home.

A Student-Built Unit

Another intriguing possibility for the literature program is a unit in which students take principal responsibility for locating reading materials and for defining and executing their own assignments. Teachers are thus freed to move to a consultative or resource role more quickly than if they were carrying primary responsibility for creating the unit.

One such unit is called a "Probe." To initiate the unit, the teacher simply asks, "What concerns you as a class and what do you propose to do about it?" From a guided discussion emerges a concerted effort on the part of the class to learn about an issue or problem and to take action on it. Some successful Probe topics include:

Noise	Civil Rights
Waste	Individuality
The Government	Censorship
Victorian Morals	Clocks
Our Town 100 Years Ago	Russia (or any country)
Old Age	Religions
Human Relationships	Earthquakes
2050	Electronics

The basic steps in organizing a Probe include the following:

1. *Choosing a general chair.* This student will serve as a coordinator for the program. Often the chair will need one or more assistants or helpers.
2. *Brainstorming.* Working in groups of four or five, the students talk over three questions:

   What do we know about this topic already?
   What do we want to know?
   Where can we find out what we want to know?
3. *Setting priority questions.* The fruits of the brainstorming session are evaluated by the whole class and reduced to, say, six or eight main questions or issues. The students break up into teams according to interests, each team with the central task of finding an answer to its question.
4. *Probing.* The teams probe the question—reading, interviewing, watching, observing—following plans worked out by the team and approved by the chair. The teacher serves as a consultant to each team.
5. *Production.* Each team produces reports and other documents—perhaps essays, films, tapes, or advertisements—that help translate its

findings for the class. Depending on the nature of the Probe, the teams may present material to the class or go outside the class to take action.

The kinds and amounts of reading and writing which the students do will, of course, vary with the topic. Some Probe topics will lead principally to reading in expository prose; others will focus more on drama, poetry, and fiction. The teacher will need to help the students see alternatives and possibilities and guide them toward new and unperceived directions.

INTEGRATION OF THE LANGUAGE ARTS THROUGH LITERATURE

It is no doubt clear by now that the literature programs described here are, in essence, *English* programs—they involve at least as much composing, speaking, and listening as they do reading and literary study. This integration seems to us highly desirable: teachers should encourage a natural flow from one form of language to another. By offering writing options as part of a literature unit, the teacher makes the *producing* of language a comfortable outcome of *consuming* it. Similarly, when reading is focused toward an actual task—learning something or persuading someone—it too becomes natural and purposeful and leads easily to related language arts activities.

In fact, it is perhaps inaccurate to call these *English* units at all, since they involve experiences outside the dimensions of the traditional English course; they are genuinely interdisciplinary. In the history of education, English has often been an umbrella subject, with the teacher trying to hold the umbrella straight while teaching basic reading, the history of Western civilization, spelling, the business letter, the necessary skills for success in college, and the difference between Elizabethan and Petrarchan sonnets. We suggest that integrated literature units, particularly with a thematic emphasis, provide a way to pull together diverse demands, while actually enlivening study and providing students with useful training for other fields. There seems to be no reason why the English teacher should not incorporate the materials of science, history, math, business and industry, politics, psychology, sociology, vocational education, art, music, journalism, and theater, since they can be used to provide a genuinely humane, broadly practical literature and reading program. (More on this in Chapter 15.)

EXPLORATIONS

• To run a good literature course, one must be bibliographically agile, knowing sources. Teachers need not always know the fine details of what is in the literature, but the knowledge must be sufficient to allow them to make recommendations with confidence. Here are three projects a teacher can undertake to develop bibliographic agility:

1. *Spend time browsing in a paperback bookstore looking at books that might be useful with students.* Don't limit your thinking to traditional literature. Check out the sociology section, the history paperbacks, the joke books, and the science section. Examine the handicrafts department and the sports books. Check cookbooks. Practice scanning for content so you can form quick, reliable judgments about a book's applicability.
2. *Do the same with the magazine section of a bookstore.* There is a phenomenal number of magazines on which you can draw regularly. Check such titles as *Gem Collector* and *Czechoslovakia Today* for possible use.
3. *Learn about pamphlet and brochure sources.* Enormous amounts of such material are printed each year in this country. For starters, familiarize yourself with the publications available from the Superintendent of Documents in Washington, D.C., and from your state's printing office. Then check travel agencies, public service institutions, universities, county agriculture agents, and the pamphlet files at your local library.

• Pick a topic that you think would interest students of the age you like to teach and create a reading ladder—in effect, a book list—of related books of increasing sophistication and difficulty.

• Learn how to give a book talk, a 15- to 30- minute review of books on a topic for young people.

• Try letting a class (or a few students) embark on a totally free reading program, with you serving only as a guide or coach. Stay with it long enough to see patterns of growth and development emerging. Do students grow as readers when left on their own? Do they enjoy the program?

• Design a record-keeping system for an individualized reading program.

• Choose a book that you think a small group of students could read on their own and develop a study guide to assist them in their reading.

• Get together with two or three other teachers and build a resource unit, just to find out how it's done and how much or how little work it involves. Flip a coin to see who gets to test it first.

• Study a conventional literature anthology in terms of its adaptability to thematic teaching. For example, if you find a British literature anthology that is organized chronologically, consider ways in which its literary selections could be restructured along thematic lines.

• Start your collection of individualized reading folders.

• Create introductory activities for a novel you know well. The next time you use the novel, see which activities work best at piquing student interest.

• Sketch out plans for a two- or three-week unit on a specific novel. Include several activities for whole class novels mentioned in the chapter and create several of your own.

• Read several young adult novels and decide which one you think is most suited for whole class use. Jot down notes on what you can do with the novel, connections you could help make to students' lives, and why you think this would be a good book for the whole class to read.

• Look through an anthology and find two or three selections you could do a mini-unit on. Generate as many teaching ideas as you can on these selections.

RELATED READINGS

D. W. Harding's essay "Response to Literature" (In *Response to Literature,* edited by James Squire [Urbana, Ill.: National Council of Teachers of English, 1968]) is a concise and practical discussion of literature and reading programs. Note especially Harding's comments on the ways in which reading patterns change as students grow, thus creating a need for the teacher to alter the modes of approach to literature. Daniel Fader and Elton McNeil's *Hooked on Books* (New York: Berkeley-Medallion, 1974) is a modern classic which helped revolutionize teaching with its recommendations for saturating a school with reading matter, especially newspapers and magazines.

The NCTE's Theory and Research into Practice series includes two publications that are very helpful to the teacher of literature. The first, *Explorations—Introductory Activities for Literature and Composition, 7–12,* by Peter Smagorinsky, Tom McCann, and Stephen Kern (1987), offers excellent strategies aimed at involving students in the literature they are to read. The second booklet, *Writing about Literature,* by Elizabeth A. Kahn, Carolyn Calhoun Walter, and Larry R. Johannessen (1984), offers many concrete suggestions on how to get students to write about and interpret the literature they read.

Teaching Writing

9

THE teaching and learning of writing are among the most difficult and even controversial components of the English program. Even the most dedicated writers have times when they agree with Scott Bates in saying "I hate wrighting" (Figure 9.1), and our profession is notorious for saying "I hate teaching writing, too." It is well known that school and college teachers prefer teaching literature to composition, and the place of writing in the English program has never been particularly secure. One need only look back a few years to see a curious love/hate affair with writing: to the 1950s, when there was a general lamenting of students' writing skills; to the 1960s, when writing skills were seen to be in pretty good shape, so much so that some colleges and universities dropped their freshman writing courses; to the 1970s and 1980s, when the concern for an alleged withering away of writing skills resurfaced. Much of that vacillation came from outside the English profession, to be sure, but to some extent it reflects plain uncertainty about approaches to and obvious dislike of teaching "wrighting."

The times have changed, however. The late 1970s and 1980s have seen an extraordinary interest in writing develop both inside and outside the English profession. A great deal of composition research has been done, so much that Professor Stephen North could write a book on *The Making of Knowledge in Composition* (Montclair, N.J.: Boynton/Cook, 1987). Summer institutes for teachers of writing have been filled to capacity, and expanded writing programs in the schools and colleges have been developed around a sound and evolving understanding of composition.

Much of the current development in theory and practice comes from

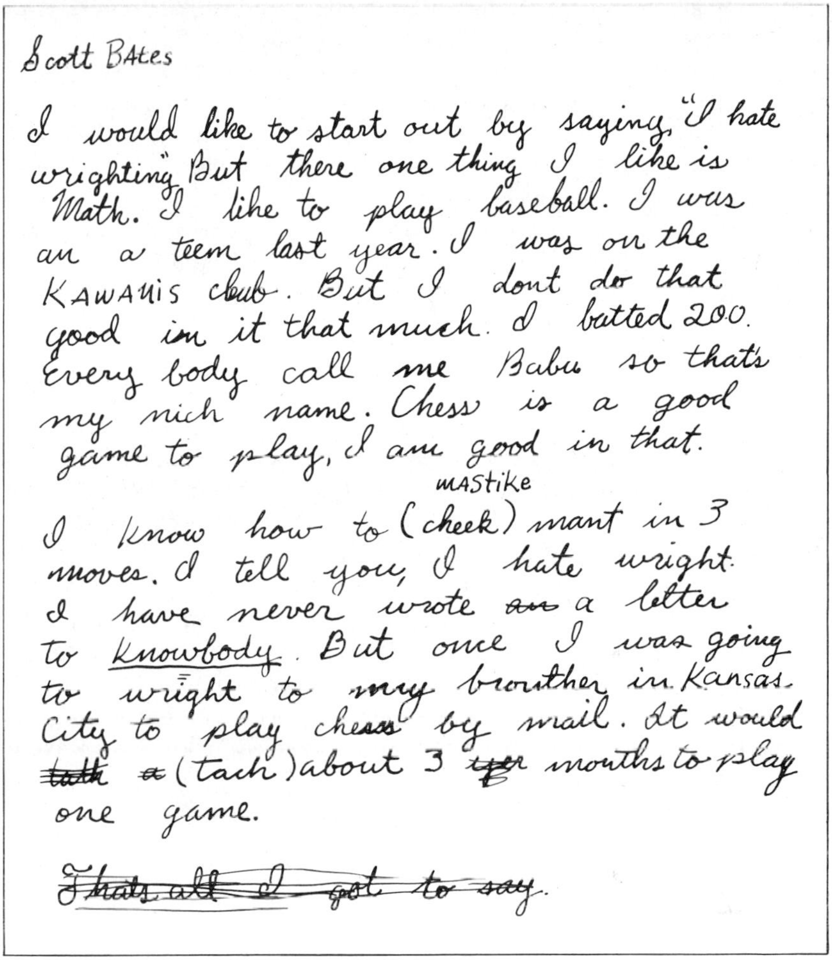

Scott Bates

I would like to start out by saying, "I hate wrighting" But there one thing I like is Math. I like to play baseball. I was an a teem last year. I was on the KAWANIS club. But I dont do that good in it that much. I batted 200. Every body call me Babu so thats my nich name. Chess is a good game to play, I am good in that.

mAStike

I know how to (cheek) mant in 3 moves. I tell you, I hate wright. I have never wrote an a letter to knowbody. But once I was going to wright to my brouther in Kansas. City to play chess by mail. It would tath a (tach) about 3 yer mouths to play one game.

~~Thats all I got to say.~~

FIGURE 9.1

recent understanding of writing as process rather than product. Professor Wallace Douglas of Northwestern University (to whom this book is dedicated) was one of the pioneers in this movement. In the early 1960s, while directing the Curriculum Center in English at Northwestern, Douglas wrote about the astonishingly complex body of skills which a student/writer must master, from the physical act of penmanship itself through the stages of marshaling ideas, getting them down on paper, editing, proofreading, and finally, receiving the response of an audience. Douglas studied the works of professional writers, including their notes and drafts, to develop a multistage view of the writing process from idea to finished page. He argued, as well, that in the schools teachers should be much more concerned with helping students master the essential skills and general processes of writing than with teaching specific forms or products.

Like any creative effort, writing requires energy and time. Few writers are able to dash off something in final form, and most of us find writing rather a struggle. Further, in writing, people put something of their soul down for close scrutiny by others; there can be a feeling of exposure in writing, especially if an audience is sharply critical.

At the same time, there are many processes in a young person's life that require complex skills, an investment of time, or public exposure: mounting a butterfly, mastering a bicycle, playing football, painting a picture, being in a play. Although writing differs in many ways from these activities, there seems to be no reason why students should find the single task of composing so difficult.

An obvious explanation is that writing has the distinction of being the only one of those activities that usually takes place in a schoolroom, and there can be little question that much of the distrust and fear of young people comes from previous classroom writing experiences. Often when students have opened up their souls in writing, the teacher has merely commented on spelling. While busy preparing students for college, teachers have overemphasized the value of impromptu writing, implying that to be good, a writer must be able to bat out polished prose within the span of forty minutes or an hour. Writing activities have often been aimless: "For tomorrow, I want you to write four paragraphs comparing and contrasting the poetic styles of John Keats and Percy Bysshe Shelley." Why? We leave it to the reader to fill in the explanation "_____."

From Larry Levinger, "The Human Side of Illiteracy," *The English Journal,* 67 (November 1978), p. 28. Reprinted by permission of the publisher.

It may be safe to say that the poor writing student has at some critical stage in his life experienced trauma in his attempts to communicate, and has, as a result, turned off to the natural and authentic elements of language.

One consistent exception to the "I hate writing" syndrome is the writing journal, a form that has received great attention in the past few years. Teaching techniques vary; but in general, the journal gives students a *choice of writing topics,* remains *private* or *semiprivate* (the teacher may be the only reader, or the student may choose to read selected elements to classmates), and is *not graded* (usually the only grade is a blanket grade for successful completion of the task).

In the experience of most teachers, student response to the journal has been almost universally positive, making it the closest thing yet to a surefire teaching device. So-called nonwriters seem to enjoy writing journals, while writers go berserk writing in them. Teachers generally enjoy reading journals. Many of the problems traditionally associated with writing seem to be almost magically solved when teachers use the journal.

An exception: A teacher told us she had tried the journal and abandoned it. "Didn't work," she said, somewhat sourly. When pressed for further information, she explained, "Well, they wrote very well in the journals—better than they ever had written before—but I found there was no transfer of writing skills to their Chaucer papers." This "failure" was not surprising. The teacher had seen the journal as something apart from the mainstream of the English—as a gimmick or time killer, not as a regular form of instruction. Steve's proposal—one that she rejected as "antiacademic"—was that if something had to be dropped in the class, the ominous Chaucer paper ought to be the first to go.

In retrospect, Steve argues that what he and the teacher should have discussed was why the journal succeeded where other kinds of writing often fail. We've come to realize that the journal "works" because it is closer to the "real" writing process than many academic writing assignments. Journals encourage students to engage deeply with topics of their own selection, and we're convinced that even academic assignments can come to have this quality of engagement for students if the setting for learning is right. Too, journals invite a different kind of response from the teacher, the response of an interested adult rather than a grammar corrector, and that too can be brought to academic assignments.

From Janet Emig, "Writing as a Mode of Learning," *College Composition and Communication,* 1977. Copyright © 1977 by the National Council of Teachers of English.

Writing represents a unique mode of learning—not merely valuable, not merely special, but unique.

Writing can, as Emig says, be a kind of learning in itself. It is a way to help students get more control over their lives and experience. The reflecting that takes place before and during the writing is also part of the learning that goes on for the student. Thus journal writing is an excellent way to ask students to grapple with their thoughts and so with their lives. It can be a vehicle through which students can grow as people. Diana did some classroom research on journal writing in a class of tenth graders who had previously failed English. She came to the following conclusions:

Journals are an important tool to use in the English classroom, especially with disaffected students.

Suggesting possibilities for topics is very important, especially with students who feel they have nothing to say.

Response to journals seems less important as times goes on. As long as students know that their work is being read, they will keep on writing.

When students feel the topic is important, their writing is at its clearest and most focused.

There are different purposes for writing. Journals allow students to explore those purposes (and different aspects of their lives) without the immediate fear of being criticized for comma placement.

Students must write about direct personal experiences until they feel they have gained a measure of control over these experiences. They can write about topics and issues outside their immediate world, but they cannot be forced to be exocentric. When they are grappling with problems in their own environment, they simply can't pay much attention to anything else. There must be a bridge between problems with a girlfriend or boyfriend and the language of Geoffrey Chaucer. (Readers will promptly anticipate what that bridge can be: It involves treating Chaucer as the sometimes bawdy stuff of experience rather than as fodder for linguistic analysis.)

Students need to be encouraged to worry about the "correctness" of their writing in the editing stage, not in the composing stage. Even though Diana did not criticize errors in the journal writing, some students were still concerned with correctness, no doubt a result of previous instruction. That seemed to diminish their ability to write freely. It reduced their willingness to use words they couldn't spell, and it cut down on their inventive use of language.

Since the journal seems to "work," teachers need to find ways to apply its techniques to the regular work of writing. This does *not* mean giving students a twelve-year diet of journal writing or abandoning "regular" assignments. In many schools, in fact, the journal has been so overworked that it no longer provides a satisfying experience for students. We've been concerned, too, with the evolution of a verb form, "journaling," to cover all of impromptu writing, including forced writing for purposes of teaching students to recall academic facts.

As often happens with educational innovations, teachers have emphasized the trimmings (the loose-leaf binding and diary format) and ignored the essence of the journal (its freedom and naturalness). There is something we call the Sherwood Anderson phenomenon, after his *Andersonville,* where characters become obsessed with one aspect of life and become grotesques. If teachers become obsessed with the journal, it, too, can lead to grotesqueries.

Surely there is nothing so unique about writing in a notebook that the principles of success cannot be discovered and applied elsewhere. In the following sections, we'll examine what our own experience and the growing body of research on composition suggest those principles might be.

WRITING: PERSONAL AND CREATIVE

It is cliché that "the best writing comes from personal experience." For decades teachers have offered students the advice, "Write about something you know." We think the cliché is basically correct, but at times it is applied in curious ways that lead to grotesquerie. For example, we have the "Summer Vacation" theme, which draws groans from kids in school and adults in memory. Writing about vacations is not a bad idea at all, but the in-school version of the theme tends to create a routine travelogue rather than deep engagement with experience.

Writing instruction works when students draw on not only personal experience but also *substantial* experience—things that hurt or worry, that delight and please. As Donald Murray has observed, we teach writing because it is a useful skill, both inside school and outside. But most important is that writing involves self-discovery and satisfies a person's need to communicate.

Abridged from Donald Murray, "Why Teach Writing—and How?" *The English Journal,* December 1973, pp. 1234–1237. Copyright © 1973 by the National Council of Teachers of English. Reprinted by permission of the publisher and the author.

WHY TEACH WRITING?

1. Writing is a skill which is important in school and after school. . . .
2. Writing for many students is a skill which can unlock the language arts. Students who have never read before often begin to read in the writing program. They have to read their own words to find out what they've said and decide how to say it more effectively.
3. Writing is thinking. . . .
4. Writing is an ethical act, because the single most important quality in writing is honesty. . . .
5. Writing is a process of self-discovery. . . .
6. Writing satisfies man's primitive hunger to communicate. . . .
7. Writing is an art, and art is profound play. . . .

Writing provides a way for students to sort through their experiences, to make sense of their world, and to share their observations with others. When students are deeply engaged in this process, it is often revealed in the intensity and vibrancy of their language. It is little wonder that writing skills don't seem to transfer from the journal to pseudoacademic papers. Unless composing is real and personal, it is aimless, and people learn nothing from it.

Another way to phrase this idea is to borrow another cliché, one that has been ignored in practice: "All writing is creative." The distinction between "creative" composition and its opposite (uncreative? noncreative? counter-creative?) is an unfortunate one. There are obvious differences in form and process between composing a poem and composing an essay, but the similarities are also great. Creative, or what we prefer to call *imaginative,* writing involves a writer successfully assimilating a personal experience and sharing it with someone else. A good memo, for instance, can be an imaginative piece of writing. The results of a teacher-imposed sonnet-writing lesson often aren't.

Evoking personal, imaginative writing in the classroom is not easy. Students are accustomed to look for "what the teacher wants," for in the past this has been the route to successful grades. One way to describe good topics is to suggest that they grow from basic open-ended questions about human experience:

How do you feel?
What are you thinking about?
What puzzles or bothers you?
What interesting things do you know?

If teachers ask these questions they will be getting at the personal experience that leads to strong writing. The journal accomplishes this by not stating any topics, thus forcing the students back into the reservoir of personal experience. Some current writing theorists, particularly some of the followers of Donald Graves of the University of New Hampshire (see the Bibliography), argue for a totally free choice of topics for all writing activities. They claim that students cannot achieve true ownership of material until they choose it themselves. We agree to an extent, and certainly one aim of our writing classes is getting to the point where we can say, "Write about anything you want."

But we have also found that students often come to us with their imaginations closed down; the "open" invitation to write may just bring about blankness. We encourage them to speak out on subjects of personal concern, and we use some of the "getting started" activities in Chapter 5 to create situations in which we can demonstrate interest in making the classroom an arena for the discussion of personal experiences, for the ownership of writing topics.

From William J. Moravec, University of South Florida. Written in response to this chapter in the first edition of *Explorations in the Teaching of English*. Reprinted by permission of the author.

TRYING TO READ AN ENGLISH ED TEXTBOOK (THE CHAPTER ON COMPOSITION) WHILE SITTING ON A SEAWALL AT LOW TIDE: AUTUMN

It's amazing how much windier it gets as you cross town.
(Come to think of it, there was *no* wind across town.)
The shoreline is never perfectly straight, is it?
And the whitecaps never converge, or run in unison, or fizzle
    out at the same time. They don't obey the human
    impositions on life.
(Still, they all disappear on the same shore, and I guess
    that's close enough for some people.)

A Seagull hovers, so close I can almost count its feathers!
(So, why am I worried about it being too directly overhead?)

I close the book of
ideas-for-getting-students-to-write-from-their-own-experiences
And take a walk: along the seawall, over the bridge to the
    causeway,
And stop halfway to look back.
The royal palms laugh warmly over where I was sitting.
Then they turn and laugh at me.
Even the murky green water smiles as I cross.
And now the sand and rocks and trees—the half-wild beach
    edging this dredged-up subordinate conjunction
Say, come down here and hide out awhile.

WRITING: RESEARCH BASED

Often teachers and students believe that there is a sharp division between "imaginative" writing and the more factually based expository or research writing. They worry, too, about preparation for college and the "real world" and are suspicious that this talk of "ownership" and "personal experience" is an abrogation of responsibility to teach serious writing and to teach writing seriously. However, increasingly we've come to see that the differences between journal writing and academic writing, between writing from past experience and new experience, are of degree, not kind.

Topic selection is critical in research-based writing. If the whole class is assigned to do research on a single author and to write a paper on what they find, our experience suggests that they will not approach the task with eagerness. But if students can discover topics on their own, topics such as an explanation of Houdini's greatest tricks or the history of soda pop, their writing will reflect that interest. There will, of course, be times in school and life when students must write on assigned topics; but we argue for first things first. Let's first get them to explore their own experiences and interests; then we can teach some simple strategies on how to make any topic— even the assigned research paper on the life of Tennyson—"your own."

Cliché: "You can't make bricks without straw." (Is that still true, we wonder?)

What we are suggesting, then, is that not only is all writing creative, all writing is *research based.* It involves conducting research into one's own experiences and feelings and into how knowledge "out there" fits into our understanding of the world.

SO WHAT DO I WRITE ABOUT?

Young people bubble over with ideas and experiences they want to share with one another and with adults. Yet, when given a blank sheet of paper and a writing assignment, they often claim they have nothing to say. (Adults often make the same claim, we've discovered.) Part of the problem is that students remember past writing classes: the teacher who treated them as if they were blockheads and said that everything they wrote was inadequate. Perhaps more important is that the assignments teachers offer are themselves frequently dull and uninviting. While we do not feel that every assignment given to students must be wildly innovative, novel, or clever, it is evident that the assignments the teacher offers define the dimensions of composition for students. If assignments are of the 500-words-and-three-paragraphs variety, students are obviously limited in what they will accomplish as writers.

There is no single composition assignment appropriate for all students. Steve discovered the idea of presenting multiple assignments—writing options—as a result of a bad time in a high school sophomore English class. At the time, he was interested in the notion of extending the "journal concept" to other situations, and he took the obvious route of establishing a free writing day for the class—one day each week when the students could write about anything they chose. The results were discouraging. The students sat around fussing and twitching, and most of the writing they produced was mediocre. They kept claiming they had nothing to say, and Steve couldn't persuade them otherwise.

So he began developing lists of writing options for free writing day. Each week he sketched out a half-dozen writing possibilities—some dealing with current events and ideas, others suggesting starting points for personal narratives. He tried to build in choices for writing poems or plays, as well as activities that would lead to expository writing. He tried to find something that might appeal to everyone.

The tone of the class improved enormously. Interestingly enough, the change seemed to result less from the actual topics designed than from the fact that Steve was helping the students see possibilities for writing. Whether the students used Steve's topics, modified them for their own purposes, or rejected them to strike off in new directions, they were discovering new avenues and possibilities. By offering options, Steve was saying, "These are some of the things you can do with language." This is an approach he has used ever since: with young writers in arts workshops, with high schoolers, with developmental college freshmen, in an advanced college expository writing class, with graduate classes for experienced teachers. You might say he swears by this approach.

To illustrate the wealth of options available on almost any subject, we want to play with a topic, "Human Relationships," that is popular in the schools and commonly found as a theme in both school and college literature texts.

What kinds of writing grow from this topic? The most routine, perhaps, would involve informal essays:

> Why do you think people have so much trouble getting along in the world? Write an essay giving your views.

But far more imaginative possibilities exist:

> Suppose you were the ruler of a country in which the inhabitants were constantly squabbling with one another. What kind of decree might you issue to force the people to get along better?
> Write a science fiction story in which monkeys learn to get along with one another and as a result take over the earth from quarreling human beings.

The topic can lead to low-key research projects:

> For hundreds of years some people have chosen to live in communes, intimate gatherings of people who share common ideas or beliefs. Read about some of these new communities and write a report on the human relationships that are involved.
> Read about some of the nineteenth-century experiments in communal living that were conducted in this country (the Oneida Community, for example) and look into some of the reasons why these experiments did or did not succeed.

The topic lends itself to imaginative writing assignments:

How do you feel when you are in deep conflict with another person? Try to express that feeling through a poem.

Write a short play showing a family that cannot solve its human relationships problems. What happens in the end? You might want to write an alternative ending in which things work out satisfactorily. Which seems more realistic?

It can lead to speaking assignments (after all, "composition" can be done in spoken words as well as writing), including an old debate chestnut:

Resolved: Parents nowadays are too permissive toward their children.

One could develop possibilities for dramatization or media composition (two topics we take up in Chapters 13 and 14):

Videotape two episodes from a soap opera called "The Cozy Corner," the continuing story of a family in which all the members dislike one another.

One can go on almost without end considering possibilities for photo essays, cartoons, posters, letters, telegrams, satire—even though no teacher would ever want to list all of the possibilities on a given topic. (For some examples, see Figure 9.2.)

One problem that concerns teachers who are using a system of options is that of students getting stuck in ruts, choosing only one form of composition and failing to move beyond it. Of course, this concern ignores the fact that in the past students *have* been largely stuck on one form—the expository essay. Exhausting the possibilities of other forms—say, drama or short story—can hardly be more harmful. However, given free choice, students' patterns of interest and skill change naturally with time. A choice example was presented by one of the girls in Steve's sophomore class who was hooked on drama. For months she wrote scripts—ten or fifteen pages each—about boy-girl romances. One day, when Steve was on the edge of madness at the thought of reading another John-Marcia dialogue, she presented an acid attack on America's involvement in the affairs of other countries. When asked about her playwriting interests, she replied, "Eh! . . . Plays are OK, but this stuff is a lot more important." People grow.

WHEN THEY (AND YOU) RUN OUT OF IDEAS

No matter how creative English teachers are, there sometimes comes a point during the year when they feel creativity ebbing and they

FIGURE 9.2

SOME NEGLECTED FORMS OF COMPOSITION
(OR, MUST THEY *ALWAYS* WRITE ESSAYS?)

Journals and diaries

Observation papers

Profiles and portraits (friends, enemies, adults, public figures)

Sketches (notebook jottings, gleanings)

Reminiscences and memoirs (high or low times, serious or fun)

Autobiography

Confessions (real or fictional)

Dramatic monologues (written, improvised, or recorded)

Slide presentations with tape accompaniments

Stream of consciousness

Editorial

Satire

Photo essay

Radio play

Children's stories and verse

Newspaper stories

Poetry, poetry, poetry (free forms and structured forms, rhymed and unrhymed, haiku, concrete poetry, light verse, limericks, protest verse, song lyrics, . . .)

Interviews

Policy papers

Research (a record of something seen or learned)

Fiction (short story or novel)

Light essays (Thurber, E. B. White)

Plays, plays, plays (short scenes, one-acts, improvised, full-dress productions)

Advertisements

Commercials

Imitations of established writers

Riddles

Jokes

Posters

Fliers

Independent newspaper

Letters (real or fictional)

Telegrams

Aphorisms

Graffiti	Propaganda
Reviews (books, concerts, football games, dates)	Petitions
	Films
Metaphors	
	Television scripts
Sound tapes	
	Cartoons
Monographs	
	Pamphlets
Magazines	

can't think of one writing option that sounds even remotely appealing. This is the time to turn from whatever is going on in the classroom and look to some less-often-considered sources for writing ideas.

Children's Books

One such source is children's literature. Many books can be used to model a form or kind of writing. If the book explains everything that there is to like about caterpillars or butterflies, students can follow the format of the book and tell others all the wonderful things about their own favorite topics. They can write on video games, football, pets, members of the opposite sex, or even the more serious topics of world peace, clean air, and honest government officials.

Books like Judith Viorst's *Alexander and the Terrible, Horrible, No Good, Very Bad Day* (Atheneum, 1982) provide excellent topics for students to write about in their own way. A wordless book like Chris VanAllsberg's *The Mysteries of Harris Burdick* (Boston: Houghton Mifflin, 1984). provides stimulation for students to create their own stories about the very unusual pictures in this book.

Once the teacher begins to actively browse through the children's section at the library, exciting writing ideas will begin to surface.

Interesting But Not Easily Categorized Books

Browse through the bookstore or library for interesting or odd books. If the subject matter grabs you, ideas and adaptations for writing will soon flow. Some such books we recently came across include:

• *Fat Man in Fur Coat and Other Bear Stories* collected and retold by Alvin Schwartz (Farrar, Straus, & Giroux, 1984). This book can lead the teacher to have students brainstorm ways in which a *bear* could be involved in a story, a highly bearable idea. After reading a sampling of the stories, students will write their own, with a bear as the main character. For a literary connection, one might look to the works of John Irving, starting with his whimsical early novel *Setting Free the Bears,* where a bear is the source of adventure or conflict.

• *Mother Goose in Prose* by L. Frank Baum (Crown Publishers, 1986, originally published in 1899) can inspire almost anyone to write. Baum (creator of the Wizard of Oz stories) has taken twenty-two nursery rhymes and fashioned them into full-blown stories. We see a day in the short life of Humpty Dumpty and find out why he was sitting on a wall. We learn why Mistress Mary planted all of her flowers in a row and what those flowers meant to her. Perhaps after hearing some of these stories, students will want to write not only the story behind the nursery rhyme but also the story behind a poem or even an advertisement.

• *How the Whale Became and Other Stories* by Ted Hughes (Puffin, 1963) can lead to explanations not only of the origin of animals but also of the origin of things in the students' lives. Students might want to write about where the TV came from or how an umbrella was invented or even why moles appear on the skin. Once the teacher starts paging through and reading snatches of this type of unusual book, ideas for writing will begin to come.

The Newspaper

Years ago, Steve attended a workshop sponsored by the Chicago *Sun Times* which was based on the premise that you can find articles about any topic you want to teach in any daily issue of the paper. That claim seems to have held up as far as he is concerned. In a "Writing in Transition" program now conducted at Michigan State University for entering freshmen, students are required to come to each morning class session having read a daily paper. Their free writing for the day comes from the paper, and often those sketchy responses grow into the starting point for longer works. Steve also has students use the newspaper as a starting point for research projects. He divides the paper into sections and the class into groups, then has students read stories, ads, comics, and the like and generate lists of questions they'd like to know more about. Within a single period, the class will frequently generate two hundred "researchable" ideas for writing.

The Journal

Don't forget to have your students scan their journals from time to time, looking for ideas that merit further exploration.

Writing Idea Books

No idea ever sounds quite as good as someone else's when we feel uncreative and dull. At this time such books as *The Whole Word Catalogue II* (McGraw-Hill, 1977), a book prepared by the New York Teachers and Writers Collaborative, can be very helpful. So can Marjorie Frank's *If You're Trying to Teach Kids to Write, You've Gotta Have This Book!* (Incentive Publications, 1979), which has something about every aspect of teaching writing, including a whole chapter on writing ideas for when teachers feel their students have run out. Also, each edition of *Notes Plus* (referred to in Chapter 5) has a section of writing ideas.

Of course, all of these writing ideas need to be placed in a context in your classroom. Writing projects must be integrated with the rest of classroom activities; otherwise the writing becomes disembodied and loses some of its drive. However, if you get the urge to do a little of this and a little of that, one way to structure it is simply to have students write a variety of pieces for one to two weeks and then collect the best of what's been written in a classroom booklet, reproduced for students and parents. These occasional writing breaks add a change to the classroom routine and give students a chance to try their hand at many different kinds of writing.

LEARNING TO WRITE BY WRITING

From James Britton, "Talking and Writing," in Eldonna Evertts, ed., *Explorations in Children's Writing.* Copyright © 1970 by the National Council of Teachers of English. Reprinted by permission of the publisher.

. . . children *learn* by writing. By learn I mean above all this process by which they shape their experience in order to make it available to themselves to learn from. Next it must be observed that, if they learn by writing, they also learn to write by writing. I know when it comes down to brass tacks, we have to qualify this assertion and make some exceptions, but we don't destroy the basic truth of it.

They learn by writing and they learn to write by writing. In other words I am putting forward an operational point of view. There is a whole world of experience to be interpreted, and writing is a major means of interpreting it. Why therefore as teachers do we go around looking for practice jobs, dummy runs, rigged or stage-managed situations, when in fact the whole of what requires to be worked upon is there waiting to be worked upon? Every time a child succeeds in writing about something that has happened to him or something he has been thinking, two things are likely to have happened. First, he has improved his chances of doing so the next time he tries; in other words, his piece of writing has given him practice. And secondly he has interpreted, shaped, coped with, some bit of experience.

That children learn to write by writing is another cliché, for a good reason; it has been recognized as pedagogically sound for well over one hundred years. James Britton's comment that people "learn by writing and they learn to write by writing" is simply one of its most recent restatements.

Yet curiously, when it comes to actual practice, some teachers seem to retreat from the wisdom of this learn-by-doing philosophy. In fact, they seem willing to go to great lengths to *avoid* actually having students write. Thus students engage in vocabulary study, spelling work, outlining practice, topic sentence composition, sentence construction, and error correction, but do not spend a great deal of time grappling with the task of composing. Part of this reaction on the part of teachers is self-defense. If you assign writing, you have to take time to comment on it. (This is a problem that will be taken up in the next chapter.) But a more basic cause of teachers' not relying on actual practice is that they assume students will write badly unless given all kinds of preliminary instruction on writing form: how to write an essay, how to compose a paragraph, how to vary sentences.

However, James Britton's epigraph shows a very important linkage between learning and writing. He suggests that students need to learn about the world—their personal world or the public world—in order to write, and he implies that as students learn to structure their ideas, they will also learn to structure their language. This concept is a variation of the language/experience model we presented in Chapter 2. He's suggesting that language is a learn-by-doing skill.

The same sophomore class described earlier helped Steve discover that teaching about writing was less important than helping students shape their ideas through language. While exploring the ideas of writing options, students had been encouraged to try different forms—reviews, poems, stories, satires, and the like. It dawned on Steve one day that although the students were composing in these forms, he had never given any lessons on how to write them. How had the students learned to do it?

There seemed to be two sources for these skills. First, for many of the activities, the students had an intuitive sense of form based on routine reading and TV viewing habits; they had all read or seen editorials, columns, plays, commercials. The second source was questioning. When students didn't know what something was, they naturally asked: "What's a haiku?" "What's satire?"

This discovery led to another from that same class, that questions about form are best answered in *operational,* not *definitional,* terms. When students ask, "What's satire?" they do not need to be told, "Satire is a poem or prose work holding up human vices, follies, etc. to ridicule or scorn." What proves helpful is advice on how to *make* a satire: "Well, suppose you wanted to make someone you disliked look foolish. One way might be. . . ." Or better, "Who is somebody around here who you think needs to get taken down a notch or two? Now what could we say . . . ?" This kind of answer enables students to engage productively in writing without involved discussion of abstractions.

Such a philosophy also applies to one of the traditional mainstays of the English curriculum: teaching the paragraph. A great deal of time is spent in the schools teaching this rhetorical structure and its attendants: thesis and clincher sentences. Students are taught these forms as abstractions: "The paragraph contains one main idea." "The topic sentence presents the central concern." "The clincher sentence restates the topic sentence." Occasionally the abstractions are presented through metaphors: "Think of your paragraph as a sandwich with topic and clincher sentences as the bread and your supporting evidence as the meat."

This kind of teaching does little to improve student writing and much to damage it. In the first place, very few real-life paragraphs follow the form very closely. In the second place, emphasizing paragraph structure makes students write by formula: "There are three things you should know about Abraham Lincoln and here are my reasons." "Abraham Lincoln was an honest man and here is how I know." Although it is intended to help students learn structure (a worthy aim in itself), teaching form often makes their writing lifeless. It is another example of the sort of Sherwood Andersonism we described earlier: taking a sound principle and then reducing it to a grotesquerie.

Curiously enough, composition textbooks never said anything about the paragraph until well into the nineteenth century. Before that, paragraphs were simply a natural division of discourse and followed no particular rules. That historical oddity helps to clarify the relationship between form and substance. Writers form and shape papers to reach an audience, and they seek out structures that will accomplish what they want, drawing in part on their intuitive knowledge of structure from reading, writing, speaking, and listening. Teaching structures before the fact of composition shortcircuits the process by placing form ahead of content.

As students write, struggling with ideas, paragraphs, and sentences, there are many opportunities for the teacher to suggest ways and means of structuring papers, always with the students' particular problems in mind.

The structuring of writing also is more easily learned and taught if students have a sense of purpose in writing. In schoolroom practice, however, the purpose has often been pleasing the teacher. "Think about your audience" has come to mean "Think about your teacher and the kind of writing he or she likes." Many student compositions done in schools are thus unreal—done as practice exercises.

But advice like "make writing real" is ambiguous. Does this mean that students should spend all their time filling out business forms and writing letters to real readers? We think not. Reality is something in the eye of the writer, and topics that interest and engage the student automatically become real. Part of the problem of reality is thus solved by engaging the students in writing that is truly imaginative and research based; and it is aided further by offering students a wide range of ways of expressing those ideas.

However, the students also need a *readership,* and a class should be alive with students reading to one another, reading one another's work, responding and reacting to the things that they have said and done. In the next chapter we explore some of the ways in which the teacher can supply an audience for students' work; for the moment, we simply want to note that the classroom should be a reading and publishing center, where students' work takes on reality by being given a readership. Providing readers can be done in many ways, ranging from the bulletin board to the manufacture of books and magazines.

THE WRITING WORKSHOP

Composing is not a neat, orderly process; it is highly idiosyncratic. Compositions can't be stamped out like lipstick cases or hubcaps, and writers must find their own style of working. Some writers produce a polished first draft; others—and we're both among them—pump out a crude "hack draft," something that is a cross between notes, rough draft, and a batch of odd sentences—all to be polished later. Students are no different in having a range of writing habits.

The teacher can accommodate individual styles by organizing the class as a writing workshop. Within the workshop, many diverse activities will be happening at once. On any given day, some students may be starting new projects while others are finishing. A few people will be at the stage of publication, while others may be displaying and distributing completed writing. A workshop mode encourages students to select new options, since it does not pressure them to complete a standard essay in a set time period. It also provides great freedom for the teacher, who can serve as a roving consultant—supplying help when and where needed—rather than as a monitor of thirty people writing in silence.

In the course of participating in a writing workshop, then, students may:

Talk with one another about writing assignments and possibilities.
Confer about writing ideas and sources for composition materials.
"Prewrite" papers in small groups, talking through assignments before
     actually committing pen to paper.
Write rough and polished drafts.
Work in small editorial groups.
Confer with the teacher about specific writing problems or about their
     growth in composition generally.
Read writing on the same topics: other students' or professional writers'.
Copyedit writing for publication.
Illustrate, print, and bind their work for distribution.

The workshop must be developed gradually. Only after a period of time
will it reach its peak of independent operation. For teachers who have never
used the writing workshop approach, one easy way to begin is simply to give
students a day to write in class. Time can be spent at the beginning of the
class interesting students in several kinds of topics. Once students are
excited or have concrete ideas, they are ready to write. The teacher then
gives the students the time they need. For students who finish quickly, have
another step or activity planned so they will know exactly what to do.
Usually, sharing their work with someone else is the next step.

The teacher usually begins writing workshops by having all students do
the same sort of task, perhaps "getting started" activities, journal writing,
or short common assignments. As the students and the teacher become
accustomed to working together, the class can be differentiated. Perhaps
some students would use the day for first-draft writing, while others want
response from a group. Still others might want to meet with the teacher,
and yet another group will be illustrating their work. We have also found
that providing writing options is especially useful in starting these workshops, since it invites individualized work from the beginning. Other teachers have had success with such diverse activities as free writing, contracts,
independent study, or an idea box at the back of the room.

Perhaps the best way to summarize is to suggest that the students in a
writing workshop will need to take a view of their work as *exploratory*. One
way to obtain this kind of attitude occurred to Steve quite by accident in
a college course. To encourage the students to try new ideas, he had asked
them to write a series of what he called "experimental" papers; these papers
were experiments, ventures into new territory without the threat of failure.

The student writing in the "experimentals" was excellent—good enough
that Steve canceled plans for some longer, more sustained writing projects.
He didn't realize the effect of this until the last week of the quarter, when
one of the students asked, "Say, when are we going to stop experimenting

and do some real writing?" In fact, the writing had been quite "real," and the students had become less inhibited about their writing.

There is a finality to "real" writing. Since it is the end of the process, it has usually been associated with pain and penalties, corrections and revisions, polite and/or impolite notes pointing out that the writing isn't up to adult standards. Steve has tried to encourage students to consider *everything* they write as experimental, to treat it as if there is always time for a bit more work if they want to do it. This, in turn, makes the freedom of the writing workshop something felt inside the student as well as inside the class, ultimately helping to create students who can write freely and openly.

SEQUENCING WRITING ACTIVITIES

Many teachers are skilled at developing good writing assignments, yet their assignments stand alone, bearing no discernible relationship to one another. Frequently, this problem is a side effect of isolating composition from other parts of the curriculum. If writing is a Fridays-only activity, the assignments are likely to be gimmicky, one-shot affairs. The pervasiveness of this approach is testified to by the popularity of what-shall-I-do-on-Friday lists of writing ideas. Although one learns to write by writing (and even isolated topics are better than no writing at all), writing ought to be assigned in ways that promote sustained growth as well. To this end, it is important to sequence the kinds of writing one expects from students.

The Handbook Approach

We'll start with a poor example: the typical composition/grammar handbook. It begins with the smallest language particle it can find—the word—and teaches students how to describe it syntactically, through learning the parts of speech. The naming process then continues through larger and larger units—the sentence, the paragraph, the whole essay. Along the way, students are shown techniques of structuring such as writing the formal outline. The culmination of the writing program is often the research or term paper.

While it is probably evident to the reader of this book why we think this approach is a bad one, it seems important to rehearse the weaknesses and disadvantages of the handbook approach one additional time:

1. It emphasizes mastery of terminology instead of offering actual writing experiences.
2. It is divorced from the students' own experiences.

3. It is based on a false assumption that one must write or practice short discourse units before going on to longer ones.
4. It presents a simplistic view of structure by its emphasis on the formal outline and the form of the paragraph.

Alternative Sequences for Writing

Better writing sequences have a basic principle in common: They start with the students' linguistic skill and psychological maturity and guide them along natural patterns of growth. For example, in *Writing in Reality,* a college composition text, James Miller and Steve use what might be called an *experience-centered* sequence. They assume that writers first need to explore their personal ideas and thoughts through private writing, before moving on to present ideas to a larger public.

They begin by explaining the differences between public and private writing (Chapters 1 and 2 in *Writing in Reality*), but they emphasize that all good writing, public or private, must be deeply motivated, flowing from the students' own storehouse of experiences and research. Chapters 3 through 5 have the students examine their past and present experiences and capture their unique writing voice and style. The next two chapters (6 and 7) focus on the outer world and encourage observation of people, places, and things. Then the sequence moves fully into public writing of essays and persuasive papers (8 and 9) and ends (10) by reminding the students that all writing, public or private, comes from one's "ultimate self." Although this book is aimed at college students, the basic sequence—from private to public, from personal to objective experience—is one that works well with younger students as well. *The Creative Word* English program, which is outlined in this book in Chapter 15, shows how the same principles can be used in a grade 7–12 reading and writing curriculum. The handbook approach and the experience-centered sequence are outlined in Figures 9.3 and 9.4.

Fred Morgan's writing textbook *Here and Now* shows another approach, one that emphasizes *perceptions* rather than experiences and produces a useful sequence of assignments. He argues (as does Patrick Creber, also cited in Chapter 15) that bad writing often reflects poor perception. Students don't really look at their world, and thus they write badly about it. Morgan has his students begin by reveling in their senses, rediscovering the pleasures of perceiving, before moving through a sequence of assignments that has the students observe people, places, animals, emotions, themselves, finally pulling all these skills together in "seeing the whole picture" (Figure 9.5). Like the *Writing in Reality* approach, Morgan's emphasizes informal and private writings at first, then moves on to more complex public writing.

Another approach is the *literary/thematic* one. The editors of *The Scho-*

FIGURE 9.3 THE HANDBOOK APPROACH.

Parts of Speech

The Sentence

Sentence Variety and Style

The Topic Sentence

The Paragraph

The Outline

The Essay

FIGURE 9.4 THE EXPERIENCE-CENTERED SEQUENCE.
From James E. Miller and Stephen Judy, *Writing in Reality*. New York: Harper & Row, 1978.

1. Personal Writing
2. Public Writing
3. The Creation of the Self
4. Versions of the Self
5. How Deep Can One Go?
6. Encountering the World
7. Interweaving the World
8. Exploring/Probing/Researching
9. Causes and Commitments
10. Writing and the Ultimate Self

lastic American Literature Series wanted to create a literature program that would encourage composition as well. They chose a series of major themes, "Who We Are," "What We Believe," and so on, and further divided them into subtopics such as "The Young" and "City and Country" (see Figure 9.6). Each of these subtopics creates possible composition topics that draw on the students' personal experiences. The program shows clearly (as did our Chapters 6, 7, and 8) that one can use literature as a jumping-off point for writing without having to rely exclusively on that academic standby, the essay of literary analysis.

In a fourth approach, described by James Moffett in his *Active Voices* series (Boynton/Cook, 1987), kinds of writing is the unifying theme. Stu-

FIGURE 9.5 THE PERCEPTUAL APPROACH.
From Fred Morgan, *Here and Now III*. New York: Harcourt Brace Jovanovich, 1979.

1. Enjoying Your Senses
2. Employing Your Senses
3. Being Aware of Your Surroundings
4. Observing a Scene
5. Getting the Feel of Action
6. Observing a Person
7. Perceiving Emotional Attitudes
8. Estimating a Person
9. Identifying with a Person
10. Perceiving a Relationship
11. Identifying with an Idea
12. Looking at Yourself
13. Examining a Desire
14. Seeing the Whole Picture

FIGURE 9.6 THE LITERARY/THEMATIC APPROACH.
From *The Scholastic American Literature Series*. New York: Scholastic Magazines, 1977.

Who We Are	*How We Live*
The Young	At Work
The Old	At Play
Men and Women	At War
Where We Live	*What We Believe*
City and Country	Personal Values
Journeys	American Myths and Dreams
A Sense of Place	Fantasy and Imagination

dents begin with Notation (Taking Down) and write diaries and journals. Then they move to Recollection (Looking Back) and do autobiographical writing and memoirs. In Investigation (Looking Into) they write such things as biography, factual articles, and research articles. In Imagination (Thinking Up) the writing ranges through plays, stories, and all kinds of poems. The last category, Cogitation (Thinking Over and Thinking Through), includes the writing of advice letters, editorials, analysis, and interpretation. Moffett points out that this type of writing program could easily be worked into literature courses, especially if students are reading the kinds of literature they are writing. Although we are strongly attracted to Moffett's hierarchies, it has always seemed to us that structuring a program around discourse forms rather than the development of youngsters' interests makes the program discourse- rather than student-centered. Further, the emphasis on modes, albeit more sophisticated than the traditional "four forms," nonetheless may set product before process and value form over content.

The sequences we have shown are generalized patterns, chosen by textbook writers in an attempt to reach as many students as possible. While these schema may be useful as models, teachers themselves must make the actual plans for a good sequence of assignments, and like any plan, the one chosen should be flexible, reflecting the needs and interests of the students and growing naturally from the course material. Under no circumstances should any sequence—be it the traditional handbook approach or something like the contemporary perceptual approach—be allowed to create a lockstep curriculum. The point, after all, is to take the students at their present developmental level and help them move forward, not to ensure that they have followed a prescribed pattern created by either textbook writer or teacher.

A NOTE ON PREPARATION FOR COLLEGE

Obviously, the kinds of assignments we recommend differ from the usual pattern prescribed in the schools, where work in the essay leads toward a culminating experience with the research paper. We would like to see students write more and in more diverse forms. At the same time, we emphasize that our recommendations are not neglectful of the college-bound. For supporting evidence we present two excerpts from senior high school students' papers. Both were submitted to a youth talent contest as among the best essays in their school.

The first essay was part of a research paper discussing the movement toward school standards:

The concepts of American education are continually being reassessed. One of the questions presently being raised concerns the customary practice of granting a diploma after completion of a basic twelve year education. It has been determined that a standard high school education does not necessarily warrant the issuance of a diploma. This document, if dispensed to students with inferior proficiency, ceases to signify that the possessor has gained the skills necessary to function as an acceptable adult in society. As each high school senior receives a diploma, whether or not they are fully competent, the standards of our country's educational system are decreased. Therefore, American high schools should not graduate students who do not pass minimum competency standards.

We hope the reader will agree that this paper is very badly written. It is stuffy, filled with jargon, and awkward. We believe the student is not entirely to blame that it turned out so poorly, for we suspect her teachers have encouraged this sort of writing for years, thinking it would help get her ready for college. It won't, we're afraid, and the student will have to do a great deal of unlearning before she will find success in college writing courses.

By contrast, the second essay, part of a research paper on jazz, begins with an anecdote:

I picked jazz because I play alto saxophone at school in the band, and I really like it. Another reason is that last summer I attended Blue Lake Fine Arts Camp and while there, heard the jazz band play. I loved the music and decided that was the kind of music I wanted to look into.

The language, of course, is fresher than the first example. Unfortunately, after this animated paragraph, the author plunged into essay prose of a very dull sort. Apparently she had gone to the library and looked up the facts about jazz, ignoring her personal experience and following the routine of research paper writing. As Steve read her paper, he searched in vain for any evidence that she had actually listened to some music or that she had actually followed up on her summer interest by playing some jazz. Unfortunately, the basics of the research paper—looking up books and writing down the facts—did not permit personal exploration and expression.

We believe that in the long run, a broadly based writing program, one that gives young people a sense of their own voice as writers and encourages them to trust their own perceptions, is the best preparation for college (and for writing demands outside school generally). The dummy run essays and term papers of the schools help very few students and actually stultify the writing growth of many others.

EXPLORATIONS

• Steve and Gilbert Tierney have created "The Assignment Makers," an activity that helps teachers clarify what they see as the critical factors that go into the process of initiating student writing. Nine hypothetical—but adapted from reality—writing assignments are given (Figure 9.7). You are asked to select the three assignments that you think are "best" (using any criteria you think are appropriate) and the three that are "worst." As you study the assignments, make notes on what you see as the critical strong and weak points about each and compare your notes with those of others. As an interesting follow-up, you might give "The Assignment Makers" to a group of students and compare their reactions to your own. (For those who would like to think over the choices as they read, we have included Steve and Gilbert's notes and observations about the assignments.)

• One of the best ways for teachers to prepare themselves to teach writing is to *do* some writing. Although teachers need not write every assignment along with their students, they certainly should have experience composing in many of the forms they assign for students. Try some writing. Create a poem (treat it as an *experiment*). Write an essay or a page of graffiti. Write a speech and an editorial commenting on the speech. Create a play, then make it into a story. Share your work with other people. Talk over what you learn about yourself and about composition in the process.

• Start a collection of writing ideas or assignments, preferably in collaboration with other people. It is enormously helpful to have a resource bank of good writing suggestions on hand for inspirationless moments. One good way to do this is to create a series of writing idea cards on heavy paper, posterboard, or blank file folders. Include a writing starter—a poem, a newspaper article, a photograph—and then write some composition topics for the students. These cards can be used with individual students or as the starting point for class assignments.

• Choose a topic or theme or issue—love, war, identity, politics, pets—and develop an exhaustive list of composing ideas for it. How can your topic be developed as:

story	film	essay
drama	letter	sculpture
graffiti	satire	column

Use the list of "neglected forms of composition" provided in this chapter as a guide.

FIGURE 9.7

From Gilbert Tierney and Stephen Judy, "The Assignment Makers," *The English Journal,* February 1972. Copyright © 1972 by the National Council of Teachers of English. Reprinted by permission of the publisher.

THE ASSIGNMENT MAKERS

(1) *Rosemary Clowan* brings in a dead crow to her tenth-grade English class. She explains that she found it along the side of the road and allows the students to look at it and talk about it. After a bit she asks if anybody has any writing ideas as a result of seeing the crow. She invites those who do to follow up their ideas while the rest of the class has a free reading period.

(2) *George Sears* brings in a 4' × 5' photo-poster showing a lonely old man feeding pigeons in the park. "Write about it," he tells his eleventh-grade class. "Use any form—prose, poetry, drama, or essay—that meets your needs. When you're through we'll see who has the best ideas."

(3) *Brad Merrimack* decides to take up the research paper with his college-bound senior English class. He tells the students to read James Roswell Lowell's practical text, *A Guide to Writing Academic and Research Papers,* and has the class examine some marked-up freshman college papers that his former students have collected for him. After this, he tells each student to write a short paper on any serious topic in English or history, but limited to ten pages and five references.

(4) *Rob Wesley's* junior English students come in to class one day quite angry because one of their friends has been suspended—unfairly, in their opinion. One student suggests that they picket the principal's office in protest. Rob gives them the rest of the hour and all the paper they can use to plan the activity.

(5) *Jean Vernon* is teaching philosophy in her advanced world literature class. Following discussion of essays and fiction by Sartre and Camus, she makes the following assignment:

Sartre and Camus are known as "existentialists." The word has such broad meaning, however, that few people have been able to write a precise, careful definition. Without consulting any other sources, write an essay that defines and explains your own view of existentialism, drawing on ideas and examples from Sartre and Camus when necessary. Pay particular attention to the concepts of *action, being,* and *death.*

(6) On the opening day of school, *Howard Upton* asks his eighth-grade class to "write about the most interesting thing you saw or did last summer." He says: "You probably have seen or done many interesting things during the past few months, either at home or on a trip. Pick one

of these things and tell us about it. When you're through, we'll read them and find out what you've been up to.

(7) *Sharon LeBeau* has just led the class in a reading of Frost's "Mending Wall." "Write about your interpretation of the poem," Sharon says, "remembering that a poem can be interpreted in many ways. I'll accept any interpretation as long as you can support your ideas."

(8) *Susan Schumacher* institutes a writing time in her sophomore class. Once or twice each week she says, "OK, stop what you're doing and write about anything you want for twenty minutes." At the end of that time she resumes the regular class work. She doesn't collect the papers, but the students can share them if they want to.

(9) *Fred Houston* brings *Auschwitz,* a powerful, chilling documentary film, to show to his eighth-grade class. After the students have seen the film and asked a variety of questions about prison camps and the executions, Fred asks them to write a paper on "Man's Inhumanity to Man."

Notes and Observations

(1) ROSEMARY CLOWAN. Some of the people who have done the activity have argued that it is in poor taste for Rosemary to bring in a dead crow, that many of the students may be offended by it. We rather like the idea, since few kids have ever been able to look at a bird—particularly a large one—up close. However, to us, Rosemary seems a bit cavalier in simply asking "if anybody has any ideas." By suggesting a few starting points for stories, essays, poems, and perhaps even a fable or play, she might be able to involve more students.

(2) GEORGE SEARS. In the manner of Leavitt and Sohn's *Stop, Look and Write*, the photo-poster seems like a good way of initiating writing activities. We like the way George avoids limiting his students to a single topic or even a single form by giving them unlimited ways of responding. We do think that like Rosemary Clowan, George could have supplied a few specific writing suggestions for those students who find it difficult to translate the bold instruction "Write!" into a concrete, workable writing-idea. The sharing of writing at the close of the hour builds in an audience, but why emphasize "the best" ideas in that situation?

(3) BRAD MERRIMACK. If one feel obligated to do the term paper with students, Brad's approach seems sensible. He does it with college-bound seniors; he limits the length and complexity of the project; and he bases his instruction "in reality" by bringing in actual freshman writing, complete with instructors' comments. We do question his reference to "serious" topics, which implies that all academic writing must be dull, boring, or pompous, and his failure to allow students to do work outside the area of humanities.

(4) ROB WESLEY. This has many of the basic elements of the "ideal" writing assignment. The kids are ready to work without any pressure from the teacher. The activity is *real,* and the students will be able to move well beyond the limits of the classroom walls. However, quite

aside from the fact that this will probably be Rob's *last* assignment once the principal finds out where the protest started, we wonder whether he couldn't have channeled the students' energies more productively. Rather than sending them off to what will probably prove to be a fruitless picket, Rob might help the students devise what Neil Postman and Charles Weingartner have called a "soft revolutionary" strategy, proposing and working for systematic changes in the school system.

(5) JEAN VERNON. This assignment strikes us as being "academic" in the worst sense of the word. It may help the students prepare for some of the horrors they will face in undergraduate seminars several years from now, but that doesn't seem to counteract the possible harm it can do now. It presents several serious problems. It pretends to be open-ended by inviting the student to present his "own view," but the general course of the essay is dictated by Jean's not-too-subtle reminder to include examples from Sartre and Camus, particularly concerning the concepts of *"action, being,* and *death."* It is also an *impossible* assignment; Jean acknowledges that experts can't define existentialism, yet she asks her students to do it anyway. She may unconsciously recognize this problem, since she carefully forbids "consulting outside sources"— a logical step for anyone faced with an impossible assignment. This kind of paper, because of its pseudointellectual nature, invites the cribbing, plagiarizing, and paraphrasing that sap so much of our energies.

(6) HOWARD UPTON. This assignment bothers many people because of its resemblance to the clichéd "My Summer Vacation." However, there are important differences. Howard makes the assignment open-ended but still asks the students to be fairly specific, thus avoiding the usual shotgun approach to vacation descriptions. Further, he does not favor kids who go away on trips, and he recognizes that things happen at home as well as in the Black Hills or the Poconos. He provides for sharing at the end of the hour and makes it clear to the students that they will be their own audience. However, as several teachers have pointed out to us, this might make a better *oral* than written assignment, particularly on the first day of school. Perhaps Howard should simply create a conversation circle or small groups and allow the students to share experiences informally.

(7) SHARON LeBEAU. In contrast to Jean Vernon's assignment about literature, this approach to academic writing seems quite humane. Sharon is not forcing an interpretation on the students. However, we still predict that the assignment will produce some rather dull, standardized writing that few people would voluntarily choose to read or write; e.g., "I think Robert Frost's 'Mending Wall' means . . . and here are my reasons: . . . ." If a poem can be interpreted in many ways, Sharon might consider allowing the students to *respond* in many ways rather than forcing them into an exercise in *explication de texte.* Given freedom to respond, her students might write essays, poems, and stories about such ideas as barriers, human relationships, disagreeable people, making friends, the World Crisis . . . and a few might even choose to read more Frost and write about him.

(8) SUSAN SCHUMACHER. Most of the teachers we have talked with approve of the basic direction of this assignment. Many teachers have had great success with free writing activities like a journal, and the kind of atmosphere Susan has created lends itself to an open, honest style of writing. Most, however, object to the "fire drill" nature of the writing time. Few people can write on command—even when they are free to write about anything. Perhaps Susan could establish entire days when free writing is encouraged along with free reading, free talking, and free "listening." Several people have suggested that she might also set up an "idea box" or file of composition suggestions for kids who don't come up with instant ideas during the writing time. One other problem with this approach is that if students don't think the writing "counts" for anything, some will be very reluctant to do it.

(9) FRED HOUSTON. Although eighth-graders may be somewhat young for a showing of a film like *Auschwitz*, our greatest reservations about this assignment concern the topic, "Man's Inhumanity to Man," which encourages abstract, possibly moralistic writing and seems to be several years beyond the eighth-graders. We like the way Houston goes from the film to discussion, and we imagine that the discussion would be quite lively after a film like *Auschwitz*. Perhaps he should simply end with discussion, or, like Susan Schumacher and Rosemary Clowan, invite the kids to do "free" writing—perhaps in a variety of forms—to express their responses to the film.

• Literature anthologies are notoriously weak in providing good writing assignments. Choose an anthology that is widely adopted and create some writing activities to go with the reading.

• Choose a topic or theme and create a sequence of assignments for a group of young people with whom you would like to work. What kinds of assignments should come first? In what ways should the sequence (and the students) develop? How can you end the sequence?

RELATED READINGS

The production of books for teachers interested in writing instruction has mushroomed in recent years. The Bibliography section of this book includes a number of the best new titles, but it may well be dated by the time the book is published. Two publishers, Boynton/Cook and Heinemann, have pretty much cornered the market for good writing texts, and both are firms that are clearly committed to serving teachers, not just turning a profit. We recommend that you obtain their catalogs and get on their mailing list.

A series of young adult books by Stephen and Susan Tchudi may be of interest, too, since they expand on ideas in this chapter and contain a number of ideas for actual writing projects. *Gifts of Writing* (New York: Scribner's, 1980) was the first in the series, with writing ideas plus ideas for presentation through publication. *Putting on a Play* followed (Scribner's, 1982), with a focus on ways of "writing" drama. *The Young Writer's Handbook* was next (Scribner's, 1984), with a concern for many different kinds of writing. *The Young Learner's Handbook* (Scribner's, 1987) was done by Steve alone and extends a number of ideas in writing instruction to the broader area of *learning*.

Teachers interested in writing may also want to subscribe to the New York Teachers and Writers Collaborative's magazine, *Teachers and Writers,* which discusses both theoretical and practical problems. Though intended primarily as a book for college writing classes, Miller and Judy's *Writing in Reality* (New York: Harper & Row, 1978) contains a discussion of current writing theory with an emphasis on the role of imagination in writing. It includes a number of writing options that can be used at a variety of grade levels.

Writing for the Here and Now

10

From Richard Behm, "Portrait of the English Teacher as a Tired Dog," *Exchange: A Newsletter for Teachers of Writing* no. 1. Published by the Writing Laboratory of the University of Wisconsin, Stevens Point. Reprinted by permission of the author.

PORTRAIT OF THE ENGLISH TEACHER AS A TIRED DOG

It is a November midnight, Johnny Carson has just ended, and throughout the block the last lights flick off—all but one that is. A single orange light blooms in the darkness. It is the English teacher, weary-eyed, cramped of leg, hand, and brain, sifting listlessly but doggedly through piles of themes, circling, marking, grading, commenting, guilt-ridden because the students were promised that the papers would be returned last week. The fifth cup of coffee grows cold and bitter. Just one more paper. And then one more. And then . . .

ASSESSING student compositions has been a problem for English teachers ever since writing became a regular part of the high school curriculum in the mid-nineteenth century. In his 1850s textbook, *Aids to English Composition,* Richard Green Parker was one of the first to comment on ways of evaluating writing: "Merits for composition should be predicated on their neatness, correctness, length, style, &c.; but the highest merits should be given for the production of ideas, and original sentiments, and forms of expression." In some ways, Parker's approach to the problem seems quite contemporary, with its emphasis on rewarding "the production of ideas" and "original sentiments" rather than dealing exclusively with mechanical correctness and neatness.

Like many teachers, however, Parker also found it easier to correct mechanical errors than to wrestle with abstract and nebulous concepts like "content" and "originality." His text showed far more concern for pointing out "deficiencies" than for rewarding "merits." A theme-grading guide at the end of the text dealt almost exclusively with the kinds of errors that could be indicated in the margins of a paper with "shorthand" symbols, "arbitrary marks" of the kind "used by printers in the correction of proof sheets." Parker may have been one of the first teachers to recognize that it was impossible to write out detailed comments on every student's paper and thus turned to "shorthand" methods for relief. He may, in fact, have been one of the first to offer the rationalization that using symbols was pedagogically justifiable because it encouraged students to locate their own errors.

Many of the procedures used for evaluating student writing over the years have been created less out of intellectual commitment than from the desperation of teachers faced with enormous stacks of papers. Teachers have tried both pointing out errors and allowing students to discover their own errors. They have tried blanket red-penciling and selective gray-penciling of errors. Some have emphasized the positive with occasional comments about the negative. Others have experimented with grading systems: single grades, double grades, and multiple grades. There is even a market for a twentieth-century "improvement" on Parker's proofreading symbols: a rubber stamp showing a little duckie who says "AWK!", protecting the ego of the child on whose paper it is imprinted by adding a playful touch to the revelation of compositional awkwardness. Despite the energy and ingenuity invested in these devices and procedures, student writing has not seemed to improve in corresponding ways.

EVALUATION: AIMS AND PURPOSES

Why haven't these approaches to evaluation worked? A major reason may be that from Parker's time to the present, approaches to evaluation have always been "future directed" rather than aimed at writing as something for the here and now. Evaluation has emphasized getting students ready for "next time," instead of helping them find success in the present.

For instance, with his talk of "merits" and "deficiencies" Parker sounds rather like a preacher trying to prepare his flock for the hereafter. Although many teachers have softened this kind of language to speak of "strengths" and "weaknessess," the attitude has remained much the same. Teachers have often operated on the assumption that if students write enough themes and receive enough evaluation, they will, sometime in the near or distant future, write The Perfect Theme that will be their pass through the Golden Gates of composition.

However, few students write simply for the sake of learning to write better. When an evaluation procedure implies that all the work being done is merely preparation for more work in the future, the reality of the writing situation is destroyed. Future-directed evaluation, even when done humanely and sensitively, may actually inhibit growth in writing.

A friend who is in publishing once pointed out that magazine and book editors are not interested in teaching authors how to write. When a manuscript arrives, an editor looks through it, makes comments, calls for some revisions, and submits changes. All this instruction is devoted solely to the aim of getting out a successful publication. The editor remains indifferent to whether or not the author's writing improves in the process. However, many authors acknowledge that the process does help them write better, and many writers depend quite heavily on their editors for advice. The moral here is that by concentrating on the present, editors help the writer find success, and when they do so they become, almost incidentally, "teachers of writing."

A teacher can escape the trap of future-directed evaluation by adopting the general kind of attitude an editor takes—being concerned with the product at hand. An editor, of course, works with adults who are reasonably accomplished writers to begin with. Because the teacher works with young people who are in the process of growing, the concerns will be more complicated. At times the teacher should be an editor, dealing with strengths and weaknesses in papers—in particular, as "publication time" approaches. At other points in the writing process he or she must serve in somewhat more sensitive roles: respondent, interested human being, friend, or adviser. The roles will differ with the student, the circumstances, and the state of the composition that the teacher receives.

This does not mean that a teacher must abandon all standards and accept anything with praise. The teacher does need to have criteria for good and bad; however, these should be applied as a way of helping students find success now. Some questions that can help the teacher get at the qualities of good writing include:

Does this writing have voice?
Does this writing use details well?
Are strong feelings displayed in this writing?
Does this writing show spunkiness, use colorful language, exciting words and phrases?
Does this writing elicit strong feelings from the reader?
Does this writing show an awareness of audience?
Does this writing show the writer "playing with language" or having fun with it?
Does this writing show fluency or does the writer seem to have a hard time putting down thoughts?
Is it clear where the writing is going?

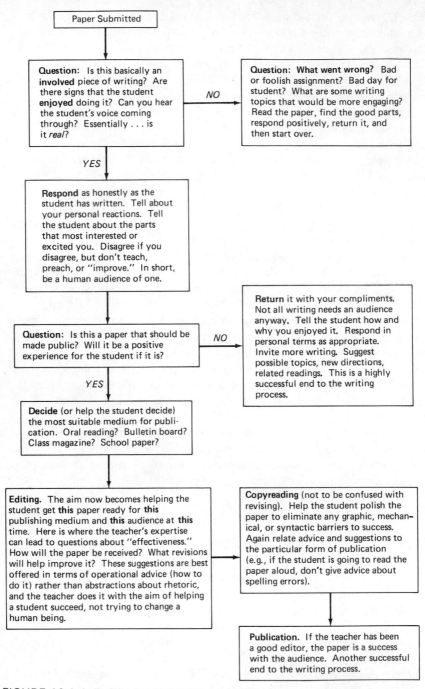

FIGURE 10.1 A FLOW CHART FOR ASSESSING STUDENT WRITING.

Is there evidence of clear thinking in the writing?
Is the writer grappling with ideas/thoughts through the writing?
Does the writer share self, thoughts, ideas, feelings?

Not all of the above criteria apply to every paper. A teacher cannot treat themes as a batch, giving every piece of work the same basic evaluative treatment. Rather, the teacher needs to find ways to individualize the responses made, rejecting the narrow role of teacher-evaluator to become a "manuscript manager" who decides on an individual basis what needs to happen for a piece of writing to bring satisfaction to the student here and now. On the next few pages, we discuss some of the key points that a teacher must consider when examining a student composition, whether essay, poem, or story. There are a number of stages or checkpoints where the teacher can pause to consider alternative ways of helping students. A summary of these stages is presented in Figure 10.1.

LISTENING FOR THE STUDENT VOICE

When a paper first comes in, the teacher should begin the assessment by trying to discover whether or not the student was excited about the activity. The teacher needs to ask if this is *authentic* communication. Can you hear the student talking when you read it? Is it a lively piece of work that reveals the student's active participation? This quality in student writing is difficult to define but rather easy to detect. Many people call it "voice"—meaning that the paper sounds as if a unique person wrote it, not a computer or a bureaucrat. In *Children's Writing* (Cambridge, England: Cambridge University Press, 1967), David Holbrook describes this as a feeling of openness, liveliness, and animation.

In approaching children's writing . . . , we need to seek beyond the problem of spelling, and the look of the writing, and get to the symbolic meaning. Once we have some sense of this, we judge it not in terms of its "psychological value" but as poetry. That is, from our experience of poetry of all kinds, we can ask ourselves, "In its symbolic exploration of inner and outer experience how sincere is this?" By "how sincere" here I think we mean how much real work is being done on problems of life: and the clue to this will be in the freshness, the energy, the rhythm and feel of the language. When anyone is really working on his inner world, he becomes excited—for he is making important discoveries and gains, as between his ego and the witches, princesses, and threatening shadows within. He sees connections and relationships, and possibilities of structures, patterns, richness of content: and in these, joy and beauty. Expression will convey the bodily feelings of experience, and the "inscape" of an inward effort. So, if we are responsive, we can usually feel this excitement in the words (as we can usually feel this excitement in a piece of music: if we look at the score we are likely to find them marked *express*).

In looking for excitement and the quality of sincerity in a student's writing, the teacher, in essence, asks, "Is there evidence that this has been a productive, reasonably enjoyable writing experience for the student?" If the answer is "yes," it will be revealed in the tone and vigor that one can sense in the language of the paper.

If the answer is negative, the teacher has reached an important decision point in assessment. Traditionally, when teachers receive flat, dull, colorless writing, they blame it on the student: "You're not trying hard enough. Do it over!" We think this blame is often misplaced. No student deliberately creates a lifeless composition. Creating dull writing is boring, and few people outside the government would choose to do very much of it. In many cases the cause of dull writing can be traced indirectly to the assignment or to an unfavorable classroom climate. Perhaps the assignment was poor—too complicated, too easy, irrelevant, or just plain silly. Perhaps the student didn't trust the teacher or the class and was unwilling to share ideas. Whatever the cause, the teacher needs to find out what went wrong, looking as much to the assignment as to the student for an explanation. The teacher can then figure out something else for the student to do. What *will* work for him? What are her interests? What are his skills? What project will excite her? How can he or she be persuaded to trust others?

But what does the teacher do with the manuscript? It seems pointless to demand revision of something that was dead to begin with. We think the teacher should, therefore, respond as positively as possible to the paper, commenting on the good parts (without faking a response). Then the paper should be returned. Often the teacher can say quite directly, "Look, I had the feeling you didn't enjoy doing this. Am I right? Let's see if we can't come up with something else you would rather do."

Here is a paper that illustrates the problem of voice. It was written in a junior high school class in which the students were asked to write a letter of application for a job they might like to have some time:

Good morning Sir I would like to apply for a banking clerk. I think I am well qualified to fill the position. I have had three years of dealing with money I know how to handle money quite well. I am a very responsible man and also very dependable. I could be trusted to handle your money without your having any uncertainty about me. And as I said before since I have been handling money. My schooling is great, I have just graduated from college, and majoring in bookkeeping which deals with a lot of money.

I can tell you how much money you are making or losing. If you were to hire me you can be certain that I will do my job to the best of my ability. Yes! This is just the kind of bank that I would like to work at.

I feel that it would be a privilege working for your bank.

"(H.) Allen Johnson"

(H.) Allen Johnson

Except for a few bright spots, this letter seems utterly lacking in voice, and I doubt that (H.) Allen Johnson profited much by doing it. Many of the phrases seem forced, unnatural, and excessively formal: "I could . . . handle your money without your having any uncertainty about me." "I feel that it would be a privilege working for your bank." Occasionally Allen's real voice comes through. His exclamation "Yes!" seems to be a victory over both the Business Letter and his own doubts about the banking business. His signature is done in playful parody of "official" looking signatures and adds an original touch. But the remainder is dull and repetitive, sounding much like a junior high school student trying to write what he imagines to be adult language.

The result is a letter that, by almost any criteria, is unsuccessful. Allen has not learned much about business letters; his letter wouldn't land him a job; and his teacher must be thoroughly frustrated by almost every aspect of his writing.

What went wrong? I suspect that despite an assignment that seemed reasonable and practical, the realities of job hunting are so far removed from the world of the junior high school student that the task became meaningless. Allen is simply not ready to worry about jobs, and there is no reason why he should be. So the assignment drove him into using a false, stuffy voice. In dealing positively with the paper, the teacher might compliment Allen on his enthusiasm and point out that he has done a good job of thinking about what a banker would want to know about a prospective employee (he *has* done a skillful job of surveying his audience, even though the topic and audience were not closely related to his current needs). The teacher should then turn Allen's attention to finding other projects that he will enjoy doing. It is conceivable that Allen might enjoy going to a bank to find out what actually happens there. We think it is more likely, however, that the teacher could find interesting writing ideas for Allen in less academic areas, topics more suitable for junior high, like writing sports stories or telling tales of the grotesque and macabre.

RESPONDING TO STUDENT WRITING

One hopes that the amount of voiceless writing that teachers receive will be small, that early in the school year they can help each student find areas where writing is profitable and interesting. Once teachers recognize that a paper has voice, it is appropriate that they take time to respond (orally or in writing). Students have spent much time writing; they need response and reaction quickly.

To respond to student writing simply means to react to a paper openly and directly, as a person rather than as a "teacher." It differs from evaluation in being a shared reaction rather than a set of future-directed instructions for improvement. In responding, teachers can tell how they reacted to the paper ("I strongly felt the fear you described when the storm hit"); they can share similar experiences ("I remember the fight I had with my parents over taking a job playing saxophone when I was a sophomore"); they can indicate their own beliefs and tell about the ways in which they agree or disagree ("I can see your point about the way newscasters operate, but I really don't agree that the networks control American thought").

Response can move beyond direct feedback to suggest new or related directions for the student to explore. ("You obviously enjoyed writing this; have you ever read any of Edgar Allan Poe's stories?" "Have you ever made a movie? I think it might be interesting for you to try to catch the same idea on film.") These more oblique comments express the honest reaction of an interested, informed adult, not just the pedagogically directed instruction of a theme grader.

In responding, however, teachers differ from the ordinary reader in a very significant way: Teachers should be willing to ignore all kinds of graphic, rhetorical, and syntactic problems that a regular reader might find frustrating or disagreeable. Teachers should fight to dig out the meaning of a page. They should puzzle over idiosyncratic spellings, ignore the fifty-word run-on sentence, forget about the fact that statistics and supporting evidence are missing, and struggle to uncoil long strings of identical loops that pass for handwriting. This is not to suggest that such problems are blithely ignored. The key point is that response should not be confused with proofreading. To comment on mechanical problems before responding to content is perverse. Such difficulties can be taken up later, after the teacher has responded fully and carefully. As David Holbrook pointed out in *Children's Writing,* looking past problems to decipher, appreciate, and enjoy student writing without having one's reaction skewed by errors and blights is extremely difficult—possibly more difficult for English teachers than for most people, since we have earned advanced degrees in linguistic flaw detecting.

Perhaps the best model for this kind of response is the letter one would write in reply to a note received from a young relative—a son, daughter, nephew, or niece. For close relatives, most of us are willing to decipher and to respond directly to meaning, and few would grade or evaluate letters.

What Else Can the Teacher Say?

Teachers who have not had a great deal of experience in writing or in responding to student writing often feel that they do not know what to look for in writing. Thus they often revert to reacting and evaluating papers only in terms of mechanics or usage. This seems to them to be an "objective" way to respond to the students' writing and they feel they won't get arguments from students if they grade papers only on mechanics. Reacting to writing and eventually judging or evaluating it often makes teachers uncomfortable if they aren't confident in their ability to recognize good writing. However, if students are to grow as writers, they need feedback on more than mechanics and spelling in their work. So teachers can start with the qualities of good writing described earlier in this chapter. Then when they respond to student papers they can begin by making comments of the following sort:

GENERAL

1. Strong writing voice—I can hear someone behind those words.
2. I can picture this.
3. I know just what you mean—I've felt this way too.
4. You're losing my attention—make this part a little more specific.

BEGINNINGS AND ENDINGS

5. Strong introduction—it makes me want to read this paper.
6. Your ending came so quickly that I felt I missed something.
7. Your wrap-up really captured the whole mood of the paper.
8. The conclusions seemed a little weak—I felt let down.

ORGANIZATION

9. This was very well organized. I could follow it easily.
10. I'm confused about how this fits in.
11. I'm not sure what the focus of the paper is.
12. How is this connected to the sentence or idea before it?
13. This sentence or paragraph seems overloaded—too much happens too fast and I can't follow you.

CLARITY

14. Can you add detail here? I just don't see the whole picture.
15. Good description—I could make a movie of this.
16. Adding some physical description would help me see this more clearly.
17. Tell me more about this—I need more information.
18. An example here would help us support your case more willingly.
19. The use of dialogue here would help me see this person more vividly.
20. I'm not sure what you mean. Let's talk.

STRUCTURE AND LANGUAGE

21. Notice that you've got a number of short sentences here—can you combine them to smooth the flow?
22. This sentence is a whopper! Break it up, please.
23. Good word choice—it really captures the essence of what you are talking about.
24. Your language seems a bit overblown; I don't hear *you* talking and that distracts me.

USAGE AND MECHANICS

25. Oops—you changed tenses and confused me.
26. You switched from the third person to the first. I can understand it, but it does distract.
27. You capitalize words randomly. Let me sit down with you in workshop and show you some things.
28. Break your work into sentences so I can more clearly see which ideas are related.

If teachers focus on their reactions to the paper and what interferes with their understanding of it, they can help students see how their paper affects others. After teachers respond to papers in this manner for a time, they will begin to be able to recognize and articulate what makes one piece of writing more effective than another and will have come a long way in building confidence in their ability to help students be successful in their writing and in their ability to evaluate writing.

Conferences on Student Writing

Another way students can grow as writers is through talking about their writing with the teacher. Conferences provide a time when the student discusses his or her writing with the teacher and asks for the kind of help he or she needs. Of course, students will not begin conferences with teachers in this way since they're used to the teacher taking the lead, so it will take a while to wean them from this dependence. In *Writing: Teachers and Children at Work* (Heinemann, 1983), Donald Graves describes how to make conferences work. He points out that "until the child speaks, nothing significant has happened in the writing conference." This is not the time for the teacher to evaluate writing but to answer questions, to respond, to suggest new directions, and to ask students about their own process.

The classroom atmosphere must be one of trust and honest concern for the learner before the conferences can succeed. Students must not feel threatened or they will not talk openly about their writing. Conferences should be kept short—from three to five minutes—and students should schedule more time if they feel they need it.

When you explain conferences to students, let them know that you will want them to talk about their writing, telling you what it's about, where they are in the writing, and what kinds of help they need. As students see that conferences can help them in their journey to say what they want to say, they will become more and more involved in them.

Some teachers like to schedule conferences as meetings between the teacher and student, perhaps at the teacher's desk. This is highly productive but, especially in the secondary classroom, it would be difficult to have a conference with every student on every piece of writing. We especially like the idea of the "miniconference," conducted as the teacher circulates around the room, making a comment to one student, asking another a question, answering a question or two from a third. In this way, the teacher can comfortably meet with each student every workshop day. Another workable approach is to hold conferences at intervals for the purpose of reviewing several student writings at once. Such conferences should lead to revisions, however, or else the discussion becomes future-directed. Some teachers even like to count a revision as another full grade, so that students feel that revision is important and make the most of their conferences.

PUBLIC OR PRIVATE?

Another question that a teacher needs to ask concerns whether a paper should be made public: "Should it be given a wider audience than just the teacher?" Although one wants to avoid writing that is merely written for the teacher, it is important to recall that not all writing is meant to be made public. The teacher should consider carefully whether providing an audience will create a positive experience for the student.

Here is a paper submitted by a high school sophomore girl:

One day me and this girl went to the store. The girl was from Chicago and she thought she was bad. She kept pointing her umbrella in my face. I told her stop but she kept pushing so I grabbed it out of her hand and stuck her with it. I felt sorry but I said no better for a person like that. Only fools fight. And when you fight you really lose whether you win or not. I believe that arguing is good because people have a way to say it without harming someone or hurting a live thing. But you can't always walk away. (You may not understand this because I haven't got the words to say it.)

—C.S.

It is possible that C.S. would find it helpful to have other students read and discuss this paper, and her classmates might be able to offer some useful or supportive advice. However, C.S. is obviously puzzled and concerned, and she may be less interested in communicating a message than exploring her own experience and seeking a response from someone else. She believes "only fools fight," and she is persuaded that people should settle disputes through argument rather than through "harming someone or hurting a live thing." Yet, as she says, "you can't always walk away," and in this situation she felt committed to action. As an adult being asked for help—a role that teachers should accept with pleasure, even if it puts them in the sometimes uncomfortable position of learning about students' problems—the teacher needs to respond directly to C.S., supporting her efforts to sort out her own beliefs and values.

If writing is judged to be private, little can be accomplished by offering instruction about writing skills. The teacher should respond—fully and helpfully—and return it to the student without any pedagogical comment. Although there may be some rhetorical problems with the writing, it becomes hollowly academic to do something about them in such a case. Here, C.S. openly expressed her feelings; the teacher read, understood, and responded. That seems to be enough.

At the same time, we need to be open to the possibility that C.S. could find an audience for the piece successfully. Perhaps it is feedback from peers that she is seeking. In this case, her writing would go "public," perhaps through sharing with a few girlfriends, perhaps as an essay for the class magazine. The teacher must then change roles to become a guide to editing and publishing.

ALTERNATIVE FORMS OF PUBLICATION

There are many different ways the teacher can provide students with a readership. Some papers are best "published" by having them read aloud to the class, either by the author or the teacher. Some writing should be read and tape-recorded to become part of a class library of recorded literature. Students' work can be posted on the board, submitted to a class newspaper or magazine, sent to the school paper or magazine, run off on ditto for the class, or circulated in manuscript form.

An excellent list of ways of publishing student writing, prepared by an Australian primary school teacher, is shown in Figure 10.2.

It is important to note that every form of writing and each kind of publication make particular, specialized demands on the writer. Students should have an audience in mind while they are writing, but often the best form of publication will not be apparent until after the writing has been completed. A short, witty poem that might bring a good laugh to the class when read aloud may die if set in print. A play that has absorbed a student's time for several weeks surely deserves presentation, but it may work better as reader's theater or a radio play than as a stage production. As an expert on writing forms, media, and styles, the teacher can help the student find the most productive forms of publication.

Here, Roman Cirillo, an eighth grader, writes about "How Airplanes Flies," and his paper presents some interesting publication problems:

Few people know why or how an airplane flies. The explanation is very simple. There no mysterious mechenism or machinery to study. You don't have to take a plane apart or crawl around inside to understand why it stays in the air. You just stand off and look at it. Airplanes flies because of the shapes of its wings. The engine and propellor have very little to do with it. The pilot has nothing to do with making the plane fly. He simply controls the flight. A glider without an engine will fly in the air for hours. The biggest airplanes will fly for a certain length of time with all the engine shut off. A plane flies and stay in the air because its wings are supported by the air just as water supports a fellow. Toss a flat piece of tin on a boat. Toss a flat piece of tin on a pond and it will sink at once. If you bend it through the middle and fasten the end together so its is watertight it will float.

There are obviously many problems with this essay. It lacks clarity and it often leaves the reader confused. But if one looks past the errors and infelicities, "How Airplanes Flies" is a clever explanation of flight. The paper has a strong, clear voice; one can hear Roman's patient instruction to someone who is ignorant of the principles of flight: "You don't have to take a plane apart or crawl around inside to understand why it stays in the air. You just stand off and look at it." Roman is a good teacher, and his explanation of how shaping metal enables the plane to fly is skillful (even though incomplete). Roman would, no doubt, fail any test on writing analogies, similes, and metaphors; but he makes excellent use of analogy in relating how things float in an invisible substance—air—to an observable phenomenon: a boat floating on water.

In its present form, however, this paper will probably not find much success with an audience. It has too many problems of clarity, too much drifting and backtracking, for a reader (particularly one who doesn't understand flight) to stay with it for long.

FIGURE 10.2

From Pat Edwards, "100 Ways to Publish Children's Writing," in R. D. Walshe, ed., *Better Reading/Writing Now!* The Primary English Association of New South Wales, Epping Public School, Epping, NSW, Australia. Copyright © 1977 by the Primary English Teaching Association of New South Wales. Reprinted by permission of the author.

100 WAYS TO PUBLISH CHILDREN'S WRITING

Books of All Kinds

1. A.B.C. Books
2. Story Books
3. Poetry Books
4. "My Best Writing"—Individual Scrapbook
5. "Introducing Our Class"
6. "Famous People" (The class as a set of VIPs)
7. Autograph Album
8. "I'd Like to Be . . ."
9. "What Do You Know About . . . ?" Series
10. Riddle and Joke Books
11. "How-to . . ." Books
12. Recipe Books
13. A Giant Book (Made from an appliance box and butcher paper)
14. "The Longest Story Ever!" (On rolls of butcher paper)
15. A "Group" Story
16. An All-School Story (With round-robin contributions)

Newspapers

17. School News
18. Family News
19. Good News
20. District News
21. "Crazy Paper" (Nursery rhymes retold)

Simple News Sheets

22. News-Writing Competition
23. About Favourite Books
24. Natural Science Reports
25. Stop Press (School news flashes)

Magazines

26. "Getting to Know You" (For a new class)
27. Specialist Magazines (From spear fishing to stamps)
28. "What Do You Want to Know about High School?" (or college)
29. Holiday Magazine
30. Class of 19— (A class reminiscence)

Letters

31. Classroom Mailbox
32. Teacher Writes Too (Personal letters to students)
33. To Mum and/or Dad
34. To Gran and/or Grandad
35. To the Principal
36. To a Person in the News
37. To a Media Personality
38. To a Librarian
39. To the School Bus Driver
40. To a Favourite Author
41. To the Local Paper

Plays

42. Begin Without Dialogue (Written instructions for mime)
43. Proceed Through Simple Dialogue
44. Dramatise Stories
45. Dramatise Poems
46. Try Melodrama
47. An End-of-Term Drama Festival

Notice Boards—Ideas for Displaying Day-to-Day Work

48. Here's Good Work!
49. Have You Read This?
50. Food for the Mind (A "thoughts" bulletin board)
51. Mail Train (Each car carries a piece of writing)
52. Garden of Poems
53. Balloons or Kites (Each with some writing)
54. All Up in the Air! (A full aeronautical display)

Special Displays to Share with Others

55. Information Charts
56. Posters

57. Conversations (Cartoon-fashion displays)
58. Patchwork Quilt (A "pastiche" of writing)
59. Sandwich Man (A walking display)
60. Advertisements

Special Displays and Exhibitions

61. Girl/Boy-of-the-Week Display
62. Rogue's Gallery (Student autobiographies or sketches of literary characters)
63. Corridor as Cemetery (in the manner of *Spoon River*)
64. Toy Exhibition (Of old or antique toys, with written histories)
65. Circus Exhibition (A history-social studies project)
66. Stamp Exhibition (Including postal history write-ups)
67. Photographic Exhibition
68. Photo Exhibition of a Field Trip

Assembly Reports

69. A Sampling of Good Writing
70. Reporting (Of newsworthy school events)
71. Celebrating Anniversaries (And national holidays)

Using Art and Craft Work

72. Mobiles of All Sorts
73. Group Production of Mobiles
74. Class Mobile
75. Enormous Posters
76. Window Craft
77. Birthday Cards
78. Congratulations Cards
79. Hand-out Cards
80. Portrait Gallery
81–85. Murals (Students write about and portray: passengers at a bus stop; performers at a concert; dancers at a discotheque; cats on a fence.)

Using Tape Recorders

86. Write–Tape–Revise
87. Tape, then Write
88. Regular Recording by Struggling Writers

Miscellaneous

89. Cartoon Show (Using overhead transparencies)
90. Run an Advertising Agency
91. Set Up a Writer's Centre
92. Form a Writer's Club
93. Hold a Writer's Barbecue (Picnic and writers' workshop)

A Wider Audience

94. A Shop Display
95. Displays for Special Events
96. Municipal Library Display
97. A Hospital Visit
98. Children's Magazines
99. P & C Readings (PTA meetings)
100. End-of-Year-Report to a Local Newspaper

Because Roman seems to have so much trouble handling the written word (one senses quite a struggle with the writing process behind this paper), we think the teacher might recommend that this project be completed as an oral "publication," particularly since Roman seems to be a good talker. Perhaps he can plan a demonstration for those members of the class who are interested. Drawing on his essay, he might bring in a dishpan and some aluminum foil to demonstrate the shaping of materials. Perhaps he can bring in some model planes or photographs or drawings to illustrate flight. An oral presentation should be a good experience for Roman, and quite significantly, it will be an experience that has its origins in writing. It might well pave the way for successful written composition in the future, but it would bring Roman success here and now.

THE CLASSROOM PUBLISHING CENTER

Back in the middle of the nineteenth century, a farsighted high school principal, John S. Hart, of Philadelphia Central High School, had a policy that the school would support any student publication that showed it could attract a modest readership. Over the period of a decade, Central had at least a dozen different school newspapers and a wide range of magazines and other student publications. Hart's wisdom was in seeing that writers quite simply need audiences. When these audiences are provided through publication, student writing improves dramatically, in both content and correctness.

Reproducing Student Work

The mass reproduction of student work seems to us so important that a review of some in-class printing and duplicating techniques is appropriate.

Spirit Duplicating. This is the old standby ditto machine. Although spirit printing produces an ordinary-looking page, usually purple, the process can be used to produce interesting magazines and fliers if you exploit the possibility of color. Using different colored ditto carbons (they come in red, green, blue, purple, and black), one can produce five-color work on a single page. It looks good and is relatively cheap and easy to do. If you are not able to requisition or steal a ditto machine for your own, you might be interested in the poor person's ditto, a device called a hectograph. It uses a tray full of gelatin and some incomprehensible magic to produce spirit copies one sheet at a time, and the last time we looked, Sears still had one for sale through the catalog. The hectograph is messy and slow, but it is also very satisfying for students to produce work on one.

Mimeograph. This is the other old standby. It produces pages that are more professional looking than spirit-purple, but most inexpensive mimeographs are also rather messy. Multiple color work can be done on mimeograph, but it is a fairly complicated procedure. You can get some interesting accessories for a mimeograph, including a tracing board to reproduce student art; lettering sets for headlines, mastheads, and the like; and specially blocked stencils cut electronically. When run on your own machine, they will give quality that is close to printed.

Computer Printing. The great breakthrough in classroom publication in our teaching lifetime has been the computer, which effectively gives you your own printing press in the classroom. Aside from the ease with which you can run copies, a new breed of "desktop publishing" programs makes it possible for students to do quite sophisticated layout and design work.

Printing. Hobbyist printing sets are available in many art and craft stores for $10 to $15. These enable the user to print with real type, one sheet of paper at a time. Setting the type is time consuming, and use of the press is probably best limited to short poems and magazine covers; but few things are more satisfying than a freshly printed page, especially if the students have set the type themselves.

Potato Printing, String Printing, Finger Painting. Anything that will pick up ink or paint and transfer it to another surface can be used to print designs, letters, and pictures.

Stencils.   These can be cut into all kinds of patterns and designs. Using spray paints, runs of one hundred can be completed quickly.

Offset Printing.   Offset is *not* a classroom process, but it deserves mention. Many instant printshops will run copies for about 6 cents per page, using the offset process. Copies look highly professional and are relatively inexpensive. Most offset houses will also "shrink" copy for you at no cost, so you can squeeze lots of print onto a single page. Also explore the possibilities that *folding* offers. For example, an 11 by 17 inch sheet (a standard two-page size), printed on both sides, can be folded three times to make a 16-page magazine measuring 8½ by 5½ inches. The total cost is $10 per hundred copies. Sold at 10 cents per copy (to students, administrators, parents), the class magazine will just break even.

One-of-a-Kind Books.   The previous techniques are all concerned with producing multiple copies of students' work. There is also value in one-of-a-kind books, done by hand, that can be passed about the class or made a part of the permanent resource center. One-of-a-kind books can often be more elaborate than duplicated materials and can include lavish use of colors and photographs, hand illumination, dry transfer printing, and special effects. Many different kinds of bindings are possible too, including cloth.

EDITING

Publishing is also important because it sets the stage for the final two parts of the response process: editing and copy reading. We have suggested that initially teachers should ignore surface errors to seek out the meaning of a page. But a concern for standards and correctness is appropriate in the context of revising and editing a paper.

Until the student and teacher have determined the audience for a paper, almost *any* instruction or advice on rhetoric or mechanics is irrelevant. However, when the form of publication has been determined, commentary about writing becomes appropriate; and the teacher and student can begin raising questions about effectiveness, clarity, organization, style, and structure. But it is critical that this commentary relate to the *particular form of publication* and the *particular audience* for the paper. Publications and readers have differing standards, and if editorial advice is to be helpful, it must be valid.

For instance, if a student writes, *"Space Outlaws* is the crummiest show on TV," the teacher's initial reaction may be to point out that "crummy" is not a standard critical term, that one cannot simply declare a show crummy without supplying reasons and supporting evidence. However, if the audience for the paper is a class of seventh graders who watch *Space Outlaws* regularly, "crummiest" may be *just* the word; the students know what the show is like and will either agree that it is crummy or argue that "it isn't all *that* crummy." In either case, the students don't need evidence or reasons; they already know the arguments. On the other hand, if the student is writing to the network president to demand that the show be removed from the air, the teacher can be genuinely helpful by pointing out that "crummiest" is inappropriate.

Advice of this kind should be operational, that is, couched in practical, "how to" terms. Abstractions about *unity, coherence, emphasis, narration, description, exposition, argumentation, topic sentences, grabber openings, clincher conclusions, brevity, antithesis, parallelism,* and *occlusion* are not likely to be of significant help to most young writers. Often, the best advice the teacher can give is simply helping the student see or discover alternatives: "Did you consider doing it this way?" or "Let me show you a couple of other ways to approach that." Although teachers may draw on their own knowledge of rhetorical principles for such advice, it isn't necessary for the student to memorize the abstraction while solving problems in the here and now.

COPYREADING

For too long, textbook writers and composition teachers have blurred the distinction between editing—changing content and form—and proofreading—polishing matters of spelling, mechanics, and usage. In their zeal to make students skillful writers of standard English, teachers have pounced on proofreading problems as early as the first draft, blithely pointing out errors in words and sentences that may well disappear entirely during the revision stage.

The discussion of mechanical and syntactic correctness should be delayed until the last possible moment in the writing process, leaving the students free to do the basic writing and revision of papers without any hesitation because of uncertainty over rules of correctness. Only after the students have edited their writing into a form that satisfies them should the teacher open the discussion of mechanics and usage. Even then, one should not charge in to red-pencil every error of mechanics, spelling, and punctuation. Rather, the teacher should concentrate on helping students put their papers into a form that will not confuse or irritate the readership. The teacher might point out to students that some audiences are offended by unclear handwriting or by language that doesn't conform to certain standards. The teacher can also note that failing to conform to some standards sometimes creates communication problems. Most students see this clearly, and if the quest for correctness has not dominated the entire writing process, they are willing to participate in a polishing session to get their paper into a form that will not cost them their readership.

Once again, however, it is important to note that the correctness demands of audiences differ widely. The teacher should not apply blanket standards of correctness or use the copyreading session as a way of slipping in standard English drill. The teacher should consider the proofreading changes that are necessary for *this* paper and *this* audience and *this* time. For instance, if the paper is simply to be read aloud or tape-recorded by the author, discussion of spelling, punctuation, or capitalization is largely a waste of time. Even if the paper is misspelled, illegibly written, and totally unpunctuated, the author can probably read it, and pointing out problems will contribute nothing to its success. If, on the other hand, the paper is going to be duplicated, it is quite legitimate for the teacher to work with the student to help get the paper into audience acceptable form. Even here, however, the teacher needs to be cautious. If "it's me" is the standard form in the dialect of a class, the teacher should probably not try to insist on "it's I" as an appropriate form. What matters is success with the audience, not a textbook illustration of "standard."

STUDENT SELF-ASSESSMENT

As we have described them, these considerations concerning assessment of student writing may seem too elaborate and time consuming for a teacher with five or six classes and 150 students. However, we have found that focusing assessment on the here and now actually speeds up the process of assessment and provides more time for the teacher to take up other classroom roles. For example, it takes less time to write a note of personal response on a paper than to mull through and write out detailed, pedagogically oriented evaluative comments. It is much faster to offer direct editorial advice keyed to specific publishing situations than it is to puzzle over the errors one will selectively attack this time.

In addition, as a class grows in the course of a quarter or semester, the students can take over more and more of the process. All this creates more time for the teacher to "float," working on a one-to-one basis with students who seek help.

There are also specific steps that the teacher can take to engage the students directly in the process of assessing their own work:

Encourage the students to talk to you and to one another about problems while they are writing.

Make it a standing invitation that any student can propose an alternative topic at any time in the class, thus reducing the number of lifeless papers.

Let the students decide which of their writing is public and which is private. In practice, most teachers find that the students are more willing to share their personal concerns with one another after initial phases of "testing" one another.

Describe the publication forms that are available. As the writing program develops and students catch on to the idea of publication, they should more often write with a specific audience and form of publication in mind.

Encourage the students to serve as one another's editors. One doesn't need to be an expert in composition and rhetoric to make useful suggestions about the clarity and effectiveness of writing. Although students may not know terminology, they are certainly capable of spotting editorial problems and talking about them in their own language: "Hey, I don't know what you're talking about." (Translation for teachers: "Lacks clarity.") "That's crazy." (Translation: "Lacks logical structure.") "I don't believe it." (Translation: "Needs more supporting evidence.") Students are highly perceptive in these ways, and when their editing has real purpose, they can take over the process and make genuinely helpful suggestions to one another.

Leave proofreading to the students. In every class there are some students who have mastered most of the proofreading skills. Often such students are simply good spellers or intuitive punctuators. Acknowledge their skill by setting them up as proofreading consultants to the class.

Treat proofreading as something to be done quickly and efficiently, rather than as a climactic step in the process of composition. Only when proofreading is made a mysterious, complex part of the mastery of standard English does it become intimidating and therefore difficult for students.

Help the students learn to react to one another's work. Small- and large-group discussion of completed compositions should be a regular part of any English class. At first, you may find that students are a bit hard on one another, no doubt imitating previous teachers of their acquaintance. It may take some practice before the students can respond to the substance of one another's writing, but it will come with time and patience.

Encourage students to develop criteria of excellence in advance for the work they are doing by putting themselves in the position of the audience and asking questions *it* would raise.

Encourage group and collaborative projects from time to time so that students can share both skills and critical knowledge.

Read some of your own writing to the class, and share your own satisfactions and dissatisfactions with it.

Encourage the students to develop lists of the problems and pleasures they associate with each project they do.

EXPLORATIONS

• Some unresolved issues and debatable questions:

What is an "error"?

Do people learn by having their errors pointed out to them? Under what conditions? Do people learn by having the errors of others pointed out?

How should assessment and evaluation procedures change as young people grow older?

Need a teacher respond to or evaluate every paper assigned?

Under what circumstances should a teacher say nothing about a bad paper? about a good one?

• The most difficult part of responding to student writing is getting over one's negative feelings about "blights" sufficiently to look at the real content of an essay. Collect some student writing and talk it over with another teacher. Share your ideas on the ways in which one could respond to it productively. Learn to look beyond mechanical and syntactic problems.

• Meet with a small group of students and engage them in a discussion of what makes good writing. To what extent do the students already have criteria of excellence of their own? How do these compare to yours?

• Develop a publishing center as recommended by Pat Edwards. Stock it with the necessary supplies to create a wide range of published books, magazines, and bulletin board displays. Then create a series of posters or activity cards that show the students how to create various publications, for example, how to make a poem mobile, how to make a giant book.

• Learn the technical ins and outs of mass reproduction of student work, from ditto to offset. Collect well-done fliers, brochures, and ads to serve as graphic examples for students. Learn how to use the desktop publishing program in the journalism department.

• Seek financial support for the publication of student writing. If the school cannot support a number of student publications, ask for contributions from local shops and industries for small and relatively inexpensive publications. Talk to the editor of your local newspaper about setting aside a page each month for student writing.

RELATED READINGS

The single best discussion of a philosophy of responding to student writing is David Holbrook's *Children's Writing* (Cambridge, England: Cambridge University Press, 1967), quoted in this chapter. Holbrook includes chapters on seeing the "real" in students' work, deciphering their handwriting, and analyzing what students are saying. Haim Ginott's books *Between Parent and Child* (New York: Macmillan, 1965) and *Between Parent and Teenager* (Macmillan, 1969) are also extremely helpful, stressing the need for parents and teachers to listen to, comprehend, and show empathy for young people's concerns before offering correction, instruction, or advice.

Teachers who want to know more about using conferences in the classroom and about helping students learn the skills they need in writing will find in Donald Graves's *Writing: Teachers and Children at Work* (Exeter, N.H.: Heinemann, 1983) a rich source of ideas. This book goes in depth into almost every aspect of teaching writing. Nancie Atwell's *In The Middle— Writing, Reading, and Learning with Adolescents* (Upper Montclair, N.J.: Boynton/Cook, 1987) is another book chock full of ideas and information on involving students in writing, responding to writing, and creating the climate for writing in the classroom. For ideas on the "miniconference" approach, see Charles Dawe and Edward A. Dornant, *One to One to Write: Resources for Conference Centered Writing* (Boston: Little, Brown, 1986). Peter Elbow's *Writing with Power* (New York: Oxford, 1981) is also a superb book with more ideas for peer editing approaches than most of us will ever employ. Brian Johnson's *Assessing English* (Sydney, Australia: St. Clair Press, 1983) is also extremely helpful in encouraging students to become editors in their own right.

Finally, teachers who are interested in expanding audiences and publication opportunities for student work might want to examine *Gifts of Writing*, by Susan and Stephen Judy (New York: Scribner's, 1980), which shows arts and crafts techniques plus writing ideas for over fifty kinds of projects.

Exploring Language

11
_____

EVERY few years politicians caught up in a difficult campaign reinvent "basics" and make their campaign theme "First Things First." They advocate "the elimination of frills" and promise a return to "old standards." Theirs is an appealing strategy that cuts to the heart of America's desire for efficiency, directness, and simplicity; and it often wins a good many votes.

English teachers also hear this cry from time to time. "Let's get back to the three Rs in school." "Why didn't someone teach my secretary to spell or punctuate?" "We here at the State U find our new students are abominably weak on fundamentals." "Of course I want my child to read literature, but after all, certain *other* things must come first." Often the demand for basics is phrased as a broad, unanswerable question: "Given all the money we spend on the schools, is it really too much to ask that the graduates be able to speak and write the Queen's English properly?"

In recent years teachers have found themselves in the middle of a basics revival. More and more parents have become upset about what they take to be a neglect of "basic skills" and have translated their concern into threats to limit funding. This, in turn, has pressured administrators and led to the movement to hold teachers accountable for listing fundamental skills and showing student improvement on test scores.

Like the appeal of the politician, a proclaimed interest in basics is very satisfying for many parents and administrators. Blue-collar parents are given a kind of assurance that their children will be able to rise in life; white-collar and suburban parents are reassured that their supremacy will not be undercut by "progressivist" English teachers who encourage "sloppy" speech and act as if "anything goes."

In a persuasive little book, *Basic Skills* (Boston: Little, Brown, 1983), Herbert Kohl has observed that traditionally, definitions of and demands for "basic skills" vary from one interest group to another. Kohl himself argues for a broad definition of basics, including learning how to use language successfully, how to compute, how to use tools and information. We like his emphasis on broad basics, but it is clear that in English/language arts teaching, "basics" almost invariably means a narrow range of surface features in language.

English teachers themselves have helped to create this overemphasis on surface correctness. Although they may not have been entirely certain of what they were trying to do in writing classes, they have stressed grammar and correctness—faithfully, consistently, without hesitation or doubt, year after year. It is unlikely that the emphasis on grammar has actually taught very much to students, but it obviously has made the graduates of our schools intensely aware of correctness. Thus parents are delighted to join in the demand for a return to basics, whether or not they ever learned anything from their own bout with grammar.

From John Dixon, *Growth Through English*. London: National Association for the Teaching of English, 1968.

Nearly a century of emphasis on the skills of English has brought almost universal literacy in our countries—a literacy dissipated, for the most part, on the impoverished literature of the popular press (which grew in answer to it). We should not be surprised. Whenever the so-called skill elements of language learning are divorced from the rest of English, the means becomes the end.

It is ironic, too, that the movement toward basics is not a new one, though its proponents act as if they were the first to discover fundamentals. The direct focus on skill instruction proves generally fruitless because it fails to concentrate on language users and their needs. The net effect of skill-building programs is often to inhibit the skill users, crippling their natural language ability and blunting their desire to do anything new with words.

A list of the most prominent claims made in behalf of the study of grammar over the years would include these: that it (1) disciplines the mind, (2) aids in the study of foreign languages, (3) helps one to use better English, (4) helps one to read better, and (5) aids in the interpretation of literature.

What does research tell us about these claims? . . . We believe the following excerpts from the *Encyclopedia of Educational Research* are worth reading:

(On disciplining the mind): Experimentation in this area failed to yield any significant evidence supporting the belief in grammar as a disciplinary subject.

(On the interpretation of literature): The result from tests in grammar, composition, and literary interpretation led to the conclusion that there was little or no relationship between grammar and composition and grammar and literary interpretation.

(On improved writing and usage): Further evidence supplementing the early studies indicated that training in formal grammar did not transfer to any significant extent to writing or to recognizing correct English. In general the experimental evidence revealed a discouraging lack of relationship between grammatical knowledge and the better utilization of expressional skills. Recently, grammar has been held to contribute to the better understanding of the sentence. Yet, even here, there is a discouraging lack of relationship between sentence sense and grammatical knowledge of subjects and predicates.

(On the study of foreign languages): In spite of the fact that the contribution of the knowledge of English grammar to achievement in foreign language has been its chief justification in the past, the experimental evidence does not support this conclusion.

(On the improvement of reading): The study of grammar has been justified because of its possible contribution to reading skills, but the evidence does not support this conclusion.

(On improved language behavior in general): No more relation exists between knowledge in a functional language situation than exists between any two totally different and unrelated subjects.

(On diagraming sentences): The use of sentence diagraming as a method of developing sentence mastery and control over certain mechanical skills closely related to the sentence has been subjected to a series of experimental investigations. In general the studies indicate that diagraming is a skill which, while responsive to instruction, has very slight value in itself. There is no point in training the pupil to diagram sentences except for the improvement it brings in his ability to create effective sentences. The evidence shows that this is insignificant.

If we accept these studies as valid, we must ask ourselves: What goes on here? For surely the meaning of these studies is that rarely have so many teachers spent so much time with so many children to accomplish so little.

Since "putting first things first" has proved unsuccessful, another possible approach—"everything, including basics, in its place"—needs to be explored. Only by considering the total language program can one avoid the obvious problems created by teaching basic skills in isolation.

GRAMMAR, USAGE, MECHANICS

The hold of grammar over the English curriculum has been strong for over one hundred years. Beginning in the fifth or sixth grade, children have received intensive instruction in grammar at annual intervals for six or seven years. Few children seem to remember much grammar from year to year, and many students quite honestly tell the teacher in June that they don't recall having studied the noun in September, despite the fact that the entire month was devoted to it. A growing body of research argues against teaching of formal grammar as a route to improved language usage. As a result, many teachers have cut down on the teaching of grammar, sometimes to the dismay of the taxpaying public. However, the decrease in grammar teaching should not be equated with a decline in standards, and there is considerable confusion on this matter.

Much of the conflict can be traced to what people expect the teacher of "grammar" to accomplish. Indeed, part of the problem simply concerns terminology, and some preliminary definitions are thus in order.

Grammar

Grammar is most simply defined as "a description of how English works." Through a process of analysis, the grammarian discovers the various components or parts of the language system and how they fit together. Grammar is a description of the language conventions that a speaker of the language has mastered in order to be able to communicate with other people. Grammar is *not* a set of rules telling how one is "supposed" to speak, and it does not prescribe behavior. It simply makes note of the language behavior that native speakers have learned. Very few people actually speak "ungrammatically," because something that is ungrammatical does not follow the basic patterns of English and therefore cannot be understood by another person. This statement is ungrammatical:

"Nobody ain't and got me ain't got nobody yet I."

It was produced by scrambling a sentence to break up English word order. Here is the grammatical version of the sentence:

"I ain't got nobody, and nobody ain't got me yet."

It follows normal English word patterns and it can therefore be understood by listeners, even though they might be somewhat offended or bothered by some of the word choices. Another word for grammar in this sense is "syntax": how sentences are constructed. Despite the kids' joke that grammar is a "sin tax," the real focus of "correctness" is a matter of usage, not grammar.

Usage

Usage is a range of socially significant choices available to a speaker *within* the grammar of a language. It is a sociological phenomenon, not linguistic, which means that it is concerned with the perceived social level of the speaker rather than with understanding or communication of messages. Either of the following can be understood:

"I ain't got nobody and nobody ain't got me yet."

"I haven't anyone, and no one has gotten me yet."

The difference between the statements is that each speaker reveals himself or herself to be a member of a particular social class. Usage is relative, and it is neither correct nor incorrect in itself. "Standard" usage is generally little more than the usage habits of the people in a country who are either (1) envied because of their superior breeding, intelligence, charm, and wit or (2) envied because of their superior wealth. The latter is more often the case. To some, this seems a cynical view of the nature of the "pure" form of our mother tongue. But the history of English shows that standard usage is a matter of convention, custom, and prestige; it is not an inherently superior dialect.

Spelling and Mechanics

iaintgotnobudyandnubudyaingotmeyet
hesaidafaintsmileplayinacrosthislips

Straighten that out, and you've got (or should it be "gotten"?) yourself an "A" for spelling and mechanics on your report card. *Mechanics* are simply transcription conventions—capitalization and punctuation—that make it possible for one person to read the writing of another. Spelling is, well, spelling, a set of conventions for noting down words which helps make connections between written and spoken English. These conventions are standardized and do not vary the way usage does. However, they are also *arbitrary* in the sense that they are merely symbols for aspects of spoken language.

The "period" used to be called a "full stop" because it marked where a speaker paused at the end of a grammatical unit. It could just as easily be called a "breather" and symbolized by an icon in the shape of a lung. Likewise, spelling is simply a way of attempting to represent speech sounds. We happen to use twenty-six letters of the alphabet to represent something like two hundred different English speech sounds. We could use different symbols altogether or strive (as some have) to create an alphabet that would represent these sounds unambiguously (an alphabet, say, where "s" always stood for a hissing sound and "c" for a hard glottal noise). Spelling is *conventional* as well; that is, over the years, "standard" forms have evolved. But it is useful to recall that this standardization has evolved with printing; in an earlier era, people spelt pretty much the way they felt like speling, and it didn't kreate partikularlie serious problems in comprehension.

Then, although spelling and mechanics are matters of convention and custom, they are nonetheless standard. A writer must follow them if he or she is to gain support of a readership. Teachers must be cautious about overteaching these codes. An exciting area of research in elementary children's language learning shows that letting kids play with "invented spellings," spelling the way they think words should be spelled, does no harm and eventually helps children come to standardized spellings. We think that in the end mechanics and spelling are learned as much from reading as from direct instruction anyway, but more on that topic later.

TEACHING GRAMMAR

For generations, teachers of English have presented lessons in grammar (the description of how English works), thinking they were teaching standard usage (the conventions of language followed by the middle and upper classes) and mechanics (the standard code of transcription conventions). The motivation behind this instruction has been to provide students with access to higher social levels. Thus students have been told such things as, "It's important for you to know grammar because you'll need it in life." It would be pleasant if life responded to laws like that, but not surprisingly, students have sensed that it doesn't and have gone on *not* learning the noun and the comma.

It seems apparent that teaching rules and laws does not significantly change performance, and most research attempts to prove otherwise have failed. As the epigraph by Postman and Weingartner describes, the connection simply isn't there. That teaching rules does not change performance is a function of the relationship between rules and performance—not of the quality of grammar or the imaginativeness of instruction. That is, from time to time you'll hear or read of a wonderful new grammar or technique for teaching. Generally such methods don't bring about the correctness millennium because grammars are not designed to change usage habits.

Teachers need to put the teaching of grammar in perspective for themselves and make their own set of judgments about what value it has in the schools. Without going into details or debating conflicting linguistic and sociolinguistic views, we will briefly present our own formula for putting grammar in its place by sketching out three areas where we think it is useful:

1. *As a source of information about language and language learning for teachers.* Grammar study, especially the study of transformational-generative grammar, provides numerous insights into the language learning process, and it is a vital part of a teacher's background. In fact, it is through the study of transformational grammar that one can most clearly see why the teaching of grammar does not promote language change. (See the recommended books at the end of this chapter for some introductory texts.)

2. *As a source of terms and tools for talking about language.* There are times when a knowledge of grammatical terminology provides a convenient way of talking about language. The discussion of language that will go on in the English class can sometimes be simplified through use of common terms. We advocate that in the junior high years the teacher offer a unit introducing most of the basic terms and definitions of grammar. However, this should be a brief unit, and the teacher should watch closely to see whether it is producing any positive results. After all, there are many ways of talking about language and composition, and grammar is only one of

them. In many cases, the time spent teaching grammar would be much more effectively given over to additional writing or speaking activities.

Several years ago, when Steve was working on some composition materials for a language arts series, the publisher told him to delay choosing a grammatical system until the publisher and another writer could settle on which kind of grammar they wanted to use for a proposed grammar strand. While they were making up their minds Steve wrote, and he discovered that he never felt handicapped by the lack of terms. Most of what he wanted to say about writing could be phrased without any reference to grammar. Obviously, *some* students can employ the abstract language of grammar to make changes in usage items. The brief introduction allows those who can to learn how, while not handicapping the others.

3. *As part of intellectual inquiry.* When divorced from concerns about usage and correctness, the study of syntax can be interesting for some students. Why is English a "word order" language? Does anyone know how German works? How does it differ? Who's studying Latin? What differences do you see between Latin and English grammars? We think that sort of study can help students gain a feeling for and an understanding of the nature of their mother tongue, but it should not be expected to eradicate "ain'ts" and "he don'ts" from the next set of papers.

TEACHING STANDARD ENGLISH

From Robert Pooley, *Teaching English Usage* (Urbana: National Council of Teachers of English, 1946), p. 14.

Good English is that form of speech which is appropriate to the purposes of the speaker, true to the language as it is, and comfortable to speaker and listener. It is the product of custom, neither cramped by rule nor freed from all restraint; it is never fixed, but changes with the organic life of the language.

Years ago Robert Pooley offered what has become a classic definition of "good English," recognizing its nature as arbitrary and conventional, but also acknowledging the role of "correctness" in "life." It was an important statement in the history of English because it recognized the sociological nature of usage and dialects, and it helped to destroy the notion of a *single* standard form of the language. Pooley's definition allows for the linguistic fact that within specific language communities, people can be quite comfortable with language forms not generally found acceptable in broader circles, and it recognized that it would be quite unnatural for speakers to change their style of speaking within that language community.

From those ideas has grown the concept of bidialectalism, which argues that the schools should not try to eradicate a natural home dialect but should encourage children to develop one or more additional dialects for use in other situations. The concept is an attempt to be humane and understanding about dialects, while at the same time allowing students to extend their linguistic capabilities.

Predators can and do use dialect differences to exploit and oppress, because ordinary people can be made to doubt their own value and to accept subservience if they can be made to despise the speech of their fathers. Obligatory bi-dialectalism for minorities is only another mode of exploitation, another way of making blacks behave as whites would like them to. It is unnecessary for communication, since the ability to understand other dialects is easily attained. . . . In the immediate present, the time and money now wasted on bi-dialectalism should be spent on teaching the children of the minorities to read . . . the direct attack on minority language, the attempt to compel bi-dialectalism, should be abandoned for an attempt to open the minds and enhance the lives of the poor and ignorant. At the same time, every attempt should be made to teach the majority to understand the life and language of the oppressed. Linguistic change is the effect and not the cause of social change. If the majority can rid itself of its prejudices, and if the minorities can get or be given an education, differences between dialects are unlikely to hurt anybody very much.

It is important to realize, as James Sledd has suggested, that teaching standard English by whatever method will not automatically open new doors to children. Often the lack of standard English is merely used as an excuse for rejecting people on racial, ethnic, or other grounds. Further, language is learned in response to needs felt by the language user. Unless students recognize a real opportunity to participate in a standard English community, they will not willingly learn its dialect. It should be noted, however, that even though speakers of different dialects do not always also speak standard English, they do have the ability to read standard English since most materials used in the schools are written in standard English.

Teachers might accomplish much more by approaching the problem indirectly. For instance, by helping students participate as fully as possible in the community of language through a variety of experiences—reading and writing, speaking and listening, role-playing—teachers can ensure that students are comfortable users of language in many situations. When and if students are given a meaningful opportunity to participate in a standard English community—through school, employment, or housing—they will be better able to adapt their language use.

Activities that can make students more aware of language differences include:

Translating the dialect they find in the fiction they read into the dialect they speak.

Choosing passages in fiction where young people are speaking to each other and showing how their language would be altered if they were speaking to a parent or a principal.

Making lists of teen slang words that most adults don't use and often don't understand and discussing why such different vocabularies come into being.

Writing a letter to a friend explaining a situation that occurred at school, then writing out the way the same situation would be explained to an adult and observing language differences.

Writing short speeches that could be presented to the class explaining what should be changed in the school, then composing a letter or petition to the principal or school board explaining needed changes.

Making dictionaries of terms and vocabulary used by specific groups of people: computer nuts, teenage girls, artists, school administrators, ministers, deep-sea divers, etc.

In addition, teachers ought to be concerned about destroying some of the old myths about good grammar, good usage, and upward mobility. If the schools spent as much time trying to end linguistic bias as they presently spend trying to enforce standard English, they might go a long way toward solving the problem. Certainly the teacher should concentrate on helping students—especially speakers of dialects other than standard English—understand what dialects are, where they come from, and what their effects on listeners are. Given such background understanding, students will be in a much better position to decide whether or not they want to change the way they talk or write.

OFFERING HELP WITH CORRECTNESS

We believe that the philosophy of writing (and, by implication, speaking) for the here and now, described in the previous chapter, offers the teacher a practical philosophy that can help resolve the dialects/correctness dilemma. The here-and-now approach strongly emphasizes the public use of language, recognizing that as students write and speak for audiences, they will realistically encounter situations where the use of a variant of standard English is appropriate.

What then? How do we provide the help students need to get their work into a form appropriate for their audience? One of Steve's former students, Judy Kortright, a teacher in Lansing, Michigan, struggled with the problem and came up with the idea of providing a variety of approaches to editing and correctness in the classroom. In *Teaching Correctness: An Alternative to Grammar* (Detroit: Michigan Council of Teachers of English, 1977), she wrote:

> Every year (at least once or twice) a nagging thought enters my brain: "Why aren't you teaching grammar, parts of speech, diagramming? Sometimes the question comes from a comment by a well-meaning parent, "When my son got to high school, he had to diagram sentences. He didn't even know where to begin." Or I am reminded that some teachers "believe in grammar" when a colleague down the hall comes running into my room, "Do you have any extra copies of *Warriner's* for eighth grade?"
>
> . . . I know, however, that there is no documented evidence in the literature to prove that the teaching of grammar improves writing skills. . . . I know, too, from personal experience that hour after hour on nouns and verbs only produces boredom, not good writers. The only students who really benefit from grammar are students who already read, write, and speak well, or those who are truly interested in how language is formed and works. For the average and especially for the marginal English student, grammar study is a waste of time.
>
> So what are the alternatives? What can I do to salve my conscience, to justify the lack of grammar drills in my classes? The answer for me, at least, is to find all the ways I can to teach correctness.

Ms. Kortright created what she called a "Correctness Corner" in her room: "this can be a table or a cubicle in the corner, a designated desk, or even a book shelf." At this activity center she provides the following kinds of materials:

Usage handbooks (either commercial handbooks or materials created by the teacher).

Usage activities (teacher-made activity cards reviewing the basic usage shibboleths: *lay-lie, sit-set,* etc).

Posters and charts (commercial and teacher-made materials that make help with correctness accessible).

Examples of good student writing.

Reference books (dictionaries, thesauruses, spelling demon lists).

Revision checklists (sequences of questions that guide students through editing and copyreading a paper).

Most important about the Correctness Corner, we think, is that it individualizes the process so that students can get the help they need at the time it is important. Further, the approach stresses independence, so that instead of the teacher constantly serving as proofreader, the students themselves become familiar with correctness aids and how to use them.

THE VOCABULARY QUESTION

Vocabulary lists have long been a staple of a large number of English classes. Teachers often feel that vocabulary work is expected of them, and then, too, they often like the structure it provides in the classroom. On Monday, students spend the period looking up assigned words, writing down definitions, and composing sentences that incorporate the words. On Friday, the class period is taken up with a test to see if students can define and spell the words. By the time the tests are corrected, another Friday has passed. As organized and fuss-free as this arrangement might seem to the English teacher, there are grave problems with this approach to learning vocabulary.

From Joan Nelson-Herber, "Expanding and Refining Vocabulary in Content Areas," *Journal of Reading,* April 1986.

Vocabulary instruction is more effective when it involves the learner in the construction of meaning through interactive processes rather than in memorizing definition or synonyms.

From Steven A. Stahl, "Principles of Effective Vocabulary Instruction," *Journal of Reading,* April 1986. Copyright © by the International Reading Association. Reprinted by permission of the publisher.

In other words, vocabulary instruction improves comprehension only when both definitions and context are given, and has the largest effect when a number of different activities or examples using the word in context are used. When only the definition is given without any examples of the word in context, or when the word is used only in context without the definition, the effects on comprehension are nonsignificant.

As Stahl and Nelson-Herber both point out, the look-up-the-word-and-know-it-for-the-test approach has virtually no effect on improving the vocabulary of students. Most research has shown that for vocabulary study to have any impact, the following conditions must be present in the instruction. Students need:

Help in relating the new words to knowledge they already have.

Assistance in developing elaborated word knowledge. Recognizing one specific definition isn't enough.

To be actively involved in learning new vocabulary. They need to do such things as thinking about new words, making up questions about them, and comparing them to other words.

Some of the following strategies can be used to meet the above conditions. Have students:

Tell what they already know about the word.

Rate new words in terms of whether they can define them, can use them, have heard of them, or have no knowledge of them.

Look at words in relationship to other words: "Can a HYPOCHONDRIAC be a MISER?

Study words in categories and discuss similarities/differences/relationships (one category might include such words as vivacious, spirited, exuberant, spry, lethargic, lassitude, languor).

Brainstorm all the ways they can think of that the word can be used.

Find words similar to a vocabulary word and grapple with shades of meaning.

Make up bumper stickers or buttons to illustrate some aspect of the vocabulary word. For example, possibilities for the word HYPOCHONDRIAC are "If you're sick—HONK!" and "Ill is in!"

Create multiple choice items about the words. An example: If you are handling CONTRABAND items:

(a) Your taxes would be high.
(b) You could end up in jail.
(c) You would advertise in the local papers.

Rank words from most desirable to least desirable, from largest to smallest, or in any other categories that would work.

Write down all the images you have about a word.

Of course, vocabulary is still best dealt with in the context of the activities or literature being used in class, and students are most interested in knowing new words when they need the word for an assignment or a piece of writing that they are committed to completing. So one of the most helpful things a teacher can do to stimulate vocabulary development is as simple as this: help students find projects and activities they can get involved in.

EXPLORING THE DIMENSIONS OF LANGUAGE

In the debates over grammar and correctness, teachers often lose sight of the fact that one of our goals as teachers of English is to help students gain more personal power through language. We want students to be articulate so that they can explain their stances and feelings, to write so that they can share their views of the world, and to read so that they can get the information or the enjoyment they seek. We want them to be curious about language and wonder how it works, to think about nonverbal communication and be aware of its effects, to be willing to take risks with language by using new words and phrases, and to be aware of how language affects a reader or listener.

We are convinced that if students knew more of language beyond correctness—that is, if they better understood how language itself functions—they would be more effective writers and readers. Many classroom activities exist to teach just that.

Many alternative forms of language study fall in the general area of "sociolinguistics"—the study of language, human beings, and their interactions—and it is an area that students find fascinating. Although knowledge of language and society will not automatically improve students' language skills, it often helps them deepen their feeling for language and how it shapes their lives.

We propose that teachers explore language through "interludes," language mini-units of a day or a week. After students have finished a major project in reading and writing, pause to let them try some of the following language explorations.

1. *Body Talk.* Study "kinesics": how people interact through physical mannerisms. The concept of body language is intriguing (and even a bit frightening), and young people of many ages enjoy talking about it and exploring its consequences. How can you tell when somebody is shy or nervous? How do you know when somebody is lying to you just by looking at him or her? How do you size up a new teacher or a new kid on the first day of school? Play "Emotional Charades," where students mime basic emotions—love, hate, excitement, fear—using only facial expressions or physical movement. Some students may enjoy observing people at a distance and trying to record their nonverbal "conversations." By being aware

of what this nonverbal form of communication can mean, students can more easily communicate because they can more accurately read the responses of other people. Body talk also offers some interesting possibilities for filmmaking and photography, both of which can supply visual data for class analysis and discussion.

2. *Artifacts.* The objects that people use and venerate tell a great deal about their value systems. Ask students to assume that your city has been covered by a giant lava flow and then unearthed by archeologists from an alien culture hundreds of years later. Have each student choose one surviving object that the aliens might find and do an analysis of the unspoken "language" of that object. What would the strangers conclude if they dug up the Golden Arches of a McDonald's hamburger palace? What might they learn from a snowmobile? From the architecture of a city? From one of its automobiles or from parks or factories? This activity encourages students to think, make generalizations, draw conclusions, and just figure out what an object alone can say about itself merely from the way it looks. As a variation, have each student bring in an object he or she prizes personally and turn it over to a partner for analysis.

3. *Baby Talk.* Psycholinguists who have examined the earliest stages of language acquisition have learned to write "baby grammars" that describe the young child's growing mastery of English. Ask students who have young brothers and sisters (age one to three years) to bring in some tape recordings of their speech. Split your students into groups and have them discover the regularities—the "grammar"—of the child's speech. How does babbling seem to work? What kinds of words do children learn first? What patterns do they use for two-word strings? How do they seem to move from two- and three-word strings to whole sentences? While students should not try to duplicate the complex work of linguists in the field, studying baby talk brings about many insights into how human beings learn and use language. They will be able to see clearly that formal instruction is not the only way a speaker learns the rules of a language.

4. *Tutoring.* Locate some younger students who have reading difficulties and arrange for interested students from your class to read with and to them. Hold frequent discussions with your team of tutors to discuss their observations and problems. Some of your students may be interested in joining a group like Literacy Volunteers of America, which works with adult nonreaders. Again, encourage your students to share their observations about how language works and is learned.

5. *Greetings.* What do we mean when we say, "How are you?" What happens if you actually answer somebody by giving a health report or an emotional summary? Give your students the task of observing and analyzing some of the hidden communications that underlie greetings and farewells. Some questions that they might seek to answer:

How do greetings and farewells differ depending on whether people are
friends, enemies, strangers, or rivals?
How do styles of ritual language differ with age? With culture or race?
What happens when people violate the unwritten rules of ritual talk (e.g.,
by *not* making a ritual greeting before speaking or by answering in
detail when asked, "How 'ya doin'?")?

This activity can help students become more aware that what we say is
not always what we mean and can help them understand why we speak that
way and how we use language to get out of uncomfortable spots.

6. *Euphemism.* George Orwell's 1946 essay "Politics and the English
Language" remains a most effective attack on the use of euphemistic language to hide a person's true intent and purposes. After having them read
the essay, send your students out to collect examples of euphemism at all
levels of school and society. Simply analyzing and laughing at euphemism
helps to make students more sensitive to it, but you can also encourage them
to explore euphemism by such activities as translating clear prose into
gobbledygook or writing instructions for a simple process—scrambling an
egg—in euphemistic language. You might also want to explore the protec-
tive aspect of euphemism so that students can see that we use language as
a way to cover up what we can't or don't want to deal with. Have the
students role-play some scenes in a society where everyone is blunt, direct,
forthright, and to the point. Does this become the best of all possible
worlds?

7. *Doublespeak.* Watergate and Iran-gate made the nation acutely conscious of "doublespeak," political language that obscures and covers up
rather than revealing the truth. In *Teaching About Doublespeak* (Urbana:
National Council of Teachers of English, 1976), a number of specialists
explore the investigation of political jargon and gobbledygook in the classroom. Why not have your students investigate the misuse of language
through published statements in your area, then possibly present a set of
Dubious Doublespeak Awards for the worst examples they find?

8. *Dialect Study.* Few people understand how or why dialects work, and
too many adults are obsessed by dialect differences. To help bring enlighten-
ment, engage the students in an informal examination of dialects. If you
have speakers of different dialects, set up groups in which the students learn
about alternative expressions. Have the two groups prepare bidialectal dictionaries. Even if you don't have a rich mixture of dialects in a class,
students can conduct a number of investigations around school and community to explore dialects. One example: Have students listen for the nefarious
"ain't" and chart its occurrences in speech.

9. *Inventing a New Language.* Many variations of this activity are possible. One is to "abolish" English and have the students design the theoretical
model for a new, ideal language. What would be the most efficient way for

this language to express relationships? What features of English would the students maintain? What aspects would they eliminate? How would the new language be written? The students might even try to develop samples of this language.

Alternatively, students can create a new lexicon based on English syntax—that is, they can invent a new vocabulary for the existing word order. "Nadsat," the teen language in Anthony Burgess's *A Clockwork Orange,* provides one example. Orwell's essay on "Newspeak" in *1984* provides another.

Students can also create pig Latin forms, systematically altering word structure so that only someone in possession of the code can translate. Developing sign languages offers additional possibilities.

10. *The Language of Personal Space.* Like body talk and the language of greetings and farewells, people have secret languages that involve the use of personal space. In two classic books, *The Silent Language* (New York: Fawcett, 1962) and *The Hidden Dimension* (Garden City: Doubleday, 1966), Edward Hall investigated some of these cultural-linguistic uses of space. As a classroom activity students can duplicate some of Hall's experiments with face-to-face conversation so that they can experience firsthand communication without words. After pointing out that various cultures find different speaking distances comfortable, ask the students to discover what their own speaking conventions are. At what distance—two feet, one foot, eighteen inches—do students become uncomfortably close to one another? At what distance are they uncomfortably far away? How do we feel toward people who stand nose-to-nose with us in conversation?

In *The Hidden Dimension,* Hall goes into more complex areas of the language of space, including such problems as overcrowding, the design and layout of floor space, the theft of urban space by automobiles, and the human's need for privacy. As with other physical languages, students can deduce much of the structure of the language of space through simple experimentation and analysis. Again, photography and filmmaking projects can easily evolve from the class study.

11. *Games and Puzzles.* Games involving language are as old as humankind, and such games often help to develop a sense of language. *Scrabble,* for instance, is a game that many students enjoy, and it serves incidentally as a vocabulary builder. Crossword puzzles, diacrostics, and anagrams are enjoyed by other students. Such games and puzzles challenge students and make them want to stretch their vocabulary and find new or more precise words. Most bookstores carry dozens of paperback collections of word games, attesting to the popularity of this pastime. Purchase a half-dozen of these books, tear them into individual sheets, and file them away to produce a game collection of several hundred activities.

12. *Analyzing Handwriting.* This activity won't necessarily improve penmanship, but it may produce a good deal more interest in it. Many hand-

writing analysis books are available in paperback stores and at supermarket checkout counters. Tell students about the basic principles of analysis, or let that be a topic for a small-group presentation, and let them go. Students can analyze one another's writing, discuss signatures of famous personalities, experiment with disguising their own handwriting, or play guessing games about signatures.

13. *Propaganda.* An examination of World War II propaganda—German, Japanese, and Allied—makes a fascinating study. Examples are readily available—from tapes of Hitler's speeches to copies of leaflets dropped from planes on enemy troops. After a study of these materials and some discussion of how they work, turn the students loose to find examples of contemporary propaganda, often more subtle but seldom using new or different techniques.

14. *Learning a Language.* For years parents and teachers have rationalized the study of grammar on the ground that it was necessary for students engaged in the study of foreign languages. Not to miss a good bet, foreign language teachers have claimed utility for their discipline in helping students understand English. Both groups have little support for their positions. English teachers should not teach grammar simply because other teachers use a grammatical method. Teaching through grammar isn't any more successful in foreign languages than it is in English. Moreover, research has yet to show any direct correlation between skill in foreign languages and skill in English.

However, when divorced from utilitarian teaching schemes, knowing— or better, using—a foreign language may well help people become more comfortable, competent users of their native language. In classes that include both native speakers of English and speakers of another language, let the two groups teach each other. Drill and exercises are not necessary. Often simply allowing the students to struggle with one another's languages over everyday concerns will be sufficient. If you don't have a mixed class of this sort, you might want to seek out tutoring opportunities for students who are interested in foreign languages and acknowledge their work as part of their regular English studies.

15. *Learning Esperanto.* A Polish linguist, L. L. Zamenhof, created Esperanto as an international language one hundred years ago. Firmly rooted in the Romance languages, it offers a simple and consistent grammar and a consistent spelling system. Millions of people speak Esperanto worldwide, and there are genuine opportunities to speak it. Write to the Esperanto League of North America, El Cirrito, California, for more information.

16. *Study of Names.* The study of names can be an interesting class project. A common approach is for students to use a desk dictionary to find out the significance or meaning of their own name. Then the students move outward, first studying names around their city—names of streets, mountains, lakes—and then names around the state and country. An excellent

resource is Alan Wolk's *The Naming of America* (New York: Thomas Nelson, 1977), which delves into place names. We especially enjoy studying the names created by developers for condominiums and malls: "Woodland Hills," which is a patch of asphalt; "Paddock Farms," which is a high-rise apartment. What do students see as the logic or hype behind such names?

17. *Logotypes.* A logotype or trademark is a self-contained message, a one-word visual language designed to identify a product or company and to project an image of it. Most industries spend a remarkable amount of time developing, testing, and marketing any new logo that they choose to use. Have students collect a number of logos (they can easily find hundreds in newspapers, magazines, and the yellow pages) and analyze the language. They can think about the impact of the shape and color and why this logo has appeal. Afterward, invite the students to develop some trademarks of their own, perhaps a new insignia or logo for the school, for your class, for fictitious companies, or for themselves.

18. *Codes and Ciphers.* -•-•/--/-••/•••/•/•••//•-/•-•/•//•-//--/-•--/••• /-/•/•-•/-•--/// (Codes are a mystery.) Codes and ciphers are as old as history, and literally thousands of ways of sending secret messages have been generated. Books for young adult readers on the subject of codes, cryptology, international code breaking, and code design appear at regular intervals, so check your library.

19. *Inductive Definitions.* Few adults or young people know much about the process of dictionary making. They don't realize that definitions grow from popular usage rather than being created arbitrarily by a panel of wordsters. Assign the class a project of defining a word—just a single word. Students are not to consult dictionaries; rather, they should collect citations—examples of the word in use—and from that evidence work inductively toward a definition. Words like "break" or "fast" (or "breakfast") are a good choice because of their functions as different parts of speech. From this activity, you can help students understand some of the ways in which words take on meaning, while helping them realize that meanings are flexible and evolutionary.

20. *Printing Processes.* The printing of books and magazines is interesting for many students, and modern printing processes are nothing short of miraculous in their speed, quality, and accuracy. Let the students investigate printing processes, beginning with hand-set, single-sheet presses and working toward computer-set type, offset presses, computer dot-matrix printers, and laser jet printers. A visit to a printing plant for the whole class or just for interested students would be appropriate. When young people learn how books, magazines, and newspapers are made, their reading interest in those publications seems to increase considerably.

21. *Electronic Communications.* The effect of modern electronics on communication systems has been as miraculous as the effect of printing. Encourage your students who have interests in science and engineering to

study electronics and the communications field. Many nontechnical volumes have been written about such devices as the transistor or diode chip and their effect on communication systems. Other topics of interest might be computer technology, miniaturization, laser beams as a form of communication, television and radio, and the electronics of the telephone.

22. *The Language of Advertising.* Although teachers often deprecate the "bad grammar" of ads, many advertisements show extremely clever use of language through wordplay and puns. In "Teaching English Through the Language of Advertising" (*The English Journal,* February 1976), Don Nilsen shows that the way advertisers break rules is highly creative. He uses ads to demonstrate everything from phonetics ("Emperor Lawnmowers: Built to Last a Lawn Time!") to ambiguities ("Salem refreshes naturally").

23. *The Language of Science.* Science books are filled with marvelous and curious terms. Where do they come from? What is the origin of such terms as *laser, biodegradable, black hole, quark, sea urchin, mollusk,* and *mesomorph?* Conduct an etymology unit on scientific words. As a variation, teach your students to read the ingredient labels on packages to learn what they are eating. Why must disodium EDTA be added to "prevent spoilage" in something that is labeled, "Fresh, Hometown, Hearth-Baked Bread"?

24. *The Language of Law.* Collect samples of legal documents: insurance policies, contracts, warranties, rules of the road. Help the students learn to decode the language, both through examining technical or specialized words and through studying the very careful wording that complicates legal writing. As a variation, have students study advertising and promotional claims and disclaimers and the use of "waffle" or "weasel" which guard a manufacturer from law suits.

25. *Idioms.* Explain to students that idioms are phrases or sayings which cannot be understood from the individual word meanings. Have students brainstorm in groups to create lists of idioms. Each student then chooses one to illustrate in a literal sense. "You're a real stick-in-the-mud." "She's got you wrapped around her little finger." Through this activity students come to be more aware that language isn't fixed in meaning and that it changes as new expressions are created.

26. *Newspaper Headlines.* Have pupils search for ambiguous and misleading headlines such as "Revolting Officers Shot" or "Giant Waves Down Liner's Funnel," metaphorical headlines such as "Reagan Faces Storm" and "Bridge Designer Blasted," and headlines where choice of words is significant or there is a play on words. (This activity was shared with us by Ken Watson of Sydney University during his visit to the States.)

27. *Comic-Cartoon Notebooks.* Bobbye Goldstein studied the language used in comics and cartoons and found that difficult words were common. She also found that students were very willing to look at language through comics and cartoons. She suggests that you have students collect cartoons and comics and put them in notebooks in such categories as figurative language, colloquial expressions, and puns. The students can identify palin-

dromes and can even make lists of multiple meanings of some of the words. Contests can be held to see which student locates the most difficult words in the comics. (See "Looking at Cartoons and Comics in a New Way," by Bobbye S. Goldstein, in the *Journal of Reading,* April 1986, pp. 657–661.)

These twenty-seven activities barely begin to scratch the surface of possible language explorations for the English class. As interludes, they change the pace of the class. As valid linguistic activities, they heighten students' critical awareness of something they consume and produce in prodigious quantities: language.

As a final activity, one that can even serve as an examination if you wish, ask your students to use their new powers of linguistic understanding to analyze the following passage from Kenneth Graham's *The Wind in the Willows:*

> The toad, having finished his breakfast, picked up a stout stick and swung it vigorously, belabouring imaginary animals. "I'll learn 'em to steam my house!" he cried. "I'll learn 'em, I'll learn 'em."
>
> "Don't say 'learn 'em,' Toad," said the Rat, greatly shocked. "It's not good English."
>
> "What are you always nagging at Toad for?" inquired the Badger rather peevishly. "What's the matter with his English? It's the same what I use myself, and if it's good enough for me, it ought to be good enough for you!"
>
> "I'm very sorry," said the Rat humbly. "I only *think* it ought to be 'teach 'em,' not 'learn 'em.'"
>
> "But we don't *want* to teach 'em," replied the Badger. "We want to *learn* 'em—learn 'em, learn 'em! And what's more, we're going to *do* it, too."

EXPLORATIONS

• If you want to be able to answer the questions of students about correctness matters, you need to have on hand a great deal of diverse material to satisfy different learners. You need the usual handbooks plus games, visuals, and self-instructional packets that present the material in many ways. Choose a skill that a student might want to master (say, how to proofread a page or how to use quotation marks) and develop a range of materials presenting it from several points of view. Field-test your materials with students. If you are working with a group of people, each person can choose a different skill and ditto or reproduce the materials to share.

• Some issues centering on altering dialects:

Can a teacher honestly preserve the home dialect while teaching an alternative school dialect?

Does possession of a standard dialect in fact give members of a society upward mobility?

• A broadly based skills program that puts grammar and correctness in their place is likely to run into some opposition from parents and administrators, who will cry "Neglect!" Interview some basics enthusiasts to explore the reasons for their concern. Develop some explanations that allow a teacher to run a broadly based language program while still providing satisfactory evidence that basics are being adequately covered.

• Create some materials for language interludes. These might be done as individual resource or activity packets, or as handouts for use with an entire class. Start with those of the twenty-seven that you found most interesting, then branch off into the recommended readings that follow and discover other possibilities.

RELATED READINGS

For the teacher seeking more information on the various grammatical systems, we recommend Constance Weaver's *Grammar for Teachers: Perspectives and Definitions* (Urbana, Ill.: National Council of Teachers of English, 1979), which explores the general nature of grammars and presents a grammar that combines aspects of traditional, structural, and transformational grammars. On dialects and usage, see Robert Pooley's *Teaching English Usage* (originally published in 1946, now available as a reprint from the National Council of Teachers of English) or Martin Joos's classic, *The Five Clocks* (New York: Harcourt Brace Jovanovich, 1967), a lucid explanation of how language usage shifts with various situations. For an excellent discussion of black English and its origins, as well as consideration of implications for schooling, read Geneva Smitherman's *Talkin' and Testifyin'* (New York: Holt, Rinehart & Winston, 1977). Douglas Barnes's *Language, the Learner, and the School* (London: Penguin, 1972), also a modern classic, is useful in the context of this chapter by focusing broadly on the social acquisition of language in the schools.

In the practical domain, Herbert Kohl's *Book of Puzzlements* (New York: Schocken, 1981) is an outstanding collection of word games and teasers. *The Journal of Reading,* April 1986, is a special issue on vocabulary and includes articles that give strategies for helping students pay attention to and hypothesize about words, as well as articles that describe effective ways to involve students in vocabulary work. S. I. Hayakawa's *Language in Thought and Action* (Harcourt Brace Jovanovich, 1982) is also packed with ideas for language experiments.

The Spoken Language

The development of the personality is inextricably bound up with the development of language. Language is the basic and essential instrument in the humanising of the species: without it thought above very primitive levels is impossible. Language and man are in continual interaction; change the man in some way and you change the language he uses; change the language he uses and you change the man. On the one hand the process of growth through education and experience causes him to reach out for new language in which to understand and communicate. On the other hand this language contains new thought and shades of thought, new feeling and shades of feeling, which help to determine such growth. His ability to direct rather than to be directed by experience, his ability to establish human relationships, are intimately related to his capacity for language; the frustrations of the inarticulate go deep. And it must be borne in mind that "language" in this context is overwhelmingly the spoken language; even in the (historically) rare literate societies such as our own this remains true. Without oracy human fulfillment is impossible; speech and personality are one.

WHETHER its form is conversation, lecture, gossip, discussion, or monologue, spoken English is one of the most central and ubiquitous skills that a member of the community of language masters. From birth, people acquire information, clarify their thoughts and beliefs, and transmit ideas and information to others principally by means of talk and conversation. By far the greatest part of our use of language involves oral English, either receptive or productive. Even nonreaders and haters of writing have been known to enjoy talking—over Coke or telephone—for hours. As James Britton has remarked, our lives are "afloat on a sea of talk."

Despite the pervasiveness of oral language in our lives, it has seldom been given much attention in the schools. Speech activities are often isolated in separate courses or brought into the English class only as enrichment units. Further, speech instruction seldom moves beyond a round of five-minute talks—the impromptu speech—rather than dealing with the full spectrum of spoken languages.

Nor do we necessarily do much with the spoken language that goes on in school. How often does a "discussion" class turn out to be dominated by a teacher, for whom discussion is merely another way of delivering his or her view of the truth, rather than an exploratory use of language. It is interesting to observe that the term *discuss* has even taken on a meaning in written English. A typical essay or examination question will ask the student to "discuss the effects of the French Revolution. . . ." In this context, "discuss" in fact means "explicate." In many classes, oral discussion is little more than an explication by the teacher, with occasional token questions tossed out to the students.

This neglect and abuse of oral English may well grow from a kind of blindness to our linguistic environment. Marshall McLuhan once observed that "One thing about which a fish knows absolutely nothing is water." It can be said with equal accuracy, "One thing about which talkers know next to nothing is talk."

TEACHING ORAL ENGLISH

"Teaching" oral language is no easy task. Linguists and sociologists are only beginning to understand the complexity of the spoken. Oral language involves a complex interaction of speaker and listener, of voice, tone, style, intonation, nonverbal expression. For example, experts in kinesics—body language—recognize that a person sends out hundreds of nonverbal signals—eyebrow twitches, frowns, leg crossings and uncrossings—every second while he or she is speaking and listening. When teachers try to "contain," to teach oral English, they are driven to present oversimplified advice on eye contact, holding note cards, and speaking in a firm, clear voice.

To put it boldly: the spoken language cannot truly be "taught." People learn to speak and listen by doing it successfully. Conversely, they become inarticulate and inept when their oral language experiences are unsuccessful or constrained. Our pedagogical focus in this chapter, then, will not be on the "how" of teaching; rather we will be concerned with ways of enriching classroom talk so that growth takes place naturally. (The same philosophy, of course, has driven our approach to reading and writing in Chapters 6 through 10.)

Learning the skills of oral English is closely related to using them, and we believe the teacher should focus attention on making the classroom a place where the use of spoken language is strongly supported. The student who is experienced in many speech areas—conversation, dialogue, discussion—is likely to be a fuller participant in the community of language than one who has spent the school years uttering one-sentence answers to recitation questions.

A wide range of spoken language activities is valuable in a classroom. These include speech that is principally expressive—done for the purposes and needs of the speaker—and productive, aimed at communicating with an audience or a listener. Some activities are spontaneous and occur without the teacher; others must be planned and structured.

THE USES OF CONVERSATION

It is especially important that the teacher consider the underlying motivation behind speech activities. Through attempting to understand what happens when people talk, teachers are best able to structure a classroom setting that supports spoken language. For instance, conversation—chat, gossip, rappin', shootin' the breeze—has sometimes been seen as something outside the educational process. Teachers cut off student conversations at the beginning of a class: "Alright now, let's get down to *business.*" The fact is, conversation is "business" of a very serious kind, albeit not always academic business. Chat serves a great many different functions in a person's life, many of which are not obvious at a superficial level of examination.

For instance, sociologists and linguists have identified a number of uses of conversation by black youngsters, each style serving a different kind of psychological-sociological function. There are such variants as "rapping" (talking to express one's personality), "jiving" or "shucking" (putting someone on, usually a white person), "running it down" (giving information or advice), "gripping" (acknowledging a superior without losing face), "copping a plea" (surrendering and pleading for mercy), and "sounding" (trying to arouse or release emotions through boasts, insults, and accusations).

Most of us recognize a similar range of language use in our own conversations. We use chat and gossip in many ways to establish our own self-esteem, to make initial contact with others, to assess feelings, to form relationships, and to seek information—in essence, to structure our world and to compare it to the worlds of others. Chat is the spoken equivalent of the writing journal, a language form that operates on the borderline between a person's inner and outer worlds.

This is not intended to glorify chitchat or to suggest that teachers are doing a good job helping students become orally literate if they merely let them exchange trivia. However, a teacher must recognize the critical role of conversation in people's lives and support it—welcome it—inside the classroom. In fact, one of the major ways in which people will become good conversationalists instead of gossipmongers is for the school to allow them to chat about matters of more than a trivial nature. People can discuss complex ideas as comfortably as they gossip about a new hairstyle. Through experiences in literature and composing, the teacher can provide students with a steadily expanding series of topics for conversation.

Students should feel free to discuss personal and academic problems, projects, books, television programs, films, one another, people, and world problems. When acknowledged as important, conversation will become the foundation for the entire spoken language program. Indeed, without students who are secure and competent conversationalists, other oral language activities will be dull, static, or ineffectual.

While conversation is not something easily structured, the teacher can demonstrate support for it by a device like the *question box*. Set up a container somewhere in your class in which students can deposit questions that they would like to discuss. From time to time, open up the question box and let the students hash over one of the topics—as an entire class or in small groups. Even the room environment can contribute to the ease with which chat takes place, and the teacher might want to set up a conversation corner where students can go to talk when their regular classwork is done.

STORYTELLING

John Rouse has suggested the intriguing idea that "we are all storytellers, and our lives are the fictions we have made" (*The Completed Gesture: Myth, Character, and Education.* New York: Skyline Books, 1978). As "fiction makers," he suggests, people abstract from their past experiences to create stories, and they use stories both to access that experience and to sketch out scenarios for their future lives. Rouse's formula for teaching language use is simple and effective: Get people to tell you a good story and you will have released the real language power that they have inside themselves. Storytelling, like the less formal forms of conversing, serves many functions. It is often as important to the storyteller as to the listener.

Stories can be told in many ways—in speech and writing, in poetry, prose, and drama—but the most fundamental kind of storytelling is done face-to-face. Like conversation, storytelling is more easily promoted than taught, better encouraged than demanded. But a number of experiences can be provided to get it started.

One technique used by Rouse is to have students interview each other, with the listener/interviewer assigned the task of digging out the other person's "real" story. Eventually the *listener* retells the story to others, with the original storyteller having the option of correcting and amplifying.

Reminiscing is a natural starting point for storytelling. Without drifting to the summer vacation motif, the teacher can often lead off a class with a story about his or her own past that invites students to share some of their experiences.

Literature—especially stories by and about adolescents—provides innumerable starting points. Following the reading of a good story, the teacher can simply ask, "Has anything like this ever happened to you?"

Tall tales, boasting, and exaggeration have an important storytelling function, since in creating an exaggerated tale, the students draw upon, expand, and develop their own view of the world.

Scary stories are among the common property of humankind: everyone has one and everyone wants to share one. After bringing in a book such as Alvin Schwartz's *More Scary Stories to Tell in the Dark* (Harper & Row, 1984) and reading a few stories, give students a chance to discuss the real and imaginary terrors of their lives.

Storytelling is a natural extension of conversation, and often the teacher can initiate it simply by saying "tell me more" when an incident or anecdote flashes by in informal conversation.

In many classes, once the storytelling concept is introduced, the students become hooked on the idea and become habitual storytellers and story collectors.

DIALOGUES AND PARTNERSHIPS

The dialogue—a conversation between two people—is a fundamental unit of spoken English. Dialogue is simple and direct, an especially efficient form for productive work. Unfortunately, the dynamics of the two-member group has been neglected. Typically, students work together only to correct papers ("Exchange papers, class"). Indeed, *collaboration* is a term that to some teachers is synonymous with "cheating." While two-member groups have occasional problems with freeloading, inbreeding, or compounding of errors, they also avoid many of the problems that evolve in larger groups. Their use should be fully exploited in the classroom. The following are among the good ways to launch partnership projects.

1. *Collaborative Writing (version 1)*. Students work together as coauthors of a piece of writing—poem, play, story, or essay. This technique allows

students to share writing skills with each other and to produce a stronger piece of writing than either could alone.

2. *Collaborative Writing (version 2).* Students work on their own writing in partnership with another person, who serves as a writing coach in:

Prewriting. (The students share ideas and talk over what they plan to write.)

Writing. (The partners coach each other through rough spots and listen to readings of the drafts.)

Postwriting. (The collaborators serve as editors and proofreaders for one another, each taking responsibility for getting the other's work in the best possible shape.)

3. *Minidebates.* Students take opposite sides of an issue and discuss it, either for themselves alone or before an audience.

4. *Response to Literature.* Partners read the same poem, story, or novel and work out their interpretation and response to it.

5. *Interviews (1).* One student interviews another about an area of expertise.

6. *Interviews (2).* As a team, students interview an outside expert: a parent, someone in business or industry, a community leader, a guest speaker.

7. *Dramatic Presentations.* The partners prepare a dramatic presentation of some of their work—say, a collection of poems or a two-character play.

A number of writers have discussed the values of education in the old-time one-room schoolhouse, pointing out that in those schools, children gained a sense of community that may have been lost in large public schools. Much of that sense of community grew from collaborative learning and partnership projects, sometimes by pedagogical default. The teacher in the one-room schoolhouse was simply too busy to work with every child as often as necessary, and partnerships were set up with older children teaching younger, the skilled teaching the unskilled. Although a few specialists have argued for a return to the one-room schoolhouse as a cure for our educational woes, the advantages of a strong collaborative learning program should not be ignored within the present system. The teacher can recreate the one-room schoolhouse, in spirit if not in fact, through the extensive use of partnership learning activities.

TEACHER-LED DISCUSSIONS

One of the most difficult skills for a teacher to master, and one that must be refined throughout a teaching career, is that of leading whole class discussions. The teacher faces a collection of thirty or more students and somehow must get them to *talk.* In its weakest form (which also happens to be a negative by-product of one-room schooling), teacher-led discussion is *recitation,* with students supplying answers to questions in order to demonstrate mastery of a text. One of our students described teacher-led discussions this way: "Too often in my experience these were exercises in getting to a predetermined conclusion with the teacher acting as the herder." But at its best, class discussion takes on a momentum of its own under the gentle guidance of the teacher, with talk helping to generate new knowledge and understanding.

The heart of the teacher-led discussion is *the discussion question,* and the quality and kinds of questions that teachers ask will make or break any class session.

Robert Nash and David Shiman have cited research that shows how unaware teachers are of the kinds and frequency of questions that they ask: "Summarizing the few research studies done on the questioning process, Seymour Sarason reports that while elementary teachers thought they averaged between twelve and twenty questions per half hour, actually the number ranged between *forty-five* and *one hundred and fifty.* " This is obviously a pattern drill and recitation, not that of a sustained classroom discussion.

Like most teachers, English teachers spend far too little time learning to ask effective questions. In college programs, teacher educators rarely take the time to teach questioning skills; when they do, the questioning process is often treated either in a cursory manner or in such a highly technical way that it loses any practical value. Further, prospective and in-service teachers seldom have the opportunity to observe a good questioner at work. Yet, questioning is perhaps the central skill in the teaching-learning experience, because, whether we are aware of it or not, we bombard our students with all kinds of inquiries throughout the day.

Nash and Shiman describe three kinds of questioning categories and suggest that teachers become conscious of how often they use questions of each type:

1. *Factual.* Such questions call for right/wrong answers. While they may occasionally be useful to warm up a class or to check on comprehension or

understanding, factual questions are a conversational dead end, and sustained discussions seldom grow from them.

2. *Conceptual.* These ask students to move beyond mere facts to make generalizations. The key word in these questions is often *why,* since it asks the students to generalize and to draw on their own values. (The reader may have noted that in science fiction films and books, a common way to make a computer self-destruct is to ask it the simple question, "Why?" Computers, which are basically fact processors, do not like to answer what we in education call "thought questions.")

3. *Contextual.* These questions combine both factual and conceptual questions by having the students draw on their own perceptions to reach generalizations and to make conclusions of their own. Thus, instead of simply asking factual questions—"What is the rhyme scheme of this poem?" "What do adjectives modify?"—the teacher draws on facts as they are perceived by the student: "How does the rhyme of this poem affect *you?*" "Why do you suppose the author used 'purple' to describe the girl's eyes?" The contextual question takes facts, perceived in context, and encourages the student to create generalizations. (Readers will recognize a strong parallel between these three types of questions and the plan of questioning about literature we presented in Chapter 6. The two schemata were developed independently but get at an underlying hierarchy of questions that have been recognized by researchers.)

We find that we can often subsume all these question categories under the *open-ended* question, the question *to which the asker doesn't necessarily know the answer.* The open-ended question encourages students to explore new territory and even to carry the teacher along with them. Factual questions—"What time is it?" "Where did you put the dustpan?" "How much is the British pound worth these days?"—are usually closed. Without diminishing the importance of such questions at times, we must observe that they terminate discussion rather than opening it up.

But not all nonfactual questions are open-ended. Socrates is widely praised for his use of the questioning or inductive method, yet, for all his skill, he seldom asked open-ended questions. Like a trial lawyer (or a good many teachers), Socrates simply kept on asking questions until he had elicited the single statement or concept he had in mind, at which point the discussion came to a close. The "Socratic method" so widely praised in education is sometimes just another way of leading students to predetermined answers.

But can one always ask open-ended questions? Aren't there times when the teacher will know the answer or lead the students toward an accepted concept? Of course there are, but here it is helpful to recall Nash and Shiman's emphasis on *personal* interpretation of information through contextual questions. If teachers phrase questions in terms of the students' perceptions—"What did *you* think of the ending of the poem?" "What do *you* see as the key words in the passage?" "What do *you* think are the most important facts in the case?"—then discussion flows, even if teachers have in mind some basic ideas and concepts of their own. Similarly, when academic concepts are phrased in contextual questions, students assimilate knowledge: "How do *you* see the law of supply and demand operating in your own life?" "What are some of the ways you might be able to use minimum/maximum calculations in developing a personal spending budget?"

When teachers begin to think about formulating good questions, they need to think in terms of questions that first of all strike a responsive chord in themselves, that seem interesting to them as learners in their own right. If the teacher isn't interested and intrigued by the questions, chances are that the students won't be either. Student reaction will quickly confirm whether the question was a good one or not.

In fact, one of the most useful ways for the teacher to avoid asking closed questions is to avoid taking sole responsibility for asking questions at all. As educators from John Dewey on have argued, learning how to ask a good question is even more difficult than learning how to answer one. The schools characteristically do very little to help students become good question askers. Perhaps the most important role a teacher can play in leading group discussion is not that of setting the agenda of questions but that of helping students channel and direct their own questions for investigation.

THE SMALL GROUP

Small group work offers enormous potential to the teacher. Such groups have many of the advantages of whole class talk activities without the disadvantages of large size and unwieldiness. Further, small groups encourage a conversational tone that the large class does not. Groups allow the sharing of ideas and common learning. They are more effective than the large group in pooling knowledge, because the small group draws out the quiet people who do not contribute to the whole class. Above all, small groups foster conversational autonomy by keeping the teacher out of the picture: students must structure their own ideas and experiences.

Volumes have been written about small group dynamics and leadership, and any teacher who wants to use small groups effectively ought to study one of those books in detail. Several are listed at the end of the chapter. However, a few general considerations are appropriate for all small group work.

Group Size and Composition

To work well, a group must have compatible membership and be of appropriate size, two factors that are at best unpredictable. Research is delightfully circuitous on this matter. We read once that research had established *five* as the perfect number for groups, but we read on to discover this merely meant that researchers have learned that people in groups of four seldom feel that the group is too large, while people in groups of six don't seem to feel the group is too small.

Many research workers have observed that groups with odd-numbered membership—three, five, and seven—seem to be more productive than even-numbered groups, simply because no tie votes or "hung juries" are possible. Unfortunately, most research cannot deal with the critical membership variable: what the group is trying to accomplish. A group of five may be too large for many tasks, while a group of nine may be too small for many others. At the risk of sounding eclectic or atheoretical, we suggest that this is largely a matter for the teacher to discover with time and experience.

Group composition or makeup is equally reluctant to obey rules. Should students be allowed to choose group membership themselves, or should the teacher make assignments? Should groups be permanent or rearranged regularly? Should one member of a group be selected as the leader, or can groups work their way to their own leadership patterns? Steve's experiences suggest that self-selected groups operate better than arbitrarily appointed or contrived groups, that leadership emerges without elections, that groups need to be rearranged from time to time. He has also had experiences that refuted each of those generalizations—assigned groups that worked well, groups that foundered until a chair was selected, groups that worked together successfully for long periods of time. Diana usually begins group work by selecting membership herself. This takes the burden off students who may feel pressured to work with friends but don't really want to or the student whom nobody picks. She also asks students at the beginning of the year to write down the names of students they would like to work with or those with whom they might have conflicts. Using this confidential information, she can appoint groups that will function successfully.

The Teacher Role

The small group dynamic is a naturalistic one, and teachers need to be cautious about trying to rigidly control group behavior. Nor can small groups be used to achieve ends that might not be worth achieving in the first place. For example, "separating friends" who talk too much in whole class discussion will probably just lead to friends who talk across their separate groups. Nor will pedagogically unsound projects suddenly become workable—"Let's split up into small groups and diagram these troublesome sentences." Good luck to all.

The most satisfactory teacher group-role that we have discovered is simply teacher-as-coach, drifting from group to group, joining in when there is something substantial to contribute. This role is a difficult one to manage. More than once each of us has joined a dynamic group only to see the conversation wither because of our presence.

The Group Task

Without a sense of task or purpose, any group will founder. Thus many teachers have divided students into small groups with the assignment insufficiently described. Without a clear aim, the students talk pointlessly (or to the point of events and personalities unconnected with English). Sometimes the task or goal can be as simple as reporting back to the class. It is also useful to have groups prepare something for presentation to the class: a discussion, perhaps, or a demonstration, role-play, or panel. On the whole, groups function better on tasks they devise themselves—that is, when the assignment is for the group to come up with and execute its own assignment.

Assessing Group Work

Some analysis of the group process—by the group or an outsider— can be helpful in improving group work and aiding people to become more effective participants. A good list of questions for such an analysis is Halbert E. Gulley's "Running Record of 'Groupness'," shown in Figure 12.1.

VARIATIONS ON THE SMALL GROUP THEME

Group work rapidly grows dull if the tasks and the nature of the small group activity are not changed regularly. One can very quickly run a class to the point where students react to group work negatively, "Not groups *again!* C'mon, give us a break." A number of small group variations are possible. Some of many, ranging from informal to formal, are suggested here.

1. *Brainstorming.* The aim of a brainstorming session is to produce as many ideas as possible in a short period of time. A topic for inquiry is selected—"How can one build a better can opener?" "How can we get more kids to participate in the bake sale?" "What are some good ways to structure a story?" "What does this screwy poem mean?"—and the participants suggest as many ideas as they can, building, borrowing, stealing one an-

FIGURE 12.1

From *Discussion, Conference and Group Process*, second edition, by Halbert E. Gulley. Copyright © 1960, 1968 by Holt, Rinehart & Winston, Inc. Reprinted by permission of Holt, Rinehart & Winston.

RUNNING RECORD OF "GROUPNESS"

The questions to be answered concern such elements as these:

I. To what extent does the group climate promote free, permissive talk?
   A. Is the atmosphere informal rather than rigidly stiff?
   B. Does every member participate?
   C. Do members react to contributions in ways that encourage the communicator to talk again later?
   D. Do high-power members react to contributions in ways that encourage lower-power members to talk again later?
   E. Are the physical surroundings pleasant and conducive to enthusiastic talk?
   F. Do members seem enthusiastic about the importance of discussing the problem and do they consider participation worthwhile?

II. To what extent are members compatible?
   A. Are members friendly to each other?
   B. Do members seem to like each other?
   C. Do members seem to enjoy talking with each other?
   D. Do members smile occasionally as they talk to others?
   E. Do members behave in ways which generally minimize the threat to others' egos?

III. To what extent does the group operate as a cohesive unit?
   A. Is there mutual helpfulness among members?
   B. Do members seem to be dependent upon each other for support?
   C. Do members seem eager to hear the group's reactions rather than proceeding on their own?
   D. Is there effort to bring deviates back into agreement with this group?
   E. Do members seem more concerned with group interests than self-interests?
   F. Do members seem cooperative rather than competitive?
   G. Do members seem pleased when other members are congratulated for superior contribution?

IV. To what extent is there efficient communicative inter-action?
   A. Which members contribute most and which least?
   B. Which members' contributions are most helpful to the group?
   C. What kinds of information-opinion are contributed by each member?

> D. To which members are most communications directed?
> E. What proportion of communications are directed to the whole group?
> F. Are members attentive listeners?
> G. Do contributions relate to and build upon earlier contributions?

other's ideas freely. No criticism or evaluation is permitted; the aim of the group is idea production, not evaluation, and all ideas are recorded, since even silly ideas may prove to have a seed of a workable solution.

2. *Buzz Groups.* These are short discussions, limited to perhaps ten or fifteen minutes, based on a single well-defined topic. Buzz groups move along quickly and actively and break the routine of longer, sustained discussions.

3. *Committees.* The committee is the bane of American clubs and politics, not to mention school faculties, but perhaps this is because so few people have ever worked on productive committees. Appointing or asking for committees on all kinds of topics can add considerably to the class if the committee is engaged in a task it finds important.

4. *Task Forces* or *Problem-Solving Groups.* These are committees with a purpose, whose aim is to solve a particular problem or complete a project. Because of the emphasis on some kind of final product, a task force is often very strongly self-directed.

5. *Representative* or *Administrative Groups.* The school is filled with them: senior class officers, the prom site selection committee, the officers of the Latin Club. While representative groups are principally characteristic of extracurricular activities, there is no reason why they cannot be established within English classes, with tasks ranging from selecting books for an in-class library to assisting in the establishment of grading or evaluation standards.

6. *Seminars.* "Seminar" may conjure up images of stuffy gatherings of Ph.D. candidates. But separated from some of its academicism, the seminar is a helpful device to use with many levels of students, as students engage in examination of an idea, a topic, or an issue and deliberate to reach conclusions, propositions, or proposals.

FORMAL SPEECHES

Declamation, oratory, and forensics have declined in this country with the growth of radio and TV, and so has interest in their classroom use. The mainstream of oral English is informal talk, and few adults actually ever give a formal speech. Thus, the speech-making practice supplied in the schools is not always directly helpful. But *practice* is the problem word here. As it is with writing, when speech activities are "future-directed," aimed toward distant speaking engagements somewhere in time, they tend to become divorced from students' realities. (This trivialization is illustrated by a remark one of Steve's students once made while urging prospective teachers to give frequent impromptu speaking assignments: "This is really important because the student never knows when he will be at a dinner or a banquet and be asked to say a few words.")

All kinds of speech activities become appropriate and enjoyable when they are made a regular option within an English program. In fact, many students will select spoken English options in preference to writing and other forms *if* the speaking is not made too formal. For instance, the "presentation"—a five-minute review of a book, a ten-minute slide program accompanied by a tape—provides functional but not necessarily dull practice in public speaking. The panel discussion can be a lively small group form of public speaking. Debates are a form of speech that genuinely excite many students, and minidebates, staged in a short period of time without the formalities of judges and timekeepers, are almost a surefire teaching technique. Even parliamentary procedure, evolved through role-playing or actual decision-making activities, can be exciting. The spectrum of talk—from chat to lecture—will emerge naturally if the teacher is successful in creating an environment that welcomes spoken English.

EXPLORATIONS

• Do some eavesdropping. Listen to people engaged in an argument and think over their skill in speaking with and listening to each other. Observe the oral English competencies of speakers at a town meeting or caucus. Listen to politicians talking over their program with reporters. What percentage of the people you listen to are, in fact, orally literate?

• Explore oral history and storytelling as a starting point for a spoken English unit. Have students recall and tell significant stories from their past. Then have them do the same through interviews with their parents and grandparents, either taping or transcribing the tales and anecdotes. Bring a local storyteller to class!

• Examine the implications of the questions you ask in class or plan to ask via your teaching notes. What percentage of your questions fall into Nash and Shiman's three categories: *factual, conceptual,* and *contextual?* What are the implications for the kinds of discussions you will promote? It might also be interesting to divide the questions along other lines: into questions that catalyze *divergent* rather than *convergent* thinking (leading to original conclusions rather than coming to a fixed point) or into *cognitive* versus *affective* (questions that emphasize knowledge versus those that are concerned with values and subjective responses). Again consider the implications of your division for the way student talk is likely to flow.

• Develop some conversation starters for a class—a list of, say, twenty or thirty topics. Or ask the students to propose a set of topics. Experiment with conversation sessions—five minutes to begin with—in which the students can talk over things informally.

• Experiment with small group patterns, perhaps inviting students to join the investigation by proposing new techniques and structures. Try groups of three, four, five, and six. Test out leaderless groups, groups with appointed leaders, and groups that choose their own leaders. See what happens when groups do and do not have to report back. Try giving detailed assignments; broad, general assignments; and no assignments.

• Some Australian teachers Steve met while on a teaching exchange said that their "methods" instructor in university told them never to assemble the class as a whole except for announcements. That is, the class was to make use of small groups and solo work exclusively. Evaluate that advice.

• Videotape a class discussion, either small or large group. Then replay the tape and ask the students to analyze it in terms of Gulley's "Running Record of 'Groupness'." This is a good activity to help students become aware of the group process. It is equally useful to teachers in helping them analyze their own role in promoting the classroom flow of talk.

• Devise a set of oral English activities that call for a range of formal and informal speech forms on a single topic. For instance, for a topic like "Religion in Today's Society," how could you provide opportunities for chat, dialogue, small group discussion, brainstorming, debates, panels, and talks?

RELATED READINGS

Three books by Andrew Wilkinson provide a comprehensive, pioneering examination of oral English (Wilkinson calls it "oracy") and ways of teaching it: *Some Aspects of Oracy* (Birmingham, England: Birmingham University Press, 1965), *The State of Language* (Birmingham: *Educational Review*, 1969), and *Spoken English* (Birmingham University Press, 1965). Unfortunately, since Wilkinson introduced the concept of oracy in the 1960s, not a lot has been done other than to pay lip service to it. The growth this profession has experienced in writing instruction in the past twenty years has not been matched by sophistication in handling oral English.

Consider joining the National Association for the Preservation and Perpetuation of Storytelling, Jonesboro, Tennessee. Its journal, *Storytelling,* provides many classroom applications and lists of storytellers in your area.

Important insights into oral language in the development of thinking as well as using language are offered in *What's Going On: Language Learning Episodes,* by Mary Barr, Pat D'Arcy, and Mary K. Healy (Upper Montclair, N.J.: Boynton/Cook, 1982), and in Margaret Donaldson's powerful *Children's Minds* (New York: Norton, 1978). M. A. K. Halliday's *Spoken and Written Language* (Victoria, Australia: Deakin University Press, 1985) compares these two modes of language and offers theoretical insights into the importance of classroom talk, both in itself and as a starting point for writing. Stephen Krashen's *Principles of Second Language Acquisition* (New York: Pergamon, 1982) offers an extremely helpful model of language learning that is applicable far beyond the needs of students whose language is not English. Finally, Richard Budd and Brent D. Ruben's *Interdisciplinary Approaches to Human Communication* (Rochelle Park, N.J.: Hayden, 1979) reviews communications and speech theory from the points of view of such diverse fields as zoology, anthropology, general semantics, systems theory, neurophysiology, and sociology.

Classroom Drama

13

From Carol Korty, *Writing Your Own Plays: Creating Adapting Improvising.* New York: Charles Scribner's Sons, 1986, p. xi.

I believe the urge to make a play comes from the desire to go beyond enjoying an experience in our own minds to sharing it in communion with others. Sharing an event in communion means experiencing it in common with others at the same time. . . . This is what makes theater.

MANY people perceive drama as formal theater—something others present and we pay admission to see—or as something false or insincere: "Don't you think you're being a bit dramatic?" But as Carol Korty has observed, drama involves a "communion" of experience. Whenever two people meet—to talk, to exchange ideas, to interact—a kind of drama results. Unless people live in utter isolation they cannot avoid daily participation in the human drama.

But our concern here is with the more restricted sense of playmaking, which is intimately connected with personal growth and development. Young children engage in dramatic play spontaneously, using it to test out roles and identities, to explore facets of their personality. Although formal dramatic play diminishes as one enters adulthood, new forms of role-playing develop, and mature adults skillfully manipulate dozens of different roles as they move through society and interact with others.

The place of drama in the elementary grades and nursery schools is relatively secure; creative dramatics, children's theater, playacting, and dramatic play have been part of the lower schools' curriculum since the early part of this century. It is only in the past two decades that secondary teachers have come to recognize the usefulness of drama for the values that Arthur Eastman describes. Here it is especially helpful in allowing students to explore potential roles and aspects of their personality, as well as to establish their values and beliefs.

Drama is larger than literacy—and earlier. It is mime and talk as well as script. It opens to the inarticulate and illiterate that engagement with experience on which literature rests. It permits them, and people in general, to discover their private human potentialities, to participate in and share the experience of the group, to make experience public.

Further, drama is a ubiquitous teaching tool. Creative drama, for example, develops a host of spoken English skills. Writing plays draws on skills ranging from description to dialogue. Reader's theater and play production engage students in the study, analysis, and evaluation of literature. One could quite easily create a drama-centered curriculum that would encompass all areas that usually fall in the language arts. Finally, but pedagogically important, drama is the *lively* art, energizing the class where it is in use. Drama is *doing,* not sitting, listening, or note taking.

The urge to question, to invent, and to perform has been stifled in millions of schoolchildren now grown up, and their final cultural pattern can be seen all around us. But within this culture which in the past has tended toward rigidity, there are now definite needs for adaptability to rapid social change and a flexibility which will allow us to cope with problems as yet to appear. Ours is a society which is finding habits, precedents, and traditions insufficient to guide and set courses for the future. For this reason alone we need, more than ever before, to place a high priority upon the development of creative expression.

IMPROVISATION AND ROLE-PLAYING

These forms of drama, sometimes subsumed under the heading "creative dramatics," represent playmaking activities in which the actors and actresses create a drama as they proceed. In its simplest form, this might be an impromptu sketch or dialogue done to illustrate or extend a litcrary concept. Or it might be a full-blown play, carefully rehearsed (but still "scriptless"), with costumes and stage props.

Although the research into this area is, by their description, "wobbly," Julie Massey and Stephen Koziol have shown that drama develops a wide range of skills and abilities, including language development and cognitive development, and even creates attitude changes. English teachers have been especially interested in role-playing as useful in values clarification, where students explore through improvised scenes various decision-making processes and the implications of choices for the development of a value system. (See, for example, *Value Exploration Through Roleplaying,* by Robert C. Hawley [Amherst: ERA Press, 1974].)

Initial Experiences with Drama

Initiating drama is especially difficult. For the first few times, students—especially those of high school age—may be edgy, nervous, and frightened, and the teacher must be very careful to make the activities pleasant and nonthreatening. Many experts in the field advocate opening classes with informal warm-up exercises designed to release tensions and get people into the mood for drama. Typical warm-ups include:

Rhythm and Movement. The leader beats out a rhythm—slow, fast, in between—and the students respond, sometimes following instructions—"Walk in time to the beat," "Move your arms only"—other times creating their own plan for movement. This activity can also be done with students responding to a musical composition.

Relaxation Exercises. As in yoga, the students stretch and relax their bodies. Many yoga postures take their names from objects and animals in nature—the Lotus, the Lion, the Bridge—so students are already playacting and imitating as they relax.

Mime. Wordlessly, the students imitate objects, actions, and feelings, for instance:

Pantomime. Participants imitate common actions: brushing teeth, talking on the phone, a person trying to keep from falling asleep at a lecture.

Objects and animals. "Be a teacup." "Be a butterfly emerging from a cocoon." "Be a sunrise." "Be a melting snowman."

Moods. Students pantomime joy, happiness, anger, sadness, or a kaleidoscope of moods.

Some teachers' experiences with warm-ups have been mixed. Often they succeed well, and drama proceeds successfully. But in some groups the warm-ups have had the contrary effect of inhibiting people and raising tension. Most people feel somewhat inadequate when drama is first introduced, and something unfamiliar like "Be a butterfly" can intimidate them thoroughly. The people who thrive on these warm-ups are often the natural hams, and their successes can create further problems for those who are shy or cautious. Many people are so locked into themselves that even these simple warm-ups cause problems. The teacher must present them with great caution.

STRUCTURING CREATIVE DRAMA EXPERIENCES

Since drama pervades all areas of life, almost any issue, problem, or idea that concerns young people can work its way into a dramatic experience of one kind or another. Writing in *The English Journal* ("Dramatic Improvisation: Path to Discovery," *The English Journal,* April 1965, pp. 323–327), Marianne and Sidney Simon described three major sources of drama topics:

1. *School.* Including "conflicts with peers; conflicts with teachers; conflicts with administration; problems within the classroom; boy-girl relationships in school; cliques and scapegoating; [and] events of urgent interest."
2. *Home.* Including family relationships; problems concerning the generations; and rules and regulations.
3. *Society.* Including issues of broad concern like "racial tensions; religious conflicts; social class barriers; and fears related to war and destruction."

Topics can grow from small group discussions, literature readings, current events, and human relations problems (inside and outside the class). Most critical is that teachers must learn to integrate drama naturally into the classroom structure, so that it is not simply a thing done occasionally or only on set days. Thus, the teacher should make it a point to offer a drama option—improvisation, say, or mime—as part of many assignments. Similarly, teachers should make it a point to draw on the dramatic possibilities in literature, moving as freely into dramatic interpretations as they would into direct discussion of a novel.

The principal aim of classroom drama is to help students understand, interpret, and talk about their world and themselves. It is not to train actors or produce theatrical experiences of professional quality. An audience at the theater does not especially care whether an actor grows through the acting experience; the teacher of classroom drama cares very much and ultimately bases evaluation of the drama on the extent to which it has helped the actor/student grow.

In planning the structure for improvisation, teachers can use as a formula the "4 Cs": character, containment, conflict, and conclusion. These provide a useful way of seeing and organizing classroom drama.

1. *Character.* Obviously the drama will be made up of people (or animals like people)—characters, in short. A central concern for the teacher is the extent to which it is necessary to predetermine the role of a character, rather than letting the actor work it out in process. As a rule, the more familiar a character is to the students, the less direction and preplanning will be necessary to help them fit that role. Most students can role-play young people, teachers, parents, and well-known public figures or celebrities with little preplanning. Other characters—older people, people from different generations or social classes—may require prior discussion. The teacher can conduct concentration sessions to help students feel the part:

> Close your eyes. Think about the character you will be. Think about his appearance—how does he look? How does she feel? Is he satisfied with his life and himself? Who are her friends? Visualize what they look like.

2. *Conflict.* The source of any dramatic action must be conflict of one sort or another. The conflict is essentially the topic of the drama. It may concern the characters—conflicts between young people and/or their parents—or it may center on situations—say, conflicts of interest and ambition.

For drama to be integrated into the mainstream of a class, the conflicts should grow from the activities and feelings of the class. Drama ideas can thus be derived from:

> Human relations problems with the class.
> Struggles that emerge in stories and plays.
> Problems or themes that appear in poetry or essays.
> The students' own writing.

3. *Containment.* This is the physical contrivance of putting all one's characters and conflict into one box so that they have to bump into one another. It is the age-old setting with an emphasis on close fit. The containment of a drama can take place anywhere—in a room, the back seat of a car, a telephone booth, a dance floor. Containment can also cross over periods of time—2001, 1930, 1776—to provide focus. Once you contain characters and conflicts, the drama is spontaneous. It *must* happen.

4. *Conclusion.* The first three Cs provide the essential structure for a drama. If they are present, drama happens. The fourth C, conclusion, is the escape clause. It commonly happens in improvisation that the actors become so deeply involved in their roles that the drama becomes endless. The participants will not compromise, and the actors remain hopelessly deadlocked. Sometimes the actors simply forget to plan a conclusion. In any event, improvised theater pales very quickly when this happens. As a regular part of planning for drama, the teacher should stress the need for some

sort of conclusion that will help to resolve the conflict—not, however, by providing a *deus ex machina* or a contrived happy ending.

To visualize how the 4 Cs work, select several characters, give them a conflict, and provide containment from the suggestions in Figure 13.1.

WHOLE CLASS DRAMA

Creative dramatics need not always involve small groups and small scenes. Steve enjoys organizing dramas that engage the entire class in a play for which there is no audience or, more accurately, in a drama in which the actors are also the audience. One form of the whole class drama involves asking the students to visualize themselves in a place where people gather— a department store, a jail, a rock concert, a football game—and to choose a role and act it out. The teacher or selected students can help to catalyze the drama by taking on a stimulating role—a shoplifter, tough cop, angry guitarist, football coach's wife—and using that role to generate and focus the drama. A variant of the whole class drama that we have used is the "partially scripted drama." On entering the class, each student receives a card with a character's name and description. At the beginning of the drama, each student acts the assigned role. A partially scripted drama for an improvisation at an airport is shown in Figure 13.2.

Other good partially scripted dramas that we have seen in schools include *The Dog Show,* with participants miming dog owners showing off their animals; *Supermarket,* with actors and actresses finding imaginary goods in imaginary rows; and *University General International Incorporated,* with people role-playing busy bureaucrats in a mad company that makes *nothing.*

By planning the characters of the drama carefully, the teacher can engineer some conflicts and confrontations. Britain's Dorothy Heathcote, whose book is mentioned at the close of this chapter, is particularly skilled at the sort of "side coaching" that this entails.

Many variations of the drama that involves everyone in the group are possible. Steve's students introduced him to *The Big Machine,* a group role-play in which everyone becomes a cog, gear, or lever in a giant Rube Goldbergian human machine devoted to some trivial task such as snapping open a peanut shell. Classes can become movie audiences, an orchestra, angels on the head of a pin, marooned victims of a shipwreck, or a group of parents worrying about what's wrong with the younger generation.

THE ROLE OF THE TEACHER IN CREATIVE DRAMA

The teacher's role is, above all, delicate. The role of organizer is reasonably clear, but there are also times—many times—when the teacher

FIGURE 13.1   THE ELEMENTS OF DRAMA

Characters

Baby	Sports hero(ine)	Butcher
Old man/woman	Movie star	Baker
Martian	Rock singer	Astronaut
Teenager	Literary character	Ship captain
Parent	Historical figure	Coach
Yourself	The president	Sitcom character
Principal	Spy	Brat
Taxpayer	Master criminal	Know-it-all
Police chief	Superhero(ine)	Engineer
Professor	Animal	God(dess)

Conflicts

Missing property	Faulty merchandise
Stolen property	Car troubles
Human rights	Curfew
New students	Homework
Friends and enemies	Parents
Race relations	International relations
Current events	Absurd happenings
Page one stories	Housecleaning
Election fraud	Homecoming queen

Broken things	Sports	
Cheating	Love	
Jealousy	Hero worship	
Dirty clothes		

Containment

2001	Mars	1920s
Hospital	Tree house	Old West
Department store	Jail	Rome
1812	Garage	Novel setting
Zoo	School	Prehistoric times
Car	Crowded bus	A test tube
Czarist Russia	Home	Your lungs
Movie theater	Fire station	Seaside
Classroom		

must contribute to an ongoing dramatic presentation to make it work. For instance, if a play seems to lack a conclusion, the teacher may need to intervene, suggesting that a character do something that will force a resolution. At other times, the teacher may need to nudge the participants into heightened conflict or say something that will keep a student from drifting out of a part. This intervention or side coaching, as it is sometimes called, must be done with caution lest the students sense it as merely a teacherly interruption. Perhaps the easiest way for it to happen is for the teacher to be prepared to assume a role and become a participant in the drama, acting as an additional character inserted into the play to help shape its direction.

The teacher should plainly not become a director. As Richard Crosscup has suggested, the teacher's role should be perceived as that of helping the students grow through drama, and the principal outcome is less the play than the growth of the students engaged in it.

From Richard Crosscup, *Children and Dramatics*. New York: Scribner's, 1966.

The leader of children's dramatics activity . . . will not be a "director." . . . The play director's creation is the play. But for the person concerned with the growth of children, it is not the play that is the end, but the child.

There are also many problems and pitfalls in creative drama, and in contrast to writing, where failures can easily be kept private, failures in drama are obvious and public. Douglas Barnes, a British teacher who has experimented extensively with drama in the classroom, reminds us of some of these problems.

From Douglas Barnes, "The Final Word," in Douglas Barnes, ed., *Drama in the Classroom*. Copyright © 1968 by the National Council of Teachers of English. Reprinted by permission.

DRAMA AS THREAT

We have all seen pupils blossom or shrink in dramatic activities. We must acknowledge our powerlessness in controlling the dramatic interplay. In the playground the pupils are finding their groups and subgroups—or their isolation—and taking up roles within them that provide some security and protection. But in the drama room we break down these temporary stabilities and safeties and make the children try other roles. Those who can will grow, but what of those who are not yet ready? In the playground they will escape from the intolerable situation, but not in our drama lesson. So we risk serious harm to them.

When people are deeply engaged in creative drama, feelings are released quickly and easily, and desirable though this may be, such openness needs to be handled carefully. Drama offers no hiding places and little opportunity for revision. The teacher must be sufficiently in control—without "controlling"—to be able to anticipate and avoid problems. Although experimentalism is desirable in creative drama, as it is in all areas of teaching, the teacher needs to be especially cautious; unsuccessful experiments may be deeply harmful to students.

FIGURE 13.2   PARTIALLY SCRIPTED AIRPORT IMPROVISATION

You are RON STRONG: member of the airport security guard. It's your job to keep trouble from springing up. In addition to helping out people in distress, look out for troublemakers, terrorists, loiterers, and stray dogs.

You are LANCE FARR, veteran pilot. It is your job to stroll around the airport chatting with customers in order to build the company's image (and, no doubt, to feed your king-sized ego).

You are little SHIRLEY TREMBLE, traveling all by yourself for the first time. You're not lost; you're not hungry; you're not hurt or scared. But it sure would be nice if people would pay a lot of attention to you. Take turns being hopelessly cute or breaking down into hysterical weeping.

Your name is MILDRED GLEE, and you are the Chief Ticket Agent. Set up shop at the front of the room and make reservations for people. Take your time. Don't make any mistakes and don't let anybody be rude to you.

You are EUDORA PRY, ace reporter for WFLY, and you are here interviewing people who are at the airport. Get the portable tape recorder and do an on-the-scene broadcast. Talk to people who look interesting. Ask them what they're doing here. Afterward, play back your tape as an instant replay of the drama.

Other characters can include: a lost little boy, someone who has lost his baggage, someone who has lost her dog, a movie actress, an obnoxious old man, taxi drivers, baggage handlers, smugglers, etc. Simply make up enough characters (30 or so), divided by sex, to match your class distribution.

To initiate the drama, simply announce that the classroom has become the central terminal at _____ Airport.

PUPPETRY

In one of Steve's teacher education courses, a student did a project investigating puppetry as a way of introducing dramatic work. She constructed several simple glove puppets, wrote up some starter situations, and asked members of the class to put on the puppets and improvise. The two volunteers (draftees, actually) crouched down behind a table—a crude stage—and began improvising, a bit edgily at first but gaining enthusiasm as they entered into the play. Steve happened to be sitting to the side so that he could see both the puppets and puppeteers, and as the drama unfolded, an interesting thing happened: The puppeteers gradually became less conscious of the puppets and began to watch and speak to each other. A two-level drama emerged—one onstage, one behind stage.

This process intrigued Steve because these two students, seated on the floor, holding puppets in the air, shouting lines at each other, were among the shy members of the class; under no circumstances would it have been possible for Steve to get them this excited about an improvisation presented directly to the class. The puppets had released these students' dramatic talents.

Since then, Steve has used puppets with many groups at all age levels, and the results have been remarkably consistent. Puppets provide a mask— some basic protection— that allows people to open up to a high degree in dramatic work. Even older students, who Steve feared might see puppetry as juvenile, seem to enjoy it. Steve has even been forced to retire one set of classroom puppets that were demolished in a lively drama by two graduate students who had previously made a point of telling him what quiet, reserved people they were.

Secondary students react positively to using puppets too, especially if they are used as a regular part of the course and not just brought out once a year. Puppets allow students to step outside themselves and become someone else. All eyes are focused on the puppet, not on the person, and this adds to the ease students feel when they use puppets.

Students can use puppets to:

Introduce themselves at the beginning of the year.

Read a poem that the puppet chose. After the poem is read, the puppet tells why it appealed to him or her.

Talk to literary characters. One puppet might take on the persona of Edward Thatcher in *A Day No Pigs Would Die* and explain why he made fun of Rob.

Enact a dialogue. After reading Jonathan Edwards' "Sinners in the Hands of an Angry God," one student can write up the Puritan puppet's response to the sermon while another student writes up responses from a puppet of the twentieth century. The puppets can then discuss their viewpoints with each other in front of the class.

Be the characters in brief plays they write. First they would have to decide on a conflict and on the characterization of each puppet; then small groups could write and have the puppets enact their play.

Teachers can also include puppetry as a part of the writing options or project activities. For example, students can create puppet characters to respond to characters in a novel or story or to verbalize a reaction to a poem.

The equipment for puppetry is simple. The puppets themselves can be made from paper bags, paper plates, cloth remnants, clay, or papier-mâché. They can be made in sizes ranging from finger puppets—simple tubes of cloth or paper—to the superpuppet, a variation on the pillowcase that the puppeteer wears. Some teachers like the idea of Sesame Street's "anything people"—faceless puppets that can be decorated with features fastened on with double-sided transparent tape—and keep on hand some blank mitten puppets that their students use to build a character they want.

The sources of puppet plays are endless. Improvisation is the obvious starting point, using 4 Cs as a basic guideline. The students can also present puppet pantomimes, ballets, dramatic readings, plays, television programs, discussions, panels, debates, interviews, and conversations. Puppetry also makes a good road show, and students often enjoy taking a puppet repertory company to other classes, to other schools, or to libraries.

ORAL INTERPRETATION

Literature is a performing art, and we often overlook the dramatic excitement that oral reading—by individuals or groups—can bring to a class. Teachers have traditionally acted as if silent reading is the only proper kind, intimating that somehow students are cheating if they listen to literature. It is shocking to observe that all but a few of the best student writers are almost totally incapable of doing an equally good oral reading of what they have written.

Students need not be polished readers or have theatrical experience in order to do successful dramatic reading. To the contrary, many students are put off or embarrassed by doing or listening to a formal theatrical reading. What is essential is a message—poem, story, play, essay—and a desire to communicate it to other people. In reading sincerely and naturally, most readers will be sufficiently dramatic to interest an audience.

The teacher can initiate an interest in oral interpretation simply by reading aloud regularly. Students of all levels seem to enjoy being read to, and it is unfortunate that oral experiences like story hour are abandoned after the early grades. A long novel, one that might be out of range for many students, can be read, a chapter at a time, over a period of several weeks or months. Literature to supplement a topical or thematic unit can be read to a class. Recordings of dramatic readings should be brought in as well, and all teachers should get a copy of the record and tapes catalog of Caedmon, a company that specializes in recordings of authors reading their own work.

The teacher should not be the only reader, of course, and students can be involved in oral interpretation. At first, the readings should be relatively short, and the student should have ample time to look over the material, though not necessarily to rehearse it, before reading aloud. By all means avoid "going around the class," having each student read a paragraph or two, in what often becomes a dull parade of uninvolved readings. If the teachers want to have students read aloud, they should organize it, prepare for it, and help the students do a polished job of it.

Having students read their own work is also a good oral interpretation project, since the reader begins by being familiar with the meaning of the work. Oral reading can also be encouraged by sponsoring activities like informal poetry readings or coffeehouse readings, in which writers come together to read and talk over their work. We like the idea of having a schoolwide festival involving the reading of student work on an annual or a semester basis. Good writing from all over the school is collected, and either the writers themselves or good oral readers read the work to the entire school or to groups of parents. This kind of festival not only honors student writers but gives your good readers a chance for public recognition as well.

GROUP THEATER

Group theater goes under a number of different names, described below, but moves beyond pure oral interpretation to involve several readers or actors.

Typically in *reader's theater* a literary work—short story, one-act play, television script—is read aloud by a group of readers, each of whom takes a part. A narrator is included if necessary. No lines must be memorized; nor are any sets or stage props needed. Reader's theater can even be done as a mock radio play, complete with sound effects. It is also an effective way to present student writing.

In *chamber theater* the literature (usually a short story) is acted out, so students actually learn their lines. In effect, chamber theater simply converts a piece of fiction into something that can be presented as a work of drama.

In *improvisational theater* the students start with a set text—a story or play or dramatic poem—and, having read and understood the work, they act it out, creating their own lines and actions. A popular variation of this approach is *story theater,* in which students pantomime the events of a story while a student or teacher reads it aloud.

None of these approaches, except possibly chamber theater, is as complex as launching a full stage play. Group theater allows students to read from scripts and thus avoid the time-consuming process of learning lines, or it allows the actors and actresses to make up their own lines. Using group theater frequently aids enormously in bringing literature to life while helping students extend their own range of dramatic experience.

PLAY PRESENTATION

Because of the many limitations that classroom preparation of a play imposes, few plays will reach the point of a full-dress production in an

English class. However, there are many occasions when a play can and should be worked up into a full presentation, especially in the case of student-written works. One-act plays also make a good classroom presentation. Generally, the guidelines for preparing a classroom play are similar to those for any formal drama: The teacher needs to provide ample time for preparation and rehearsal and to participate in the process of shaping the play, helping the students see its full dramatic potential. The classroom presentation also provides opportunities for involvement by technically oriented students—technicians, stagehands, managers, effects people, prop people, and lighting experts. Once the work of a presentation has been done, the class play probably should be taken on the road to other classes or schools.

In general, we would like to see the schools place less emphasis on whole school dramatic productions and more on presentations by small groups and classes. While the senior class play or school musical is often an impressive show, the whole school drama involves relatively few students and is often quite expensive. In the interest of involving more students, we think administrators and secondary English departments might consider investing their funds in a number of small theater groups or providing money to support dramatic productions in individual classes.

DRAMA AS LITERATURE

Drama is also usually part of any literature anthology. However, many teachers breathe a sigh of relief that they can't get to the drama section (it's almost always at the end of the book) because they don't know what to do with a play besides having it read aloud. If drama is viewed as another kind of literature, the teacher will quickly see that students should be able to get involved with the characters, the issues, and the conflicts as with any other type of literature. Moreover, students can discuss the differences in action, language, and setting due to the performing nature of drama as well as consider what drama does more or less successfully than other genres.

After plays have been read in the classroom, consider having students engage in some of the following kinds of activities, which represent a range of improvisational drama, scripted theater, and discussion possibilities:

Change one element (plot, character, dialogue, setting) and write a bit, showing how this changes the play.

Choose one character and then skim the play to find lines that character says that tell us a lot about him or her. Then go back through the play and find ten lines that others say in reference to the character. Record these quotations. Now write a brief sketch of the character you chose, using the evidence you just collected. Then look at the character in terms of what you do and do not know about him or her.

Compared to literature, does drama as a form let us know more or less about characters?

Select two or three plays and look for symbolism in them. If symbolism exists, how is it present in drama (scenery, characters, language)? Discuss your conclusions.

Sketch out the main events and conflicts in one or more plays; then rewrite the play in an oral form, the rap. Discuss what this new form adds to or takes away from the drama.

Discuss themes present in the plays—are they similar to or different from themes we've discovered in the other literature we have read?

From the anthology pick out five poems and five short stories that deal with the same theme as one of the plays.

Turn a play into a TV drama. How would it be different?

Invite eight people from different plays to an imaginary dinner. What issues or themes would they talk about? What human concerns would they share?

Choose a theme present in at least two of the plays and write a poem or an editorial about it.

Write a folktale or fairy tale based on a play.

Write a dialogue between two major characters from different plays.

Write a script for a talk show with three characters from different plays who can respond to a similar issue.

Write a "Dating Game" episode with three male or three female characters. Compose the questions the members of the opposite sex would ask them and write the contestants' responses.

Write a speech for one of the characters (such as Iago) as either a presidential candidate or a TV evangelist.

You are in charge of creating Tony award categories and of awarding the Tonys to characters from the plays you have read. Explain your choices. Some suggestions: Strongest Female Character, Most Unfortunate Character, Most Mentally Disturbed Character.

Write a letter to one of the characters whom you feel strongly about. Explain to him or her what bothers you about his or her behavior or what you find particularly appealing.

Create a product that several characters might want or need and then write a commercial or advertisement enticing them to buy it. State which characters are your intended audience and why.

Create and present an evening news show using incidents and characters from selected plays.

Create a radio drama complete with an announcer and sound effects on a dramatic portion of one of the plays.

Become characters from a play and let the class interview you.

GAMES AND SIMULATIONS

The value of games and simulations has only recently been recognized, and educational games are rapidly being developed in many fields. While not "drama" in a formal sense, games nonetheless draw students into new roles and identities by engaging them in simulated situations. There are games to teach color and shape, to engage students in a reenactment of Colonial shipping problems, to simulate urban planning, and to develop an understanding of the political process. Video games and computer simulations put students into airplanes, automobiles, and decision-making situations. Although many commercially prepared games are available, teachers and students can also enjoy creating their own.

Steve and his students have designed a number of games including "Newsprint" (which simulates the operation of a daily newspaper); "Tenure Track," a year in the life of a new teacher; "The Pollution Solution," a large group role-playing people of a town faced with a pollution problem; and "Soap," involving the writing of a soap opera.

There are no hard-and-fast rules for designing simulations and games. Perhaps the best approach for interested teachers is to examine some commercial games like "Monopoly," "Clue," "Sorry," or "Bermuda Triangle," study how they work, and then apply the format of the game to the chosen topic.

Here are some guidelines that are helpful to people designing a game for the first time:

1. *Describe the learning objectives for the game.* Do you want students to read, write, speak, or listen? What do you want them to gain from the game?

2. *Find a source of dramatic tension in the game.* For the game to progress, there must be a basic conflict or motivation. (In "Newsprint," for example, the drama is created by having rival newspapers competing for success.)

3. *Find a model for the game.* Using as a model "Hollywood Squares," "Authors," "Wiff'N Proof," "Monopoly," or any other game that seems to fit your purposes, draft a set of rules and procedures for your game.

4. *Create any needed materials.* These can include boards, spinners, decks of cards, and so on.

5. *Play the game experimentally.* (Do this some Friday or Saturday evening at a party with friends.) Find out what doesn't work in the game as you designed it.

6. *Play the game with your students.*

To our way of thinking, for a game to be a legitimate part of English, it should in one way or another directly engage students in examining or using language. While it might be fun to bring in a game that simulates, say, life in the roaring twenties or male/female role problems, the game should have some connections with language use in order to be worth the time of the teacher and students.

A list of games that have potential for use in an English class is shown in Figure 13.3. To the best of our knowledge, none of these games exist, at least not in commercial or published form. We will simply present the titles and allow the reader to figure out what the game might be.

EXPLORATIONS

• To draw on drama freely and easily, one needs to feel comfortable with it. Try some improvisations and a dramatic reading with some colleagues. Talk over the feelings you experience and consider ways of making drama pleasant for students. Be especially conscious of the initial feelings you have when improvising.

• Visit an actors' studio or class, observe the teaching, and consider applications for the English class.

• Talk over some of the problems that arise in a drama-oriented class. What should the teacher do about:

Students who are shy?
Students who probably would enjoy drama but seem reluctant to participate?
Students whose physical appearance—for example, overweight, tall, plain—
   might cause embarrassment if they were assigned to inappropriate roles?
A drama that becomes too serious, with the barrier between real life and drama
   dissolving?

• Design a series of creative activities for a unit of literary work you are interested in teaching. Try to include some possibilities for wordless drama (pantomime), role-playing, and full-fledged skits or playlets. Also consider the possibilities the unit offers for group theater presentations.

• Make some puppets and put on a play.

• Practice your oral interpretation skills by reading aloud to your students. Don't try to become theatrical; simply relax and enjoy reading to others.

• Locate a good sound library close to where you live or teach and examine its holdings in dramatic readings and recorded theater.

FIGURE 13.3   GAMES FOR THE ENGLISH CLASSROOM

The Debate Game

Censorship

Sitcom

Town Meeting

The Sexist Language Game

The Doublespeak Game

The Language of Advertising

Sign Language

Family Reunion

Discover a Dialect

Discover Your Dialect

The Lexicographer's Dilemma

The (Beat/Romantic/Victorian) Poetry Game

Name That Poem!

The Canterbury Tales Game

The Learn a New Language Game

Codes and Ciphers

The Library Game

The Hardy Boys/Nancy Drew Write Your Own Thriller Game

The Epistle Game

Esperanto in Action

Intergalactic Communication

• If you are interested in developing games and simulations, begin by conducting a one- or two-day "Tournament of Games" in which students bring in a range of games, play them, and share the results. From this discussion, evolve some ideas about game structure, including answers to some of the following questions:

How are winners and losers determined?

How does the game simulate or imitate a real situation?

How is the flow of play directed and controlled by such devices as dice, cards, and a game board?

• Design one of the games in Figure 13.3 and play it with friends or a group of students.

RELATED READINGS

Viola Spolin's *Improvisation for the Theater* (Evanston, Ill.: Northwestern University Press, 1967) is a classic in its field, including a strong section on the art side of coaching. A good book for use with elementary children is Elizabeth Kelly's *The Magic If* (Baltimore, Md.: National Educational Press, 1973). Charles Duke's *Creative Dramatics English Teaching* (NCTE, 1974) is conveniently divided into two parts: one presenting the basic theory of creative dramatic work, the other discussing classroom strategies.

For a complete guide to the use of reader's theater in the classroom take a look at Shirlee Sloyer's *Readers Theatre: Story Dramatization in the Classroom* (Urbana, Ill.: National Council of Teachers of English, 1982). She talks about selecting appropriate material, how to adapt material, and classroom procedures for reader's theater. For teachers who need concrete examples of reader's theater scripts based on literature before they have students write their own scripts, Reader's Theater Script Service (P.O. Box 178333, San Diego, CA 92117) and Contemporary Drama Service (Box 7710-H4, Colorado Springs, CO 80933) offer a wide variety of such scripts. Write to the above addresses for catalogs. Another resource that shows drama is the classroom in *How Tall Is This Ghost, John?* by David Mallick (Australian Association for the Teaching of English, 1984 [distributed in the United States by Boynton/Cook]). This book focuses on making the classroom a workshop where students understand meaning through action. Shakespeare's plays are the material being worked with.

Teachers may also want to examine *Games in the Classroom,* edited by Ken Davis and John Hollowell (NCTE, 1978), which provides good advice on making and playing games and on their use in English classes. Dorothy

Heathcote's writings have now been collected as *Drama as Context* (Upper Montclair, N.J.: Boynton/Cook, 1980). Finally, if you are interested in puppetry, check your library for a book on puppet making or see *Putting on a Play,* by Stephen and Susan Judy (New York: Scribner's, 1982), which also contains ideas for radio plays as well as neighborhood theater production.

English:
A Mass Medium

14

From Edmund Carpenter, *Oh, What a Blow That Phantom Gave Me!* New York: Bantam Books, 1974, p.3.

Electricity has made angels of us all—not angels in the Sunday school sense of being good or having wings, but spirits freed from flesh, capable of instant transportation anywhere.

From Marshall McLuhan, "Explorations Number Seven," a broadcast of the Canadian Broadcasting Corporation, May 1957. Copyright © 1957 by the CBC. Reprinted by permission of Corinne McLuhan.

It's natural today to speak
of "audio and visual aids" to teaching,
for we still think of the book as norm,
of other media as incidental.
We also think of the new media
—press, radio, movies, TV—
as MASS MEDIA
& think of the book
as an individualistic form. . . .

Today in our cities,
most learning occurs outside the classroom.
The sheer quantity of information conveyed by
press-mags-film TV-radio
far exceeds
the quantity of information conveyed by
school instruction & texts.
This challenge has destroyed
the monopoly of the book as a teaching aid

& cracked the very walls of the classroom,
so suddenly,
we're confused, baffled. . . .

In this violently upsetting social situation,
many teachers naturally view
the offerings of the new media
as entertainment,
rather than education.
But this view carries
no conviction to the student.
Find a classic
which wasn't first regarded
as light entertainment. . . .
The movie is to dramatic representation
what the book was to the manuscript.
It makes available
to many & at many times & places
what otherwise would be restricted
to a few at few times & places.
The movie, like the book,
is a ditto device.
TV shows to 50,000,000 simultaneously.
Some feel that the value
of experiencing a book
is diminished by being extended
to many minds.
This notion is always implicit
in the phrases "mass media," "mass entertainment"—
useless phrases of obscuring the fact THAT
English itself
is a mass medium.

ENGLISH DISCOVERS THE MEDIA: A PLAY IN FIVE SCENES

SCENE 1

A teacher leads a class discussing the merits of the film version of a novel the class has just completed reading. After carefully guided debate, the students reach the conclusion that the filmmaker took too many liberties with the novel and that reading is more interesting than filmgoing anyway, since reading forces you to use your imagination. Later in the week, the students all go to the flicks instead of reading their English assignment.

SCENE 2

A class begins a newspaper unit. Each day the students bring in a paper and study its journalistic techniques. They discover biased and unbiased editorials, colorful sports writing, and a number of typographical errors. Some students read the want ads and the comics on the sly. After the newspaper unit, the class resumes its perusal of the history of British literature.

SCENE 3

The school gets into computers in a big way. New book purchases for the library come to a halt so that the school can purchase a bunch of Peachy II's. The software purchased for/by the English department includes "How Now, Nouns," "Getting Rid of Comma Faults," and a "Talking Speller" in which a computerized voice dictates a spelling list to the students.

SCENE 4

An *au courant* teacher who has read Marshall McLuhan decides to teach film study. He opens his course by lecturing on the nature of visual symbolism and assigning a paper on the structural analysis of a film currently showing at the local cinema.

SCENE 5

The principal sets aside a portion of the school budget for film rental, something the teachers have long requested. Unfortunately, all films must be requisitioned the spring prior to the year in which they will be used. Since teachers cannot possibly plan that far ahead, the film budget is never spent.

McLuhan is right when he says that the media confuse us. After years of either ignoring media or using them merely as audiovisual aids, teachers have, in the past two decades, come to realize that media are a part of language and belong in the English classroom. But what to do with media remains a puzzle. Some teachers have simply put old content into new forms, as McLuhan predicts, gussying up the old curriculum with videotape and floppy disks. A few teachers draw on videos as a natural part of the curriculum; others declare TV and film an abomination and stick exclusively to print.

As we look to the future, we can see that the fully functioning members of the community of language will draw on many different media, including print. They will be able to use telephone (car, portable, or videophone); computer; video (for both viewing and production); and old-fashioned letters and newfangled electronic mail, depending on the demands of time, situation, and cost. They will be able to see and become involved in a film and perhaps not worry that it was or was not true to the book, appreciating it for what the experience *is,* not for what it is *not.* "English is a mass medium," McLuhan suggested. That is, it's time to recognize that the language is larger than *any* of the media used to transmit it and will be larger than any media which arise in the future. To turn McLuhan's phrase, we can also add, "The media are English" (and all other languages).

McLuhan suggested further:

The educational task
is not only
to provide
basic tools
of perception,
but to develop
judgment & discrimination
with ordinary social experience.

The form of McLuhan's statement provides a witty example of his point. In writing his essay in the visual shape of a poem, he traps us in a superficiality—judging content in terms of the medium. Often we lack the judgment and discrimination to look toward the language and content rather than superficial form.

Taking a clue from the previous passage, we want to suggest that what matters is the student and his or her use of language discriminatingly, not the choice of media forms. Our aim as teachers must be to help the students develop powers of "perception . . . judgment & discrimination with ordinary social experience." (We ought to be concerned with discriminating among academic experiences as well.) Such discrimination is based in language, as young people observe their world and describe it in language.

Today's students are born in an electronic world, one that, as Edmund Carpenter suggests, has made "angels of us all," capable of instant flight to any place in the globe. With their horizons expanded, young people need to be able to respond to the media creatively and critically and to use them to communicate with others successfully. Those two aims—*responding to* and *using* the media—are the focus of this chapter. We will not even begin to describe all of the possible media uses that are open to the elementary or secondary language arts teacher. But we will present a sampler of activities that can strengthen students' media skills by concentrating, first and foremost, on the student as a creator and consumer of language.

Although we have isolated the consideration of media in a single chapter in an obvious but structurally necessary violation of McLuhan's principle of integration, the teacher should be able to incorporate media in class smoothly and comfortably, just as with practice and experimentation, drama becomes a regular part of the class, not something that is taken up on isolated days or in specialized units. The value of media comes in using them, either as sources of ideas and information or as forms of composition.

RESPONDING TO MEDIA: TELEVISION

What are we to make of television? Its worst critics blast it as being not only destructive but downright evil, creating a false set of standards and values for its watcher-victims. Others point to the informational and instructional value of many television programs, not just limited to public television and non-prime-time hours, and argue for selective viewing. The networks present themselves as brokers to public taste, offering whatever forms of instruction and entertainment the public will support.

It is perhaps most useful for a teacher *not* to take a two-value stand on television, but to help students become aware of the way it affects their lives. As McLuhan has argued, we tend to lose consciousness of familiar media, and television is the most familiar medium of all. Some of the following projects can help students rediscover the familiar on the tube and evaluate its effects on themselves.

TV-Watching Log

We've all read statistics on the number of hours students spend in front of the television set. Let your students analyze their own tube time by having them keep a complete log of their viewing for a single week. How many hours do they watch? How many hours on school days? On weekends? Have them discuss planned versus unplanned watching. How often do they turn on the set just to see what is happening? Encourage the students to break their watching into categories: news, adventure, comedy, cartoons, sports, movies, and so on. Put your categories and figures on a large sheet of butcher paper and tack it on a bulletin board so that your students can see at a glance how the hours add up.

This activity will generate all kinds of follow-up discussion. Often young people will show considerable savvy as they discuss their viewing. Students can also consider alternative ways of spending their time. Steve thinks he had some impact on a middle school class by pointing out that if they cut their TV viewing time in half until the time they graduated from high school, they would have time to jog 12,000 miles, to read the *Hardy Boys* or *Nancy Drew* books cover to cover 16 times, or to earn enough by baby-sitting to pay cash for a new car!

TV Review Sheet

As a follow-up to the TV log, students can begin to critique the shows they watch. On a one-page ditto, students can review, say, the five best and five worst shows for a given week. This is a good project to do with small groups, with a fresh group of critics being assigned each week. Students might also want to send their review sheets to the managers of local television stations. "Criticism" in this case can be as informal or formal as the teacher and students wish. At first, it may be best simply to let students react informally, but as the term or year progresses they should become more and more skilled at explaining just what triggered their reactions.

Study TV Conventions

Because of its domination by commercial interests, TV is highly repetitive and unimaginative. Once a new show succeeds, others follow the pattern. Have your students investigate a TV genre: police shows, situation comedies, cartoons, superhero shows, soap operas, made-for-TV movies. Encourage them to look for the stereotypes of character and plot that emerge. As a follow-up, let the students write satires of the genres they have been studying. These satires might even be presented for the class through improvised drama or recorded on videotape for showing around the school.

The Image of America on TV

Stereotypes are not limited to characters in the TV genre shows. Television also creates stereotypes of Americans. Have the students keep track of stereotypes for a week or more. Tell them to look at the roles of men and women, children, husbands and wives, singles, racial minorities, lawyers, doctors, blue-collar workers, and so on. It has been said that TV is a revolutionary medium because it shows the lower economic classes what the upper crust has and lives like. It has also been observed that despite efforts of people in the women's movement, television offers dated stereotypes of women as homemakers and/or sex objects. Do your students agree?

TV Commercials

Many people argue that on TV the ads are both better and worse than the programs: better, because they are developed with great skill to achieve high impact through brief exposure; worse, because they are highly exploitative, frequently verging on the dishonest. Conduct a TV commercial unit with your students, having them watch, analyze, and critique the commercials they see. This, too, is a unit that can be followed up with a video or stage production, with students writing and taping their own satirical commercials.

TV Tie-Ins

In a positive vein, in recent years promoters have discovered the TV tie-in, in which a novel is made over for television or a popular television program is turned into a novel. While the quality of the by-product—either TV show or new book—varies considerably, in general the tie-ins spur interest in literacy. Many paperback bookstores now have a "TV Novels" section with a hundred or more titles that have been or are being televised. Draw on the interest that the tie-ins produce by teaching some of the books or by assigning the show for discussion and analysis.

RESPONDING TO MEDIA: FILM

Film has come into its own in English and language arts classes in the past two decades. Where once films were used almost exclusively as visual aids, presenting instructional information rather than being used as entertainment or aesthetic experience, now they enter the class as a source of experience for reading/writing activities and as a communications medium in their own right. In addition, film forms a significant part of the common culture of young people, so a teacher can safely refer to many feature films shown outside the school with a degree of certainty that students will have seen or heard about them.

At the same time, as film has become respectable, it has also suffered from "academization." That is, because teachers and (especially) college professors feel a need to teach, rather than simply to let students view and respond, they often try to legitimize the film experience by engaging in formal analysis and criticism. In many film classes, much time is spent on detailed analysis of the technical properties of film and on the naming of film techniques and strategies. While some knowledge of how films are made is obviously useful, too much analysis simply has the effect of spoiling the viewer's pleasure. Sound familiar? English teachers have done the same thing with literature for years. Similarly, many teachers of English have drawn on their knowledge of literary criticism to lead their students in, say, a search for symbolism or the study of recurring motifs in films. As McLuhan would say, such analysis is a matter of viewing a new medium in terms of an old one.

From Pauline Kael, "On the Future of Movies," *The New Yorker,* 1974. Reprinted by permission.

There are a few exceptions, but in general it can be said that the public no longer discovers movies, the public no longer makes a picture a hit. If the advertising for a movie doesn't build up an overwhelming desire to be part of the event, people just don't go. They don't listen to their own instincts, they don't listen to the critics—they listen to the advertising. Or, to put it more precisely, they do listen to their instincts, but their instincts are now controlled by advertising. It seeps through everything—talk shows, game shows, magazine and newspaper stories. Museums organize retrospectives of a movie director's work to coordinate with the opening of his latest film, and publish monographs paid for by the movie companies. College editors travel at a movie company's expense to see its big new film and to meet the director, and directors preview their new pictures at colleges. The public-relations event becomes part of the national consciousness. You don't hear anybody say, "I saw the most wonderful movie you never heard of"; when you hear people talking it's about the same blasted movie that everybody's going to—the one that's flooding the media.

One of the big problems with film viewing today is that the enormous public relations efforts of the filmmakers discourage independent judgment. Instead of seeing a movie and responding to it in personal terms, the viewer is predisposed to take a particular stance toward it. (These days, PR departments begin to "hype" a film as an Academy Award winner even before a single scene has been shot.) Students need opportunities to develop their own responses to "the language of film" and to form, in language, their own responses. Just as with television, we want to help them become independent judges of film, not just miniature critics.

The Video Revolution

The development of home video players and the explosion of video stores can be a genuine boon to the English teacher. Whereas in times past teachers often had access and scheduling problems with films, they can now go to a video store and, for a dollar or two, rent the film they want to show when they want to show it. Some teachers, too, have extensive tape libraries of their own, with copies made from the television movie channels for nonprofit educational use in their classes. (As of this writing, the jury is still out on whether or not such use is a violation of copyright.) In any case, video equipment now makes the dream of using films in the classroom a practical reality. You can bring in filmed versions of novels, sometimes two filmed versions of the same novel; you can show films that reflect on a theme or topic; you can find documentaries as well as dramas to fit with your teaching units. Exploit the possibilities!

Filmgoers Polls

As a test of the responses and reactions of other young people and adults, have your students develop filmgoers polls. They might interview people going into and leaving a theater. (The theater owner's permission might be required.) Why are people going to the movie? What do they expect to see? Where did they first hear about the film? Do they already know how it ends? Are they pleased or disappointed afterward? Will they recommend the picture to their friends?

Such interviews can yield statistical data for tabulation or material for a student-written feature article about film. Both kinds of writing are a natural for a school paper. If actually traveling to the theater is not possible, students can conduct similar kinds of polls around school, asking fellow students what they watch and why.

Fads and Fancies in Film

Encourage your students to study film types or genres, particularly the more faddish sorts. For instance, the last two decades have seen a number of film fads: disaster films (subdivided into airplane disasters, deep-sea calamities, and natural catastrophes—earthquakes, fires, comets); occult films, scare-the-daylights-out-of-you movies; highway high jinks (with foolish-looking police officers pursuing roguish heroes and heroines at high speed); the police academies; outer space superfilms; the beat-'em-Rockys; and others too gross to mention. Ask your students to search out the formulas of such films and try to explain the appeal they have for viewers.

Studying Response to Film

Teachers can help students become independent film viewers by encouraging them to be aware of how they respond to film and why. The questions following any film—including films shown on television—might run as follows.

1. *Response.* What is your response? How did you react? What did the film make you think or feel? Did you want to laugh? To cry? Where did the film touch your own life, your own experience? Did you relate to any

of the characters in the film? Were any of the problems or characters just like life for you?

2. *Discussion.* Let's look at the film itself. Why did you react the way you did? What was it: the action? the characters? the pictures? (Without a lot of technical jargon, the teacher can help the students see how their responses were directed by the strip of acetate rolling through the projector.)

3. *Evaluation.* Did the film have an impact on you *skillfully?* Were the characters realistic? Did they need to be? Did the film hold together? (Again without introducing a great deal of sophisticated terminology, the teacher can help students engage in criticism that will help them clarify their own values and responses to cinema.)

RESPONDING TO MEDIA: STUDYING THE NEWSPAPER

Students usually enjoy a newspaper unit, and the materials are readily available to the teacher. Often local newsstands carry both local and out-of-town papers, so the teacher can show a range of journalistic approaches. In addition, a great many papers have education programs that will supply your class with papers and you with a variety of teaching aids and guidelines.

From Jeffrey Shrank, *Understanding Mass Media*. Lincolnwood, Ill.: National Textbook Company, 1975. Reprinted by permission.

American newspapers began with bulletins hung on tavern walls or printed sheets from the local postmaster or printer. Anyone could start a newspaper, and this fact was most important in the development of a free press. Most schools have small newspapers that cover only events in school, but there is no legal reason why these papers could not be expanded to become neighborhood newspapers. On the other hand, a school radio or TV station cannot broadcast to the public without a government license. New, inexpensive offset printing systems make it possible for anyone with a few hundred dollars to produce a small newspaper with a circulation in the thousands.

However, analyzing the content of a paper does not teach as much as learning the ins and outs of journalism through actual experience. Instead of the conventional newspaper study unit, the teacher might consider a simulation game, "Newsprint," where the class is divided into teams of five or six students, each team forming the staff of a newspaper. Within the ground rules established by the teacher, each team develops a paper that is run off in multiple copies. The newspapers are taken to another cooperating class whose students are asked one question: "If you were going to buy one newspaper, which of these would you purchase?" The resulting "circulation figures" determine the winner. The game is best played in several rounds, each group producing a fresh paper for each round and adapting its style and format to attract more readers. The basic rules for newsprint are shown in Figure 14.1.

Like most simulation games, "Newsprint" does not require a great deal of analysis after the fact; competitors learn in the process. As a follow-up, however, the teacher can spend some time reviewing the events of the competition and helping the students relate their experiences to the problems of the daily paper in America. One way to focus the follow-up is to have the students evaluate a local newspaper and send their suggested changes to the editor. In fact, the editor might want to respond to your students' suggestions and could possibly be prevailed on to analyze and critique the papers they produce.

If "Newsprint" works well, you might also try variations with other media and forms. Instead of newspapers, have the students develop a magazine on a topic of their choice—sports, home living, fashion, cars—and market their magazine in cooperating classes. Alternatively, conduct a literary magazine contest based on the students' own writing.

EXPLORING THE MEDIA OF PERSUASION

The analysis of persuasive language—advertising and propaganda—is a productive and intrinsically interesting study for English classes. Students enjoy sifting through newspapers and magazines and studying TV commercials to gain a sense of how mass media are used to market beliefs, ideas, values, personalities, and products. Rather than simply having students analyze, however, you might want to try to engage them in developing a persuasive campaign, an activity that can be done by a whole class or by small groups. "The Campaign" can be done as a simulation, with the students themselves serving as an audience, or in reality, with an audience selected from the school or community.

The students select an issue or a topic that they see as important in the school, community, or world; they identify a target audience that *dis*agrees with their point of view; and they develop a multimedia campaign to persuade that audience. Thus the students might campaign for more student privileges with the faculty as target; for better recreation areas with the town council as target; for a cleanup of a stream or river with landowners and industries as target. As a simulation, "The Campaign" might be aimed

FIGURE 14.1   TEACHER'S MANUAL FOR "NEWSPRINT."

The Aim: For students to simulate competing newspapers by creating several papers based on differing editorial concepts. The papers are evaluated by another class to create simulated circulation figures.

Ground Rules

Few limits need to be placed on the actual content or form of the newspapers since the aim of the game is for students to discover a form and content that will win them a readership. The teacher does need to ensure that the same production materials, printing process, etc. are available to each group and set the common limits:

Length.   Two-, three-, or four-page papers seem to work best, though sometimes longer papers can be produced.

Form of reproduction.   Probably ditto, mimeograph, photocopy, or computer printout.

Special Limitations.   The teacher may want to ban or encourage the use of typewriters or word processors, depending on availability, or to set special limits on content of the newspapers. It may be necessary to limit the source of news—school only, city only etc.—and to establish time limits—two days, four days, or whatever fits the schedule best.

Procedures

Round I.   Forming newspaper teams can be done by self-selection, teacher appointments, or choosing up sides by editors. After the students understand the ground rules, set them to work. You might want to bring in examples of newspapers, preferably of many different styles and patterns, and leave them about the class for reference. You can serve as a consultant or not, depending on your interests and those of the students. When the papers are finished, rush them off to the cooperating class and wait for the results. (In addition to asking the cooperating students to indicate their first choice, you might want to have them rank the newspapers and/or fill out a simple feedback form telling what they saw as the strengths and weaknesses of each.)

Round II.   Self-evaluation takes place. The winners bask in glory; the losers scramble about finding ways to increase circulation. The students study the feedback from their readership (or poll the other students in person), learn from one another's first editions, adapt ideas, beef up strong points, cut out losing ideas. The same evaluation procedure applies to winners as to losers, and it proves interesting to see what changes in circulation figures take place after the evaluation. Often the first-round winner will stay with the tried-and-true and be dethroned by an innovative former loser.

Additional Rounds. The game can continue as long as the newspapers evolve in new directions and as long as the students remain interested.

at passage of gun control legislation, with the class itself role-playing Congress.

After helping the students find a topic and target, simply present a list of a few of the many possible means of persuasion:

Buttons	Video documentaries
Placards	Radio shows
Editorials	Improvisational theater
Essays	Strikes
Laws	Position papers
Oratory	Propaganda
Petitions	Rumors
Sit-ins	Threats
Bumper stickers	Blackmail
Interviews	Films
Debates	Slide tapes
Letters	Media shows
Letters to editors	Appeals
Recall drives	Lobbying
Advertisements	

Some teachers are bothered by seeing unconventional and unethical persuasion forms like "threats" and "blackmail" on the list. The intent here is not to teach these forms but to help students recognize that both ethical and unethical means are not only considered but also used on them every day of their lives. In this sort of analysis, they will naturally engage in a wide range of classic questions about persuasion:

What forms of perusasion are most effective with the various target audiences? Why?
Is it possible to be immoral or unfair when campaigning?
Is it wrong to make the worse appear the better cause?

The actual presentation of the campaign creates a spectacle. Students come to class armed with posters, placards, banners, and buttons. Their presentations—at least in our experience—are animated and involved.

When all the commotion has died down, it is important to include a follow-up discussion, so that the activity isn't just fun and games. Ask the students to evaluate the impact of the various campaigns: Which were most successful? Why? Which fell short of the mark? What went wrong?

At this time, too, the teacher might want to refer to models of professional persuasion in newspapers and magazines to enlarge the discussion.

COMMUNICATING THROUGH MEDIA

In the previous sections, we have outlined a few of the many ways teachers can use the mass media as a source of study in English classes. The task remains in this section to sketch some of the possibilities for media composition—using media to send a message or to create a work of art. Of course, responding to media and creating in them cannot be completely separated. In the previous section, both "Newsprint" and "The Campaign" involved students in preparing media materials as a way of understanding how they work. By analogy, as young people communicate through various mass media, they can be expected to understand more completely how the media work and to increase their ability to react critically.

Video Making

This has become one of the more popular media activities in English classes, because today's students are visually oriented as a result of the popularity of television and top-quality films, and film is a language they find quite comfortable. Producing a video is also immensely satisfying; it is a tangible and visible accomplishment. Because of the high quality of contemporary equipment, video making often produces results that are apparently more professional than those of other modes of composition. What is a bit surprising is that today's "lazy" students who allegedly have "short attention spans" and need to be "entertained constantly" by TV are delighted to spend the time necessary making a good video. The process is quite time consuming—a short video can easily require twenty to thirty hours of preparation time.

We like to begin video work by having students simply "play" with the camera—panning back and forth slowly and rapidly, walking with the camera, shooting out of automobile windows, zooming in and out, shooting in dim or bright light. These exercises will help to diminish errors on the final run-through and give your students some feel for the medium.

Topics for videos are limitless. Almost any idea, feeling, poem, play, or song can lead to a short film. Some of the better topics are those that lend themselves to montage effects, collections of thematically related shots. This kind of effect can be achieved for subjects such as people, animals, feet, moods and emotions, the seasons, poem interpretations, leaves, and songs. Most difficult to do are dramas—serious or funny—because of the precision of acting and taping that is required.

Some video projects your students might find interesting are:

Tape an improvised drama. Replay the tape for discussion. Then have the students do the improvisation a second time.

Prepare a documentary videotape. Have students investigate an issue or problem around town or school and report on it.

Put on a puppet show for the cameras.

Stage a play, either chamber theater or a form in which students learn lines. (Video makes memorizing easier, since it can be done a scene at a time.)

Tape instructional materials. Get some of your good writers to plan a tape showing how they write and revise a paper.

Tape a panel discussion.

Make a tape of a simulation game in progress.

Prepare a program on a favorite author, with a student dressing up as the writer.

We recommend that kids start with *short* videos, perhaps just a minute or two in length, before launching into thirty-minute shows. Among the better models for the videomaker are commercials and short art films, both of which are based on creating and sustaining a mood, feeling, or theme over a short period of time.

Planning a video is critical. Productions shot at random or solely on inspiration look it. In working out a formal or informal shooting script, the students should consider the scenes they want and how they will obtain them. To the fullest extent possible, students should try to edit in the camera—that is, to plan their sequence of shots so that, barring mistakes, little editing will need to be done. If editing is required, you'll have to line up a second video deck and have the students carefully transfer the sequences they want to a single tape.

To complete the video experience, talk to the program director of your local public access cable channel or the school's video channel and arrange to have student works shown on prime time. Or, failing that, arrange to have a video player and monitor set up in the cafeteria at lunchtime so others can see your students' work.

The Slide Tape

Very effective projects and presentations can be done with the slide tape—a series of colored transparencies accompanied by a taped sound track. During presentation, the tape recording is played while the presenter/projectionist controls the showing of slides to match the tape. The medium offers some unique possibilities. Because the projectionist can control the pace of the slides, many of the problems of film sound tracks are eliminated, providing precise sound-image correspondence, even to the point of having images change in time to music or poetry. In addition, newer slide projection equipment makes changing slides easy, providing a rapid series of image changes and exposures of one second or less. Because the pace can be controlled, slide tapes are often longer and more complex in content than films. For students seriously interested in photography, the medium of the transparency provides a much more professional outlet. Good as student videos can be, they seldom have the visual quality of a good slide tape.

Most of the topics suitable for videos can be explored through a slide tape in different but equally interesting ways. In addition, the slide tape opens up possibilities for such topics as:

Documentaries—substantial narrative discussions of problems and issues.

Literature presentations—with perhaps a dozen poems or poets represented in a sustained literary experience.

Readings of student works—with accompaniment of music and photography.

Reader's theater—a literary work read aloud with appropriate photographs shown on the screen.

Preplanning a slide tape is important. Because of the ease of changing the order of a deck of slides, editing a slide tape is much easier than working with video. The final presentation of the slide tape requires a good deal of planning and rehearsal. It is possible to obtain a gadget that will automate the process, resulting in a perfectly synchronized show time after time. This is easier, but in some ways it limits the spontaneity and adventure of the slide show.

Radio Plays

It is unfortunate that the radio drama is almost dead, because radio plays developed an audience involvement that has never been and cannot be matched by film and/or television. But the aural concepts behind radio plays are alive and well in many English classes in the form of tape-recorded simulations of radio programs.

Not all students will find *live* classroom drama as described in Chapter 13 to be their medium. Not all students can perform comfortably in a dramatic reading. Radio plays—done with a tape recorder—offer a productive outlet for such students, as well as being interesting for most other students in a class. Although radio dramas have all the advantages of improvisation, they leave room for mistakes, which can be erased and retaped until the students are satisfied. Tapes also provide a kind of anonymity for the student who wishes it.

Radio plays offer realism not available in other dramatic forms. No matter how skilled the actor, a 17-year-old impersonating a 70-year-old on stage still *looks* 17, and putting on greasepaint doesn't help. But a 17-year-old speaking into a tape recorder can be any age, so that with radio plays students have available a wider range of roles that can be explored realistically. The very boundaries of the drama can be extended through the radio play—three students tape-recording in a small room can become a roaring party, the crew of a spaceship, or the entire cast of *Our Town*.

Radio also opens up the possibilities of using sound effects to create impressions of mood and place. Many stores sell sound effects records that contain a wide range of interesting noises—ping-pong games, marching bands, leaky faucets, cavalry charges. However, much of the fun comes in creating one's own sound effects, either by collecting real sounds on a tape recorder or developing in-class machinery that will duplicate the sound desired—say, an airplane, a truck, or an explosion.

Producing a radio drama is time consuming. The students can improvise or work from prepared scripts, using their own stories or adapting materials from other media. The basic studio tool is the tape recorder. Supplementary equipment can include additional microphones, linked together through a mixing device, and various patch cords that allow the tape deck to be wired directly to a record player, radio, or other tape recorder. Many of the students in your class will understand the electronics even if you don't. Also explore the possibility of using one of the newer stereo recorders that has the capability of layering "sound on sound," providing for many interesting stereo effects and complex mixes of voice and music.

For examples of radio plays, in case your students are not familiar with the medium, bring in an album on the history of radio, with such gems as "The Shadow," "One Man's Family," and "The Lone Ranger."

In addition to the radio play, the tape recorder can be used to recreate any number of other radio forms such as interviews and panels, documentaries, and news and sports broadcasts. Survey the programs of a good FM station for samples, and investigate the AM filler broadcasts with shows like "Ask the Doctor," "Dear Abby," "On the Road," "Perspectives," and "Sports Shorts."

Finally, explore the use of the school's public address system for wider distribution of your students' radio work. Many schools have student-run radio stations that play through the PA system into lounges, halls, and lunchrooms. Your students' creative radio programs might well fit into the schedule.

TOWARD A MEDIA CURRICULUM

We have presented a sampler of media forms in this chapter. There are many, many more possibilities, and David Burmester spells out 101 more of them in Figure 14.2. Many more ideas are also described in the references at the close of the chapter. It is important to stress that media instruction will not succeed if it is treated simply as a novelty or gimmick. Media options should be blended with other options as part of the curriculum of the class and used in English and language arts classes regularly so that students become very comfortable with these types of activities. James Morrow and Murray Suid have developed the outline for a K–12 media curriculum. (They include print and drama as well as electronic and visual media.) Whether or not a school system has such an elaborate curriculum, their program provides a model that can be used by teachers at any level as a guide to classroom media use (Figure 14.3).

THE COMPUTER

We've included computers as a mass medium because we see them functioning in most respects as language collection and dissemination devices, "mass media" in the best sense of the word. And just as people have worried in the past about the ways in which film and TV might affect values, so there is increasing concern over what computers will "do to us." We're in the midst of an information explosion, of course, and the amount of data that computers can hold is downright spooky as we think about the invasion of human rights and privacies.

It is more important, we think, to explore the ways in which computers are coming to shape our perceptions unconsciously. Like any medium, computers have their own message. Despite their sophistication, they are, as the cliché goes, "programmed by people." Further, the people who program them have *their* perceptions shaped, in part, by what the computer will "accept" or do most successfully. Thus, as we become a society molded, in part, by computer programmers, those programmers are molded, in part, by the machines they work with. That shaping, of course, influences computer design, so even as we think of future generations of computers and what they can do for us, we are limited by what computers have already

FIGURE 14.2

From David Burmester, "Mainstreaming Media: 101 Ways to Use Media in the English Classroom," *The English Journal*, February 1983, pp. 109–111. Copyright © 1983 by the National Council of Teachers of English. Reprinted by permission of the publisher and the author.

MAINSTREAMING MEDIA: 101 WAYS TO USE MEDIA IN THE ENGLISH CLASSROOM

1. Show a film as motivation for free writing.
2. Show a film such as "Hunger" or "Essay on War" that attempts to make a point. Have students respond in writing.
3. Show a short, impressionistic film such as "Sky." Have students write phrases depicting imagery from the film. Turn these into poetry.
4. After doing #3, record the students reading their writing and play it along with the film.
5. Use a film as a model for a writing assignment (e.g., show "The Weapons of Gordon Parks" to students writing personal profiles).
6. Show a film or TV show. Have students write reviews.
7. Have students review current movies or TV shows. Publish the reviews for the class.
8. Show a film and discuss it. You don't always have to have your students write.
9. Show a film and do nothing. Sometimes we make students believe that the only reason we use film is to make them do something.
10. Audio tape a film soundtrack. Play it and have students write what they see in the mind's eye. Show the film and compare to the writings.
11. Show a film twice, once with its own soundtrack, once with something else you've chosen. Discuss how sound affects film.
12. Read a piece of literature and see a film based on it. Discuss or write about how different artists approach the same material.
13. When you're studying literature (e.g., science fiction), supplement the reading with films of short stories (i.e., "The Veldt").
14. Use film to augment literary experiences (e.g., show "Night and Fog" after reading *The Diary of a Young Girl*).
15. Use a fact film as background for reading.
16. Show a film about an author or poet.
17. Show a film produced by a corporation (find these listed in *Educator's Guide to Free Films*). Is there a hidden agenda, or was the film made for truly altruistic reasons?
18. Borrow an armed forces film (see your local recruiter) and try to see what assumptions it makes about its audiences. Does the narrator refer to an "enemy"? Who *is* the enemy?

19. Show a film (or part of one) backwards. Discuss the experience. Have students write a backwards version of a film cliche (e.g., the shoot-out on Main Street, the south seas volcano eruption). (For an example, see pp. 73–75 in the paperback edition of Kurt Vonnegut's *Slaughterhouse-Five*.

20. Assignment: Think of the movies you've seen. Which was your favorite? Tell why in fewer than 100 written words.

21. Have students make a Super-8 film complete with titles and a soundtrack.

22. If you can't actually make films, have students do the pre-shoot steps (write a treatment, make story-boards, write a shooting script).

23. Have students make flip books.

24. Experiment with drawing on blank 16mm film. Project and add sound using a record.

25. Get news outtakes for a local TV station. Have students edit them to make a film.

26. Assign the class to watch a particular TV show and discuss it the next day. One of the nice things is that since almost every household in America has a TV set, you can study the medium without having the hardware in class.

27. Contrast a TV drama with a similar situation comedy (*Hill Street Blues* and *Barney Miller,* for example). How are they alike? Different?

28. Compare the characters in the TV version of M*A*S*H with those in the original film. Which are better developed? Why?

29. Watch three episodes of a popular TV show featuring a strong hero. Compare with a strong hero in literature. How are they alike? How do they differ?

30. Watch a soap opera or situation comedy. Discuss why it gets good ratings.

31. Have students watch children's TV. What values are promoted by programs and advertising?

32. Have students write about sex and violence on TV. Do they have residual effects?

33. Have students watch TV for an entire evening and write mini-reviews of everything seen.

34. Discuss the question "What would happen if all the television sets in the world stopped working and couldn't be replaced?"

35. Do a survey of student viewing habits. Discuss what they would do with the time saved by cutting their viewing in half.

36. Direct student viewing by publishing a weekly guide. It doesn't always have to be PBS; include something light once in a while.

37. News often mirrors literature. Have students be alert for news items which relate to literary works being read.

38. Have students write and then tape (video or audio) their own news broadcast. What editorial decisions had to be made?

39. Have students watch TV news and collect examples of euphemism and slippery language.
40. Have students make videotape documentaries.
41. Have students make commercials on tape.
42. Choose a particular advertising assumption (e.g., children are always "cute") and see how often it crops up during a week's viewing.
43. Show a TV commercial. Have students write about the assumptions they discover. Are all women dedicated housewives? Do all men drink beer?
44. Have students collect examples of stereotyping in advertising. Discuss how stereotypes affect our attitudes about men, women, minorities, occupations, and so forth.
45. How is bias important in advertising? Take some time to discuss bias and its influence on people. Why do Japanese enjoy squid while most Americans blanch at the thought?
46. Collect advertisements from magazines directed at special audiences (men, farmers, sports fans, etc.).
47. Find ads for the same product in magazines geared to various audiences (*Seventeen, Esquire, Sport,* etc.). Do the ads change tone? Does the language change? Is there a different sales pitch depending on the audiences?
48. Do the same thing with TV advertising.
49. What is the advertiser's view of America? Have students use magazine ads to construct collages entitled "The American Dream." Write about what is and is not pictured.
50. Choose a product which has been on the market for years and compare advertisements over time (perhaps at five- or ten-year intervals). What do advertisements say about our culture?
51. Show a TV commercial. Have students critique its effectiveness.
52. Compile a list of advertising slogans. Reproduce them and have students attempt to identify the products. Discuss the results.
53. Product names are not chosen capriciously. Some merely indicate the use or nature of the product *(Head and Shoulders, Cool Whip)* while others seem to go beyond mere labeling and imply value or quality *(Imperial, Zest).* Have students collect names of products and study the motivation behind the naming game.
54. Study automobile names. Some styles are named for weapons *(Dart, LeSabre),* others for animals *(Impala, Pinto).* What psychological impact do these names have on consumers?
55. Audiotape a TV commercial. Write a description of the visuals. Play the tape for your students and have them write paragraphs in which they attempt to design the video tract.
56. Have your students follow a political campaign and see if the candidate is being marketed as though he/she were a product.
57. Give students an imaginary product. Have them devise an ad campaign including TV sports, print ads, packaging, and so forth. This can be done by individuals or group "ad agencies."

58. Plan an ad campaign for a school event.
59. Have students design an ad for an idea.
60. Use different types of music (rock, jazz, classical) to stimulate free writing. Discuss how music affects mood and, therefore, writing.
61. Study song lyrics (but don't call them poetry). What do contemporary songwriters say about life?
62. Have students write new lyrics for old songs.
63. Play recordings of Bill Cosby's childhood recollections. Have the students write their own childhood memories patterned after his.
64. Play a recording of Hal Holbrook as Mark Twain. How can an actor add to the experience of reading a great writer's work?
65. Play recordings of poets reading their own poetry. How do the readings add or detract from the experience of reading the poetry?
66. Read a musical like *West Side Story* and act it out on audiotape using the original cast recording for the songs.
67. Many great "Golden Age" radio programs were adapted from literature. Use recordings of these as you would readings in a literature unit.
68. Have students adapt short stories as radio plays and then record them on audiotape.
69. Have students listen to contemporary radio drama. How does it compare to television drama?
70. Have students listen to radio talk shows and write about the people they hear.
71. Tape portions of "All Things Considered," radio network news, and Top 40 news headlines. How does coverage and news selection differ?
72. Have students produce a sound collage to create a mood, depict a situation, or promote an idea.
73. Have students use tape recorders to collect oral history. Then produce a local version of *Foxfire* or one of Studs Terkel's books.
74. Your *voice* is a sound medium. Read aloud to your students. Even though they can read, they need to hear *good* language used well.
75. Have your students make a sound filmstrip or slide show. We once did a S/FS about internment of Japanese-Americans. Pictures were photographed from books while the soundtrack combined interviews with a student written script.
76. Make a slide show to go along with a popular song. Have each student illustrate a line from the song. Photograph on 35mm slide film.
77. Have students use instant cameras to take pictures of community problems. Have them paste these in their journals and write about them.

78. Have students use photographs to illustrate writing. How do they add to the meaning?
79. Use fine art slides to motivate writing.
80. Have students make funny captions for movie stills.
81. Have students make up titles for photos from magazines as practice in writing titles.
82. Have students make poetry posters using photos taken specially or clipped from magazines.
83. Take candid pictures of all the members of the class. Distribute these and have students write about others as if they were characters from books or movies.
84. Use a multi-media show (film, music, slides, etc.) as motivation for a writing assignment.
85. Have a class publish a periodical newsletter about media (reviews of movies, TV shows, commercials, etc.).
86. Have your class offer to do a regular media column for the school newspaper (or, if there is a high school page in your local newspaper, offer to do a column there).
87. Have students collect examples of literary allusions in advertisements, cartoons, etc.
88. Have students compile a list of expressions which have entered the language because of media (advertising slogans, popular songs, etc.).
89. Have each student read a newspaper from one end to the other, every word. Have them discuss and write about this once in a lifetime event.
90. Visit a newspaper plant or TV studio.
91. Invite as guest speakers people who grew up when there was only radio (or even before). What did they do with their free time?
92. As a group book report, have students role-play a TV talk show with each of them as a different character and the moderator playing the author.
93. Capitalize on the video game craze; have students design and write about their own games.
94. Make a Scrabble board transparency for the overhead projector and use a Scrabble set to play the game with the whole class, pitting small groups against each other.
95. Encourage students who can to do their class writing on word processors.
96. Try to get a word processor for your classroom. They're expensive but can open new dimensions for student writers.
97. Research the history of a mass medium.
98. Assignment: What records, videotapes, and films would you take to a desert island?
99. Assignment: If you were going to colonize a new planet, which media would you allow? Which would you ban? Why?

> 100. Assignment: Develop a survival strategy for humans living in a media ecology.
> 101. Compile a list of 101 more ways to use media in the English classroom.

done. All that is by way of suggesting our belief that computer technology will be used most successfully in the English class as it contributes to the fundamental goal (as described by McLuhan) of teaching judgment and discrimination.

The earliest uses of computers in the English classroom did anything but that. The very first pieces of software to hit the market were distinctly of the "old wine in new bottles" variety, skill and drill put onto a computer. At one point, Steve was reviewing regularly for *Rainbow* magazine, dedicated to the Radio Shack color computer. He gave that up because he found that most of his reviews were negative, including one of the "Talking Speller" alluded to in the playlet that begins this chapter. He found a great many language arts programs for computers doing well that which should not be done at all. If one wants to teach traditional grammar, it is probably more effective to do it through a computer game, where kids shoot down *adverbs* but must avoid shooting themselves in the *verb,* and where *dangling participles* leave them dangling from a cliff. But if the research is correct (and there is every reason to believe it is) in showing that parts-of-speech grammar teaching is not an effective route to improved language usage, the computer sophistication is wasted. We think that in the end there will be place for such programs, probably in remedial centers, but they certainly shouldn't be in mainstream English classes.

A notch above the skill-and-drill programs in pedagogical soundness were the editing programs which emerged. These "grammar checkers" would analyze your writing sentence by sentence and supply data on average sentence length, passive voices, and certain nonstandard constructions (e.g., "he don't"). Such programs do, in fact, successfully identify potential language problems, but they make a fundamental (but computerly necessary) error of separating form and content. Passive voice is to be avoided in much writing, of course, but there are times when it is perfectly acceptable, as in the first clause of this sentence. Yet "grammar checkers" identify all instances of a problem. In our experience, only the students who were "better" writers in the first place could successfully use the information supplied. The less able writers were simply confused. What those writers need, we think, is not a computer but a writing coach, somebody who can read text, think about content, and supply suggestions for improvement in context.

Spelling checkers receive our stamp of approval; we think they are a

FIGURE 14.3
From James Morrow and Murray Suid, "Media in the English Classroom, Some Pedagogical Issues," *The English Journal,* October 1974, pp.41–43. Copyright © 1974 by the National Council of Teachers of English. Reprinted by permission of the publisher and the authors.

A MEDIA CURRICULUM

Kindergarten and Grade 1

Stage: Playlets and skits improvised for live performance before other class members.

Design: Greeting cards, illustrations for original stories, one-panel cartoons.

Print: Simple dictated stories, poems, and picture captions.

Photography: Slide tapes made by teacher or older children with class members supplying drawings or body language for the camera and voices for the tape recorder.

Radio: Playlets and skits acted out for tape recorder operated by teacher or older children.

Movies: Movie stories acted out before equipment operated by teacher or older children.

Television: Playlets and skits acted out before equipment operated by teacher or older children.

Grades 2 and 3

Stage: Magic shows, comedy routines, acts, speeches, and other prepared productions.

Design: Comic strips (not books), posters, ads, fun houses, and game boards.

Photography: Complete slide tape production, including creation of script, visual materials (drawings, collages, etc.), and sound track, but with older children or teacher holding the camera or tape recorder if necessary.

Radio: Complete radio production (including script, sound effects, and acting) can now include class members operating uncomplicated cassette recorders.

Movies: Complete movie production, with sets, costumes, props, and script devised by class members, but with teacher or older children running camera. Elementary cutout and object animation with teacher or older children setting up the camera and class members clicking off the frames.

Television: Studio production of plays and skits but with teacher or older children operating the equipment. Portable video production can now include kids aiming the camera.

Grades 4,5, and 6

Stage: Preparation can now include formal rehearsal of a formal script (memorizing lines).

Design: Comic books running to several pages (not just strips), conscious use of propaganda in magazine ads and posters.

Print: Stories and plays running to several pages, poems of several verses, review of books read and movies seen.

Photography: Slide tape production can now include class members operating simple "Instamatic" cameras. Class members can also create photo exhibits and photo essays with Instamatic prints.

Radio: Complete radio production, with class members operating reel-to-reel tape recorders and taking battery-operated cassette recorders outside to make "sound essays."

Movies: Live action movie production can now include class members operating "Instamatic" cameras. Sophisticated cutout or object animation, with teacher or older children setting up the camera and class members clicking off the frames and checking out the shots.

Television: Portable video production, with class members using the camera with only casual supervision by teacher. Studio equipment still operated by teacher or older children with occasional placing of class members in the driver's seat.

Grades 7, 8 and 9

Stage: Complete play production, sustained improvisations, speeches before large groups.

Design: A wide range of design and art activities, including posters, magazine designing, advertising, etc.

Print: Stories, plays, and poems of greater sophistication, plus the beginnings of personal essays, newspaper and magazine forms, and the like.

Photography: Slide tape production can now include 35mm slide photography and sound track mixing (music under voice, etc.) by class members. Photo exhibits and books can include 35mm prints.

Radio:	Radio plays running to 15 or 20 minutes in a full studio setup, with several microphone inputs mixed by class members onto one tape.
Movies:	Live action and animation with class members running the camera and teacher checking out shots occasionally.
Television:	Studio and portable production with class members running all the equipment under teacher supervision.

Grades 10,11, and 12

A few students really take off. They write novels and plays, produce hour specials for television, and make feature length 8mm movies. More commonly, teachers work toward increasing sophistication and high standards in all the productions named thus far: skits, routines, acts, bits, comic books, posters, greeting cards, fun houses, game boards, magazine ads, stories, poems, plays, essays, reviews, scripts, captions, photobooks, photo exhibits, slide tapes, radio plays, sound essays, live action films, animated films, portable television programs, and studio television programs.

useful addition to a computerized English classroom. By identifying possibly misspelt words, they serve as an aid in proofreading; and they may have some carryover to writing by, first, relieving youngsters' worries about spelling, and second, helping them identify their own spelling "demons." Indeed, we were interested to hear of one proposal for a spelling checker program that would check only the words which a person habitually misused, instead of an 80,000-word dictionary—a personalized spelling checker which would be considerably faster than some of the commercial models. However, spelling checkers are only a minor-league contribution to the computer revolution in the English classroom.

Word processing is a big-league contribution and, to date, has contributed most strongly to changing the face of English instruction. Word processors simply make it easier for kids to write and revise; they take a big chunk of the agony from writing and therefore encourage it. A word processor is an open-ended tool as well; it is designed to let the user create with it rather than lead the user to a predetermined conclusion (as so many of the skill-and-drill programs have been). Along with word processors are emerging "outline processors," which simply let one organize flexibly and erase plans freely, and even "thought processors" and "invention programs," which encourage writers to generate a wide range of ideas before writing.

Many school districts and even state boards of education have now mandated courses in "computer literacy," in what might, at first, be seen as striking close to the notion of teaching judgment and discrimination. Certainly, the idea of such courses seems sound: Students generally learn a little about how computers function and do some programming, often in *Basic* or *Logo.* However, writing a simple program that will say, "HI, *YOUR NAME,*" or getting a Logo turtle to run in circles still does not come very close to getting students to use computers and computer information with judgment and discrimination—which brings us to the concept of the "hypertext": the networking of computer resources, a pulling together of various media. As computer memories and storage grow greater, computer specialists foresee linkups of various information sources, not only numbers and texts but also resource centers, files of photographs and videos, even audio recordings. Experiments with "interactive computers" are already solidly under way and promise to be a major development in the 1990s. Computers will be able to bring the world to a student's fingertips. Every school, even one in remote regions, will be able to tap rich sources of information and images. The English class will become more naturally interdisciplinary, and the kinds of information available will make the underbooked library a thing of the past.

In a sense, then, all the media uses we have discussed in this chapter will come together through the computer keyboard and monitor. The question with which we close will be a question for teachers to answer over the next decades: "Given the dream-come-true of resources, what will English teachers do to broaden literacy?"

EXPLORATIONS

• Using media effectively in a class depends in part on the extent to which the teacher feels comfortable with them. If you have never done so, make a video or a slide tape so you can learn the intricacies and problems of using cameras and tape. Find out where a videotape machine is kept, and experiment. If your busy schedule won't permit this, offer media as an option for some of your students and apprentice yourself to them.

• Still photography also offers some interesting media opportunities. Explore and experiment with such forms as photo essay, photo journal, thematic photography, and sequence photos.

• Simulations, games, and real-life experiences are possible for virtually all media and help one come to understand any medium better. Design and test an activity that would engage students in considering the problems and quality of, say, television programs and films. One possibility for television:

In a simulation mode, have small groups write (and, ideally, videotape) 15-minute pilots for a new television series.

• Sponsor a video festival. Get the neighborhood video store to donate prizes.

• McLuhan said, "The medium is the message." By that he meant that every media—print, television, radio, film, telephone—shapes and limits the messages it carries and the effects of those messages on a listener. Thus, you can "do things" in some media that you can't do in others, and each media "messages" the audience in different ways. Engage some students in an examination of media messages. Some questions that might be raised:

What does this medium do best (e.g., spread news, present literature, inform, amuse, entertain)?
What worst?
In what ways, if any, does it "bend" or "distort" reality in sending its message?
How is the reader/listener likely to be influenced by this medium?

An interesting variation of this activity is to have students examine the media messages of various types of literature. A poem, like a television set, has certain ways of "messaging" people. Have students ask the same set of questions about poems, essays, stories, plays.

• Design the media component for a course you plan to teach. Include as rich a range of media forms—for both response and communication—as you can.

RELATED READINGS

One could prepare an extremely long bibliography for this chapter, but growth and development happen so rapidly that it would be out of date quickly. We'll mention just a few books that seem to us to be excellent, are reasonably recent, and are representative of the best thinking in the field.

For an overview of the impact of media, see Edmund Carpenter's *Oh, What a Blow That Phantom Gave Me!* (New York: Bantam Books, 1974), which takes an anthropological view of the ways in which media shape our culture and values. The same theme is the topic of Marshall McLuhan's *City as Classroom* (with Kathryn Hutchon and Eric McLuhan [Agincourt, Ontario: Book Society of Canada, Ltd., 1977]), a textbook for students that leads them to investigate the impact of contemporary media from the television set to computers. Also directly useful in the classroom is Jeffrey Schrank's *Understanding Mass Media* (Skokie, Ill.: National Textbook

Company, 1975). Anthony Adams and Esmor Jones's *Teaching Humanities in the Microelectronic Age* (Milton Keynes, U.K.: Open University, 1983) is an excellent primer on the implications of the newer technologies for instruction in English and the liberal arts. William Wresch's *The Computer in Composition Instruction* (Urbana, Ill.: National Council of Teachers of English, 1984) is also an excellent primer on the implications of computer technology for the English classroom.

The Dimensions of the English Curriculum

ABOLISH ENGLISH!

We have arrived at a point in American education where brutal frankness might help us all clear the air and clear the mush out of our heads . . . English as a subject is dead. Ninety percent of our students killed it decades ago, but it has been denied interment by a tough band of necrophiliacs called English teachers. They have finally failed. They know now what their students knew decades ago.

But before the moment of truth, they made many attempts at resurrection. They withdrew the classics in favor of contemporary literature; they switched from formal grammar to functional grammar to no grammar at all; they tried linguistics; they choked on generative grammar. They tried anthologies, but they were too remote, too heavy. They tried paperbacks but they were too expendable and too lightweight. They tried formal writing, just plain writing; they even abandoned writing. They tried audio-visual aids and found out that for students a picture was worth one million words. The success of the projector hastened the demise of English, just as the arrival of television speeded up the twentieth century.

Right now, English is defined as whatever you can do in an English class just as long as you can get away with it.

Abolish English? Those are strong words. The man can't be serious. English has been around forever and will be around forever. It's as American as. . . .

When August Franza wrote his essay "Abolish English," he generated a storm of protest. An English teacher himself, Franza intended to satirize some of the failings of the English curriculum. But a great many people thought his proposal was serious and wrote strong letters of protest.

His tongue-in-cheek argument presents a number of points that *could* be taken seriously by teachers, administrators, and parents. For example, many people have argued that English is irrelevant in the age of media. Kids watch television nowadays and don't read books. They pick up a telephone and call long distance rather than write letters. Adults' reading sometimes seems limited to cereal boxes, while writing is relegated to grocery-length lists. While people obviously need to learn to read and write, the critics argue, the age of English, with its emphasis on books, pens, and paper, is over. If we teach "literacy," critics suggest, we ought to teach media literacy or computer literacy or scientific and technological literacy.

Other people cast a different argument in favor of the abolition of English. English, they say, is too filled with frills and nonessentials like the historical study of literature or vague goals like the "appreciation" of literature as art. Let's stick to the basics; abolish English and replace it with something called "communications skills": how to send and receive messages clearly and precisely. List the basics you want to teach; teach them; then measure your students to see whether you've succeeded.

We have no particular quarrel with the integration of contemporary literacies in the English classroom; nor are we opposed to ensuring that students who graduate from our schools have competence in basic communications skills. But it seems to us that critics err badly when they claim that print is dead and when they imagine that future cultures will rely on electronic communications media to the exclusion of reading and writing. Further, those people who would reduce English to a laundry list of basic skills are ignoring broad areas of competence in their zeal to make English functional.

Even though it seems fair to suggest that English teaching has had many failures, one must still ask, "To what end have all these methods and techniques and strategies been tried? What were people trying to accomplish with paperbacks or anthologies or formal writing or not writing or anything they could get away with?" The answer that comes back is clear. Whether using the new technology or the old, paperbacks or hardback anthologies, teachers have consistently and steadfastly had the adult standards discussed in Chapter 2 in mind.

For instance, when the use of film first became popular in English classes, one of the first texts to appear on the market was a glossary called "A Grammar of Film." The assumption—very old and really quite traditional—was that until students knew about film terminology—"pan," "fade," "wipe," "dolly in," "zoom," "cut," "take"—they couldn't properly understand or appreciate a film. Similarly, although the paperback revolution brought interesting, relevant literature to the English class, one still has the feeling that many teachers introduce paperbacks only as a new route to an age-old goal: "If we let them read what they want, perhaps we can eventually get them back to the 'good' books." Musical lyrics too often enter the classroom only as an oblique way of presenting poetry: "These popular song lyrics, class, are actually *poetry.* You see, poetry *is* something you've been enjoying all along without even knowing it. Now, let's look at the metaphors in the first line of this song. . . ." When "computer literacy" came into vogue, many schools and states followed an age-old curriculum pattern: Put all the new knowledge in a new course, isolated from all other subjects in the curriculum; then teach the "fundamentals" one at a time.

Marshall McLuhan has noted that we approach the future by looking in a rearview mirror. New media, he says, are often filled with the content of the old rather than used for fresh purposes. And so it is with innovation in education. Teachers discover film, then use it to teach traditional literary terms; curriculum reformers decide that it is innovative to make teachers list objectives, then settle for objectives whose origins are two hundred years old and whose underlying principles have long since been discredited. They decide every kid should use computers, then put all the computers in a single room where the non-computer teachers can't get at them. Under such circumstances, it is hardly surprising that "new," "revolutionary," "innovative" ideas don't seem to work better than did their predecessors.

If the teaching of English is to grow, and if the critics are to be answered, English teachers must deal with some first principles, asking themselves precisely what they are about. "What is English?" is a question that provokes debate whenever it is raised, but it is a question that must be considered by English teachers every time they enter their classrooms. What the teacher does—whether teaching metaphors and similes or trying to get students to write about their personal experiences—defines the subject not only for the teacher but for the student as well.

From Benjamin DeMott, "Reading, Writing, Reality, Unreality . . . ," in James Squire, ed., *Response to Literature* (Urbana: National Council of Teachers of English, 1968), p. 36. Copyright © 1968 by The National Council of Teachers of English. Reprinted by permission of the publisher and the author.

"English" is not centrally about the difference between good books and bad. It is not centrally about poetics, metrics, mysteries of versification, or the study of balance and antithesis in the Ciceronian sentence. It is not centrally about the history of literature, not centrally about changes in moral and philosophical systems as these can be deduced from abstracts of selected Great Works. Still more negatives: the English classroom is not primarily the place where students learn of the majesty of Shakespeare and alas for Beaumont and Fletcher. It is not primarily the place where students learn to talk about the structure of a poem or about the logic of the octave and sestet, or about the relation between the narrator and author and speaker and mock-speaker and reader and mock-reader of the poem. It is not primarily the place where students learn to mind their proper manners at the spelling table or to expand their vocabulary or to write Correct like nice folks. It is not a finishing school, not a laff riot with a "swinging prof," not an archeological site.

It is the place—there is no other in most schools—the place wherein the chief matters of concern are particulars of humanness—individual human feeling, human response, and human time, as these can be known through the written expression (at many literary levels) of men living and dead, and as they can be discovered by student writers seeking through words to name and compose their own experience. English in sum is about my distinctness and the distinctness of other human beings. Its function, like that of some books called great, is to provide an arena in which the separate man, the single ego, can strive at once to know the world through art, to know what if anything he uniquely is, and what some brothers uniquely are. The instruments employed are the imagination, the intellect, and texts or events that rouse the former to life.

The most articulate answer we've ever found to the question "What is English?" was written by Benjamin DeMott, a professor of English at Amherst College. DeMott's statement is a remarkably coherent and complex observation. It is important to note that he does not discard the traditions of the English profession. He values studies as diverse as the reading of great works and the learning of vocabulary. Yet he is unwilling to let the traditional studies completely dominate the discipline. English, he says, is centrally about humanness as it can be known and explored through language.

As we demonstrated in Chapter 2, language interpenetrates every part of our lives. DeMott is right in saying that there is no other place in most schools where the concern for the individual human being and his or her language is central. Most important perhaps is that he puts the various components of English into perspective by relating them to the personal growth of the individual. Does "correctness" matter? Of course it does, but it cannot be allowed to engulf students in mechanical matters so that the human voice is lost. Should students study the media and computers? Of course, since these technologies play an important role in structuring and shaping our lives; but students should study other human uses of language as well, including reading and writing.

If we accept the concept that English is a study of humanness—of humanity—we can see some important implications for the English program:

1. *"English" is more than just reading and writing.* While the first two Rs are a major concern of English teaching, the subject must broaden its

scope to include *all* uses of language, from short memos to long examination papers, from the "language" of television to the language of computers. English cannot afford to limit itself to the writing of school essays and the reading of school textbooks.

2. *"English" is not limited to the English classroom.* There has been growing awareness in recent years of something called "language across the curriculum," and English teachers have argued forcefully that reading and writing must be a focal point in every classroom, in every field or discipline. There seems to be a strong movement in schools and colleges toward interdisciplinary studies, and even in schools where interdepartmental cooperation is not easy, English teachers can take it upon themselves to include other subject fields in their work, inviting students to read about science, to write about social studies, to role-play and dramatize from history, to talk about consumer concerns, politics, and world affairs.

3. *"English" is a way of perceiving, knowing, learning, and becoming.* English is not simply a matter of mastering the language, for language is a part of all aspects of human experience. Martin Mystrand has described the English class as a place where one uses "language to know," not just studies the uses of language. Actually, the two are bound up with each other. Borrowing from Benjamin DeMott, we can say that English as a school subject is "not centrally" about the learning of language, either language structures or applications, that it is "centrally" about the processes of perceiving, knowing, learning, and becoming as these involve language. The point of connection, of course, is that in learning to use language to explore, to know, to become, one masters the forms and structures of the language as well.

THE ENGLISH CURRICULUM: THE STATE OF THE ART

The heretic spoke: "The only thing holding most educational institutions together is the brickwork and the heating and plumbing. Schools find it convenient to centralize the purchase of books, fuel oil, and hamburger meat, and economical to gather children in blocks of five hundred or two thousand for the purpose of educating them. But aside from these considerations (and perhaps a winning football team), most schools are simply physical conveniences—like bathrooms—with no spiritual or intellectual relationship to draw people or to hold them there."

"Hold on there!" Up the aisle came the assistant superintendent for instruction, struggling under the weight of a heavy volume. "This book provides our unity here. It is the curriculum guide that we have developed."

The book that the superintendent displayed was three hundred mimeographed pages long, bound in apple green paper, and held together with oversized brads. The preface included a letter from the school board, thanking the members of the curriculum committee for their dedication and long hours of work in preparing the guide, along with a note from the principal adding some comments about the tradition of excellence that the school had long enjoyed. Inside the guide could be found a pie diagram showing the components of English, a list of the textbooks shelved in the book room, charts of grammar objectives by grade levels, a list of senior high units, a bibliography of books approved for supplemental reading, sample lesson plans for teaching *The Pigman,* a list of spelling demons, and a map showing fire escape routes.

Had anyone asked, it would have been noted that the assistant superintendent's was the only extant copy, the others having been lost or misplaced almost as soon as they were issued.

Examining a typical curriculum guide often reveals an incredible amount of inconsistency and disarray, carefully masked by a good typing or printing job. In preparing this chapter, we reviewed approximately three dozen curriculum guides from elementary, junior, and senior high schools around the country, guides we collected at national meetings or through one of the national information retrieval systems. While there is obviously no national curriculum or "typical" school, we think it might be useful to present some generalizations about the common characteristics of these guides in order to create a view of the current state of the English curriculum.

The Elementary Years

"English" does not exist for the elementary teacher. It is either called "language arts" or is broken down into its various components: reading, writing, spelling, vocabulary, etc. And here is perhaps the greatest weakness of the elementary curriculum, for despite the opportunity for integrated studies presented by the self-contained classroom, elementary teachers tend to fragment language, presenting it to children in small bits and pieces. "Spelling" becomes a component all to itself (9:20 on Tuesdays and Thursdays). "Writing" becomes penmanship, which is different from composition. Elementary school children even pick up these distinctions. When Steve's son was in third grade, he was careful to distinguish "reading," which meant going to the library, from "reading workbook," which involved learning to alphabetize. While a great many elementary school teachers do a superb job of teaching language, we believe it is fair to say that in all too many cases, the English curriculum of the elementary grades is dominated by workbooks, work sheets, and fill-in-the-blank activities rather than by actual language production.

The Junior High/Middle School Years

At the risk of alienating a number of good, well-organized school staffs, it appears to us that the junior high English curriculum can best be characterized as "Basic Hodgepodge." While some middle schools and junior highs have established topical or thematic courses, most simply have an "English" or a "Language Arts," a general course, with teachers moving from one instructional unit to another without purpose or focus. This leads to a blend, or hodgepodge, characterized by the following list of units from a junior high school curriculum:

Building Blocks of Communication
Curtain Up!
Focus on Life
Man in Conflict
Power of the Paragraph
Western Sampler
Reinforcing Language Skills
Aquanauts and Astronauts
Communications Through Mass Media
Encounter and Insights
Laughter and Legends
Creative Composition

We do not wish to detract from the content of these units, for many seem sound, clever, and imaginative. The flaw it seems to us is the inconsistency in the definition of "English" that emerges from the list. Why must "Creative Composition" be isolated from the literature units? Why must instruction in language basics always be isolated in "Building Blocks" units? If mass media are important, why are they set apart in a unit of their own rather than integrated with either literature or composition work? Children characteristically take many, many such units of work during their junior high years, but we fear that often in the schools there is no real cumulative effect, no real sense of purpose and direction in the English that students "do."

The Senior High Years

Now we will risk alienating the English staffs of some top-notch schools by generalizing that in contrast to the junior high, the senior high English curriculum comes off as being "Advanced Hodgepodge." Most commonly, high schools offer a "general" or basic first-year English course, sometimes offered in different sections with students grouped by ability levels. Such courses have a twin aim of remediating what the high schools commonly conceive of as the misspent years of elementary and junior high schools, plus providing material to prepare students for the coming years. The content of the course may range from mythology—so they will understand classical allusions in literature—to grammar—so they will presumably learn to write and speak "correct" English. Like the junior high curriculum, the general courses tend to alternate a series of units in literature, language, and composition, often without apparent connections.

For upper-level students, we settle into the familiar pattern of the survey course: British, American, and world literature. In the late 1960s and early 1970s, elective courses broadened the offerings in the high school program, but in many cases electives presented too many choices so that topics and decisions overwhelmed the students. Too, in the heyday of electives, many courses of dubious intellectual merit with only marginal content in English crept into the curriculum. In recent years, the trend has been toward consolidation, eliminating some of the spurious choices, and, in some instances, replacing electives altogether and returning to the traditional survey.

In a report of the NCTE Curriculum Commission, Barret Mandel identified three basic orientations of the English curriculum: *basic skills, literary heritage,* and *personal growth,* each with its advocates, each with its particular strengths. The commission called for discussion of the three approaches and for philosophical and practical fusion if possible. As the reader well knows, we are clearly in the "personal growth" camp, but we would argue strongly that such an approach excludes neither *basics* nor *heritage.* We further claim, and will show on the following pages, that it is quite possible to develop a model of curriculum based on principles of personal growth and development that is rigorous and inclusive.

CURRICULUM: NOUN OR VERB?

In a great many elementary, junior high, and senior schools (as well as the colleges), the curriculum is static. When asked about the school's curriculum, many teachers will produce a *document,* a listing of courses, aims, and requirements, rather than describing what they *do* in the school. Thus "curriculum" has become a noun—an object—that is changed only when the documents are rewritten. Often a rewriting really means a reshuffling, so that all the old familiar parts settle, largely undisturbed, into new but more comfortable settings.

By contrast, curriculum can be conceived as a verb—something dynamic and changing—consisting of a set of flexible relationships and activities that evolve from a group of adults—the teachers; a larger number of young people—the students; and a set of resources—bricks and mortar, books, desks, pencils, and paper. When these parts function well together, they produce a community of language, a place where students read, write, and talk about concerns of their own, steadily increasing the range and complexity of their language skills. The English curriculum, in short, is a process— something *happening*—rather than a product or object, and its dimensions grow and shift just as surely as the needs and interests of the students change.

In order to become a verb instead of a noun, a curriculum must be both *collaborative* and *experimental*. We think too few teachers in the schools and colleges seem to be exploring their teaching systematically. As often as not, "innovation" consists of adopting a new textbook that covers the old material in new, or superficially different, ways. Few teachers are willing to experiment and share the results of their experiments with other teachers. Teachers tend to work alone, in silence, often masking their failures and sharing only their successes.

A faculty must find a common meeting ground where people can talk to one another, share their successes and failures openly, and search productively for new ways to solve common problems. This common ground does not mean that the faculty must be monolithic. To the contrary, the most productive schools are those that not only are diverse but also capitalize on the diversity of their members.

An experimental curriculum involving collaboration among teachers will obviously lead to constant development, evolution, and sharing. Although curriculum artifacts—written statements of ideas, units, aims, goals, and approaches—will be available, there may not be any single, dated "guide." Ideally, no formal revision will take place either, because revision will be constant, and the members of the department will look forward to new experiments rather than back to the documentation of a tradition.

It is also obvious that no standard curriculum will do for all or even for most schools. Any evolutionary curriculum will be shaped around the qualities of the participants. One can, however, talk about the curriculum-building process and about some of the stages through which faculties need to proceed as they evolve the curriculum and courses.

FORMING A THEORY OF INSTRUCTION

In *Toward a Theory of Instruction* (Belknap, 1967), Jerome Bruner makes a valuable distinction between a "theory of instruction" and a "curriculum." A *theory of instruction*, he suggests, is a consistent, coherent, if tentative, statement about what young people need to learn and about how they learn it, "a theory of how growth and development are assisted by diverse means." A *curriculum,* on the other hand, is a specific set of goals, methods, and materials.

Unfortunately, many educators are reluctant to deal with the necessarily difficult and abstract issues that come up in the process of developing a theory of instruction. Rather, they prefer to get to the "nuts and bolts," the practical business of mapping out a course of study. It is understandably tempting to avoid the "idealistic" stage in order to get on with the course outlining and the text adoption. But dealing with basic issues is critical, and unless a faculty is willing to grapple with them, the time spent planning is often wasted. Without a theory of instruction—even one that sometimes says, "We don't know" or "We can't agree"—the curriculum becomes fragmented.

The actual form that a theory of instruction takes is variable. It may consist of an essay about English teaching written by one member of the faculty; it may be a collection of individual statements submitted by individual teachers; or it may be an inventory of teacher talents in which the members of the faculty describe what they feel they can bring to the language community. Perhaps most useful, it may be an unwritten spirit of understanding that grows among staff members as a result of discussions and debates. What it cannot or should not be is the typical broad statement of "philosophy" for a school system—something so vague that any member of the department can seek refuge under it—a statement laced with meaningless platitudes about citizenship, morality, and the basic skills of language.

Gray Cavanagh has evaluated some of the questions that departments typically consider when planning curriculum (Figure 15.1). The questions for concern that he *rejects*—"How can the teacher best teach?" "What are the best ways of teaching the student our literary heritage?"—are the nuts-and-bolts questions. The questions he proposes instead—"How can the student best learn?" "What curriculum approach best assures the emotional and imaginative development of the student?"—are the broader questions that are the concern of a theory of instruction. Only after those have been answered adequately should the department begin moving on to more practical matters.

LEARNERS AND THEIR LANGUAGE

Perhaps the most neglected aspect of curriculum building has been the learner. Though most guides and catalogs are filled with statements about what the school plans to do with, to, about, and for the students, one seldom sees any overt indication of the teachers' understanding of the students and what they bring to school. Lack of concern with the learner is characteristic of the adult standards approach, since the overwhelming

FIGURE 15.1

From Gray Cavanagh, "Sanity and Balance in the English Program," *The English Journal,* February 1972. Copyright © 1972 by the National Council of Teachers of English. Slightly abridged. Reprinted by permission of the publisher and the author.

The Questions for Concern Should Not be	*The Questions for Concern Should Be*
How can the teacher best teach? What is the best course of studies?	How can the student best learn? What are the most effective ways of involving the student in the learning experience?
What are the best texts for teaching English?	How can the student be motivated to develop a taste for reading a wide range of books and magazines?
What are the best ways of teaching the student our literary heritage?	How do we teach the student to select and to teach himself those elements important to his personal understanding of the past and present?
What is the best way and sequence in which to teach basic skills of English?	How do we lead the student to master the processes necessary to his full development and to accept his responsibility to himself to select and perfect these skills in a developmental pattern?
How do we make the student learn efficiently those subjects and skills in which he is weakest?	By what approaches can we best enable the student to develop his talents and abilities in his areas of greatest interest and aptitude?
What curriculum approach best assures the cognitive development of the student?	What curriculum approach best assures the emotional and imaginative development of the student?
By what methods can the student best be taught standard English usage?	By what methods can the student best learn to express himself orally and in written form with power and individuality?

The Questions for Concern Should Not be	The Questions for Concern Should Be
How can teachers best work together to produce a valid course of studies?	What are the most effective ways in which the student can be enabled to direct his own learning?

interest of that approach is not in what the student *is,* but in what he or she supposedly should be.

In *Sense and Sensitivity* (London: University of London Press, 1965), J. W. Patrick Creber has argued that failing to look at the student has led to a split between "the interests of the pupil and the interests of the discipline." Curricula are constructed with the discipline—grammar, rhetoric, criticism—at the center, and students and their interests simply must be fit in around this center. Creber contends that the needs of students and the knowledge of the discipline must coincide. If they do not, he suggests, then the discipline or course content must be reshaped to fit the needs of the individual student.

From J. W. Patrick Creber, *Sense and Sensitivity.* Copyright © 1965 by J. W. Patrick Creber. Reprinted by permission of the publisher, The University of London Press.

The whole approach to [English] has encouraged [the child] to pass over vast areas of familiar but interesting experience—to bury it forever, without realizing its significance, without ever having an inkling of its connection with the subject he has been trying, so painfully, to learn.

We cannot, however, accept any such sacrifice—any dichotomy between the interests of the pupil and the interests of the subject. Such a distinction seems based on the false premise that the two are mutually exclusive or radically opposed. On the contrary, that method which is of greatest benefit to the child seems to be precisely the method which makes for the greatest vitality and sensitivity of language.

This view leads Creber to a simple but ingenious approach to developing a course of instruction. First, the teacher must study the students in terms of their psychological, emotional, cognitive, and linguistic development. Then he or she can sensibly select experiences that will both meet the students' needs and help them develop within the disciplines of English.

This curriculum process leads him to a program of "imaginative work" for students. After analyzing the interests and needs of his students, he perceives three developmental levels: the "rediscovery of the familiar" for 11-year-olds; "the expanding consciousness" for 12- and 13-year-olds, who are entering puberty and becoming more aware of themselves in relation to others; and "imagination and morality" for the older students, who are expanding their interests and concerns to encompass more and more of the world. Having selected these broad themes, Creber then chooses literature and writing activities that will help students explore the theme (Figure 15.2).

To implement this kind of approach, a school should take a very close look at the students it serves. One way of doing this, of course, is through interest inventories and surveys. A survey might include the following kinds of questions:

What are the principal common interests of the students at this age: animals and pets? boys? girls? the world outside? college?

What are the principal concerns that the students feel? What do they worry about most: themselves? their relationships with peers? their relationships with adults?

Where are they in the process of becoming adults? In what ways are they adultlike? In what ways are they operating under different patterns?

In addition, teachers should draw on their own experiences with students at the appropriate grade level, using all of their past experiences to focus on what can be happening in the English class.

Which books, poems, stories have proven "sure fire" with this group? Why?

Which books appeal to special interests?

What kinds of writing topics and speaking topics have worked well? What kinds haven't? Why?

Given completely free choice of language activities, which ones will students choose? What does this tell us about these students?

Teachers might also want to look directly at the language skills that the students already have mastered to discuss the direction those skills seem to be taking. One way to approach this would be for the teacher to think in terms of ten or so students whom he or she would regard as competent users of language for their own purposes at their present age, students who seem to be getting along well in the community of language—talking comfortably with peers and adults, writing successfully in the tasks they select, reading and generally enjoying it. Then the teacher might ask himself or herself:

What are the skills in language that these students have mastered to date? What can they do with language? What are they learning to do?

FIGURE 15.2

From J. W. Patrick Creber, *Sense and Sensitivity*. Copyright © 1965 by J. W. Patrick Creber. Reprinted by permission of the author. Published by the Exeter University Curriculum Centre.

CREBER'S PROGRAM FOR IMAGINATIVE WORK

First Year [Age 11]: The Rediscovery of the Familiar

For several reasons the training of the imagination to recapture visual impressions is a good starting point with children entering the secondary school. In the first place, such children tend to interpret the injunction "use your imagination" in a purely visual sense. . . . Secondly, the visual element is very obviously dominant in our society, particularly in entertainment. . . . One often has the feeling, when dealing with fourteen- and fifteen-year-olds, that much adolescent inarticulateness has its roots in a visual incapacity, or at any rate in a blunted sensibility; children appear to grow up without really seeing anything. . . . [p.23]

Topics for imaginative work:

Concentration exercises

Memories from nature (rainy days, Christmas morning)

Responding to pictures and photographs from nature

Responding to nature poetry

Second and Third Years [Ages 12–13]: The Growth of Consciousness

The stages outlined here are somewhat arbitrary and the division I am now making between the work for first- and second-year children is a case in point. Nevertheless, this division may serve to emphasize two general truths about children's development:

1. in this second year we may expect to see the nascence of adolescent self-consciousness
2. by this time the children are readier to be "art conscious"—to look at their work more critically and to learn some simple concepts of form and style.

. . . Though the main characteristic of this year's work will be its increased complexity, it will also differ from what has gone before in its greater stress on people as opposed to things. [p.48]

Topics for imaginative work:

Scenes describing people, especially familiar people

Descriptions of their own feelings in real situations

Descriptions of feelings in imagined situations

Critical or workshop examination of writing

The Final Stage [Age 14]: Imagination and Morality

Children of this age are becoming, as they move into the difficult period of adolescence, much more vividly aware not only of internal stresses but also of their relations with other people, whose behavior interests them deeply. The greater complexity and disintegration of their lives and the sharper intensity of their personal problems lead normally to a much greater degree of inhibition and self-consciousness. . . . A further characteristic of this age is of fundamental importance. Morality, for most children . . . as for most adults . . . is largely a matter of precepts and rules of thumb, which, though they may be modified or even rejected, are very rarely questioned fundamentally. . . . I believe that the only satisfactory method of making a real impact on the moral standards of the children is through the imagination by utilizing their already lively interest in people's behavior. They should now be ready to attempt subjects the aim of which is to make "reciprocity of viewpoint" part of their own attitude to people. [pp. 73–75]

Topics for imaginative work:

Responding to literature of human experience

Objectifying some of the difficulties of adolescence through literature

Thinking and writing about people in other situations

Dramatization of diametrically opposed roles

Writing from the point of view of others

From this discussion will emerge a developmental portrait of young people, a rather complex and detailed one if the curriculum group is serious about trying to determine student needs. Like the theory of instruction, it will be tentative; and it will recognize, furthermore, that not all students will or should fit precisely into the pattern that has been identified.

PLANNING AND DESIGN

In a follow-up to the article cited previously, Gray Cavanagh and Ken Styles have suggested in "Design for English in the 1980's" (*The English Journal,* September 1978, pp. 40–44) that curriculum design in the future will consist of three basic elements:

1. *Core program elements as determined by governmental education authority.* In this country, for example, both state and local boards of education have engaged in preparing lists of minimum basic skills for each grade level. Often such lists cover just a bare minimum. A curriculum planning group will need to include those skills but make certain they do not dominate the curriculum.

2. *Local program elements determined by team planning and individually by the classroom teacher.* In 1986 a commission convened by the Carnegie Corporation of New York strongly reinforced this notion of responsible planning, with a proposal for greater autonomy and increased accountability for teachers. Two components need to be considered in this notion of planning:

   a. *Team planning.* The local group—school staff, English faculty, districtwide planning group—meets to make some basic curriculum decisions. Such planning should go beyond adopting a series of textbooks or approving a free reading list. A good planning team will take into consideration the surveys described in the previous section and will be concerned with meeting student needs and monitoring growth, not just with sequencing course structures.
   b. *Teacher planning.* At the very best (or worst, depending on one's point of view), the government-mandated and locally planned curricula will account for perhaps 25 percent of a teacher's time. The individual teacher always has done and probably always will do the bulk of planning.

3. *Personalized program projects designed and contracted by students working individually or in small gorups.* Styles and Cavanagh involve students in the curriculum design, allowing for individualized and student-initiated work done individually or in small groups.

(A diagram of the Styles-Cavanagh program, including a balance of reading/writing/listening/speaking projects, is shown in Figure 15.3.)

The Curriculum Design

The next step is to select a curriculum design or "package," a way of dividing students and teachers into units or courses of a workable size

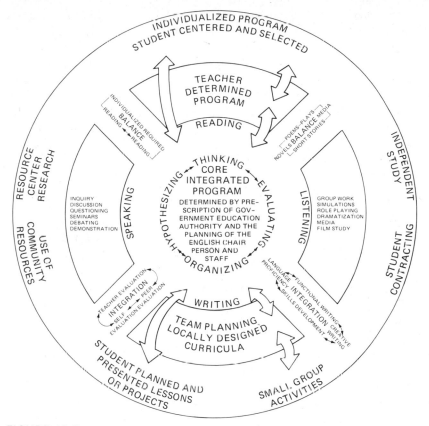

FIGURE 15.3

(From Ken Styles and Gray Cavanagh, "Design for English in the 1980s," chart appearing in *The English Journal,* September 1978, p. 40. Copyright © 1978 by the National Council of Teachers of English. Reprinted by permission.)

and content. A committee established by the Michigan Department of Education spent considerable time in 1985 reviewing various curriculum patterns being used within the state and nationwide. They found that virtually all curricula included provisions for four basic kinds of study in English: (1) literature and reading, (2) writing, (3) listening and speaking, and (4) language study. Most commonly, high schools emphasized grade level English as an organizing pattern (English I, II, III, IV), with a focus on introductory basics in the four areas above during the first two years and specialized literary study in years three and four. Urban schools and schools with low percentages of college-bound students tended to focus instruction more on job-related language skills in years three and four. Junior highs and middle schools tended to organize around themes and topics, not always in a pattern whose rationale could clearly be distinguished.

But many more curriculum options exist at all levels, and curriculum groups should probably consider some of the following possibilities.

• *Team Teaching.* Fashionable in the sixties, interest in teaming seems to have declined in the schools, partly because it often degenerated into lecture swapping, with team members taking turns lecturing to hordes of students on specialized topics of the team member's choice. The advantage of teaming is flexibility of grouping and the capacity for individualizing instruction. Through "buying time" by means of making presentations to large groups, the team members create more time for seminars and individual conferences. Thus, without disturbing schedule makers, schools create a kind of flexible scheduling. Many variations on teaming are possible. An appealing idea is that of clustering teachers of differing skills and experiences in single classes—a team consisting of master teacher, new teacher, a teacher aide, and perhaps a student teacher or group of tutors.

One area where teaming is on the upswing is in the middle school, usually grades 6, 7, and 8, where cross-age, interdisciplinary teams are growing in popularity. Junior high and senior high teachers might well study these experiments to see if they are applicable at the higher levels as well.

• *Small Group/Large Group.* This scheduling system allows the teacher to meet with a class as a whole once or twice a week and then in tutorial sessions several more times, usually for shorter periods of time. Such a plan allows for a high degree of individualization and helps to get the teacher out of the lecture mode.

• *Modular Scheduling.* Instead of relying on traditional 50-minute periods, modular scheduling breaks the day into a number of 15- or 20-minute modules. These "mods" can be combined in various ways to create long or short "periods" for small or large numbers of students. Unfortunately, many modular scheduling programs were a victim of the back-to-basics movement because flexible scheduling was seen as linked to "progressivist" programs; advocates of basics like standardized 40-minute class periods.

Given the realities of present-day English, our recommendation is for:

• *Themes Within Grade Levels.* This model maintains the year-long (or two-semester) pattern common in most junior and senior high schools, but creates themes and topics as the center of design, rather than literary nationalities or isolated basics such as grammar, writing, and reading. A model of this approach is provided by the high schools of Hampton, Virginia.

Steve had an opportunity to work with the Hampton teachers and with their outstanding English supervisor, Dr. Betty Swiggett, for over three years while this program was developed. The Hampton teachers began by surveying community and school needs and even met with a large number of community members who had previously been concerned about English instruction in the district. Several key parents from those meetings were then selected to serve as members of the actual curriculum planning group.

Following the kinds of processes outlined in this chapter, the curriculum builders first assessed the nature of the kids in the Hampton system, what they were like, how their skills and abilities varied. From this discussion grew a list of themes and topics for exploration. Although Dr. Swiggett offered the teachers the option of a textbook-free curriculum, based solely on paperback readings, the teachers felt they needed the support given by an adopted literature anthology. However, they chose *not* to follow the chronological/national pattern of instruction set out by this book and, in summer workshops, developed teaching units as shown in Figure 15.4. The program was implemented and evaluated with very positive marks by students, community members, teachers, and external reviewers. It stands as a clear example of how curriculum can be developed along sound, developmental lines.

EVALUATING A CURRICULUM

The curriculum development process ends with evaluation. Figure 15.5 shows a list of twenty questions developed for use in the Hampton project. The questions are designed so that the more positive replies given, the "better" the curriculum. However, not all curriculum specialists and teachers would agree that all the components and elements described are desirable. For example, though we believe basic skills instruction should be integrated throughout the program, many people are persuaded that skills must be taught in isolation to guarantee that they are properly covered. Thus people evaluating an English curriculum should revise, adapt, and rewrite the list to fit their own theory of instruction and particular interests.

LANGUAGE ACROSS THE CURRICULUM

We will not, in this chapter, attempt to go into great detail on the "Language Across the Curriculum" movement. Steve has written a series of monographs on this topic for the National Education Association: *Teaching Writing in the Content Areas (Elementary,* with Susan Tchudi; *Junior High Middle School,* with Margie Huerta; *High School,* with Joanne Yates; and *College).* That series is accompanied by an in-service resource kit that some school districts have found helpful in training both English teachers and teachers of other disciplines to "do more" with English and content. Briefly, our philosophy is this: There is every reason to support the language across the curriculum movement and every reason to suppose that it will remain an unfulfilled idea during our and the readers' teaching lifetime. Great progress has been made in the past two decades in attracting content area teachers to this interest area, and there is good reason to believe

FIGURE 15.4 HAMPTON CURRICULUM.
From the Hampton, Virginia, English Curriculum Guide.

THEMES FOR STUDY

Grade 7

Mythological Heroes

Folk Heroes and Folk Craft

Popular Heroes and Conflicts

Family Courage and Challenges

Grade 8

Identity/Self-Fulfillment

Communication/Interpersonal Relationships

Compassion and Common Struggle

Facing Reality

Grade 9

Struggles and Conflicts

Freedom and Responsibility

Hopes and Aspirations

Media and Modern Man

Grade 10

What's in a Name?

School Days

Who Am I Now?

What Am I Good For?

Grade 11

America's Dream and Promise

Inner Struggle

Struggle for Justice

Search for Values

Man and Nature

Grade 12

Know Thyself

Conflicts of Will

Choice and Consequence

Foibles

Critics of Society

the movement will continue. At the same time, it may be many decades before anything like *all* members of the teaching profession subscribe to it. (Witness, for example, the difficulty we've had just within our own ranks as English teachers over the matter of *grammar*.) We think it is prudent, then, for the English teacher not only to promote reading and writing in

FIGURE 15.5

QUESTIONS FOR CURRICULUM EVALUATION

1. Does the curriculum have a clearly stated, specific philosophy or theory of instruction?
2. Does the theory of instruction grow from observation and research into the growth and development of young people?
3. Does the philosophy reflect current, "state of the art" theory and research on language learning?
4. Do course and curriculum objectives grow from the philosophy so that they are consistent with it?
5. If a common core of objectives is suppled by either the school district or the state, do the objectives go beyond mere basics to encompass the full range of language activities?
6. Do common objectives leave room for individual teachers to develop courses around the individual needs of their students?
7. Does the curriculum reflect the expressed concerns and interests of parents and other community members?
8. Does the curriculum reflect the stated interests and concerns of the students?
9. Does the curriculum provide opportunities for students to assume some responsibility for their own education?
10. Do the courses or instructional units integrate the language arts rather than isolating them as separate components, that is, reading, literature, writing, skills?
11. Are students encouraged to read and write in a wide variety of discourse forms?
12. Are oral language activities—speaking, listening, dramatics, role playing—an integral part of language arts courses and units?
13. Are contemporary media—film, television, radio—a natural part of English work?
14. Does the curriculum include provisions for interdisciplinary work, either within English courses or through interdepartmental units and courses?
15. Does the curriculum make connections with the "real" world through community-based activities?
16. Does the curriculum directly or indirectly state or imply a concern for lifelong literacy?
17. Is the curriculum fully multicultural?
18. Does the curriculum pattern provide for sequence, growth, articulation, and natural relationships from one course or unit to another?
19. Does the curriculum provide for evaluation and assessment, both of students and the curriculum itself?
20. Does the curriculum provide for and encourage its own evolution?

the content areas for other teachers, but to do so within his or her class as well. We've found our own teaching enormously enriched in recent years as we have included interdisciplinary content and concerns. We now see ourselves as teachers of math, science, and history along with English and other disciplines.

Here is a sampler of some of the interdisciplinary connections that are possible:

Mathematics and Science

Neil Ellman, a former English/reading teacher who is now an assistant principal in New Jersey, has shown a few of the exciting possibilities for English/science work (see Figure 15.6). His focus here is on science in the English classroom, but one could easily share these innovative ideas with a colleague in science, whose own teaching would be enlivened by them.

History and Humanities

Experiments in History Teaching (Cambridge, Mass.: Danforth Foundation, 1967) is a collection of innovative programs being conducted by history teachers. But it takes little imagination to see how the topics listed in Figure 15.7 could be extended to include considerable reading and a good deal of imaginative writing.

Other Disciplines

Any field can be explored for reading and writing possibilities. The general formula that we use in looking for language/teaching ideas in the disciplines is this:

1. *Identify the basic concepts to be taught in the discipline.* We must start by finding out what is to be taught and learned, whether how to run a lathe or the characteristics of nonpermeable membranes.

2. *Review the basic text used in the course for readability.* What can the teacher do to make certain that students make contact with the text? Are there difficult words? New concepts to be pretaught?

3. *Look for related readings in popular, professional, or trade publications.* Chances are there will be related stories in the newspaper, even this very week. Teachers can look for instruction manuals, young adult trade books, adult books, and monographs for supplementary material. This can be read to the class as a whole or left for individualized reading.

FIGURE 15.6   SCIENCE IN THE ENGLISH CLASSROOM.
Excerpted from Neil Ellman, "Science in an English Classroom," *The English Journal,* April 1978, p. 64. Copyright © 1978 by the National Council of Teachers of English. Reprinted by permission.

READING [The students read:]

Literary and scientific journals to compare them to each other for stylistic and organizational characteristics;

Biographies of scientists and literary creators to discover the similarities and differences between such individuals;

Literary works written by scientists themselves to determine their particular ways of looking at life, if indeed differences exist;

Newspaper accounts of scientific breakthroughs to determine how the press communicates difficult concepts to a mass audience;

Science fiction to compare it to science fact and futurism;

Science articles and texts to uncover their subtle biases of language and thought;

And literature about scientists to study how they are portrayed by their literary counterparts. . . .

LISTENING AND SPEAKING [The students engage in:]

Panel discussions and debates on contemporary scientific issues and problems, particularly concerning the moral and ethical dilemmas created by scientific advances;

Oral reports on recent discoveries and inventions;

Listening exercises involving tonal quality, decibel level, animal sounds, etc.;

Interviews with local scientists, science teachers, and ordinary people affected by scientific advances;

And role playing of hypothetical meetings between great scientists and politicians, religious leaders, or literary intellectuals. What would happen, for example, if Charles Darwin could debate with Plato or

Pope Paul, or if Ptolemy could discuss the nature of the universe with Copernicus or Einstein? . . .

WRITING [The students write:]

Research reports on scientific and technological subjects;

Technical materials rewritten into language more suitable for the layperson, or more suitable for a child;

Imaginary conversations with and letters to scientific innovators;

Real letters to famous scientists, or letters-to-the-editor about current problems caused by technology;

Essays on the impact of science and technology;

Haiku capturing the precise moment of a scientific phenomenon, e.g., the moment of fertilization, binary fission, nuclear fusion, or osmosis;

Mystery stories in which the puzzle depends on a scientific principle;

"Found Poetry" from science textbooks and journals;

Futuristic scenarios in the manner of Herman Kahn and the Hudson Institute;

And journalistic accounts of the activities in the school's own science program.

4. *Identify some of the writing forms that are characteristically identified with this area.* Number 3 above makes this easier. The question is, "What do practitioners in the field write?" texts? manuals? letters to the editor? how-to guides?

5. *Cast some writing assignments in those modes.* Students write their own how-to manual for lathe operation. They write their own scientific report on nonpermeable membranes.

6. *Look for imaginative expansions for writing, speaking, dramatizing.* At this point students might be invited to do something a bit more creative, say, dramatizing a molecule faced with a nonpermeable membrane or speculating about how a lathe would function aboard a satellite in a weightless environment.

FIGURE 15.7   EXPERIMENTS IN HISTORY TEACHING.
Topics from *Experiments in History Teaching* Cambridge, Mass.: Danforth Center, 1977.

Artifacts in the Classroom [Studying historically important films, e.g., a 1934 German propaganda film.]

American Experience [Examining historical themes in the past one hundred years of American history through art, music, museum resources, and observation of historical artifacts.]

Landscape History [Using one's hometown or neighborhood.]

Afro-American Folk Culture [Through music, art, slave narratives, current street corner lore.]

Mass Culture and Country Music [Themes and concerns of Americans as expressed through their music.]

Historical Biography [Researching and writing a biography of a famous American.]

Simulating the Past [Role playing key events in history: the signing of the Treaty of Versailles, the trial of Galileo, Civil War diplomacy.]

The World of Work [Historical study of the work ethic.]

Industrialization in America [Investigating the evolution of technology in America with discussion of its side effects.]

Violence [Covert and overt violence in American history, with a discussion of implications about our values.]

Women's History [Examined through literature, film, journals, diaries.]

Baseball [A discovery unit on the history and evolution of the game.]

Language in Curriculum Design

It is possible, too, for the principles of curriculum design in this chapter to be extended to other disciplines. Just as there are developmental patterns within language development, there are patterns in the development of academic interests as well. Indeed, there is good reason to argue that growth patterns in other disciplines will follow those sketched out for

English if only because language and the cognitive processes that support it are central to learning in the disciplines. Steve's *ABC's of Literacy* (New York: Oxford University Press, 1980) sketches out such a program.

EXPLORATIONS

• Articulate a response to August Franza's modest proposal to abolish English.

• What is your answer to the question, "What is English?" Consider it from one or several points of view:

What *was* "English" for one of your favorite English teachers in high school or college? How did his or her teaching define it?
What *is* "English" for you now, either as you have experienced it in college or as you define it through your teaching?
What *could* "English" be if it fulfilled its potential?
What do you *want* it to be for future generations of students?

• What is your theory of learning, your "theory of how growth and development are assisted by diverse means"? You might find Gray Cavanagh's list of "questions for concern" given in Figure 15.1 helpful in pinning down your answers.

• The administrative structures of a school both simplify instruction and make it more complex. In your opinion, which of the following structures are worthy of being preserved or saved? Which should be discarded? Which would, with some modification, be useful? To whom?

	Preserve	Discard	Modify
Schools	( )	( )	( )
Classes	( )	( )	( )
Courses	( )	( )	( )
Grades	( )	( )	( )
Teachers	( )	( )	( )
Academic departments	( )	( )	( )
Diplomas	( )	( )	( )
Semesters or terms	( )	( )	( )
Administrators	( )	( )	( )
Class periods	( )	( )	( )
Counselors	( )	( )	( )
Recess	( )	( )	( )

• The Canterbury Schools Simulation. This game simulates the development of an English/language arts curriculum for the public schools of Canterbury, U.S.A. The superintendent of schools, Alton Grandstaff, has invited educational consultant firms to submit designs for the curriculum in any of the district's three schools: Chaucer High, Pardoner JHS, and Pilgrim Elementary School (Figure 15.8).

A minimum of ten people can play this game as part of a college "meth-

---

FIGURE 15.8

THE CANTERBURY PUBLIC SCHOOLS Canterbury, U.S.A.

Alton P. Grandstaff, Superintendent

New Instructional Program in English

Deeply concerned about the quality of literacy education, the Board of Education of Canterbury, U.S.A. is authorizing the development of new English/language arts curricula for Geoffrey Chaucer Senior High School, Pardoner Junior High School, and Pilgrim Elementary School. The Board seeks proposals from reliable educational consultant firms for the new program.

The town of Canterbury has been described as "Everytown" and was once named an All-American City by the National Chamber of Commerce. It is supported through a variety of forms of industry. It is known internationally as the Safety Pin Capital of the world, and the city also manufactures clocks and watches, lipstick cases, link chains, and comic books. This industry has also created an active business district and a need for a number of professionals in law, medicine, and related fields. In short, the town and its schools represent all walks of life.

Thirty-four percent of the students in the schools are members of racial or ethnic minorities, and the school district is committed to equality of educational opportunity for all. Approximately fifty percent of the graduating class of Chaucer High will go on to college, many to Canterbury Junior College, but a high percentage to the State university or other four-year colleges. Most of the remaining fifty percent will receive some form of vocational or career training after they graduate. The district is concerned about meeting the future needs of all students.

The Board of Education has no particular model or pattern of instruction in mind and invites consultant firms to develop highly imaginative, but sound innovative programs.

Proposals will be discussed at a public hearing.

ods" class or as a school or departmental in-service activity. Divide into teams of three, four, or five members. One group will role-play the Panel of Judges, whose duties are described below.

Each of the other groups becomes an educational consultant firm and chooses a name for itself like *Creative English Associates, Supergrammar Think Tank,* or *Tomorrow's Words Today.* In a predetermined period of time (ninety minutes to two hours seems to be a minimum), the educational consultant firms develop a proposal for the Canterbury school closest to the members' area of interest, either elementary, junior high, or senior high. Each firm makes a twenty-minute presentation to the Panel of Judges. The panel may select "best" proposals from among those submitted or merely quiz and question the presenters, asking them to explain and justify their decisions and proposals. The Panel of Judges must represent all segments of the Canterbury population as well as the superintendent's office. A typical cast for a panel of five might include:

1. A representative of the superintendent's office: a bright young person with a fresh Ph.D. in Administration and Curriculum. Reform is this person's stock in trade; nothing is good unless *innovative.*
2. A representative of the minority groups, preferably someone fairly militant and activist.
3. A member of the white blue-collar work force, someone who sees the schools as functional and doesn't want to see hard-earned tax dollars wasted.
4. A liberal parent from a professional background who wants to see the schools in Canterbury become just as imaginative as those in Kensington Hills, a neighboring wealthy suburb.
5. A representative of the English teachers, someone well informed about new trends in the field.

While the consultant firms are at work on their proposals, the Panel of Judges meets to develop a list of criteria for evaluating the proposals, possibly drawing on the evaluative questions listed previously. It must decide what kinds of educational features it sees as important, and it needs to settle on some ideas concerning whether or not the program is meeting the needs of the Canterbury students.

RELATED READINGS

Barret Mandel's *Three Language Arts Curriculum Models* (Urbana, Ill.: National Council of Teachers of English, 1980) is the most recent professional statement seriously surveying curriculum models. Although it is now a bit dated, it makes useful reading. We especially recommend David Jackson's *Continuity in Secondary English* (London: Methuen, 1982) because of its emphasis on a developmental process of curriculum development. Peter Medway's *Finding a Language: Autonomy and Learning in School* (London: Chameleon, 1980) is especially good for its discussion of how a faculty developed a systematic language-across-the-curriculum program. Medway is also candid in assessing failures. Peter Abb's *English Within the Arts* (London: Stodder and Houghton, 1982) is challenging because of its view that English belongs with the fine and creative arts rather than its traditional base with history/humanities/literature faculties. Finally, one should put "curriculum" in perspective with a reading or rereading of Ivan Illich's *Deschooling Society* (New York: Harper Colophon, 1971), which offers the radical view that we should not only abolish English, we should abolish schools, too.

Managing the English Classroom

16

A tall, athletic boy chases a smaller fellow around the classroom, grabs his blue denim jacket, and unceremoniously throws it out the third floor window. Other students leap from their seats and flock to the windows to see whether the jacket landed in the green garbage dumpster or became snagged on the protruding granite window ledges of the floors below. In tears and desperation, the teacher frantically calls the assistant principal for help.

THIS scenario—the out-of-control class—is a recurring nightmare for many newer teachers, but this incident happened to a teacher in the *ninth* year of her teaching career. It was, however, her first year in a junior high and her first year of English teaching. Prior to this, she had been a successful teacher of social studies in the high school, but now she felt like a total failure. A part of the problem was that in tenth through twelfth grades she had never encountered truly unruly classes and simply did not have the organizational skills to handle the energy and the need for frequent changes of activity that junior high age students seem to need.

Perhaps equally important, she had no strong sense of how to go about teaching English: She simply divided English up into three days of reading stories and two days of working on spelling and mechanics, all from the text or work sheets. She was not making any effort to connect aspects of instruction, and thus students felt no purpose or direction. In addition, the teacher had no idea how to teach and evaluate writing, so she limited her class to having students write answers to the study questions at the end of the stories.

In case the reader hasn't already read between the lines, this scenario actually describes what happened to Diana fourteen years ago, when she made the shift from high school social studies to junior high English. In retrospect, it is amazing that there weren't *more* problems in those first weeks of junior high teaching. After crying every night that first miserable ten weeks, she began to review her management in the classroom and examined what she was doing with content. She didn't learn how to teach English all at once; nor did she instantly understand the connections between how content is handled and how students behave. She did, however, learn enough to survive.

From Charles Greiner, "To Confess a Fault Freely." *The English Journal,* 66 (May 1977), p. 6. Copyright © 1977 by the National Council of Teachers of English. Reprinted by permission.

I was . . . a rather shy and quiet young man, very proper and given to blushing. The year was 1951. The shabby school was located in a small depressed mill town on the dark and gloomy fringe of Pittsburgh. The students were a scruffy lot of eighth graders whose experience in the real world was infinitely various and new, and in spite of their tender ages, far deeper and much broader than mine. . . .

Since it was the first week of school, I'd been lulled into a false sense of security. Things were going along without any enthusiasm, to be sure, but in the plodding, listless, orderly way my own school experience led me to believe was normal. Fortified with Warriner's sturdy grammar, I solemnly directed my charges through the confusing mazes of irregular verbs. Then we came, on a grey September afternoon, to the nemesis of all beginning English teachers. They were coiled there on page thirty-four like twin copperheads ready to strike—"To lie and to lay."

It was as if Whistler's mother had leaped from her rocking chair, thrown off her black dress, and stood revealed before our very eyes as Linda Lovelace! I initiated the apocalypse by innocently asking what the kids took to be highly suggestive questions.

"Now you lie down to rest, but the verb *lay* requires an object. Albert, can you think of something you could lay?" Rowdy laughter, catcalls, and Albert turning scarlet. "Here, here, class. Settle down! Complete this sentence, 'After school I intend to lay. . . .' "

Wild shouting, personal allegations regarding the horizontal activities of the class couple, lusty Albert and busty Mary Jane. These resulted in Mary Jane's screaming denials and a fist fight during which Albert broke a chair and someone tossed my new briefcase through the window.

I confess to the cardinal sin of never having taught lie and lay again.

In our years of teaching school and college students, we have found that a well-managed class is based on principles that go deeper than the issues of *control* and *discipline,* important as they may be. Classroom management requires a strong theoretical framework of what English is as a discipline and as a set of processes, and it demands an evolving understanding of what produces growth in students, as well as a clear set of personal values, sound teaching ideas, and good classroom organization. This chapter, then, is a summary of the organizing strategies and other bits of practical information we have gleaned from our years in the classroom. These can help blend content and teaching methodology into a workable whole so that learning can take place in the classroom and disruption is minimized. This chapter is also intended to offer suggestions to teachers, both new and experienced, who, sufficiently overwhelmed by the annoying details of classroom life such as attendance taking, paperwork, hall passes, and pencil handouts, simply have little energy or patience to even think about group work or classroom drama or creating resource areas or a publication of student writing. We'd like to remove some of the managerial roadblocks so the teacher can focus on effective strategies to involve students more deeply in their learning.

TEACHING STRATEGIES AND PRACTICES

Motivating students is essential to a well-run classroom, because the more fully students are involved in their work, the less desire they will have to be disruptive. When students are difficult to manage and are not responding to anything planned, a teacher's immediate instinct may be to crack down and show them who's boss. Fantasies of the military dictator bloom in your mind, and you see yourself marching down aisles, swagger stick in hand, giving orders, and watching students obey unquestioningly, doing assignments with care, watching you with awe mixed with respect and fear. Unfortunately, punitive measures seldom get the desired results; indeed, cracking down often leads to more and more rebellion. (Who ever said school isn't like "real life"?) Under the generalissimo system, teachers (and dictators) spend all their time controlling the class and monitoring every little piece of inattentive or annoying behavior.

One productive solution to the difficult class is to focus on ways of involving the very students who most irritate us. Since we believe that content, in the best sense of language and living, is at the heart of the matter of discipline, we try to involve students—all students, not just disruptive ones—by drawing on their own experiences and the language skills they have in hand, rather than dwelling on deficiencies.

CAPTURING AND MAINTAINING STUDENT INTEREST

Some ideas and strategies that have worked for us:

Use group work. Aside from being a sound way to operate instructionally, grouping helps with classroom management because you can "divide and conquer." Many behavior problems occur when students are expected to quietly listen to the teacher; that's when many students try to show off for their peers, and that's when it's easy to make a teacher look inept or foolish. When students are involved in groups, their focus is on others in the groups and on the work and they get fewer chances to show off to the whole class. (Of course, group work invites other kinds of behavior problems, and we'll offer more on how to make group work productive elsewhere in this chapter.)

Change activities frequently. Especially in middle school and junior high, kids need a change of pace. We reject the notion that kids of that age are incapable of maintaining interest for sustained periods of time, but we know only too well that lively, growing youngsters ("transescents" as they're called in some professional literature) need to be up and about, physically and intellectually. So instead of expending energy on keeping students doing one single task the whole hour, we plan two or three shorter activities. The class might start off with a written response to what has been read, then move to discussion groups, and conclude the hour with a whole class discussion on what was brought out in the groups. Or a class period might begin with a listing on the board of possible writing topics, move into writing time, and then wrap up with shared writing, with the whole class or with a partner or small group.

Interest students in what they are being asked to do. Student curiosity and engagement can be piqued by telling them something about a reading that will raise their interest quotient or by brainstorming and discussing possible topics. Stories can be left hanging at the end of the hour, "to be continued." The teacher can discuss his or her own responses to a book under discussion or challenge students to refute the teacher's "accepted" or conventional view of a plot, character, or theme. Literature, language, and life are, for all but the Living Dead, filled with excitement; the teacher needs to work on helping students become more curious about all three.

Find a range of materials for students to explore. Bring in magazines, newspapers, comic books, book carts, new paperbacks, bulletins and brochures, posters, videos, cassettes, or a set of moose antlers. Encourage the students to bring materials to share as well. Link these materials to the topic under discussion; find connections between the themes explored in literature and the stuff that people find interesting in their daily lives (the two often converge).

Do projects that have a genuine payoff. Exchanging projects with other grades or classes for reaction and response works well, providing an honest audience and a visible end point to a class unit. Diana had particular success with a poetry project in which eighth graders selected ten to fifteen poems that they thought third graders would like. At first the older students were skeptical, but by the second day they were gleefully reading poems aloud to one another from poetry books borrowed from the library. The students then copied the selected poems, made a cover, and sent the books to the third grade classroom. The third graders replied with letters commenting on selections and even on neatness and handwriting!

Demonstrate that student work is important and valued. Refer to it often and display some of it in the classroom. If students are asked to list all the ideas Mrs. Joe had on child rearing in *Great Expectations,* then compile the best ideas and post or announce the results in class. Sharing work done by the students will usually get good results in the English classroom because students perceive that they are doing something for more than the teacher.

PROMOTING STUDENT SUCCESS

It is axiomatic that nothing succeeds like success. More important and more subtle is that success demonstrates a growing body of skills and knowledge and is thus a direct indication of learning. We don't believe in piling on vague or half-felt praise, and we certainly don't advocate giving students a false impression of their own skills and abilities. Rather, we like to build on what students concretely accomplish in our classrooms.

Start with what they know. Students already feel that they have a lot to learn without the teacher telling them so all the time. To get positive results, begin with assignments the students can respond to successfully, then gradually move to areas that are less familiar. If the teacher is interested in teaching a specific form of writing, for instance, lead students into the assignment by letting them explore some writing they can do already. The formal persuasive paper, for example, can more easily be taught if students are first asked to write a letter to their parents persuading them to let them have, do, be into, or get out of something.

Make assignments at which students can succeed. We can all remember the intimidation of the "impossible assignment" in college. (Our negative favorite is the college prof who lectured on the enormous complexity of "existentialism," then asked us to summarize its essence in a single paragraph.) After reading a student's first writing assignment, the teacher will often recognize the student's strengths and weaknesses. If we are truly interested in the learning of students, it becomes obvious that asking them to do something that is far beyond their skill level is self-defeating for student and teacher. For instance, assigning a research paper to a student who has no idea of how to search for and gather information is frustrating for the student and discouraging for the teacher. Instead, ask the novices to put together a dictionary on topics which interest them: hunting, music, UFOs, dreams, astrology, or cockroaches. Next the students create appropriate definitions for each term. As they put together the dictionary, they will naturally interview one another on word meanings and do some elementary research in the library. This project, then, builds their confidence in research skills and prepares the students for further research projects.

Give good directions and concrete assignments. Before asking students to write a "response" to a story, tell them what a response is and what kind you expect. Tell them you want them to react to or summarize the story, to detail what they didn't understand, to describe what made a strong impression on them, to explain what they would like to say to the author or a character in the story. Vague assignments will elicit vague and often boring work.

Help students make sense of what they are doing in class. The ever-present "Why are we doing this?" should be answered. If you can't answer this convincingly (to yourself as well as the students) you may need to think more about what you're about. Teachers who understand the links between reading, writing, thinking, and speaking and can convey information about purpose to students will usually get a better response from them. Students also need to be shown how plans fit in or expand on what they've already done. Presenting material without providing a context not only confuses students, but often makes them angry because they can't see the point. They resent "busy work," not only because it is usually boring but also because they don't see what they will gain from it.

Help students know what kinds of resources are available in the library. But don't just take them on one more grand tour of the card catalog and the *Reader's Guide.* Help students identify a topic they're excited about, then explore the resources. Show them vertical files, reference books, the catalog, bibliographies. Use your expertise as a library user to help them find what they need. Then ask them to report back, not only on what they found, but on where and how they found it.

Encourage artwork and drawing to embellish stories and projects. This can build commitment on the part of the student to completing the project. Many students enjoy art as a change of pace, and even the least talented can do scissors-and-paste work with colored paper or magazine photographs. Too, artwork is the only thing some students feel they can do successfully. Such projects help build pride in classwork and add to audience impact.

PROMOTING INVOLVEMENT IN WRITING

In the teaching of writing we are concerned first with the relationship between student and self. Writing is an act of self-discovery that engages the deepest elements of identity. For the writing student, literacy is achieved when the continuity of self is articulated well. The skills so vital to this process are not confined to the pages of texts; nor do they rest solely as a body of knowledge within the minds of teachers. Human beings are born with them; the impulse to speak, to make language, is natural and is the most distinguishable quality of the human species. When we consider the writing problem, we must remind ourselves that writing has origins independent of the educational process.

Larry Levinger reminds us of the "human side" of illiteracy, that writing grows from inside and is a reflection of the self. He proposes further that "the poor writing student has at some critical stage in his life experienced trauma in his attempts to communicate, and has, as a result, turned off to the natural and authentic elements of language." The student becomes blocked, in short. Although we think "trauma" may be too strong a word, it's clear to us that many nonwriters have, in fact, suffered embarrassment and even humiliation over their attempts to write in the past. No wonder these people frequently become "discipline problems" in the writing class. Some antidotes to the poison of writer's blocks:

Read student work aloud as a way of modeling good writing. Besides giving some recognition to students, this lets students know clearly what is expected of them while showing that individual responses are valued.

Establish a dialogue with students through journal writing. Make sure students receive frequent responses from you to their journals, even short notes. Journal writing is an excellent way to build trust and to get students writing. Discuss possible topics at the beginning of the week or class period so students will feel they have something to write about.

Use short writing assignments. For especially disruptive classes this works well. Ask them to write a sentence or paragraph that begins with "School is. . . ." After a few minutes of writing let students share orally what they have written. Other beginnings that get a response are: "Teachers are . . . ," "Parents are . . . ," "Music is . . . ," and "Fun is. . . ." Students become quite involved in discussing what they have written and often want to compile the most interesting sentences and post them in the room or make them part of a classroom booklet of writing.

Compose on the overhead projector. Diana used this technique in a class of tenth graders, all of whom failed English the term before. They had just completed *Of Mice and Men* and were trying to write a character sketch that would do justice to Lenny. They loved Lenny and wanted to make sure it sounded right. Diana started by writing the first sentence on overhead acetate, then called on students to continue. The class had great debates about how phrases sounded and which words captured the meaning they intended. It took two days to complete this character sketch because the students were so involved. Students were then responsible for copying down the finished product and commenting on the parts they liked best/least.

Draw on students' memories. Everyone has memories of childhood jokes and games. Encourage each student to write up the jokes and games they remember from second or third grade. If possible, send these students to an elementary school to interview youngsters on current jokes and games. Then use these rich resources for writing projects.

GETTING STUDENTS INVOLVED WITH READING

Most English teachers are in this business because they value books and like to read. The savvy teacher also comes to recognize that reading can be a powerful aid in class discipline, even in classes consisting of less able readers.

Read aloud to the class. Find high-powered, engrossing, fast-moving stories or novels and read them as dramatically as possible to the class. Even the oldest, most jaded students will generally listen quietly and even become involved in the story. In Diana's tenth grade class, mentioned previously, reading *Of Mice and Men* aloud gained class involvement. The students were startled that she actually seemed to *like* the book, and they commented that they never had teachers who seem to like what they were doing in class. Oftentimes, the students in classes that tend to be disruptive have never read a whole book before and respond positively to oral reading. Some young adult novels that work particularly well for usually disinterested students include *A Day No Pigs Would Die* by Robert Newton Peck, *Ace Hits the Big Time* by Barbara Beasley Murphy and Judie Wolkoff, *Slake's Limbo* by Felice Limbo, *Dear Lola, or How to Build Your Own Family* by Judie Angell, *Roll of Thunder, Hear My Cry* by Mildred Taylor, and *Where the Red Fern Grows* by Wilson Rawls.

Find ways to involve students in response to their reading. Do more with short stories or novels than having them answer comprehension questions at the end and get ready for a test. Start with their response or reactions to what they've read and build activities that help them respond even more. (See Chapter 7 for more specific ideas.)

Ask for students' evaluation of what they've read. For instance, bring in a batch of young adult books from the library; have students choose one to read; then have them post their evaluation of the book on a class or library bulletin board.

INVOLVE STUDENTS IN ORAL LANGUAGE

Talk, chatter, gossip, hootin' and hollerin' are the bane of the classroom disciplinarian's life. Most teachers are agreed that students' strongest skills in language are oral and that we need to "do more" with oral language in the classroom. Here are some ideas for channeling classroom talk productively:

Encourage oral storytelling. Students are very willing to share a ghost story, or a scary story, a recurring dream, family myths and legends, school or community myths and legends. After the telling, students can write them up or (lest writing be seen as punishment for volunteering to talk) tape-record them so that students in other classes can hear them.

Involve students in scripting stories and reading them aloud. (See Chapter 13 for details on reader's theater.) Begin by showing them what this kind of scripting involves, perhaps having them perform a script prepared by you or by last year's students. Scripting draws on students' intuitive knowledge of speech patterns in transforming a story into a play, then allows them to use that knowledge in dramatic presentations.

Capitalize on young people's speaking abilities. If students want to write and perform an oral "rap" or rhymed chant as a response to a story, encourage them to do so.

Discuss what's on students' minds; then channel this energy into productive talk. Let them air their gripes and pet peeves, then let them discuss productive solutions and remedies. Also keep in touch with specific events that students are concerned about in school. For example, if lunch hours are suddenly shortened or the absence policy is abruptly changed, hold a discussion or debate the issue in class. Frequently this sort of discussion will lead into writing, reading, and even research activities.

ESTABLISHING PROCEDURES IN THE ENGLISH CLASSROOM

We've stressed that helping students achieve a strong sense of purpose and involving them in the content of a course is crucial to their (and your) success, but this will not happen unless the English classroom is well organized, so that students know what they can expect and see that the teacher has procedures to follow. Without careful organization, chaos often erupts, especially at the beginning and end of the class period. When this happens at the start of class, the teacher has to use much energy to get the class settled down and on task, and much valuable time is wasted.

Beginnings and Endings

Seating charts can be extremely helpful to even the most experienced teacher. If the teacher is dealing with mature groups of eleventh and twelfth graders or very small groups, this may not be necessary by the end of the term. However, if the teacher is to take roll quickly and efficiently, a seating chart is invaluable. Seating charts also allow the teacher to learn names quickly and to identify noisy cliques from the first day of class. One useful technique Diana has developed is to make a miniature copy of the seating chart, which is then taped into the attendance book—the chart folds out for attendance taking and saves the teacher a lot of time that would otherwise be spent flipping back to the seating chart or hunting for it on the desk. Steve now uses a computer data processing program to record student names and sundry kinds of relevant information; this list can be reformatted in various ways without retyping, so the master list can produce a seating chart, attendance log, phone and address list, and even individual summaries of course progress.

In peppier classes it is important to structure activities for the early moments when attendance is being taken or other class business is being transacted. Students can routinely:

- Write in their journals.
- Copy assignments from the board into their notebooks.
- Write a mini-essay on the quotation of the day.
- Take turns being responsible for telling a suitable joke or story.
- Take turns reading favorite poems.
- Offer brief reviews of last night's TV.

Sometimes, however, with classes that can handle it, it is good to let kids chitchat while roll is being taken so that their social needs will be met and they'll be more willing to settle down and start work.

The end of the class hour is another sticky time. If closing details are not handled smoothly, students can become an instant mob, racing to the door and jockeying for position. We'll sometimes offer such quickie activities as filling in *Mad Libs,* reading humorous poetry, or asking students to figure out two or three limericks.

Distributing Materials

Even passing out books or work sheets and collecting student work need to be handled carefully or the room can quickly erupt into pandemonium. These cautions are not necessary for the more mature classes, but organization makes distribution easier in any case. If books in the room are to be passed out to everyone (a common practice in schools with a text shortage or in classes where teachers use supplemental works), a good plan is to have one student from each row come to the front to get enough books for the entire row. Use the reverse procedure to collect books, and rotate this responsibility so that no student feels overburdened.

Passing back papers can be a nightmare that begins with calling out student names, continues with students jumping up to get their papers, and ends with the whole room in an uproar because student attention has been diverted. It's inviting for kids to watch all the action—the moans and exclamations—as their cronies respond to the evaluation. Whispers of "whad ja get?" soon turn into the infamous dull roar. A simple procedural matter is to have students put their row or group number on their papers, along with their name and class hour. You can even set up routines where students know to place their papers on the bottom or top of the stack as papers are passed up the row, so you can keep them in order and pass them back without sorting. It works especially well to have these stacks of papers on the students' desks as they enter the class so that the usual before-class activity and paper-passing-back activity are combined into one.

For especially high energy classes you can even place books and materials on front desks before students arrive. This way there is no reason to move around the room, and poking and pushing and shouting are minimized.

MISCELLANEOUS BOTHERS AND PROCEDURES

One teacher we know had to develop guidelines for the use of the pencil sharpener, which became a place of impromptu conferencing among the inmates. Friskier students loved to frequent the pencil sharpener so they could either bop other students on their way or meet their friends for a bit of quick but often loud gossip. The English teacher of our acquaintance was so harried by pencil-sharpening issues that she removed the pencil sharpener from her room. However, now she often has to deal with almost unreadable papers written with very dull pencils! We suggest allowing students to use the pencil sharpener only before class or allowing only one person at the sharpener at a time.

Now, pencil sharpeners may seem far removed from the glories of Wordsworth and Shakespeare, but given the nature of the captive audience, it is amazing how much teacher time these seemingly minor issues require unless teachers very quickly come up with procedures they can live with. You don't want a classroom that is bogged down in rules and regulations, either. The key decision each teacher must make centers on which procedures are necessary to make classroom management smooth and efficient.

Order in the classroom is enhanced if materials, books, and supplies are organized in such a way that students know where things are without asking the teacher. Markers, tape, scissors, and pencils can be kept in coffee cans on the teacher's desk or on a table nearby. Dictionaries and other reference materials are accessible if they're clearly labeled and on reachable shelves.

Student journals, which many teachers have their students leave in the classroom, are stored on shelves or in boxes by hour and by row. That way students can easily pick up their journals on the way into the classroom. Keeping a small box on the teacher's desk clearly marked for incoming work encourages students to put their drafts in an identified place rather than in the middle of the teacher's desk or in his or her hands. If student writing is to be collected in a portfolio throughout the year, a file drawer or collection of cardboard boxes set aside for this purpose will ensure that students can easily find the work they need.

Some teachers shy away from individualized reading programs because of fears about record keeping. This need not be as complicated as it might seem if the teacher utilizes the student manpower available in the classroom. Diana has found it effective to appoint one student to be in charge of counting any library books in the class at the end of the hour and making sure all students have returned the books to the front of the room. To keep in-room free reading books organized, have students make a file card for each book, writing the title and author's name on the card. These cards are put in a small file box, alphabetized by the author's last name, and kept near the front of the room. When new books arrive, they can be distributed for student perusal while the students write book cards.

A student can also be in charge of the in-class paperback library checkout system: Students simply sign the card of the book they choose and place the card in another small file box for books in circulation. When books are returned, the student in charge finds the card, crosses out the borrower's name, and refiles the book on the shelves.

To alphabetize books or not? Diana has collected at least three hundred books in her classroom, and she has students shelve them by the author's last name. Bookshelves are organized by portions of the alphabet, A–E, F–M, etc. If your in-class library is small, or if you know it well, you may prefer random shelving, since you can spot books quickly. Still, some students love to help keep the room organized, and using them as librarians pleases them and eases the burden on the teacher.

Steve always thought the problem of "pencil thieves" was limited to the elementary and secondary schools until his university department chair sent 'round a somber note saying that so many pencils had disappeared that the department could no longer supply them for students to use in completing course evaluations. The supply of pencils is precisely the sort of problem that can drive the English teacher into early retirement or an early grave. Many students simply do not bring pencils to class. Teachers rant, rave, and gnash their teeth, but the problem persists. Elaborate systems have been devised, ranging from securing collateral for borrowed writing implements (a method that leaves the teacher with a drawer full of lunch cards, broken watches, bracelets, sunglasses, but no pencils) to the obviously self-destructive system of forbidding pencil-less students to do any work in the class. One teacher used a sign-out system and soon found the class hour shot with thirty-three students signing out and checking in pencils every day. Diana always has eight to ten loaner pens and pencils available and puts a student in charge of collecting and distributing them. Steve suspects that system might even work at the college level, since students also can borrow from classmates and seem more committed to returning the pencils to their peers than to the teacher.

MANAGING ACTIVITY IN THE CLASSROOM

For teachers who have resource areas in their rooms, it also takes forethought to figure out how to move students to these different areas in the room without having traffic jams or bickering over resources. On days when students will be working on different activities, the easiest way to handle movement is to call groups of students alphabetically or by rows to select materials. Some will get books from the poetry center or writing ideas from the writing file; others will retrieve a piece of their own writing from their writing portfolio for further work; while still others may be getting supplies to put the finishing touches on a project that will be displayed in the library.

Group Work

To a teacher who has never had students work in groups, the whole process may seem potentially chaotic: desks being pushed willy-nilly around the room, loud student voices, the irritating sounds of scraping furniture, books being flung to earth. Our commitment to group work is based on the experience that careful planning can not only eliminate these problems but also involve students more deeply than if they were working alone. Initially, small group discussion and projects take a great deal of careful planning by the teacher to figure out how to move students around the class and how to keep them involved in the group work. When students are used to groups, they can move to them quickly—but training *is* required. Sometimes the teacher can arrange the desks in circles before the students arrive, perhaps listing group assignments on the board. It's also a good idea initially for the teacher to choose group membership until the students have built skill in the group process and can see the positive outcomes.

Once seated, students need specific directions about what they are to accomplish and how they should go about it. Asking them to do anything as general as "discuss the story" will not usually work. As we've suggested in Chapter 12, task-oriented groups work best, and this can often be enhanced by a handout or summary sheet for the students to prepare. Limit group work at first by giving groups ten or fifteen minutes to solve a problem; then extend the amount of time in groups. It's better at the beginning to stop before everyone is done than to wait until each group has finished and run the risk of having students sitting and not quite knowing what to do. Always follow up with group reports so that students know they are accountable for the assigned work. Students can help put desks back where they belong if your next class needs a different room arrangement. Giving students this responsibility frees the teacher from one more detail of group organization. After several sessions of small group work, the teacher will probably find that students prefer this kind of classroom organization because they get a chance to be involved and can voice their opinions and ideas.

Writing Conferences

Books on writing instruction frequently make conferencing sound effortless and glitch-free. The experienced teacher, however, quickly raises an obvious question: "What do I do with the other twenty-nine students?" Steve likes to use silent reading days for conferences, though Diana prefers to maintain the silence and even read along with the students. A good time to conference is when students are working in pairs or alone, perhaps on an assignment or a piece of writing. A conference may involve calling students up to the teacher's desk for five or ten minutes, but we also like to do "miniconferencing," where we float about the room while students work and engage in thirty-second discussions on particular points.

PLANNING FOR INSTRUCTION

Good planning goes hand in hand with good teaching and organizing strategies in contributing to a successful English classroom. Teachers have to be ready for almost anything on a given day, since administrative decisions can change the bell schedule drastically on very little notice. Too, because English is a required course, this is the class commonly selected for testing or other schoolwide activities and announcements. School pictures may be taken during the English classes, and there is the usual list of interruptions common to all classes: school assemblies, announcements, pep rallies. Such distractions can consume student energy and make it difficult to interest students in any kind of academic endeavors for the day.

Fragmented Days

It's a good idea, then, to have on hand a supply of short, language-related activities for disrupted days. Students can become engrossed in completing crossword puzzles, finding words that rhyme with a list of words given, or seeing who can make the most words out of the letters in *architecture* or who can come up with the longest list of homonyms. These kinds of days are also good for listing activities: Who can come up with the longest lists of annoying behavior or things to hate about vegetables or despicable traits of siblings? Students can make lists of major actions in a novel or traits of characters; they can even turn lists into short scripts or conversations. List making works on fragmented days because each item is short and doesn't require sustained thinking; it tolerates interruptions.

Individualizing

Planning for the English classroom also involves having extra material available for students who finish early or who want to do something for extra credit. At times like this, having puzzles, word searches, or other word games, as well as having books for browsing, can absorb energy and maintain the interest of those who are done with the work for the day.

It's also good to keep on hand a supply of material for the genuinely disruptive student, the kid who needs to be moved. Keep on hand the *Guinness Book of World Records,* books of sports facts, and catalogs or indexes of free materials by mail. Paging through the *Guinness,* with its many pages of pictures and amazing records, has "soothed many a savage soul."

Class Discussions

Imaginative planning is also essential for successful class discussions. The prepared teacher will ask students at the beginning of the hour to jot down a sentence or two on whatever is to be discussed. Then discussion can begin by the teacher asking a sampling of students to read their responses. After a few of these are read, other students will begin to react to fellow students' statements and lively discussions can follow. Discussions also can die or never come to life at all if the teacher asks general questions. Instead of asking students "Do you have any questions?" or "What's your reaction to this?" (two questions which always seem to produce blank stares) begin with a concrete question: "What appealed to you or bothered you about Gene's behavior in Chapter Five?" or "Have you ever been ashamed of anyone the way Pip was ashamed of Joe?"

Silent Reading

English teachers are told to give students time to read in class, but often they have little idea about how to actually get kids to read. Given a choice, most students would rather socialize or do homework for other classes. Students should come to see that the reading time is connected to their classwork and is a normal and legitimate procedure for English classes. If students know they will be sharing their book with others through an informal book talk or completing a project that will "count," they are much more likely to take the silent reading seriously.

The first few times students have class time to read, the teacher needs to be very precise about the ground rules; it sometimes may even be necessary to have students clear their desks of everything but the book they are reading so they won't be tempted to do homework for other classes. It may take students a while to settle down, and the teacher should remind them that there is to be no stray talk. If the teacher reads along with the students, this modeling of behavior may help bring order to the class, since once students see that the teacher is engrossed in a book they are much more likely to settle down and get into their own book.

TEACHER ATTITUDES AND BEHAVIOR

Teachers set the tone of a class not only through management procedures and instructional strategies but also through their own attitudes and behavior. Our experience suggests the following general guidelines for English teachers to follow:

Consistency. Students like to know where they stand. If gum chewing or failing to put their names in the upper left-hand corner of their papers doesn't bother the teacher on most days, students will not understand when the teacher suddenly becomes enraged by these acts.

Fairness. Students like to feel that they are being judged on their own merits and are upset if a teacher assumes that because a sibling was a troublemaker or a good writer, the present student will be like that too.

Interest and involvement. Teachers who seem genuinely interested in their work will generally receive positive responses from students, who like teachers who interact with them and show their willingness to help them. It is helpful if teachers remember that they are not simply servers who dish out assignments and then sit at the table until the meal is over. If students see that teachers are willing to be involved, they'll be more willing to be involved too.

Sense of humor. Humor in the classroom can save the day for both the teacher and the students. The ability to see the humor in a situation says something about the teacher's willingness to be human, and students respond positively to that trait.

Willingness to listen. Everyone likes to be listened to and have their ideas and opinions count for something. Students are no exception. They have little tolerance for teachers who exhibit a know-it-all attitude and refuse to listen to them.

Liking students. Teachers who view adolescents as subhumans will not get as far with them. Good teachers appreciate adolescents for their uniqueness and vitality.

Willingness to be the adult. Although we have written of the ideal of student-centeredness, this concept does not imply that one refuses to take on authority. As the adult, the teacher makes the classroom a place where students can work without being bothered by excessive noise or by teasing. Students need to feel that someone will set guidelines in the classroom and they look to the teacher to do this. They often do not feel they can set limits on themselves, and they rely on the teacher to help them do this.

Taking actions to match feelings. When Diana first began teaching junior high she would tell students in a very pleasant voice that she was angry at their behavior. They simply didn't believe her and continued with their disruptive behavior. As she learned to show through her voice and facial expressions that she was unhappy with their behavior, they would listen.

Showing students what kind of behavior is appropriate. If students are getting a little too noisy, the teacher reminds them to keep the noise level down before it gets out of hand. If a student walks in front of the teacher while she is talking, the teacher reminds the student that that is not appropriate. A willingness to deal with seemingly minor issues goes a long way in maintaining a classroom where students respect each other's right to learn.

IF ALL ELSE FAILS

In spite of all the best plans and strategies and attitudes, there are times when nothing seems to work with individual students and they continue to be disruptive. For behavior that does disrupt the class:

- Firmly ask the student to stop doing whatever is disruptive.
- Move the student to another seat or another part of the room.
- Follow up after school with a phone call to the student's parents.

Some behavior is more serious and needs to be dealt with more swiftly. In these cases have the student wait in the hall outside the class until you can step outside and discuss the behavior. Confronting a student in class will usually escalate the problem, and the student will not back down for fear of losing face with peers. The hallway provides a more neutral and private place.

- If behavior involves fighting with another student or verbal abuse of either the teacher or another student, send the student to the office. Do not admit the student back to class until you have had a conference with the administrator and the student to discuss the behavior that caused the student to be sent to the office.

EXPLORATIONS

- Go to several bookstores and make a list of the "word play" books or other books you think could fill those empty moments in the English classroom. Include crossword puzzles, word searches, and any other books that encourage using and looking at language.

- Ask other teachers about what they consider their best organizing strategies. List these ideas and consider their potential usefulness to you.

- Interview students on what teacher behavior most affects their learning in a positive or negative way. Why do they want to work harder for some teachers than for others? Draw conclusions.

- Brainstorm for a list of art activities that could be used and tied into an English classroom. Ask other teachers for feedback on your list.

- Try some of the activities suggested in this chapter in a class that is considered not to be well motivated. Or, see if you can observe a teacher who has a reputation for good classroom management.

- The end of the school year is also a difficult time to plan for because summer vacation is on everyone's mind. Construct a week's worth of high-interest activities that would work at that time of year. (Consider using it early in the year, too, but keep a good supply in reserve.)

RELATED READINGS

We quite honestly cannot recommend any books on "classroom management" in the abstract. Such books (which are widely available in bookstores and teacher centers) seem to us to concentrate on advice that is independent of content and rules which are either simplistic or inappropriate for a wide range of situations. In this chapter, we've tried to suggest ideas for you to try in the classroom, invariably linking management to content. While we don't claim that this chapter is the last word in classroom management, we think you're much more likely to find thoughtful words growing from your own experience than in the pages of books devoted to managerial techniques.

Evaluation, Grading, Assessment, and Research

HOMEROOM TEACHER_____	**STUDENT PROGRESS REPORT**					_____SEMESTER	

STUDENT_____YEAR 197____ - 197____GRADE_____

SUBJECT	TEACHER	1		2		SEM. EXAM	SEM. GRADE
		GRADE	COMMENTS	GRADE	COMMENTS		
DAYS ABSENT							
TIMES TARDY							

KEY TO MARKS
A—Excellent
B—Good
C—Average
D—Below Average
E—Failure
I Incomplete

21-M—10-71—RIEGLE PRESS INC.—DR-9992

KEY TO TEACHER'S COMMENTS (T. C.)

1. Excellent all-around student
2. Follows directions
3. Is able to give and accept constructive criticism
4. Volunteers for extras
5. Shows improvement
6. Consistently courteous and co-operative
7. Takes pride in work

8. Attentive in class
9. Good attitude
10. Tests unsatisfactory
11. Capable of doing better
12. Talks too much
13. Disturbs others
14. Does not bring required materials to class
15. Wastes time

16. Careless with school property
17. Absent too much
18. Needs supervision of home study
19. Does not pay attention
20. Does not meet assignments
21. Careless work habits
22. Lack of respect for others

FIGURE 17,1   STUDENT PROGRESS REPORT.

WE sometimes think the educational system of this country is a house of straw, bound together by the grading system. If Ph.D. candidates stopped hustling for grades in advanced seminars, if M.A. candidates didn't want good grades in order to gain entrance to a doctoral program, if undergraduates lost interest in high grade point averages, if the high school students didn't grade-hunt to impress their way into colleges (or at least try to get passing grades to avoid expulsion or parental wrath), if elementary school students were no longer threatened by the thought of failing to be passed along to the next grade, and if mommies and daddies stopped giving children quarters for every "A" on the report card (Figure 17.1), the entire structure might collapse in a tangle of arms, legs, minds, and intellectual fodder.

The metaphor is extreme, but it points out the principal objections that many of us have to the grading system. Grades often deal with trivial matters; students may be graded down as easily for their failure to "show respect for school property" as for their propensity to "talk too much" (especially ironic if this happens in a class dealing with language). Grades induce a false competitiveness in many children, producing students skilled at playing the grading game and unskilled at meeting the more substantial goals of education. Worst of all, grades are often used as mere binder for straw houses that *ought* to be blown away, supporting poor educational practice by threatening to fail those who do not acquiesce or perform.

Grades are also difficult to give. Sally Brown puts her finger on the problem very nicely in Figure 17.2: "How could anyone get a 'C' [or an 'A' or 'B'] in coat-hanger sculpture [or essay writing or novel reading]?" What does a "C" or an "A" or a "B" grade mean anyway? It is easy enough to grade automobile performance in acceleration or to rank the order of teams in a baseball league—one simply derives a scale of performance and tests it. It is much more difficult for teachers to derive accurate, consistent criteria of measurement and evaluation. Almost any system employed becomes either unworkable or unfair. Studies of theme grading, for instance, show that given a randomly selected group of evaluators, almost any composition will receive a range of grades from excellent to poor.

Finally, grades have a negative effect on many students' self-esteem. Obviously any grade less than "A" means that failure of one kind or another is being perceived by the teacher. Thus in a class where, say, 25 percent of the students receive "A," the true failure is a painful 75 percent, despite the fact that the schools only acknowledge the "Fs" as failing.

THE GRADING SYNDROME

Given all this rather obvious evidence that grades are both harmful and ill-founded, why has grading survived so long? The answer, we think, is that grades have so permeated the school system that everyone has become addicted to their use. We chose the word "addicted" carefully, because we think it is appropriate. In the typical school, few people can live without grades. Despite the obvious harmful effects, students have become hooked on grades. When papers come back the students immediately scan to the end to find out what the grade is, ignoring the teacher's comments. When assignments are given out, the students want to know more about how the grade will be given than how to approach the task. When teachers try to de-emphasize the letter grade, they hear a howl of protest from the students. For the good students, grades are a prize and a goal, and they resent any attempt to devalue their "As" and "A-minuses." Somewhat surprisingly, the average students are equally addicted, and unless they too receive their daily dose of "Cs" and "B-minuses," they start getting jumpy.

Teachers are often addicted, but in somewhat different ways. The teacher's habit comes from the use of grades to compel youngsters to do

FIGURE 17.2

(From Charles Schultz, "Peanuts," March 26, 1972 © 1972 by United Feature Syndicate, Inc. Reprinted by permission.)

things. The teachers' lounge talk is infamous: "I always start them out with 'Ds' and 'Cs'; that scares them and they work harder." "Wait till they get a look at the test I've cooked up for them this time! It'll keep the grades down." Of course, teachers faithfully disavow the addiction by offering rationalizations: "My students want to know where they stand." "People are evaluated all the time in life, so it's important for the students to be evaluated in school."

The addiction to grades is obviously highly destructive to the kind of English and language arts programs described in this book. Students will learn language when they are using it for their own purposes, and it is doubtful that grading adds much to that reality. As often as not, grades are merely a distraction that interferes with the normal feedback and self-evaluation processes that will operate in a well-functioning English class.

KICKING THE GRADING HABIT

There are some good alternatives to grades. A few elementary schools, for example, have gotten rid of grades in favor of written comments and/or conferences with parents and teachers, a method that focuses on assessment and helpful feedback rather than a single symbolic grade. Such a system is not altogether impossible at the secondary level, although the larger numbers enrolled in most high schools create difficulties. Further, it would be quite possible to put most schools on a Pass-Fail or Credit-No Credit system, which would take significance away from individual grades and focus attention where it belongs, on assessment of performance. Such systems have been tried successfully in a handful of institutions.

But realistically, we have to say that if grades were to be abolished tomorrow, most teachers would flounder badly, since they have become so attuned to graded teaching, and many parents would be up in arms, possibly followed or led by their grade-hungry children. Our first choice of states of affairs would be a grade-free system, but in this chapter we'll focus on alternative ways of assessing student growth. Our interest is in eliminating some of the negative aspects of grading and attempting to make what is a poor system work as well as it can under the circumstances.

ALTERNATIVES IN EVALUATION AND ASSESSMENT

Many teachers have been exploring alternative forms of grading for years. For a person compelled by a school to give grades, this can be a frustrating task. No alternative grading system entirely satisfies students or teachers. Some unfairness or inadequacy always creeps in. Further, if one doesn't believe in the efficacy of grades in the first place, exploring alternatives is a frustrating diversion of energies.

As teachers examine alternatives, it is useful for them to keep in mind a distinction between *grading* and the broader concept of *evaluation*. Few English teachers would disagree that there is a need to evaluate students' work in one way or another. The difficulty enters in when a single symbol—the grade—is allowed or intended to stand for a wide range of students' performances in class. The following alternatives to traditional grading systems do not eliminate the concept of evaluation. Rather, they first attempt to evolve systems of letting the students know about the kind of progress they are making, and only second do they try to translate that performance into some mark for a report card or transcript.

Self-Evaluation

Steve has experimented widely with a form of self-evaluation in both college and high school classes. He believes it is possibly more important for students to learn to judge their own work than for them to understand teacher's assessments. Thus he provides many opportunities for self-assessment. After students complete a paper, he asks them to describe their "pleasures and pains" in writing—in effect, describing what they think they did well and what they did badly. At the end of the term, he has them write an informal "intellectual history" of themselves in the course, summarizing what they have read, thought about, talked about, and achieved.

We think that this kind of self-assessment program is valuable for two reasons.

First, it gives students a true sense of their achievements in a course, so that no grade can substitute for their deeper understanding of what they have done.

Second, it provides a more solid basis for grading than any simple numerical system. If the only form of evaluation in a course is a series of numbers in the teacher's grade book, it is not surprising that students become grade conscious. In a self-evaluation system, the foundation is far more solid, so that the grade comes as a confirmation of what the student already knows through self-examination.

Students can even be involved in the grading process. At the end of the term, they can be asked to review the criteria that the teacher has established for the course and to suggest how they see themselves as measuring up. On that basis, students can *recommend* a grade (not "pick one"), and the teacher takes final responsibility for assigning a grade. When Steve uses this system, he usually states that he will accept any recommendation that is written "in good faith"—that is, that makes an honest attempt at evaluation. Bad faith recommendations, described in advance for the class, include such problems as comparative grading ("All the rest of those people want 'As' so why shouldn't I have one?"), task avoidance ("I really don't know what to say, so I'll ask for a 'B'."), or failure to discuss concrete accomplishments ("They say that you get out of a course what you put into it. Well, I must have put a lot into this course because I sure got a lot out of it!"). Steve also spends time discussing the range of grades that might be possible, given the basic expectations and requirements of the course. On the whole, the recommended-grade system works well. Occasionally students try to take it for a ride, recommending unreasonably high grades, but Steve has had more problems with students recommending a low grade out of false modesty.

Here are several other variations on the self-evaluation plan:

Matched Grades. The student and the teacher make up grade recommendations independently and compare notes. If the grades match (which they often do), all is well. For mismatches, a difference of opinion of one grade or more, a conference is called to settle the difference.

Conferences. The student and the teacher meet to work out the grade. The student brings along samples of the work for the term, and the two arrive at an evaluation.

Journal Evaluation. The student keeps a detailed log of accomplishments in the class, a kind of running record in support of a grade recommendation.

Contract Grading

Contract grading provides a convenient alternative system that specifies two main components:

1. The amount of work a student must do to achieve a given grade, "C," "B," or "A."
2. The quality of acceptability for that work.

The student designs a program of work aiming toward a specific grade and discusses it with the teacher. When agreement has been reached, the student begins to execute his or her contract. Thus the method is appealing because of the way it provides for individual work.

The most obvious disadvantage of contracts was brought home to Steve when he experimented with the system in a high school English class. He passed out contract forms and with the students hashed out the agreements. All plans looked good on paper. One student planned to read seven novels and two magazines; another was going to write a collection of short stories; a third planned to do a film. About two weeks into the term, however, it became apparent that enthusiasm had decreased, or more accurately, that nobody was proceeding toward successful contract completion. Steve asked one of his student confidants about this, and he said with brutal directness, "Ah hell, we just filled those out to satisfy you." Had the students been truly free to choose their course of study, they would have chosen not to write contracts. In short, contract grading still keeps a high degree of control in the hands of the teacher.

Further, depending on how it is established, a contract system may also turn the students into what one teacher called "point grubbers." Knowing the number of "points" or books or stories required for a given grade, the students complete that work, and only that work, necessary to achieve the grade they want. In this situation, even though some negative aspects of the grading system have been eliminated, they have been replaced by others that may be just as bad in terms of increasing student dependence as learners. (That indictment also applies, by the way, to programs that use rewards—tokens, candy bars, toys, "kid cash," and prizes—as a way of inducing student motivation.)

NONGRADED SYSTEMS

A number of schools have experimented with nongraded systems. We hope that in coming years more and more schools will want to experiment with them.

Pass-Fail

We've mentioned our preference for Pass-Fail and the related Credit-No Credit plans. If we ran the schools, we'd install such a plan immediately, for both are examples of a workable nongraded system. Credit-No Credit has slight advantages because of its avoiding any mention of "passing" or "failing." Under these plans, the teacher can establish minimum levels of performance, allowing for both quantity and quality, without getting into the knotty and impossible situation of deciding on gradations of quality.

There are a few problems with the system. For instance, "Pass" or "Credit" can cover a wide range of performances, lumping good students in with those whose performances are only satisfactory. However, if one is truly devoted to eliminating grade evaluations, such distinctions should not seem important.

The P-F/Cr-NCr system cannot be compromised, a practice that is rather common. Some schools, for instance, introduce a third level—"Pass *with Honor*" or "Credit *with Distinction*"—as a way of separating the good from the mediocre. Obviously such a distinction merely reintroduces grades; it matters little whether one uses letters of the alphabet, "A-B-C," or phrases: "cum laude," "magna cum laude," "summa cum laude."

Another unworkable compromise is putting a school on two systems—one graded, the other P-F/Cr-NCr—and allowing students and teachers to choose which they prefer. This merely introduces gamesmanship and actually heightens rather than lessens concern for grades. The students try to take easy courses for grades, tough ones for Pass-Fail. Teachers who are inclined to see a P-F system as a watering down of standards tend to want their own courses to be on the grade system while other teachers use P-F.

Some people have argued that P-F and other nongraded systems are a bad idea because colleges "need grades to process admissions requests." While it is correct that secondary school grades are the single best predictor of college success, this is slim justification for maintaining a poor system in the schools. Convenient though grades may be, the colleges ought to be willing to look for better examples of student performance.

The Portfolio

The most complex and perhaps the most valid alternative to grading is to give the children empty file folders when they enter school and have them fill the folders with documents describing and evaluating their experiences in school. This portfolio can be revised and updated from time to time, so that the students have a constant, manageable record of their school work.

For instance, at the end of a course, term, or year, the teacher might file three items:

1. A description of the course, its goals, and the kinds of experiences it provides.
2. A self-assessment statement by the student.
3. An assessment of the student's work by the teacher.

The teacher and student might meet in conference to discuss their assessments, and appropriate appeals could be made by the student or teacher if wide differences of perception exist.

The portfolio would not be strictly limited to formal school experiences. The student might also request assessments from employers and include descriptions of out-of-school activities—from sports and camp to volunteer work.

The advantages of the portfolio system are many. It eliminates much of the concern for credits and grades. It also provides a comprehensive record of the student's work, and it can be far more useful to colleges and employers than are the present grade point averages.

Critics of the portfolio system raise many objections. What if teachers are unfair in their evaluations? Maintaining portfolios seems complicated—who wants to write or read all that stuff? Who would make decisions about which documents go in and which are left out?

But most of these objections can be reduced to one problem: Most schools and school systems are simply not ready for the portfolio yet. This does not invalidate the concept of a portfolio or similar system; it simply reemphasizes the point that time and experimentation will be required before the letter grade goes down for the last time.

STUDENTS AND GRADES

The main concern of many students when they are asked to do an assignment or a task in class is "does this count?" Their concern is not as often focused on "will this be graded" as on "will this be worth something?" Anything they view as not helping them toward their goal of eventually getting a grade in class becomes meaningless to them. Students are very efficient. They have busy lives and so want to know exactly how each assignment will count toward their grade. Students will infrequently do something for their own enrichment or pleasure. This is the kind of attitude the grading system has brought us. So in classes students need to know that checks, or credit, or grades are given for each scrap of work they do, or they see no reason for doing it. They have learned to "play the game," and we must take this into account in our response to their work.

If we do decide to try some of the alternative systems suggested, part of our job is to explain to students what we're doing, why we're doing it, and how this will help them grow as learners. We may also need to explain our views on learning as we wean them away from the idea that a good grade on a multiple-choice test is evidence of real learning.

GRADING PLANS AND PUBLIC RELATIONS

Teachers and students are not the only ones addicted to grades. Parents are often nearly fanatic about them, an especially dangerous situation because parents seldom understand the discrepancies and inconsistencies of grading systems. All too many parents, we fear, are most satisfied by what they see as a stern grading system with high standards (just like the one they seem to recall from their own school days), but one that tends to give their child high marks, thus reaffirming their sense of genetic superiority. (Someone once offered the interesting thesis that standardized tests are nothing more than a compendium of what test makers' children know. This person argued that if the children of test makers were to slip to the lower percentiles, the tests would evolve until those children were on top again. Whether correct or not, that hypothesis does help to point out that the middle and upper classes put much stock in a grading system that has consistently helped to discriminate in favor of their children.)

A teacher who wants to experiment with new grading systems or to abolish grades altogether must proceed cautiously, conquering public relations problems while solving the already knotty problem of developing a better evaluation scheme.

For the lone teacher, experimentation must be done with great care and a good deal of record keeping. If teachers move toward a recommended grade system, they should still keep detailed notes or charts describing what students are doing—preparing for the day when a parent asks the principal, "What's this I hear about kids getting any grade they ask for?" Even the students themselves may present some problems, since grade comparing is popular, and superficial discrepancies are bound to appear in any highly individualized teaching plan: "Jack only wrote two essays and three poems, and I wrote one essay and six poems. Why is his grade higher?" Again, record keeping, along with a prepared defense explaining that what Jack got is his own business, can help support the teacher's evaluation.

Much less risky, and ultimately far more valuable, are departmental or schoolwide discussions on grading, complete with public meetings with the parents. A major parental concern will be college entrance, and it might be useful to invite a college admissions officer to answer the critical question: "Will our students be at any disadvantage with our proposed new system?" Answers to that will vary, but in general a school will receive favorable replies *if* the new grading system is well founded and provides an adequate amount of information about the student. Many alternative systems—especially the portfolio plan—actually provide *more* information for the colleges than do grades (which only correlate about 50 percent with college performance anyway).

Above all, parents need to be told that the new system is experimental and exploratory, that the school is not irrevocably bound to it. Often establishing pilot programs run on a comparative basis with the traditional grading plan proves useful. If the alternative is well designed and anticipates the concerns of parents, the results of comparisons will be satisfactory, even down to student evaluations of the new system.

ON SELF-ASSESSMENT AND EVALUATION

In a sense, this chapter has been a digression from the real purposes of *Explorations in the Teaching of English*. Grades are an impediment; they contribute little if anything to the schooling process, and they cause innumerable problems. Up to this point in the chapter we have simply been concerned with exploring ways of eliminating these negative effects as efficiently as possible so that the teacher can get on with the process of teaching.

As part of teaching, however, the teacher does need to consider the role of evaluation (not "grading"). In itself, evaluation is not a negative concept, and careful evaluation is a natural part of learning. For example, there are things a violinist cannot learn without being told, "That's not good; that's not the way to do it." However, in the schools we have traditionally neglected the end to which this feedback naturally aims, that is, to sharpen a person's ability to do self-assessment. What distinguishes the concert violinist from the hack is, in part, the ability to make discriminations, to recognize when things are and are not being done well. Ultimately, evaluation must become internal rather than external.

What the schools need to teach, McLuhan has suggested, is "social discrimination"—that is, the ability to judge experiences and activities independently, determining less whether things are good or bad than what they are good or bad *for*.

Specifically, in English, this introduces a whole new order of discriminations. The teacher must be more concerned about helping students learn to make their own personal assessments of novels than about judging enduring literary qualities. In writing, it means helping the students to the point where they have confidence that a way of saying things reflects well what they believe.

These refinements of judgment will also change with age. For the preschooler, value judgments are broad, fairly selfish, and unequivocal, as in the predictable response to "No, Henrietta, you may not have an ice cream cone." As students mature, their interests expand outward and their determinations of "good" and "bad" shift. A teacher needs to be especially concerned with observing the extent to which students are capable of involving outsiders in their considerations of value. Generally, for younger students, pleasing oneself is enough, so that attempts to make the student consider an audience are relatively pointless. Only for older students does satisfying the reader become a strong internalized part of a value system. Similarly, the judgmental criteria applied to reading will differ with age, and it may well be that only for the oldest are matters of style and form significant.

If teachers will keep that kind of developmental need in mind and plan appropriate self-evaluation activities for young people at all levels, much of the pain, confusion, and negative effects traditionally associated with grades will diminish. After all, if the students can truly learn to know "what they're worth," they won't be dependent on teachers and other adults for formal evaluations. And that, in our judgment, is what good teaching is all about.

THE ENGLISH TEACHER AND INFORMAL RESEARCH

"Research" does not have positive connotations for a good many teachers. Often, college level courses in research deal with abstractions only dimly related to classroom experiences. Many teachers—math haters all—have had to struggle through elementary research statistics courses, puzzling over and never quite comprehending the value of T-tests, chi-squares, and product-moment correlations.

But "research" in its general sense simply means "systematic inquiry into a subject in order to discover or revise facts, theories, etc." *(The Random House College Dictionary).* Teachers ought to engage in that kind of research every day they walk into the classroom. It is a matter of exploring new options and possibilities and testing out their effectiveness. But a great many teachers lack an experimental attitude, tending to operate mainly on intuition, hunch, and gut level reaction rather than systematically reviewing their work. When that happens, administrators and parents rightfully complain that teachers "don't seem to know what they are doing" and look to accountability programs for a measure of protection or a guarantee of competence.

We believe that if teachers were to do systematic evaluation of and informal research into their own programs, they would not only be better teachers, they might well satisfy the outsiders as well.

An informal research procedure that Steve has used in his own teaching follows a basic pattern for formal educational research but modifies it for classroom use (Figure 17.3). Using it, the teacher can systematically phrase questions about instructional effectiveness and seek out answers. We will take these five stages in order:

1. *Asking Research Questions.* A research scientist once remarked that a great deal of research seems to be a test of which is the worse of two bad

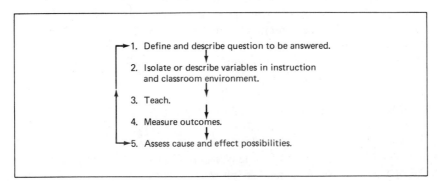

FIGURE 17.3   DESIGN FOR CLASSROOM RESEARCH

ways of doing things. He implied that researchers often fail to ask *significant* questions. For example, "Which of these two grammars is better?" is a question often asked, but one that is limited in its value. A much better, more comprehensive question is, "Does grammar—any grammar—produce change in students' language use?"

Steve was guilty of this kind of sin in planning his M.A. research thesis. He compared two methods—lecture and small group discussion—for teaching a Shakespearean play. Unfortunately, the play was well beyond the range of all of his students. Both experimental *and* control groups scored about 42 out of a possible 100 on the follow-up quiz. Instead of doing research into those two different methods, he should have been raising questions about the appropriateness of Shakespeare for his students.

What is a good research question? To us, it is a question that does not rely on unstated or unproven assumptions or unsubstantiated educational wisdom—for example, "All students 'need' this skill I want to teach." Most of the Explorations suggested at chapter end in this book imply what we take to be good practical research questions, exploring the domains of composition, literature, language, and so on. Ultimately, most research questions will center on student performance: "If I do X, will the students be better able to do Y?"

2. *Isolate Variables.* Educational research seems complicated to many teachers because of attempts to control variables. In seeking out controls to achieve what's called "validity" and "replicability" in the research jargon, researchers must take extreme steps to isolate the technique under investigation. Often this results in making classroom settings contrived and unnatural, which in itself can produce false measurements.

Informal classroom researchers must be aware of variables but should not attempt to control them rigidly. The teacher can, however, try to describe all of the different factors that enter into the question under consideration. For example, if you are teaching a poem to several classes in different ways, your results may be influenced by the different performance levels of the classes: Your second hour class is bright and aggressive; your third hour kids are ready for lunch; the sixth hour people just want to go home. In conducting research you should try to describe all the different elements that are contributing to and shaping the class. A journal or teacher log is especially useful for this purpose, containing a running record of your observations.

3. *Teach.* A self-evident step. Less self-evident: Make certain you have kept accurate records of what you are teaching. Lesson plans, notes, and, once again, a journal are useful.

4. *Measure Outcomes.* Assessment here might be as simple as quizzing students at the end of the hour, or it might be a more complicated unit test. In an excellent article on classroom evaluation, Alan Purves describes three basic kinds of measurement:

1. *Objective.* Results are measured as right/wrong or true/false.
2. *Formal Performance.* Students perform the task in a staged or contrived setting, for example, an essay test. Presumably this performance also reflects their ability to execute the task in the real world.
3. *Naturalistic.* The teacher observes students performing in real-life settings. For example, if oral skills are being taught, the teacher watches the students work in small groups to determine if the skills are being learned.

Any of these forms of assessment may be used, alone or in combination, to determine your results. In addition, most assessment measures can be attached to grading procedures described earlier in the chapter, so that the evaluation of students and the evaluation of the new technique and method need not be done separately.

5. *Assess Cause and Effect.* Here informal research becomes tricky. The formal researcher uses statistical evidence and controls to eliminate variables and point the way toward analysis of cause and effect. Because informal researchers have no such controls, they must be cautious. So your fifth hour class responded well to your method—how do you know it was your teaching? Was there anything else that could have caused the response you observed? Here teachers must be downright cynical in looking for reasons other than their methods: "Of course they performed better—it's right after lunch!" "No wonder it didn't work—we had a fire drill right in the middle of the dramatic reading."

Attributing causality where none exists is a major sin in educational research. You can never be altogether certain that your results show causality—a necessary connection between what you teach and what students know or can do—but if you are appropriately but not excessively suspicious, the odds are you'll draw good, sound conclusions from your informal research.

In the process of conducting informal research, we predict that you will not only become a better teacher, you will also find that matters of evaluation and assessment in your classes will go more smoothly. The previous topic sentence provides the basis for a good informal research question. We'll need to check it out.

EXPLORATIONS

• The grading plans described in this chapter—recommended grades, contracts, pass-fail—are only a few of many possible alternative grading systems, and even those can be used in many combinations. Work out plans for a grading arrangement that you find livable. Test it with students.

• Organize a schoolwide committee to review grading, whose principal function is to investigate the effects of evaluation systems and to arouse student and faculty interest in seeking alternatives to poor or destructive systems. Such a committee might also initiate public meetings designed to elicit parental support for a changed system.

• As a class project, invite students to design evaluation plans that they see as fair and workable.

• Make an informal study of the ways in which students' abilities to make discriminations change with age and experience. What does a "good" book seem to mean for a fourth grader? What evaluative criteria does the eleventh grader apply? Do the same for writing.

• Few teachers believe that students are capable of fair or reasonable self-assessments. For your own edification, introduce an experiment of having the students take full responsibility for developing the criteria for evaluation and/or grading for all project work for a period of, say, a month or two. As teacher, you will give assignments as usual. After hearing the topic or project assigned, the students will develop a set of evaluative criteria. Do their criteria change and mature?

• Create a list of good research questions: your own. Show the list to a colleague and compare notes on your views of the questions worth asking.

• Design an informal classroom research project using the pattern described in the chapter. Then conduct the project and evaluate results.

RELATED READINGS

"Wad-Ja-Get?": The Grading Game in American Education, by Howard Kirschenbaum, Sidney B. Simon, and Rodney Napier (New York: Hart, 1971) is an outstanding exploration of the topic, including detailed discussions of the negative effects of grading, pointers on public relations, and an excellent survey of alternative grading and evaluation systems. Also excellent is William Glasser's *Schools Without Failure* (New York: Harper & Row, 1969), especially for its discussion of the way in which failure distorts one's ability to perceive reality clearly. Two issues of *The English Journal* (March 1975 and October 1978) have focused exclusively on assessment and evaluation, including a variety of ways of responding to and grading student work. Involving students in the assessment process is the focus of *Assessing English,* by Brian Johnston (Sydney, NSW, Australia: St. Clair Press, 1983). This book not only looks at the whole question of the purpose of assessment but suggests specific ways to help students reflect on their own work. Malcolm Knowles's *Using Learning Contracts* (San Francisco: Jossey

Bass, 1986) provides a number of excellent models, although its audience is primarily educators of adults or teachers in nontraditional school systems. Also helpful is Pauline Chater's *Marking and Assessment in English* (New York: Methuen, 1986). For a discussion of informal and formal assessment measures, see Alan Purves's essay "Evaluating Growth in English," in James R. Squire, editor, *The Teaching of English: The Seventy-Sixth Yearbook of the National Society for the Study of Education* (Chicago: University of Chicago Press, 1977).

Professional Issues and Problems

18

From Edmund J. Farrell, "Forces at Work: English Teaching in Context, Present to Perhaps," in James R. Squire, ed., *The Teaching of English: The Seventy-Sixth Yearbook of the National Society for the Study of Education, Part I.* Chicago: University of Chicago Press, 1977, pp.310–311.

Education as institution and English as subject are markedly sensitive to and influenced by the malaises, aspirations, and commitments of society at large. During the 1960's schools were temporarily closed by such diverse events as assassinations of national leaders, students' celebrations of "Earth Day," rioting in inner cities, failures of school tax elections, and students' protest against the continued fighting of American armed forces in Vietnam, Laos, and Cambodia. In recent years the subject of English has been forced to respond to the rightful desires of ethnic minorities and women that their contributions to literature be recognized and that their lives and values be represented accurately in textbooks; it has had to accommodate rapid and continuing growth in linguistic scholarship, particularly in psycholinguistics, sociolinguistics, and dialectology; and it has been compelled to broaden its curriculum to include study of film, mass media, and popular culture. Further, legislative demands for responsible justification of tax expenditures have shaped in part both education and English during the past decade, for "accountability" brought with it the writing of performance objectives, massive programs of testing, and new budgetary systems for the schools. At present both education and the profession of English teaching are being adversely affected by inflation and budgetary cutbacks; surpluses of teachers at all levels; declining enrollments of elementary-age students; growing violence in schools, which has necessitated the policing of school halls in many cities; and censorious groups of citizens who attempt to remove from classrooms materials they find objectionable.

In short, education as institution and English as subject exist in an environment which is simultaneously global, national, and local.

"**N**o author of a single chapter of a book can do adequate justice to any one of a list of long- or short-range problems and concerns, let alone encompass them all," writes Edmund Farrell about problems and enduring issues which the teacher of English faces. Professional problems come and go (or remain); difficult situations are resolved (or left unresolved); issues are raised and forgotten (or debated without conclusion); new methods surface and have their heyday (but instructional problems persist). In this chapter on "Professional Issues and Problems," then, we will neither list all the problems today's teachers are facing nor offer solutions to them. As we stated in the Preface, teachers are in the best position to identify issues and problems and to seek solutions that fit their particular situations. ("The system is the solution," boasts a Bell Telephone commercial. How often is it that outsiders offer us their "systematic" solutions for problems we didn't know we had?)

Instead, we will address three closely related issues of a general sort that seem to us crucial for English teachers in this decade of the 1980s, problems that move beyond the vagaries of topical concerns to focus on long-range priorities for the profession. These issues are, first, reintegrating English as a subject; second, extending English in new directions; and, third, coping with the historical tendency of society to restrict rather than support teachers. Then, in the Explorations section, we will present a series of case studies dealing with contemporary issues that invite readers to propose solutions.

From Frank Smith, "The Language Arts and the Learner's Mind," *Language Arts,* February 1979, p.118. Copyright © 1979 by the National Council of Teachers of English. Reprinted by permission of the publisher and the author.

The categories of the language arts are arbitrary and artificial; they do not refer to exclusive kinds of knowledge or activity in the human brain. Reading, writing, speaking, and understanding speech are not accomplished with four different parts of the brain, nor do three of them become irrelevant if a student spends a forty-minute period on the fourth. They are not separate stages in a child's development; children do not first learn to talk, then to understand speech, then learn to read, and then to write (or any variation of that order). And the four aspects of language do not require different "levels" of cognitive development. The labels are our way of looking at language from the outside, ignoring the fact that they involve the same processes within the brain.

INTEGRATING ENGLISH

Frank Smith correctly objects to fragmenting English and the language arts into separate components. At both elementary and secondary levels, the components of English are too often taught separately from one another, and the separation increases as the students grow older. Thus, while elementary children may find themselves in a language arts block where spelling and reading are isolated and taught at different times, the high school student may be placed in a course labeled "literature" where written composition is totally ignored.

Of course, some fragmentation is inevitable as we discuss and attempt to understand the subject. "English" contains dozens of subfields and related subjects. Even in this book, committed as we are to something called "integrated" English, we found it important to write about composition separately from literature, to discuss the media in a chapter other than the one given over to language. Still, to borrow from the general semanticists, "the word is not the thing." The labels we use to discuss our subject should not be confused with the reality, stated by Frank Smith, that language processes are contiguous in the brain. We don't have separate faculties for reading, writing, listening, speaking, spelling, drama, and media viewing.

We believe the need for integration can be kept in mind if we resurrect from an earlier chapter the sketch of a student (Figure 18.1) and remind the reader that the *student,* not the *subject matter,* is at the heart of what-

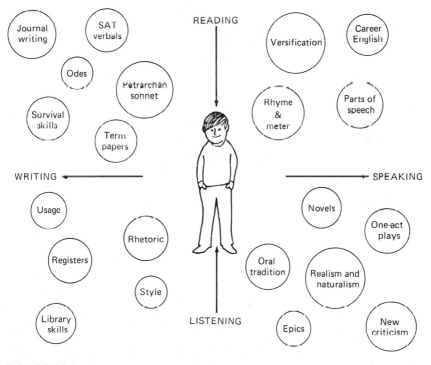

FIGURE 18.1

ever we label "English" or "language arts" or "communication skills." Further, it matters little whether the students themselves are conscious of the labels professionals use to describe the subject. What should concern teachers most is what children and young adults do with language—how they use it. (Perhaps the figure should be changed to show a young person immersed in language: watching TV while reading a book and talking on the telephone at the same time while a computer monitor glows in the background.)

Reintegrating English must be a conscious act for many teachers. If the curriculum guide dictates short stories and implies they should be taught in isolation, one must actively seek out other forms of literature—some plays, a poem or two—to avoid breaking the discipline into components. If a course is labeled "composition," the teacher will need to bring in literary selections and talk about writers as composers so that students see the connection between literature and their own experience with composition. If a unit involves media study, the teacher may take pains to include writing and books along with television and radio.

While many kinds of interconnections among the language arts are possible, the following seem to us most important for the teacher to keep in mind:

1. *From Reading into Writing.* Students' responses to what they read need not be limited to writing about books in pseudocritical ways. Most important is that students be able to relate their own experiences to the ideas they find in literature, that they make a connection with the literary work (see Chapter 6). When this happens, students write about literature in many discourse modes, from poems and short fiction to letters and scripts. Reading provides a jumping-off point for the students to enter into the full dimensions of composing in English. (See also Chapter 9.)

2. *From Writing into Reading.* David Holbrook has reminded us (Chapter 10) that student writing may differ in quality but not intent from professional writing. This, in turn, suggests that we should treat student writing as literature and that students should read one another's work not just as critics or editors, but as real audiences who respond to classroom writing just as they would to a published work. Further, students can respond in writing to one another's literature, thus bringing the language arts class full circle.

3. *Language Study.* Most contemporary English educators argue against the study of language in the abstract as a means of changing students' usage. Still, as we have pointed out (Chapter 11), exploring language in its natural state outside grammar texts can be quite exciting. Similarly, language study in literature becomes tedious if limited to the analysis of metaphor and simile or scansion of verse. A teacher can take what Jean Malmstrom, formerly of Western Michigan University, calls a "linguistic attitude" toward literature by having students examine language choices—words, syntactic structures—as they affect the reader's

response. Obviously this technique helps to integrate reading and language study. It can be used as a way of helping students respond to their own writing as well.

4. *Drama in the Classroom.* The interconnections between drama and the other language arts are too numerous to present in detail. It will suffice to note that drama has been described as the complete language art. It can involve oral composing through role-playing; written composition through scriptwriting; reading, including script reading, reader's theater, and oral interpretation; media, through television and radio production; and language, including such matters as dialects and nonverbal cues. (See Chapters 13 and 14.) Scriptwriting alone is almost a complete composition course, involving everything from the expository writing of speeches to the narrative and description of stage directions.

5. *Media Study.* English is a mass medium; there is no need for a war between English teachers and media people, between print people and nonprint people. (See Chapter 14.) In media/English, students write and read scripts, see films and write or talk about them, evaluate television programs in speech or writing, and compose in various media languages, none of which, as Frank Smith would observe, is compartmentalized separately from reading and writing in the brain.

6. *Oral English.* If drama is the complete language art, oral English (Chapter 12) is the glue that cements the language arts together. No component of English—even silent reading—can be isolated from conversation or formal speech; and any lesson—whether in composition, literature, language, or media—offers opportunities for the teacher to help students develop their oral English skills.

THE REAL WORLD OF TEACHING: RESTRICTIONS ON THE TEACHER OF ENGLISH

It is important to place this discussion of the dimensions of English in the context of actual teaching situations. For instance, although current theory promotes interdisciplinary programs that enlarge the range of English, the fact is that more and more forces are pushing the English teacher toward isolation and fragmentation. The back-to-basics people want more parts of speech and drill; parents want control over their children's reading matter and are objecting to new books; class loads are increasing despite a declining school enrollment, so that individualizing becomes increasingly difficult. Putting students at the center of the curriculum may seem important, but teachers have to think of themselves too. For many teachers, the central consideration becomes just plain survival (Figure 18.2).

FIGURE 18.2

Survival

Survival is an unfortunate word to have to apply to activities in an educational institution. But it is something with which everyone involved with schools must be concerned, for the survival rate for both teachers and students is distressingly low.

The students who don't make it have been well described here and elsewhere. Their failure to survive is reflected in dropout rates, disciplinary problems, public rejection of the schools, and above all, in a nation of adults who are marginal participants in the community of language.

Less well documented are the ways in which teachers fail to survive, perhaps because the tenure laws have a way of propping up devastated teachers and holding them in place. But it is clear that large numbers of teachers are not surviving in any real sense. One such teacher is a man Steve met during his first year of high school teaching, a history teacher who told him, "I really hate this place, and I'd rather be working on my flower gardens. I only have ten more years to go before retirement."

We are more concerned about a second kind of teacher—represented by a group with which Steve worked for a year. In September, the teachers were bright and enthusiastic, ready to try anything. They plunged into their teaching with vigor, and this was reflected in the tone of excitement in their workshop sessions. As the year progressed, however, the meetings seemed to grow less interesting, and toward the end of the year, everyone realized that a negative pall had fallen over the group. Whenever one member proposed an idea, five others would instantly offer reasons why "it'll never work." Their optimism was gone. Exploring deeper, their discouragement could be traced to a range of mildly negative experiences that they were having on a day-to-day basis. Nothing traumatic like a student leaping out of a window or the principal chewing out the teacher in front of the students. Little things: no supplies; not enough ditto paper; too much red tape; too many students; too many absence reports, tardy slips, admits, and hall passes; no books; gloomy classrooms. Many of these teachers also felt very much alone in their schools because of little things like mild disapproval on the part of colleagues, occasional tut-tuts from the assistant principal about discipline or decorum, lack of support for new programs, and department meetings that failed to deal with substantive issues.

They realized that they were becoming victims of "teacher burnout." Once this problem was identified, the group was able to renew itself and managed to end up the year on as high a note as they began. But Steve feared for their survival the following year. "The schools," as someone once remarked, "are an awful place for people to have to teach."

But some teachers *do* survive. Teaching next door to that history teacher who would rather garden than teach was a 62-year-old woman who could do Shakespeare in ways that deeply excited students. One sees many other teachers who have learned not only to survive but, to borrow from Faulkner, to *prevail.* Such people seem to us to have two main characteristics:

First, they have a clear, stable sense of self and purpose. They are what John Gardner calls self-renewing persons, people who do not stagnate, whose interests and ideas are always at least two or three stages beyond their present accomplishments.

Second, they know how to function within an institution. In *The Vanishing Adolescent* (New York: Dell, 1960), Edgar Friedenberg talks about a student named Stanley, a self-directed learner who had learned to use the school for his own ends, while students all around him were being stifled by it. Stanley used the school like a railroad, Friedenberg said, checking out the scheduling possibilities until he found something that would take him where he wanted to go.

Too many teachers come to see the institution as a barrier rather than a form of transportation. In many cases, the train is not a luxury one. Often it is an ancient couch with sprung seats, torn upholstery, and dim lighting. This train often fails to run on time. While some of the passengers become depressed and spend their time fussing with the conductor, the survival-oriented traveler searches out the softest seat and, pulling out a supply of magazines, settles in to read, having informed friends at the end of the line not to expect the train to be on time. Surviving teachers just don't allow problems and pressures to place them on the defensive; they are alert to problems and aggressively work to take positive, even anticipatory, action. They are, in a very real sense, "idealistic."

Idealism is a badly understood concept. Most people take it to mean "naive optimism," the kind of thinking traditionally engaged in by liberals, free thinkers, and professors of education. In fact, idealism simply means having a set of ideas—a vision, if you will—of the way things can be and should be.

Advice to teachers wanting to survive: Keep your idealism. (Please note that we didn't say *youthful* idealism. Any teacher—twenty to sixty-five—needs to have ideals.) Don't change destinations simply because you don't like the conductor or the seating accommodations. Define your ideals carefully and don't let "them"—circumstances, clerks, administrators, and frustrations—force you to reject valid ideals.

Already we seem to hear a voice muttering at the back of the lecture hall: "Who are they kidding? It's not realistic to be idealistic!" To the contrary, we submit that it is actually not practical to be narrowly "realistic." If teachers do not have an idealized vision of what they want their teaching to be, and if they cannot see the remotest possibility of approximating that ideal by hook or by crook in the near or distant future, the only "realistic" thing for them to do is abandon teaching in favor of a "practical" profession like spot welding or steam fitting.

It would be naive to base one's vision on the assumption that next year unlimited funds will be available to every teacher for any teaching purpose, that in September all students will trot into classes eager to learn and capable of plunging into independent self-directed work. It would be equally naive to base a vision on the belief that a revolutionary storm is about to sweep across this country to dissolve the present system of education and to lead to something better. But it is both realistic and idealistic to visualize good, imaginative classes being taught under the present, less-than-ideal conditions.

Reality limits the ease and potential for accomplishing one's ideals overnight. Nevertheless, too few teachers are aggressive in fighting the limitations of their situation. They limit themselves by making false assumptions about their school. Too many teachers assume they will be fired if they don't teach *the noun,* but they never investigate whether or not the school actually checks up on teachers; they assume that the principal will not provide funds for student writing awards, but no one has ever submitted a proposal; they assume that students aren't interested in books, but nobody has actually *tried* a full-scale reading program.

Teachers often fail to exploit the available resources, even if minimal, losing sight of their ideal in the process: "My desks are bolted to the floor, so I guess I can't make an interesting environment for English." (Can't the walls be decorated?) "I'd like to let kids make videos, but the school won't buy a recorder." Has the teacher pounded on the door of the video store to ask for a loaner in exchange for publicity?

Teachers can work toward their visions if they actively fight reality and refuse to take an all or nothing stance. The ideal can be approached only in stages, through successive approximations. Too many teachers quit after their first failure, or do not recognize a crude approximation as a first step rather than as a terminal plateau.

No chart or outline can conquer the limitations of one's situation, but we want to offer a three-step procedure for analyzing any situation, a procedure that should help to sort out the variables and lead you toward successive approximations of the ideal.

IDEALISM AND SUCCESSIVE APPROXIMATION

Step I

State the goal (the ideal) in detailed terms, without a thought for the limitations of reality. *Don't* compromise when thinking about your vision.

Example

I want a classroom library. An excellent one. I want 1000 brand-new paperback titles, subscriptions to 25 magazines and 5 newspapers, and a pamphlet file of 500 up-to-date monographs on every conceivable subject. And I want a comfortable display and lounge area where the students can browse and read.

Step II

List all the obstacles to that ideal. Don't leave any out. (This procedure, by the way, is an excellent way of releasing tensions.) But do not list any false or imagined obstacles; make certain that the barriers actually exist.

Example
1. There's practically no money in the book budget.
2. The department chairman has the book budget neatly tied up for his own classes.

3. The curriculum committee publishes a very limited list of approved books.
4. I have no place to store books, and I don't even have my own class-room.
5. There isn't any furniture for a reading center.

And so on. You can probably add ten more obstacles to the list, all of them valid.

Step III

Systematically design ways of approximating your goal, attacking the obstacles one by one, aggressively seeking ways to leap past them to approximate the ideal.

Solutions for obstacles 1 and 2 are relatively easy: You simply will have to look elsewhere for books. (You also have the option of demanding a greater share of the budget and wrestling with the department chairman for control of the English department, but let's assume for the moment that this is too dangerous to try.) First, of course, you can bring in titles from your own paperback collection, a hundred or more that have accumulated over the years, tomes that simply build up dust and moving expense. You can ask the students to bring in books (with their parents' approval, of course). Some of your friends may be willing to contribute, and you can accost the manager of the paperback bookstore for samples, damaged stock, and left-over magazines and newspapers. You can get the students to join a paper-back book club, knowing that they always have 50 cents or so in loose change. You can start a paperback cooperative with other teachers in order to pool your meager resources. You can also help the student council set up a paperback bookstore. And so on. Any teacher can quickly build up resources of this sort in reasonable—though not ideal—quantities.

Obstacle 3—the curriculum committee—presents more of a challenge. First, you should do a little precensorship of the titles you have accumulated to pull out some harmless but censorially dangerous literature, like the well-thumbed copy of *The Amboy Dukes* that one student contributed and the U.S. Department of Agriculture Bulletin on sheep breeding. Having removed the most obvious sore spots, you can skim some professional book lists—*Books for You,* the Arbuthnot anthology, and *Reading Ladders for Human Relations,* for example—looking for references to the titles you have accumulated. It's unlikely that the curriculum committee will raise too many objections if books are recognized in nationally approved guides for reading. With this data in hand, you can approach the curriculum commit-tee with this question:

Is there any reason why I cannot supplement the curriculum selections with these titles, many of which have been approved as being suitable for reading by young people?

(Note that the question is *not* "Do I have to stick to your list?"—one that would bring a prompt, insulted, affirmative answer.)

It may be that the committee will reject the list in toto. If so, its judgment is suspect, and if you wanted to, you could make a mighty fuss about blanket censorship. More likely is that the committee will accept much of the list, rejecting a few titles to keep up its self-image. If they reject an unreasonable number, you can still try the old ploy of asking for reasons. Some sticky questions: "Why do you think the book is unsuitable?" "On what pages are the unsuitable passages?" and the clincher, "Have you read the entire book?"

Obstacles 4 and 5—concerning the facilities—are relatively easy ones to overcome. You can turn the problem of the reading center over to the students, explaining the idea and asking them to propose solutions. Some possibilities:

A cabinet on wheels that can be opened during class time, rolled aside
    or to other classes, built by the shop class.
The same thing, supplied by the local paperback distributor.
Rug remnants for seating.
Inflatable furniture that can be deflated and stored in the cabinet.
Seating cushions made by the home economics class.

We do not mean to imply that these solutions are complete. Perhaps they won't work at all. But if they don't, the process is simply begun anew, with the newer obstacles listed.

We are convinced, then, that the ideal of integrated, experience-based English can be realized (or approximated) even in these difficult times for English teachers.

Science fiction, it has been explained, is not so much a vision of a different future as it is an extension of our current view of the possible. Thus at the turn of the century, H. G. Wells correctly prophesied that the new "aero plane" would be used for warfare, but because one part of his vision was cramped, he failed to realize the speed and sophisticated weaponry of air combat and visualized planes filled with armed sharpshooters, plugging away at one another with small arms. As often as not, the real limits placed on English teachers are their own imaginations. Once they have visualized something as possible, they can find ways to make it practical.

SEEKING SUPPORT

A new teacher or an experienced teacher assigned to a different building often feels lost in the first days. They're not sure how things are done, where the ditto machine is, who to ask for staples, how the curriculum is taught, or what novels are used in which courses. The easiest way to quickly gain a sense of the building is to find an involved teacher who is willing to answer questions and share the nitty-gritty of how things are done, how most English teachers go about teaching the curriculum, who gets to use what books when, how to order supplementary material, and the other myriad of questions that come up.

It will take a teacher new to a building a while to sense where other English teachers are coming from and to know who can be counted on for support and for sharing ideas compatible with their own philosophy of teaching. The best thing is to listen and say little. Announcing your own philosophy loudly in the teachers' lounge ("I think grammar is overemphasized by most English teachers") will do nothing but antagonize others and may seem very defensive on your part. One of the hardest problems for the involved, idealistic teacher to come to terms with is that some teachers, for whatever reasons, are no longer interested in doing anything but getting through the day without a hassle. They will use textbooks page by page, and they aren't interested in the enthusiasm and workable teaching ideas of others. The less they think about teaching, the happier they are. These are the people to stay away from. Teachers who constantly berate the youth of today and bemoan the low level of their skills are not the people who will help the committed teacher be more successful in the classroom. Instead, look for upbeat, positive people to get to know, no matter what subject they teach. The positive, caring attitudes of these colleagues can help us keep our equilibrium and provide us with support when we need it.

When support in your building seems sparse, or for a refuge in times of stress, we suggest that every English language arts teacher ought to join, and if possible attend conferences of, the National Council of Teachers of English (1111 Kenyon Road, Urbana, Illinois 61801) or your state or local affiliate professional organization. (A list of local groups is available from the NCTE.) Attending conferences and interacting with other English teachers who care can be a big morale booster. First of all, conferences make us feel less isolated; we see that others have the same problems and struggles that we do. Second, we can see from talking and listening to others that we are doing a lot of things right and are indeed on the right track. Third, we can meet people from districts near our own to whom we can turn for advice and ideas. Fourth, we can take many useful ideas away from the conference with us. Fifth, we can build a sense of camaraderie with other teachers throughout our state (or nation) and know that we have support "out there" even though we get little support at our own building. Sixth, going to conferences keeps us up on the latest research in the field and on new directions our profession is taking. And lastly, going to conferences is just plain fun. Conferences can provide a big shot of energy and nourishment all at once.

The NCTE, it should be added, maintains an excellent list of professional books on topics ranging from censorship to teaching Shakespeare and thus is a good source for up-to-date readings on problem areas.

ENCOURAGING SUPPORT

Many parents and administrators want to support the goals of the English teacher and want to know what they can do to encourage reading and writing and speaking at home and at school. Figure 18.3 gives suggestions not only to parents and administrators but also to English teachers and teachers of other subjects. So whenever a principal or a parent or another teacher asks "What can I do to improve literacy?" this list can act as a handy reference to help you formulate some suggestions.

At this point, the text of *Explorations in the Teaching of English* draws to a close. If we were having a final examination, this would be it. Take as much time as you need:

1. Be an education-fiction writer and describe a best-of-all-possible-worlds school for the year 2001, including the role of English language work prominently in your description.
2. Realistically describe the barriers that stand in the way of bringing that vision into reality.
3. Describe what you as a teacher can expect to do during your teaching career (whether you plan to teach two years or forty) to start your classes on the way toward realizing that vision.

EXPLORATIONS

• The explorations in this section involve a series of case studies centering on some of the problems discussed in the chapter. In several instances they may remind you of situations you have encountered or heard about. If so, substitute your real-life case studies for ours.

GETTING BACK TO BASICS

Sandra Farmer is teaching in a relatively conservative urban school, one run by a principal who used to be a mathematics teacher. The school prides itself on giving good courses in fundamentals, and one of the things that the principal likes to do

FIGURE 18.3
From Stephen Judy, *The ABC's of Literacy.* New York: Oxford, 1980.

100 PROJECTS FOR IMPROVING LITERACY

For School Boards and Administrators

1. Declare a commitment to literacy instruction; then act on it.
2. Form a committee to design an ideal literacy program.
3. Form a committee to implement #2 as realistically as possible.
4. Make a needs assessment of the community—how do people *use* language?
5. Assess student interests and needs. Is this the nonliterate generation?
6. Evaluate the existing literacy curriculum.
7. Invite interest groups to develop portions of #3—a piece of the pie.
8. Provide funds for study groups and committees.
9. Reassess current district spending for literacy (and football and computers).
10. Support teacher development of curriculum and pilot projects.
11. Provide time for experimental course planning and development.
12. Search for outside grants for literacy programs.
13. Sponsor articulation meetings: school-to-school, parent-to-teacher.
14. Involve the press, service clubs, community experts.
15. Celebrate the accomplishments of student writers.
16. Get paperback books and magazines into every classroom, English and other.
17. Support smaller class loads for teachers of literacy.

For Parents and Community Members

18. Create conversations with your youngsters.
19. Ask kids open-ended questions.
20. Listen to youngsters' stories and respond to them.
21. Play word games.
22. Put youngsters with storytelling oldsters.
23. Read aloud to your kids.
24. Let your kids see you reading.
25. Tell about your reading; share books with youngsters.
26. Share newly discovered words with children.
27. Tell stories: true and made up.
28. Leave notes and letters around the house.
29. Leave reading material around the house.
30. Take your children to the library; help them learn to use it.

31. Provide help with reading and writing homework (with teacher approval).
32. Stock a bookshelf with reference tools: almanacs, dictionaries, encyclopedia.
33. Leave a dictionary out and open.
34. Explore story hour and other educational opportunities at the library.
35. Take your family to a play.
36. Take your family for ice cream after the play. Discuss.
37. Subscribe to periodicals.
38. Discuss political and other cartoons at the supper table.
39. Let kids stay up after *lights out* to read.
40. Show gentle interest in grammar and pronunciation.
41. Watch your own language. Be precise.
42. Make puns and engage in wordplay.
43. Give books as gifts.
44. Give some of your own writing as a gift.
45. Don't let kids turn on the TV just to see what's on.
46. Encourage selective TV viewing.
47. Selectively critique what kids are watching.
48. Watch some TV with the kids and discuss its value(s).
49. Make up a family list of favorite shows and discuss.
50. Read *TV Guide* with an eye toward recommending good programs.
51. Write letters of praise and complaint to TV stations; read them to the kids.
52. Encourage children to write letters of their own to the media.
53. Declare your active support for a schoolwide literacy program.
54. Find out about the schools firsthand. (Don't trust media broadsides.)
55. Join a parent/teacher group working for better literacy instruction.
56. Volunteer as a reading/writing tutor or teacher aide.

For English Teachers and Librarians

57. Saturate the school with the materials of literacy.
58. Use the library as a media center and learning center, not just a bookshelf.
59. Create schoolrooms that invite reading and writing.
60. Create English programs based on the actual use of language.
61. Start mini- or pilot projects based on the actual use of language.
62. Extend the dimensions of literacy beyond "classic" books, expository writing.
63. Teach writing as process, not product.
64. Teach reading as process, not comprehension.
65. Read and write with your students; listen and talk to them.

66. Base the language program on knowledge of contemporary linguistics.
67. Capture the dramatic potential of literature.
68. Teach oral English.
69. Teach students to be their own editors.
70. Use collaborative learning projects.
71. Publish student work constantly.
72. Extend the range of school-sponsored publications.
73. Treat student writing as literature.
74. Establish literacy HELP centers staffed by parent aides.
75. Create after-school reading and writing clubs.
76. Assign subject matter reading in English classes.
77. Develop interdisciplinary and team-taught units and courses.
78. Consult with content teachers on reading/writing problems in their classes.
79. Seek real-world connections with the English program.
80. Develop alternatives to conventional schoolroom English programs.
81. Open the English classroom to community members.

For Teachers of Other Subjects

82. Stock the classroom with books related to your subject.
83. Include popular subject matter magazines in your classroom teaching.
84. Teach the writing and reading skills needed for your class.
85. Offer alternatives within writing assignments.
86. Include *purpose* and *audience* in your writing assignments.
87. Introduce journal writing in your classes.
88. Discuss the writing of major figures in your field.
89. Encourage interviews as a way of learning.
90. Use oral English as a mode of learning and sharing knowledge.
91. Respond to student writing as a subject matter expert, not as a theme grader.
92. Find publishing avenues for your students' writing.
93. Have students create a guide to writing in your field.
94. Bring in fiction and poetry about your subject. (Get help from the English department.)
95. Bring in biographies and autobiographies of major figures.
96. Read and write about your field; get something published yourself.
97. Study the origins of specialized vocabulary in your field.
98. Compare the language in popular and technical writing in your field.
99. Have students write about their knowledge for younger children.
100. Have lunch with an English teacher.

is quiz teachers (informally, of course) about how they are getting along with "basics." "We don't need poets," he says, "we need plumbers, and the guy who fixes my pipes better know how to read and write. When I taught Latin. . . ."

Here are a few excerpts from the school's tenth grade curriculum:

Grammar and Word Forms

Noun forms: Plurals, possessives.
Pronoun forms: Subject and object, possessives, using pronouns to refer to indefinites, using pronouns with gerunds.
Modifiers: Forms, adjective or adverb, position of adverbs, comparison.
Verb forms: Tenses, confusing pairs of verbs, tenses of verbals, agreement with the subject.

Writing Your Paragraphs

Writing narrative paragraphs
Writing descriptive paragraphs
Writing expository paragraphs
Topic sentences
Supplying details
Adequate development
Unity
Continuity
Orderly arrangement
Tying sentences together
Emphasis through proportion

Sandra doesn't really have much use for all this, but she does feel under pressure. Devise a composition program for average tenth graders that will allow her to teach her ideal of personal, experience oriented writing while still being able to tell the principal, in some detail, how she is covering basics.

THE PURSUIT OF LITERATURE

[Materials needed: Some conventional literature anthologies]

Jack Hawkins discovers, to his dismay, that the school to which he has transferred has a very traditional view of literary study, with sophomore year stressing literary types; junior year, American literature; senior year, British. The department chairman makes it clear that he wants the basic materials in the text covered, and he distributes a model syllabus that blocks out the main aims of each year's work.

Jack searches for alternatives. But when he goes to the book room, he finds mostly dusty anthologies and a few old copies of *Julius Caesar.* He can't depart from the text even if he wants to.

Look through a conventional literature anthology and figure out how one could use the materials inside—less the critical apparatus and discussion questions—to teach in a response-centered, issue-oriented way. In short, redesign the book the way you might teach the materials. Suggestion: First look through the book and identify every piece you would genuinely like to teach. Then think about themes, issues, and problems of interest to students that will relate to the selections you've chosen.

MAKING IT!

Samuel Gordon has had what he regards as a successful first year of teaching. The students seemed to like him and they did some interesting and creative things in class. He stressed free and individualized reading programs, lots of journal writing, and did units on science fiction, women in literature, and minorities. He did not do grammar; he did not assign book reports; he did not pay much attention to the required literature anthology. He let the students grade themselves, and the grades were higher than usual for general English classes.

Now, at the end of the year, trouble is emerging. Aside from just giving him disapproving looks, the department chairman is becoming actively hostile. The principal has, on two occasions, been seen shaking his head in concern at the noise level coming from Sam's classes. As part of the school policy, Sam must face the principal and chairman in the annual "conference," a meeting that will lead directly to a hiring (or firing) recommendation.

Role-play the tenure hearing, showing how Sam presents his case.

As an alternative assignment, devise a strategy whereby Sam could have avoided the confrontation altogether.

CENSORSHIP

Jean Miller teaches Richard Wright's *Black Boy* in an eleventh grade general English class in a conservative school district. One day the roof falls in. A minister and a mother show up to complain to the principal about the book's contents—in particular the "damns" and "hells" and the intercourse scene when Richard was six. Shortly after that, the president of the PTA calls to complain that the book white washes [sic] bad boys and makes all parents look dumb and tyrannical. Finally, a member of a racist political group calls to claim that the book is "black racist," giving a false picture of white people and ignoring all they have done for the Negro.

Role-play the public hearing at which *Black Boy* is discussed, with members of your group taking on the various roles. Assign two or three people to counsel Jean, helping her work out an anticensorship case and self-defense.

INTERDISCIPLINARY ENGLISH

The English department at Whitman High is being besieged with complaints from other departments about the reading and writing skills of students. "They can't read the text," complains a physics teacher. "They can barely write a complete sentence," observes the business education teacher.

Design an interdisciplinary English plan for Whitman High that might help to satisfy other departments without turning English into a mere service department with its own interests absorbed by prepping students for other classes.

EXTENDING THE RANGE

Karen Wexler has been assigned to the junior American literature survey second semester—from Ralph Waldo Emerson to Kurt Vonnegut, Jr. The text she has been given treats literature chronologically and conventionally, but the school's library is a good one.

Brainstorm for ways in which Karen could make her course truly interdisciplinary, including science, history, art, music, etc. Consider, too, the kinds of community-based projects she might design for her course.

RELATED READINGS

Just when you thought we were finished . . . we have yet another final examination for you. Go back to Chapter 1 of this book and do the Exploration again, reviewing a series of statements about the teaching of English. We suggested that you save your first responses for comparison, and now is the time to do that.

Then, after you have thought about the ways in which your philosophy and values have and have not changed, flip to the Bibliography of the book. This includes references to related readings we have mentioned in the text and quite a few more. To keep yourself professionally active and alive— becoming a survivor—you'll probably want to read a variety of professional books. Make a list of the titles from the bibliography that you think might be particularly helpful to you and use them as the base for your professional library.

Bibliography

Abbs, Peter. *Autobiography in Education.* London: Heinemann, 1974.

Abbs, Peter. *English Within the Arts.* London: Hodder and Stoughton, 1982.

Adams, Anthony, and Esmor Jones. *Teaching Humanities in the Microelectronic Age.* Milton Keynes, UK: Open University, 1983.

Allen, David. *Teaching English Since 1965.* Exeter, N.H.: Heinemann, 1980.

Allen, Roach Van. *Language Experiences in Communication.* Boston: Houghton Mifflin, 1976.

Applebee, Arthur. *The Child's Concept of Story.* Chicago: University of Chicago Press, 1980.

Applebee, Arthur. *Tradition and Reform in Teaching English.* Urbana, Ill.: National Council of Teachers of English, 1974.

Applebee, Arthur. *A Survey of Teaching Conditions.* Urbana, Ill.: National Council of Teachers of English, 1978.

Ashton-Warner, Sylvia. *Teacher.* New York: Simon & Schuster.

Atwell, Nancie. *In the Middle.* Upper Montclair, N.J.: Boynton/Cook, 1987.

Barnes, Douglas, and Dorothy Barnes, with Stephen Clarke. *Versions of English.* Exeter, N.H.: Heinemann, 1984.

Barnes, Douglas, James Britton, and Mike Torbe. *Language, the Learner and the School.* London: Penguin, 1986.

Barr, Mary, Pat D'Arcy, and Mary K. Healy. *What's Going On? Language Learning Episodes.* Upper Montclair, N.J.: Boynton/Cook, 1982.

Berthoff, Ann. *Forming/Think-*

ing/Writing. Upper Montclair, N.J.: Boynton/Cook, 1978.

Bettelheim, Bruno, and Karen Zelan. *On Learning to Read.* New York: Vintage, 1981.

Bleich, David. *Readings and Feelings.* Urbana, Ill.: National Council of Teachers of English, 1975.

Bogojavlensky, Anna Rahnast, and others. *The Great Learning Book.* Reading, Mass.: Addison-Wesley, 1977.

Boomer, Garth. *Fair Dinkum Teaching and Learning.* Upper Montclair, N.J.: Boynton/Cook, 1985.

Bosma, Betty. *Fairy Tales, Fables, Legends, Myths.* New York: Teachers College Press, 1986.

Botein, Stephen, ed. *Experiments in History Teaching.* Cambridge, Mass.: Danforth Center, 1977.

Boyer, Ernest. *High School.* New York: Harper & Row, 1983.

Braddock, Richard, and others. *Research in Written Composition.* Urbana, Ill.: National Council of Teachers of English, 1963.

Britton, James. *Prospect and Retrospect.* Upper Montclair, N.J.: Boynton/Cook, 1982.

Britton, James. *Language, the Learner, and the School.* London: Penguin, 1971.

Britton, James, et al. *English Teaching: An International Exchange.* Exeter, N.H.: Heinemann, 1984.

Bruner, Jerome. *The Process of Education.* New York: Vintage Books 1960.

Budd, Richard, and Brent D. Ruben. *Interdisciplinary Approaches to Human Communication.* Rochelle Park, N.J.: Hayden, 1979.

Byron, Ken. *Drama in the English Classroom.* New York: Methuen, 1986.

Calkins, Lucy McCormick. *The Art of Teaching Writing.* Exeter, N.H.: Heinemann, 1986.

Carpenter, Edmund. *Oh, What a Blow That Phantom Gave Me!* New York: Bantam, 1974.

Cassedy, Sylvia. *In Your Own Words: A Beginner's Guide to Writing.* New York: Doubleday, 1979.

Chater, Pauline. *Marking and Assessment in English.* New York: Methuen, 1984.

Chomsky, Noam. *Language and Mind.* New York: Harcourt Brace Jovanovich, 1972.

Chukovsky, Kornei. *From Two to Five.* Berkeley: University of California, 1962.

Clay, Marie. *What Did I Write?* Exeter, N.H.: Heinemann, 1975.

Clegg, A. B. *The Excitement of Writing.* London: Chatto & Windus, 1965.

Cooper, Charles, and Lee Odell. *Evaluating Writing.* Urbana, Ill.: National Council of Teachers of English, 1977.

Cooper, Charles, and Lee Odell. *Research on Composing.* Urbana, Ill.: National Council of Teachers of English, 1973.

Cooper, Charles, ed. *The Nature and Measurement of Competency in English.* Urbana, Ill.:

National Council of Teachers of English, 1981.

Corcoran, William, and Emrys Evans, eds. *Reading, Texts, Teaching.* Upper Montclair, N.J.: Boynton/Cook, 1987.

Creber, J. W. Patrick. *Sense and Sensitivity.* London: University of London, 1965.

Crosscup, Richard. *Children and Dramatics.* New York: Scribner's, 1964.

Davis, Kenneth, and John Hollowel, eds. *Games in the English Classroom.* Urbana, Ill: National Council of Teachers of English, 1978.

Dawe, Charles W., and Edward A. Dornana. *One to One: Resources for Conference Centered Writing.* Boston: Little, Brown, 1987.

Dewey, John. *School and Society.* Chicago: University of Chicago Press, 1956.

Diederich, Paul. *Measuring Growth in English.* Urbana, Ill.: National Council of Teachers of English, 1974.

Diederick, Daniel, ed. *Teaching About Doublespeak.* Urbana, Ill.: National Council of Teachers of English, 1972.

Dixon, John. *Growth Through English.* Urbana, Ill.: National Council of Teachers of English, 1975.

Donaldson, Margaret. *Children's Minds.* New York: Norton, 1978.

Donovan, Tim, and Ben McClelland, eds. *Eight Approaches to Teaching Composition.* Urbana,

Ill.: National Council of Teachers of English, 1981.

Dreyer, Sharon Spredemann. *The Bookfinder: A Guide to Children's Literature About the Needs and Problems of Youth.* Circle Pines, Minn.: American Guidance Service.

Duke, Charles. *Creative Dramatics and English Teaching.* Urbana, Ill.: National Council of Teachers of English, 1974.

Elbow, Peter. *Writing With Power.* New York: Oxford University Press, 1981.

Emig, Janet. *The Composing Processes of Twelfth Graders.* Urbana, Ill.: National Council of Teachers of English, 1971.

England, David, and Stephen Judy. *An Historical Primer on the Teaching of English.* Urbana, Ill.: English Journal, 1979.

Erickson, Erik. *Childhood and Society.* New York: Berkeley, 1976.

Fagan, William T., Julie Jensen, and Charles Cooper. *Measures for Research and Evaluation in the English Language Arts.* Urbana, Ill.: NCTE/ERIC, 1985.

Farmer, Marjorie, ed. *Consensus and Dissent in Teaching English.* Urbana, Ill.: National Council of Teachers of English, 1986.

Fox, Mem. *Teaching Drama to Young Children.* Exeter, N.H.: Heinemann, 1986.

Friedenberg, Edgar. *Coming of Age in America.* New York: Random House, 1963.

Fulwiler, Toby, and Art Young.

Language Connections. Urbana, Ill.: National Council of Teachers of English, 1982.

Fulwiler, Toby, ed. *The Journal Book.* Upper Montclair, N.J.: Boynton/Cook, 1987.

Galvin, Kathleen, and Cassandra Book, *Person to Person.* Skokie, Ill.: National Textbook Company, 1978.

Gere, Anne. *Roots in the Sawdust.* Urbana, Ill.: National Council of Teachers of English, 1982.

Glasser, William. *Schools Without Failure.* New York: Harper & Row, 1969.

Goodman, Ken. *What's Whole in Whole Language.* Exeter, N.H.: Heinemann, 1986.

Goodman, Paul. *Growing Up Absurd.* New York: Random House, 1960.

Graves, Donald. *Writing: Teachers and Children at Work.* Exeter, N.H.: Heinemann, 1983.

Grugeon, Elizabeth, and Peter Walden, eds. *Literature and Learning.* London: Ward Lock Educational, 1978.

Gulley, Halbert E. *Discussion, Conference, and Group Process.* New York: Scribner's, 1966.

Halliday, M. A. K. *Spoken and Written Language.* Deakin, Victoria: Deakin University Press, 1985.

Hayakawa, S. I. *Language and Thought in Action.* New York: Harcourt, Brace, 1982.

Heathcote, Dorothy. *Drama as Context.* Upper Montclair, N.J.: Boynton/Cook, 1980.

Hillocks, George, Jr. *Research on Written Composition.* Urbana, Ill.: National Council of Teachers of English, 1986.

Holbrook, David. *Children's Writing.* Cambridge, England: Cambridge University Press.

Holbrook, David. *English for Meaning.* Atlantic Highlands, N.J.: Humanities Press, 1979.

Hook, J. N. *A Long Way Together.* Urbana, Ill.: National Council of Teachers of English, 1979.

Hosic, James Fleming. *Reorganization of English in Secondary Education.* Washington, D.C.: U.S.O.E., 1917.

Huey, E. B. *The Psychology and Pedagogy of Reading (1908).* New York: Macmillan, 1968.

Illich, Ivan. *Deschooling Society.* New York: Harper Colophon, 1971.

Ireland, Norma Olin. *Index to Fairy Tales 1949–1972.* Westwood, Mass.: Faxon Company, 1973.

Jackson, David. *Continuity in Secondary English.* New York: Methuen, 1982.

Jensen, Julie, ed. *Composing and Comprehending.* Urbana, Ill.: National Council of Teachers of English, 1984.

Johnson, Brian. *Assessing English: Helping Students Reflect on Their Work.* Sydney, NSW: St. Clair Press, 1983.

Johnson, Liz, and Cecily O'Neill, eds. *Dorothy Heathcote: Collected Writings.* Exeter, N.H.: Heinemann, 1984.

Judy, Stephen, ed. *Teaching En-*

glish: Reflections on the State of the Art. Rochelle Park, N.J.: Boynton/Cook, 1979.

Kirby, Dan, and Tom Liner. *Inside Out.* Upper Montclair, N.J.: Boynton/Cook, 1981.

Knowles, Malcolm. *Using Learning Contracts.* San Francisco: Jossey Bass, 1986.

Kohl, Herbert. *A Book of Puzzlements: Play and Invention with Language.* New York: Schocken, 1981.

Kohl, Herbert. *Basic Skills.* Boston: Little, Brown, 1982.

Krashen, Stephen D. *Principles in Second Language Acquisition.* New York: Pergamon, 1982.

Labov, William. *Language in the Inner City.* Philadelphia: University of Pennsylvania Press, 1972.

Labov, William. *The Study of Nonstandard English.* Urbana, Ill.: National Council of Teachers of English, 1970.

Langer, Suzanne. *Philosophy in a New Key.* Cambridge, Mass.: Harvard Paperback, 1980.

Mack, Karin, and Eric Skjei. *Overcoming Writing Blocks.* Los Angeles: J. P. Tarcher, 1979.

Macrorie, Ken. *20 Teachers.* New York: Oxford, 1984.

Macrorie, Ken. *Searching Writing.* Rochelle Park, N.J.: Hayden Books, 1980.

Mandel, Barret, ed. *Three Language Arts Curriculum Models.* Urbana, Ill.: National Council of Teachers of English, 1980.

Marshall, Sybil. *An Experiment in Education.* Cambridge, UK: Cambridge University Press, 1963.

Martin, Nancy, et al. *Writing and Learning Across the Curriculum.* London: Ward Lock Educational, 1976.

Mayher, John, Nancy Lester, and Gordon Pradl. *Learning to Write: Writing to Learn.* Upper Montclair, N.J.: Boynton/Cook, 1983.

McClelland, Ben, and Timothy R. Donovan. *Research and Scholarship in Composition.* New York: Modern Language Association, 1985.

McLuhan, Marshall, and others. *City as Classroom.* Agincourt, Ont.: Book Society of Canada, 1977.

Medway, Peter. *Finding a Language: Autonomy and Learning in School.* London: Chameleon Books, 1980.

Meek, Margaret. *The Cool Web: The Pattern of Children's Reading.* London: Bodley Head, 1977.

Miller, James E., and Stephen Judy. *Writing in Reality.* New York: Harper & Row, 1978.

Milton, Ohmer, and others. *Making Sense of College Grades.* San Francisco: Jossey Bass, 1986.

Murray, Donald. *A Writer Teaches Writing.* Boston: Houghton Mifflin, 1968.

Murray, Donald. *Learning by Teaching.* Upper Montclair, N.J.: Boynton/Cook, 1982.

National Council of Teachers of English. *An Experience Curricu-*

lum in English. Chicago: National Council of Teachers of English, 1935.

National Education Association. *Report of the Committee of Ten.* Washington, D.C.: National Education Association, 1893.

Newkirk, Thomas. *Only Connect: Uniting Reading and Writing.* Upper Montclair, N.J.: Boynton/Cook, 1986.

Newkirk, Thomas. *To Compose: Teaching Writing in the High School.* Washington, D.C.: National Institute of Education, 1985.

Newman, Judith. *Whole Language: Theory in Use.* Exeter, N.H.: Heinemann, 1985.

Nilsen, Aileen Pace, and Kenneth Donelson. *Literature for Today's Young Adults.* Glencoe, Ill.: Scott, Foresman, 1985.

North, Stephen. *The Making of Knowledge in Composition.* Upper Montclair, N.J.: Boynton/Cook, 1987.

Norton, James, and Francis Gretton. *Writing Incredibly Short Plays, Poems, Stories.* New York: Harcourt Brace Jovanovich, 1972.

Ohman, Richard. *English in America: A Radical View of the Profession.* New York: Oxford University Press, 1974.

Pattison, Robert. *On Literacy.* New York: Oxford University Press, 1982.

Peterson, Bruce. *Convergences: Transactions in Reading and Writing.* Urbana, Ill.: National Council of Teachers of English, 1986.

Piaget, Jean. *The Language and Thought of the Child.* Cleveland: World Publishing, 1966.

Polanyi, Michael. *Personal Knowledge: Towards a Post-Critical Philosophy.* Chicago: University of Chicago, 1962.

Purves, Alan. *How Porcupines Make Love.* Boston: Ginn/Xerox, 1972.

Rank, Hugh. *Language and Public Policy.* Urbana, Ill.: National Council of Teachers of English, 1974.

Robinson, H. Alan. *Reading and Writing Instruction in the United States.* Newark, Del.: International Reading Association, 1977.

Rosenblatt, Louise. *Literature as Exploration.* New York: Noble & Noble, 1968.

Rosenblatt, Louise. *The Reader, The Text, The Poem.* Carbondale, Ill.: Southern Illinois University, 1978.

Rouse, John. *The Completed Gesture: Myth, Character, and Education.* New York: Skyline Books, 1978.

Rubin, Don, and Nancy A. Mead. - *Large Scale Assessment of Oral Communication Skills.* Annandale, Va.: Speech Communication Association, 1984.

Ruchlis, Hy, and Belle Sharefkin. *Reality Centered Learning.* New York: Citation, 1975.

Sapir, Edward. *Culture, Language, and Personality.* Berkeley: University of California Press, 1962.

Scribner, Sylvia, and Michael Cole. *The Psychology of Literacy.* Cambridge, Mass.: Harvard University Press, 1981.

Smith, Frank. *Comprehension and Learning.* New York: Holt, Rinehart & Winston, 1975.

Smith, Frank. *Psycholinguistics and Reading.* New York: Holt, Rinehart & Winston, 1973.

Snow, C. P. *The Two Cultures.* New York: Cambridge, 1984.

Squire, James, ed. *The Teaching of English.* Chicago: NSSE (76th Yearbook), 1977.

Stenio, Andrew, Jr. *The Testing Trap.* New York: Rawson Wade, 1982.

Stillman, Peter. *Writing Your Way.* Upper Montclair, N.J.: Boynton/Cook, 1984.

Tchudi, Stephen. *English Teachers at Work.* Upper Montclair, N.J.: Boynton/Cook, 1986.

Tchudi, Stephen. *Teaching Writing in the Content Areas.* Washington, D.C.: National Education Association, 1986.

Tchudi, Stephen, and others. - *Teaching Writing in the Content Areas* (3 vols.). Washington, D.C.: National Education Association, 1974.

Tchudi, Stephen, ed. *Language, Schooling, and Society.* Upper Montclair, N.J.: Boynton/Cook, 1985.

Thais, Christopher, and Charles Suhor, eds. *Speaking and Writing, K–12.* Urbana, Ill.: National Council of Teachers of English, 1984.

Tough, Joan. *Talk for Teaching and Learning.* London: Ward Lock Educational, 1979.

Tuttle, Frederick B. *Composition: A Media Approach.* Washington, D.C.: National Education Association, 1978.

Tway, Eileen, ed. *Reading Ladders for Human Relations.* Urbana, Ill.: National Council of Teachers of English, 1981.

Vygotsky, Lev. *Thought and Language.* Cambridge, Mass.: Cambridge University Press, 1962.

Waldrep, Tom. *Writers on Writing.* New York: Random House, 1985.

Walshe, R. D. *Every Child Can Write.* Rozelle, NSW: Primary English Teaching Association, 1982.

Walshe, R. D., ed. *Writing and Learning in Australia.* Melbourne: Oxford University Press, 1986.

Weaver, Constance. *Psycholinguistics and Reading.* Cambridge, Mass.: Winthrop Publishers, 1980.

Wilkinson, Andrew. *The Foundation of Language.* New York: Oxford, 1973.

Yarrington, David. *The Great American Reading Machine.* Rochelle Park, N.J.: Hayden Books, 1977.

Young, Art, and Toby Fulwiler. - *Writing Across the Disciplines.* Upper Montclair, N.J.: Boynton/Cook, 1986.

Index